Lecture Notes in Computer Science

Commenced Publication in 1973
Founding and Former Series Editors:
Gerhard Goos, Juris Hartmanis, and Jan van Leeuwen

Editorial Board

David Hutchison
Lancaster University, UK

Takeo Kanade
Carnegie Mellon University, Pittsburgh, PA, USA

Josef Kittler
University of Surrey, Guildford, UK

Jon M. Kleinberg
Cornell University, Ithaca, NY, USA

Alfred Kobsa
University of California, Irvine, CA, USA

Friedemann Mattern
ETH Zurich, Switzerland

John C. Mitchell
Stanford University, CA, USA

Moni Naor
Weizmann Institute of Science, Rehovot, Israel

Oscar Nierstrasz
University of Bern, Switzerland

C. Pandu Rangan
Indian Institute of Technology, Madras, India

Bernhard Steffen
University of Dortmund, Germany

Madhu Sudan
Massachusetts Institute of Technology, MA, USA

Demetri Terzopoulos
University of California, Los Angeles, CA, USA

Doug Tygar
University of California, Berkeley, CA, USA

Gerhard Weikum
Max-Planck Institute of Computer Science, Saarbruecken, Germany

Reihaneh Safavi-Naini (Ed.)

Information Theoretic Security

3rd International Conference, ICITS 2008
Calgary, Canada, August 10-13, 2008
Proceedings

 Springer

Volume Editor

Reihaneh Safavi-Naini
University of Calgary
Department of Computer Science
ICT Building, 2500 University Drive NW
Calgary, AB, T2N 1N4, Canada
E-mail: rei@cpsc.ucalgary.ca

Library of Congress Control Number: Applied for

CR Subject Classification (1998): E.3, D.4.6, F.2.1, C.2, K.4.4, K.6.5

LNCS Sublibrary: SL 4 – Security and Cryptology

ISSN   0302-9743
ISBN-10   3-540-85092-9 Springer Berlin Heidelberg New York
ISBN-13   978-3-540-85092-2 Springer Berlin Heidelberg New York

This work is subject to copyright. All rights are reserved, whether the whole or part of the material is concerned, specifically the rights of translation, reprinting, re-use of illustrations, recitation, broadcasting, reproduction on microfilms or in any other way, and storage in data banks. Duplication of this publication or parts thereof is permitted only under the provisions of the German Copyright Law of September 9, 1965, in its current version, and permission for use must always be obtained from Springer. Violations are liable to prosecution under the German Copyright Law.

Springer is a part of Springer Science+Business Media

springer.com

© Springer-Verlag Berlin Heidelberg 2008
Printed in Germany

Typesetting: Camera-ready by author, data conversion by Scientific Publishing Services, Chennai, India
Printed on acid-free paper   SPIN: 12444649   06/3180   5 4 3 2 1 0

Preface

ICITS 2008, the Third International Conference on Information Theoretic Security, was held in Calgary, Alberta, Canada, during August 10–13, 2008, at the University of Calgary. This series of conferences was started with the 2005 IEEE Information Theory Workshop on Theory and Practice in Information-Theoretic Security (ITW 2005, Japan), held on Awaji Island, Japan, October 16–19, 2005.

The conference series aims at bringing focus to security research when there is no unproven computational assumption on the adversary. This is the framework proposed by Claude Shannon in his seminal paper formalizing modern unclassified research on cryptography. Over the last few decades, Shannon's approach to formalizing security has been used in various other areas including authentication, secure communication, key exchange, multiparty computation and information hiding to name a few. Coding theory has also proven to be a powerful tool in the construction of security systems with information theoretic security.

There were 43 submitted papers of which 14 were accepted. Each contributed paper was reviewed by three members of the Program Committee. In the case of co-authorship by a Program Committee member the paper was reviewed by five members of the committee (no committee member reviewed their own submission). In addition to the accepted papers, the conference also included nine invited speakers, whose contributions were not refereed. These proceedings contain the accepted papers with any revisions required by the Program Committee as well as the contributions by invited speakers.

The invited speakers were:

João Barros	Strong Secrecy for Wireless Channels
Claude Crèpeau	Interactive Hashing: An Information Theoretic Tool
Juan Garay	Partially Connected Networks: Information Theoretically Secure Protocols and Open Problems
Venkatesan Guruswami	List Error-Correction with Optimal Information Rate
Goichiro Hanaoka	Some Information-Theoretic Arguments for Encryption: Non-malleability and Chosen-Ciphertext Security
Norbert Lütkenhaus	Theory of Quantum Key Distribution: The Road Ahead
Pierre Moulin	Perfectly Secure Information Hiding
Serge Vaudenay	The Complexity of Distinguishing Distributions
Moti Yung	Does Physical Security of Cryptographic Devices Need a Formal Study?

Submissions to ICITS 2008 were required to be anonymous. The task of selecting 14 papers out of 43 submissions was challenging. Each paper was carefully discussed until a consensus was reached. It was a great pleasure to work with such a high-caliber and meticulous Program Committee. External referees helped the Program Committee in reaching their decisions, and I thank them for their effort. A list of all external referees appears later in these proceedings.

I would like to thank the General Chair of the conference, Barry Sanders, and the Organizing Committee (listed below), whose unrelenting effort ensured the smooth running of the conference. I would like to thank Michal Sramka and Karl-Peter Marzlin, in particular, for their continued effort in maintaining the conference website and submission system (iChair), and lending a hand whenever it was required.

The conference benefited enormously from the generous financial support of the University of Calgary, the Informatics Circle of Research Excellence in Alberta, the Pacific Institute of Mathematical Sciences, the Canadian Institute for Advanced Research and Quantum Works.

Finally, I would like to thank the authors of all submitted papers for their hard work and all attendees of the conference whose support ensured the success of the conference.

August 2008   Reihaneh Safavi-Naini

ICITS 2008

The Third International Conference on Information Theoretic Security
University of Calgary, Canada
August 10–13, 2008

General Chair

Barry Sanders   QIS[1],University of Calgary, Canada

Program Chair

Reihaneh Safavi-Naini   iCIS Lab[2], University of Calgary, Canada

Program Committee

Simon Blackurn   Royal Holloway University of London, UK
Carlo Blundo   University of Salerno, Italy
Stefan Dziembowski   Universitá La Sapienza, Italy
Cunsheng Ding   Hong Kong University of Science
                             and Technology, Hong Kong

Yevgeniy Dodis   New York University, USA
Paolo D'Arco   University of Salerno, Italy
Serge Fehr   CWI, The Netherland
Matthias Fitzi   ETH, Switzerland
Hideki Imai   Chuo University, Japan
Kaoru Kurosawa   Ibaraki University, Japan
Jörn Müller-Quade   Universität Karlsruhe, Germany
Dingyi Pei   Academia Sinica, P.R. China
C. Pandu Rangan   Indian Institute of Technology, India
Renato Renner   ETH, Switzerland
Alain Tapp   Université de Montréal, Canada
Huaxiong Wang   Nanyang Technological University, Singapore
Wolfgang Tittel   University of Calgary, Canada
Moti Yung   Google and Columbia University, USA
Yuliang Zheng   University of North Carolina, USA

---

[1] Institute for Quantum Information Sciences.
[2] iCORE Information Security Laboratory.

Steering Committee

Carlo Blundo   University of Salerno, Italy
Gilles Brassard   University of Montreal, Canada
Ronald Cramer   CWI, The Netherlands
Yvo Desmedt, Chair   University College London, UK
Hideki Imai   National Institute of Advanced
                            Industrial Science and Technology, Japan
Kaoru Kurosawa   Ibaraki University, Japan
Ueli Maurer   ETH, Switzerland
Reihaneh Safavi-Naini   University of Calgary, Canada
Doug Stinson   University of Waterloo, Canada
Moti Yung   Google and Columbia University, USA
Yuliang Zheng   University of North Carolina, USA

Organizing Committee

Mina Askari   iCIS Lab, University of Calgary, Canada
Catherine Giacobbo   QIS, University of Calgary, Canada
Jeong San Kim   QIS, University of Calgary, Canada
Itzel Lucio Martinez   QIS, University of Calgary, Canada
Karl-Peter Marzlin   QIS, University of Calgary, Canada
Xiaofan Mo   QIS, University of Calgary, Canada
Michal Sramka   iCIS Lab, University of Calgary, Canada

External Referees

Nuttapong Attrapadung   Aggelos Kiayias
Kai Yuen Cheong   Varad kirtane
Ashish Choudary   Takeshi Koshiba
Yang Cui   Donggang Liu
Yvo Desmedt   Anderson C.A. Nascimento
Dejan Dukaric   Frederique Oggier
Nelly Fazio   Arpita Patra
Jun Furukawa   Krzysztof Pietrzak
Clemente Galdi   Hongsng Shi
Robbert de Haan   Takeshi Shimoyama
Manabu Hagiwara   SeongHan Shin
Martin Hirt   Hitoshi Tanuma
Shaoquan Jiang   Ashraful Tuhin
Masaru Kamada   Ivan Visconti

Table of Contents

Secure and Reliable Communication I

Quantum Information and Communication

Networks and Devices

Mulitparty Computation

Information Hiding and Tracing

Coding Theory and Security

Quantum Computation

Secure and Reliable Communication II

Foundation

Encryption

Partially Connected Networks:
Information Theoretically Secure Protocols
and Open Problems
(Invited Talk)

Juan A. Garay

Bell Labs, Alcatel-Lucent, 600 Mountain Ave., Murray Hill, NJ 07974
garay@research.bell-labs.com

Abstract. We consider networks (graphs) that are *not* fully connected, and where some of the nodes may be corrupted (and thus misbehave in arbitrarily malicious and coordinated ways) by a computationally unbounded adversary. It is well known that some fundamental tasks in information-theoretic security, such as secure communication (perfectly secure message transmission) [4], broadcast (a.k.a. Byzantine agreement) [7], and secure multi-party computation [1,2], are possible if and only the network has very large connectivity—specifically, $\Omega(t)$, where t is an upper bound on the number of corruptions [3,4]. On the other hand, typically in practical networks most nodes have a small degree, independent of the size of the network; thus, it is unavoidable that some of the nodes will be unable to perform the required task.

The notion of computation in such settings was introduced in [5], where achieving Byzantine agreement with a low number of exceptions on several classes of graphs was considered, and more recently studied in [6,8] with regards to secure multi-party computation.

In this talk we review several protocols for the above tasks, and point out some interesting problems for future research.

References

1. Ben-Or, M., Goldwasser, S., Wigderson, A.: Completeness theorems for non-cryptographic fault-tolerant distributed computation. In: Proc. 20th STOC, May 1988, pp. 1–10 (1988)
2. Chaum, D., Crepeau, C., Damgard, I.: Multiparty unconditionally secure protocols. In: Proc. 20th STOC, May 1988, pp. 11–19 (1988)
3. Dolev, D.: The Byzantine generals strike again. Journal of Algorithms 1(3), 14–30 (1982)
4. Dolev, D., Dwork, C., Waarts, O., Young, M.: Perfectly secure message transmission. Journal of ACM 1(40), 17–47 (1993)
5. Dwork, C., Peleg, D., Pippinger, N., Upfal, E.: Fault tolerance in networks of bounded degree. In: Proc. 18th STOC, May 1986, pp. 370–379 (1986)
6. Garay, J., Ostrovsky, R.: Almost-everywhere secure computation. In: Advances in Cryptology–Eurocrypt 2008, April 2008. LNCS, vol. 4965, pp. 307–323. Springer, Heidelberg (2008)
7. Pease, M., Shostak, R., Lamport, L.: Reaching agreement in the presence of faults. Journal of the ACM, JACM 27(2) (April 1980)
8. Vaya, S.: Secure computation on incomplete networks. In: Cryptology ePrint archive, Report 2007/346 (September 2007)

R. Safavi-Naini (Ed.): ICITS 2008, LNCS 5155, p. 1, 2008.
© Springer-Verlag Berlin Heidelberg 2008

Almost Secure 1-Round Message Transmission Scheme with Polynomial-Time Message Decryption

Toshinori Araki

NEC Corporation
t-araki@ek.jp.nec.com

Abstract. The model of (r-round, n-channel) message transmission scheme (MTS) was introduced by Dolev *et al.* [5]. In their model, there are n channels between a sender S and a receiver R, and they do not share any information like keys. S wants to send a message to R secretly and reliably in r-round. But, there is an adversary A who can observe and forge at most t information which sent through n-channels.

In this paper, we propose almost secure (1-round, $3t+1$-channel) MTS. Proposed scheme has following two properties. (1) If sending message is large some degree, the communication bits for transmitting messages is much more efficient with comparing to the perfectly secure (1-round, $3t+1$-channel) MTS proposed by Dolev *et.al* [5]. (2) The running time of message decryption algorithm is polynomial in n.

1   Introduction

Background. The model of (r-round, n-channel) message transmission scheme (MTS) was first introduced by Dolev *et al.* [5]. In their model, there are n channels between a sender S and a receiver R, and they do not share any information like keys. S wants to send a message $m \in \mathcal{M}$ to R secretly and reliably in r-round. But, there is an adversary A who can observe and forge at most t information which sent through n-channels.

We call a (r-round, n-channel) MTS is (t, δ)-secure if the scheme satisfies the following four conditions for any infinitely powerful adversary.

1. A can not obtain any partial information about m.
2. R never accepts $\hat{m} \neq m$.
3. R can output $\hat{m} = m$ with probability at least $1 - \delta$.
4. If the all forged informations are null strings, R can output $\hat{m} = m$.

There are three typical measures for the efficiency of (t, δ)-secure (r-round, n-channel) MTS ; that is, t : the number of channels which controlled by A, r : the number of rounds and $b(l)$: the total number of bits which sent through channels for communicating l bits message. This paper focuses on the case: $r = 1$.

With respect to 1-round MTS, Dolev *et al.* showed that the necessary and sufficient condition for achieving ($t, 0$)-security is $n \geq 3t + 1$ [5]. They also

R. Safavi-Naini (Ed.): ICITS 2008, LNCS 5155, pp. 2–13, 2008.
© Springer-Verlag Berlin Heidelberg 2008

proposed a $(t, 0)$-secure scheme for $n = 3t + 1$ whose $b(l)$ is $l \cdot n$. This scheme satisfies the bound of $b(l)$ presented in [6]. In the case of $\delta \neq 0$, some schemes are proposed [4,8,11]. However, the scheme proposed in [11] is flawed [8]. The (t, δ)-secure scheme for $n = 2t+1$ proposed in [4,8] requires decryption algorithm where running time is exponential in n.

The scheme in [4,8] is based on a kind of (k, n) threshold scheme which can detect only the fact of cheating. Inspired by the result [4,8], we think "If we use another kind of secret sharing scheme, how MTS can construct?". This is the motivation of this research. In this paper, we research about a MTS based on a (k, n) threshold scheme which can identify t cheaters.

Our Contribution. In this paper, we propose (t, δ)-secure schemes for $r = 1$ and $3t+1$ channels. This scheme is based on a secret sharing scheme proposed in [12] which can identify t-cheaters. The proposed schemes possesses the following two properties.

1. The communication bits $b(l)$ satisfies $b(l) \approx n \cdot (l/(t + 1) + \log 1/\delta)$.
2. The running time of decryption algorithm is polynomial in n.

If sending message is large some degree, proposed scheme's communication bits is much smaller than that of the scheme in [5].

Organization. The rest of the paper is organized as follows. In Section 2, we briefly review the model of (t, δ)-secure (1-round, n-channel) MTS. In Section 3, we briefly review the tools for constructing proposed schemes. In Section 4, we present a (t, δ)-secure (1-round, $3t + 1$-channel) MTS. The running time of decryption algorithm is polynomial in n. In Section 5, we present a variation of the scheme proposed in Section 4. In Section 6, we summarize our work.

2   Message Transmission Scheme

In this section, we define a model of (t, δ)-secure (1-round, n-channel) message transmission scheme (MTS). In this model, there are a sender S and a receiver R are connected by n channels $\mathcal{C} = \{C_1, \ldots, C_n\}$. They do not share any informations like keys. The sender's goal is sending a message $m \in \mathcal{M}$ to the receiver in one-round, where $\mathcal{M}$ denotes the set of messages. But there is an adversary A who can observe and forge the informations sent through at most t channels.

A (1-round, n-channel) MTS consists of a pair of two algorithms (Enc, Dec). Encryption algorithm Enc takes a message $m \in \mathcal{M}$ as input and outputs a list $(x_1, \ldots, x_n)$. Each x_i is the information sent through C_i and we call each x_i to ciphertext. Ordinarily, Enc is invoked by the S. Decryption algorithm Dec takes a list of the ciphertexts from channels $(\hat{x}_1, \ldots, \hat{x}_n)$ and outputs $\hat{m} \in \mathcal{M}$ or **failure**.

To define the security, we define the following game for any (1-round, n-channel) message transmission scheme **MTS** = (Enc, Dec) and for any (not necessarily polynomially bounded) Turing machine A = (A_1, A_2), where A represents adversary who can observe and forge the ciphertexts sent through at most t channels. Following definitions are based on the definitions in [8].

Game($\mathbf{MTS}$, A)

    $m \leftarrow \mathcal{M}$; //according to the probability distribution over $\mathcal{M}$.

    $(x_1, \ldots, x_n) \leftarrow \mathsf{Enc}(m)$;

    $(i_1, \ldots, i_t) \leftarrow \mathsf{A}_1$;

    $(x'_{i_1}, \ldots, x'_{i_t}) \leftarrow \mathsf{A}_2(x_{i_1}, \ldots, x_{i_t})$; // x' can be null string.

Definition 1. *We say* (1-*round*, n-*channel*) *message transmission scheme* $\mathbf{MTS}$ (t, δ)-*secure if the following four conditions are satisfied for any adversary* A *who can observe and forge the ciphertexts sent through at most* t *channels.*

-Privacy. *A cannot obtain any information about* m.
-General Reliability. *The receiver outputs* $\hat{m} = m$ *or* **failure**. *In the other words, the receiver never output invalid message.*
-Failure

$$\Pr(\mathsf{Dec}(\hat{x_1}, \ldots, \hat{x_n}) = \mathbf{failure}) \leq \delta$$

-Trivial Reliability. *If all forged messages are null strings, then* Dec *outputs* m. (*This is a requirement for the case* t *channel fail to deliver messages*).

With respect to $(t, 0)$-secure (1-round, $n(= 3t + 1)$-channel) message transmission scheme, the following result is already known.

Proposition 1. [5] *There exists* $(t, 0)$-*secure* (1-*round*, $n(= 3t + 1)$-*channel*) *message transmission scheme with* $b(l) = l \cdot n$.

In [4,8], a (t, δ)-secure (1-round, $n(= 2t + 1)$-channel) message transmission scheme is proposed. But, the running time of this scheme's message decryption algorithm is exponential in n.

3 Preliminaries

In this section, we review the tools for constructing proposed scheme.

3.1 (k, n) Threshold Scheme

A (k, n) threshold secret sharing scheme [2,10] is a cryptographic primitive used to distribute a secret s to n participants in such a way that a set of k or more participants can recover the secret s and a set of $k - 1$ or less participants cannot obtain any information about s. There are n participants $\mathcal{P} = \{P_1, \ldots, P_n\}$ and a dealer D in (k, n) threshold scheme.

A model consists of two algorithms: $\mathsf{ShareGen}$ and $\mathsf{Reconst}$. Share generation algorithm $\mathsf{ShareGen}$ takes a secret $s \in \mathcal{S}$ as input and outputs a list $(v_1, v_2, \ldots, v_n)$. Each v_i is called a *share* and is given to a participant P_i. Ordinarily, $\mathsf{ShareGen}$ is invoked by the D. Secret reconstruction algorithm $\mathsf{Reconst}$ takes a list of shares and outputs a secret $s \in \mathcal{S}$.

Shamir's (k, n) **Threshold Scheme.** In this paper, we use shamir's secret sharing scheme [10]. In this scheme, on input a secret $s \in GF(p)$, the D randomly choose a polynomial $f(x)$ of degree at most $k-1$ over $GF(p)$ such that $f(0) = s$, and the share $v_i = f(i)$. In case $m \geq k$, the list of shares $\{v_{i_1}, \ldots, v_{i_m}\}$ is equivalent to codeword of generalized Reed-Solomon code [9]. Moreover, in case $m = k + 2t$, we can correct shares even when t shares are forged by using efficient algorithm like Berlekamp algorithm [1] which complexity is $O(m^2)$ [9].

Ramp Scheme. In the above case, secret is only embeded to constant term of $f(x)$. In [3], Blakley proposed to embed secret to other coefficients. For example, on input a secret $s = (s_0, \ldots, s_{N-1}) \in GF(p)^N$, the D randomly choose $a_j \in GF(p)$ for $N \leq j \leq k - 1$ and generate a polynomial $f(x)$ of degree $k - 1$ over $GF(p)$ such that $f(x) = s_0 + s_1 x + \ldots + s_{N-1} x^{N-1} + a_N x^N + \ldots + a_{k-1} x^{k-1}$ and the share $v_i = f(i)$.

In above case, any k or more participants can recover s but no subset of less than $k - N$ participants can determine any partial information about s. We call this type of threshold scheme to (k, N, n) threshold scheme.

3.2 t-Cheater Identifiable (k, n) Threshold Scheme

A secret sharing scheme capable of identifying cheaters was first presented by Rabin and Ben-Or [13]. They considered the scenario in which at most t cheaters submit forged shares in the secret reconstruction phase. Such cheaters will succeed if they cannot be identified as cheaters in reconstructing the secret.

This model consists of two algorithms. The share generation algorithm ShareGen is the same as that in the ordinary secret sharing schemes.

A secret reconstruction algorithm Reconst is slightly changed: it takes a list of shares as input and outputs either a secret or a pair $(\bot, L)$ where $\bot$ is a special symbol indicating that cheating was detected, and L is a set of cheaters who submit invalid shares to Reconst. Reconst outputs $\bot$ if and only if cheating has detected.

The model can be formalized by the following simple game defined for any (k, n) threshold secret sharing scheme $\mathbf{SS} = (\mathsf{ShareGen}, \mathsf{Reconst})$ and for any (not necessarily polynomially bounded) Turing machine $\mathsf{B} = (\mathsf{B}_1, \mathsf{B}_2)$, where B represents cheaters $P_{i_1}, \ldots, P_{i_t}$ who try to cheat $P_{i_{t+1}}, \ldots, P_{i_k}$. Following definitions are based on the definitions in [12].

Game($\mathbf{SS}, \mathsf{B}$)

    $s \leftarrow \mathcal{S}$;   // according to the probability distribution over $\mathcal{S}$.
    $(v_1, \ldots, v_n) \leftarrow \mathsf{ShareGen}(s)$;
    $(i_1, \ldots, i_t) \leftarrow \mathsf{B}_1$;
    $(v'_{i_1}, \ldots, v'_{i_t}, i_{t+1}, \ldots, i_k) \leftarrow \mathsf{B}_2(v_{i_1}, \ldots, v_{i_t})$;

The advantage of each cheater P_{i_j} is expressed as $Adv(\mathbf{SS}, \mathsf{B}, P_{i_j}) = \Pr[s' \in \mathcal{S} \wedge s' \neq s \wedge i_j \notin L]$,

where s' is a secret reconstructed from $v'_{i_1}, \ldots, v'_{i_t}, v_{i_{t+1}}, \ldots, v_{i_k}$ and the probability is taken over the distribution of $\mathcal{S}$ and over the random tapes of ShareGen and B.

Definition 2. *We say* (k, n) *threshold secret sharing scheme* **SS** (t, ϵ)*-cheater identifiable if the following three conditions are satisfied for any adversary* B *who can observe and forge t shares.*

-Condition 1. Any set of k or more honest participants can recover original secret s.

-Condition 2. Any set of $k - 1$ or less participants cannot determine any information about s.

-Condition 3. $Adv(\mathbf{SS}, \mathsf{B}, P_{i_j}) \leq \epsilon$ for any adversary B and any P_{i_j} .

Above definition does not have any condition about a set of $k + 1$ or more participants containing some cheaters. A definition including this situation is given in [7]. However, we adopt a definition given in [12]. Because, the proposed scheme of this paper is based on a cheater identifiable (k, n) threshold secret sharing scheme proposed in [12] and this base scheme does not define the reconstruction algorithm for such situation.

Next, we briefly review the scheme presented in [12].

The Obana Scheme [12]

The Share Generation algorithm ShareGen and the Share Reconstruction algorithm Reconst are described as follows where p and q are a prime powers such that $q \geq np$.

-Share Generation: On input a secret $s \in GF(p)$, the share generation algorithm ShareGen outputs a list of ciphertexts $(v_1, \ldots, v_n)$ as follows:

1. Generate a random polynomial $f_s(x)$ of degree at most k over $GF(p)$ such that $f_s(0) = s$.
2. Generate a random polynomial $C(x)$ of degree at most t over $GF(q)$.
3. Compute $v_i = (f_s(i), C(p \cdot (i - 1) + f_s(i)))$ and output $(v_1, \ldots, v_n)$ where each $p \cdot (i - 1) + f_s(i)$ is computed over integer and then reduced to $GF(q)$

-Secret Reconstruction and Cheater Identification: On input a list of share $((v_{s,j_1}, v_{c,j_1}), \ldots, ((v_{s,j_k}, v_{c,j_k}))$, the reconstruction algorithm Reconst outputs a secret s or $\perp$ as follows:

1. Reconstruct $\hat{C}(x)$ from $(v_{c,j_1}, \ldots, v_{c,j_k})$ using an error correction algorithm of generalized Reed-Solomon Code (e.g. Berlekamp algorithm. [1])
2. Check if $v_{c,j_l} = \hat{C}(p \cdot (j_l - 1) + v_{s,j_l})$ holds (for $1 \leq l \leq k$.) If $v_{c,j_l} \neq \hat{C}(p \cdot (j_l - 1) + v_{s,j_l})$ then j_l is added to the list of invalid shares L.
3. If $L = \emptyset$ then compute the secret $\hat{s}$ from $(v_{s,j_1}, \ldots, v_{s,j_k})$ using Lagrange interpolation and output $\hat{s}$, otherwise Reconst outputs $(\perp, L)$.

The properties of this scheme is summarized by the following proposition.

Proposition 2. [12] *If* $k \geq 3t + 1$ *then the Obana scheme is a* (t, ϵ) *cheater identifiable* (k, n) *threshold scheme such that*

$$|S|^1 = p, \epsilon = 1/q, q \geq n \cdot p, |v_i| = p \cdot q(= |S|/\epsilon).$$

---

[1] Throughout the paper, the cardinality of the set $\mathcal{X}$ is denoted by $|\mathcal{X}|$.

By using this scheme, even if there exist t forged shares in more than $3t + 1$ shares, we can choose only valid shares with high probability.

3.3 Almost Strong Class of Universal Hash Functions

Obana scheme is using the properties of *Almost strong class of universal hash functions*. Here, we review the properties of this as follows.

A family of hash functions $H : \mathcal{A} \to \mathcal{B}$ with the properties (1) and (2) below is called *Almost strongly universal hash functions with strength t* ϵ-ASU$_t$.

1. For any $x \in \mathcal{A}$ and $y \in \mathcal{B}$, $|\{h_e \in H \mid h_e(x) = y\}| = |H|/|\mathcal{B}|$.
2. For any distinct $x_1, \ldots, x_t \in \mathcal{A}$ and for any distinct $y_1, \ldots y_t \in \mathcal{B}$,

$$\frac{|\{h_e \in H \mid h_e(x_1) = y_1, \ldots, h_e(x_t) = y_t\}|}{|\{h_e \in H \mid h_e(x_1) = y_1, \ldots, h_e(x_{t-1}) = y_{t-1}\}|} \leq \epsilon.$$

4 Proposed Scheme

As noted before, proposed scheme is based on t cheater identifiable secret sharing scheme proposed in [12].

Basically, proposed scheme's ciphertext x_i is the share v_i of [12] which set $k = 2t+1$ and $n = 3t+1$. If do so, R receive at least valid $2t+1$ ciphertexts. Moreover, by the property of t cheater identifiable secret sharing scheme, the receiver R can choose only valid ciphertexts with high probability from received ciphertexts. Clearly, in this case, R can decrypt valid message. But, there is small probability that R choose more than $2t + 1$ valid ciphertexts and some invalid ciphertexts. For satisfying "General Reliability", we must make Dec which can detect the fact perfectly and efficiently. To do so, we use the a property of Shamir's (k, n) threshold scheme such that k *valid shares determine a polynomial and invalid shares never pass this polynomial*. By using this property, we can perfectly detect the fact noted before. Because, receiver R receives at least $2t+1$ valid ciphertexts. In proposed scheme, we use $(2t + 1, t + 1, 3t + 1)$ threshold scheme for efficiency. Because, in message transmission , we may take into account adversary who can observe only t channel. So we may use $(2t + 1, t + 1, 3t + 1)$ threshold scheme.

The encryption algorithm Enc and the decryption algorithm Dec are described as follows where p and q are prime powers such that $q \geq np$.

-Enc: On input a message $m \in GF(p^{t+1})$ where $(m_0, m_1, \ldots, m_t)$ is a vector representation of m, the encryption algorithm Enc outputs a list of ciphertexts $(c_1, \ldots, c_n)$ as follows:

1. Generate a random polynomial $f_m(x)$ of degree at most $2t$ over $GF(p)$ such that

$$f_m(x) = m_0 + m_1 x + \ldots + m_t x^t + a_{t+1} x^{t+1} + \ldots + a_{2t} x^{2t}$$

where $a_{t+1}, \ldots, a_{2t}$ are ramdom elements over $GF(p)$.
2. Generate a random polynomial $C(x)$ of degree at most t over $GF(q)$.

3. Compute $c_i = (f_m(i), C(p \cdot (i-1) + f_m(i)))$ and output $(c_1, \ldots, c_n)$ where each $p \cdot (i-1) + f_m(i)$ is computed over integer and then reduced to $GF(q)$.

-Dec: On input a list of ciphertexts $((c_{m,1}, c_{c,1}), \ldots, ((c_{m,n}, c_{c,n}))$, the decryption algorithm Dec outputs a message m or $\perp$ as follows:

1. Reconstruct $\hat{C}(x)$ from $(c_{c,1}, \ldots, c_{c,n})$ using an error correction algorithm of generalized Reed-Solomon Code (e.g. Berlekamp algorithm.[1]).
2. Check if $c_{c,i} = \hat{C}(p \cdot (i-1) + c_{m,i})$ holds (for $1 \leq i \leq n$.) If $c_{c,i} = \hat{C}(p \cdot (i-1) + c_{m,i})$ then i is added to the list of valid ciphertexts L.
3. Reconstruct $\hat{f}_m(x)$ from k of $c_{m,i}$ where $i \in L$ and check all $c_{m,i}$ where $i \in L$ pass $\hat{f}_m(x)$. If all $c_{m,i}$ where $i \in L$ pass $\hat{f}_m(x)$, output the values embeded to f_m. Otherwise Dec outputs failure.

Clearly, the running time of Dec is polynomial in n and the properties of this scheme is summarized by the following theorem.

Theorem 1. *Proposed scheme is (t, δ)-secure $(1$-round, $3t+1$-channel$)$ message transmission scheme such that $\delta = t/(q-t+1)$.*

Proof. At first, $(C(x_1), C(x_2), \ldots, C(x_n))$ is a codeword of the Reed-Solomon Code with minimum distance $n - t$. Moreover, if $n - t > 2t(n = 3t + 1)$ then $C(x)$ can be reconstructed even when t ciphertexts are forged.

Privacy. We use $(2t+1, t+1, 3t+1)$ threshold scheme for encrypting messages and A can know at most $t(= 2t + 1 - (t+1))$ ciphertexts about message So, by the property of ramp scheme, A can not get any information about message.

General Reliability. A can forge at most t ciphertexts. In other words, in decryption, there are $2t + 1$ channels' informations are unforged. These informations about message determine one polynomial which encrypting message. If A want R to decrypt invalid message $\hat{m} \neq m$, at least A must forge ciphertexts such that the forged value about message is not on polynomial f. But, Dec check whether all information about message pass the same polynomial of degree $2t$. So, Dec never outputs invalid message.

Failure. Here, we prove $\delta = t/(q-t+1)$. Firstly, we show $C(x)$ is $1/q$-ASU_{t+1}. Suppose $C(x) = a_0 + a_1 \cdot x + \ldots, a_t \cdot x^t$, for any $a_1, \ldots, a_t$, x_1 and y_1, we can manipulate a_0 so as to $C(x_1) = y_1$. So, $|\{C(x) \mid C(x_1) = y_1\}| = q^t$. $|H| = q^{t+1}$ and $|B| = q$. So $C(x)$ suffices condition 1 for $1/q$-ASU_{t+1}. Similarly, for any $a_1, \ldots, a_t, x_1, \ldots, x_{t+1}$ and $y_1, \ldots, y_{t+1}$, $|\{C(x) \mid C(x_1) = y_1, \ldots, C(x_t) = y_t\}| = q$ and $|\{C(x) \mid C(x_1) = y_1, \ldots, C(x_{t+1}) = y_{t+1}\}| = 1$. So, $|\{C(x) \mid C(x_1) = y_1, \ldots, C(x_{t+1}) = y_{t+1}\}|/|\{C(x) \mid C(x_1) = y_1, \ldots, C(x_t) = y_t\}| = 1/q$. So, $C(x)$ suffices condition 2 for $1/q$-ASU_{t+1}. So, $C(x)$ is $1/q$-ASU_{t+1}.

As noted beginning of proof, C can be reconstructed even when t informations are forged. C is chosen randomly, the following equality holds for any distinct $x_1, \ldots, x_t, x_{t+1} \in GF(q)$ and for any $y_1, \ldots, y_t, y_{t+1} \in GF(q)$.

$$\Pr[C(x_{t+1}) = y_{t+1} | C(x_1) = y_1, \ldots, C(x_t) = y_t] = 1/q$$

Without loss of generality, we can assume $C_1, \ldots, C_t$ are channels which A observe and forge the ciphertexts sent through. Suppose that A try to forge c_1 to $c_1' = (c_{m,1}', c_{c,1}')$ such that $c_{m,1}' \neq c_{m,1}$, 1 is added to L in the process of decryption if $c_{c,1}' = C(c_{m,1}')$ since Enc can recover the original $C(x)$ even when t ciphertexts are forged.

Since $\{C(x)|C(x) \text{ over } GF(q) \text{ and the degree at most } t\}$ is a strong class of universal hash functions and $c_{m,1}'$ is different from any of $p \cdot (i-1) + c_{m,i}'$ ($1 \leq i \leq t$), the following equation holds:

$$\Pr[C(c_{m,1}') = c_{c,1}' | C(p \cdot (i-1) + c_{m,i}) = c_{c,i}, (\text{for} 1 \leq i \leq t)] = 1/q$$

where the probability is taken over the random choice of $C(x)$. The above discussion holds for any $c_i (1 \leq i \leq t)$ (But, we must consider that A can choose the values of forged ciphertext adaptively.) For making R output "failure", A must make pass at least one forged ciphertext. A can forge at most t informations. So, if q is sufficiently large, the probability that Enc outputs "failure" is

$$1-(1-1/q)(1-1/(q-1))\ldots(1-1/(q-t+1)) \leq 1-(1-1/(q-t+1))^t \leq t/(q-t+1).$$

Trivial Reliability. As noted above, $C(x)$ can be reconstructed correctly. In this case, information about message do not contain forged information. So, the R can correctly decrypt messages.   □

Proposed scheme is (t, δ)-secure (1-round, $3t + 1$-channel) MTS such that

$$|M| = p^{t+1}, \delta = t/(q-t+1), |x_i| = p \cdot q.$$

Now suppose $log|M| = l$, this scheme's communication bits $b(l)$ is $b(l) = n \cdot (\log p + \log q) \approx n \cdot (l/(t+1) + \log 1/\delta)$.

5   A Scheme with Flexible Parameters

There is a limitation that the δ must be smaller than $t/n|M|^{1/t}$ in section 4's scheme. This limitation is not preferable, especially when we want to send a message with large size. However, for considering sharing a secret with large size, in [12] a t-cheater identifiable secret sharing scheme is proposed. The properties of this scheme are summarized by following proposition.

Proposition 3. [12] If $k \geq 3t+1$, there exists a (t, ϵ) cheater identifiable (k, n) threshold scheme such that

$$|S| = p^N, \epsilon = (N-1)/p + 1/q \leq N/p, q \geq n \cdot p, |v_i| = p^{N+1} \cdot q.$$

Using this scheme, we can construct a (1-round, $3t + 1$-channel) message transmission scheme as follows.

-Enc: On input a message $m \in GF((p^{N \cdot (t+1)}))$ where $(m_0, m_1, \ldots, m_t)$ is a vector representation of m, the encryption algorithm Enc outputs a list of ciphertexts $(c_1, \ldots, c_n)$ as follows:

1. Generate a random polynomial $f_m(x)$ of degree at most $2t$ over $GF(p^N)$ such that

$$f_m(x) = m_0 + m_1 x + \ldots + m_t x^t + a_{t+1} x^{t+1} + \ldots + a_{2t} x^{2t}$$

   where $a_{t+1}, \ldots, a_{2t}$ are ramdom elements over $GF(p^N)$.
2. Generate $e \in GF(p)$ randomly and construct a random polynomial $C_e(x)$ of degree at most t over $GF(p)$ such that $C_e(0) = e$.
3. Generate a random polynomial $C_s(x)$ of degree at most t over $GF(q)$.
4. Compute $c_{m,i} = (c_{m,i,0}, \ldots, c_{m,i,N-1}) = f_m(i)$ where $c_{m,i,j} \in GF(p)$ (for $0 \leq j \leq N-1$), $c_{C_e,i} = C_e(i)$ and $c_{C_s,i} = C_s(p \cdot (i-1) + (\sum_{j=0}^{N-1} c_{m,i,j} \cdot e^j \bmod p))$.
5. Compute $c_i = (c_{m,i}, c_{C_e,i}, c_{C_s,i})$ and output $(c_1, \ldots, c_n)$.

-Dec: On input a list of ciphertexts $((c_{m,1}, c_{e,1}, c_{s,1}), \ldots, (c_{m,n}, c_{e,n}, c_{s,n}))$, the decryption algorithm Dec outputs a secret m or $\perp$ as follows:

1. Reconstruct $\hat{C}_e(x)$ and $\hat{C}_s(x)$ from $(c_{e,1}, \ldots, c_{e,n})$ and $(c_{s,1}, \ldots, c_{s,n})$, respectively using an error correction algorithm of Reed-Solomon Code.
2. Check if $c_{C_e,i} = \hat{C}_e(i)$ (for $1 \leq i \leq n$.) If $c_{C_e,i} = \hat{C}_e(i)$ then i is added to the list of valid ciphertexts L.
3. Compute $\hat{e} = \hat{C}_e(0)$.
4. Check if $c_{s,i} = \hat{C}_s(p \cdot (i-1) + (\sum_{l=0}^{N-1} c_{m,i,l} \cdot e^l \bmod p))$ holds (for all $i \in L$). If $c_{s,i} \neq \hat{C}_s(p \cdot (i-1) + (\sum_{l=0}^{N-1} c_{m,i,l} \cdot e^l \bmod p))$ then i is removed from the list of valid ciphertexts L.
5. Reconstruct $\hat{f}_m(x)$ from k of $c_{m,i}$ where $i \in L$ and check all $c_{m,i}$ where $i \in L$ pass $\hat{f}_m(x)$. If all $c_{m,i}$ where $i \in L$ pass $\hat{f}_m(x)$, output the values embeded to f_m. Otherwise Dec outputs failure.

Clearly, the running time of Dec is polynomial in n and the properties of this scheme is summarized by the following theorem.

Theorem 2. *Proposed scheme is (t, δ)-secure (1-round, $(3t + 1)$-channel) message transmission scheme such that $\delta = t(N-1)/(p-(N+1)(t-1))+t/(q-t+1)$.*

Proof. The proofs of Privacy, General Reliability and Trivial Reliability are the same as in the proof of Theorem 1. So, we only prove $\delta = t(N - 1)/(p - (N + 1)(t - 1)) + t/(q - t + 1)$.

As in the proof of Theorem 1, $(C_e(x_1), C_e(x_2), \ldots, C_e(x_n))$ and $(C_s(x_1), C_s(x_2), \ldots, C_s(x_n))$ are codewords of the Reed-Solomon Code with minimum distance $n - t$. Moreover, $n - t > 2t$ ($n = 3t + 1$). So, $C_e(x)$ and $C_s(x)$ can be reconstructed even when t ciphertexts are forged.

Suppose that A try to forge c_1 to $c'_1 = (c'_{m,1}, c'_{e,1}, c'_{s,1})$ such that $c'_{m,1} \neq c_{m,1}$, 1 is added to L in the process of decryption if $c'_{s,1} = C_s(\sum_{j=0}^{N-1} c'_{m,1,j} \cdot e^j \bmod p)$ where e randomly distributed over $GF(p)$. There are two cases to consider in computing such probability. In the first case suppose that $c'_{s,1} \neq c_{s,1}$. In this case, the successful probability ϵ of A who know that $c_{s,i} = C_s(p \cdot (i-1) + (\sum_{j=0}^{N-1} c_{m,i,j} \cdot$

$e^j \mod p)$) hold for $1 \le i \le t$ is computed as follows. (For simplicity we will denote $\sum_{j=0}^{N-1} c_{m,i,j} \cdot e^j \mod p$ by $g(c_{m,i}, e)$.)

$$\begin{aligned}
\epsilon &= \Pr[c'_{s,i} = C_s(g(c'_{m,i}))|c_{s,i} = C_s(g(c_{m,i}))(\text{for} 1 \le i \le t)] \\
&= \Pr[g(c_{m,i}, e) \ne g(c'_{m,i}, e)] \\
&\quad \cdot \Pr[c'_{s,i} = C_s(g(c'_{m,i}))|c_{s,i} = C_s(g(c_{m,i}))(\text{for} 1 \le i \le t), g(c_{m,i}, e) \ne g(c'_{m,i}, e)] \\
&\le 1/q
\end{aligned}$$

where the last inequality directly follows from the fact that $\{C_s\}$ is a family of a strong class of universal hash function with strength $t + 1$. (See the proof of Theorem 1 for details.)

Next we consider the second case in which $c'_{s,1} = c_{s,1}$ holds. In this case ϵ is computed as follows.

$$\begin{aligned}
\epsilon &= \Pr[c'_{s,i} = C_s(g(c'_{m,i}))|c_{s,i} = C_s(g(c_{m,i}))(\text{for} 1 \le i \le t)] \\
&= \Pr[g(c_{m,i}, e) = g(c'_{m,i}, e)] + \Pr[g(c_{m,i}, e) \ne g(c'_{m,i}, e)] \cdot \\
&\quad \Pr[c'_{s,i} = C_s(g(c'_{m,i}))|c_{s,i} = C_s(g(c_{m,i}))(\text{for} 1 \le i \le t), g(c_{m,i}, e) \ne g(c'_{m,i}, e)] \\
&\le \Pr[g(c_{m,i}, e) = g(c'_{m,i}, e)] + 1/q
\end{aligned}$$

$g(c_{m,i}, e)$ and $g(c'_{m,i}, e)$ are different polynomial of degree at most $N - 1$ about e. So, $g(c_{m,i}, e) = g(c'_{m,i}, e)$ has at most $N - 1$ roots. So,

$$\Pr[g(c_{m,i}, e) = g(c'_{m,i}, e)] + 1/q \le (N - 1)/p + 1/q$$

The above discussion holds for any $c_i (1 \le i \le t)$ (But, we must consider that A can choose the values of forged ciphertext adaptively.) For making R output "failure", A must make pass at least one forged ciphertext. A can forge at most t informations. So, if p is sufficiently large, the probability that Enc outputs "failure" is

$$\begin{aligned}
&1 - (1 - ((N-1)/p + 1/q)) \ldots (1 - ((N - 1)/(p - (N + 1)(t - 1)) + 1/(q - t + 1))) \\
&\le 1 - (1 - ((N - 1)/(p - (N + 1)(t - 1)) + 1/(q - t + 1)))^t \\
&\le t(N - 1)/(p - (N + 1)(t - 1)) + t/(q - t + 1)) \qquad \square
\end{aligned}$$

Proposed scheme is (t, δ)-secure (1-round, $3t + 1$-channel) MTS such that

$$|M| = p^{(t+1) \cdot N}, \delta = t(N - 1)/(p - (N + 1)(t - 1)) + t/(q - t + 1)), |x_i| = p^{N+1} \cdot q.$$

Now suppose $log|M| = l$, this scheme's communication bits $b(l)$ is $b(l) \approx n \cdot (N \cdot \log p + \log p + \log q) \approx n \cdot (l/(t + 1) + 2 \cdot \log 1/\delta)$.

The scheme proposed in section 4 is more efficient. But, this scheme can take more flexible parameters by controlling N.

6   Conclusion

In this paper, we present two (t, δ)-secure (1-round, $3t + 1$-channel) message transmission scheme.

Table 1. Comparison of the communication bits $b(l)$

	Scheme in § 4	Scheme in § 5 ($N = 3$)	Dolev et.al. ($\delta = 0$)
$b(512)$	$2500, \delta \approx 2^{-126}$	$2160, \delta \approx 2^{-40}$	5120
$b(1024)$	$5160, \delta \approx 2^{-254}$	$4310, \delta \approx 2^{-83}$	10240
$b(2048)$	$10280, \delta \approx 2^{-510}$	$8560, \delta \approx 2^{-168}$	20480
$b(3072)$	$15400, \delta \approx 2^{-766}$	$12810, \delta \approx 2^{-766}$	30720

Table 2. Comparison of the communication bits $b(l)$ for large message

	Scheme in § 5 ($\delta \geq 2^{-80}$)	Dolev et.al. ($\delta = 0$)
$b(1M)$	$2.5M + 2040$	$10M$
$b(2M)$	$5M + 2120$	$20M$
$b(4M)$	$10M + 2280$	$40M$

These schemes are quite simple and direct construction using (t, ϵ)-Cheater Identifiable (k, n) threshold schemes proposed by Obana [12] and ramp scheme [3]. However, if sending message is large some degree, this scheme is much more efficient with respect to the number of communication bits for transmitting messages comparing to the perfectly secure (1-round, $3t + 1$-channel) MTS proposed by Dolev et.al [5].

Table 1 compares the length of communication bits $b(l)$ and δ for the various message size where $t = 3$ and $n = 3 \cdot 3 + 1 = 10$. In Table 2, we compare the length of communication bits $b(l)$ for the large message size. It can be seen that proposed scheme has small failure probability but the bit length of communication bits is much more efficient comparing to the scheme proposed in [5].

Finding the bound of $b(l)$ of $(t, \delta(\neq 0))$-secure scheme and comparing this to our proposed scheme will be future work.

Acknowledgement

We are grateful to Matthias Fitzi for giving us many valuable comments on technical and editorial problems in the initial version of this paper. We would also like to thank the anonymous referees for useful and detailed comments.

References

1. Berlekamp, E.R.: Algebraic Coding Theory, ch. 7. McGraw-Hill, New York (1968)
2. Blakley, G.R.: Safeguarding cryptographic keys. In: Proc. AFIPS 1979, National Computer Conference, vol. 48, pp. 313–137 (1979); vol. 4(4), pp. 502–510 (1991)
3. Blakley, G.R., Meadows, C.: Security of Ramp Schemes. In: Blakely, G.R., Chaum, D. (eds.) CRYPTO 1984. LNCS, vol. 196, pp. 242–268. Springer, Heidelberg (1985)
4. Cramer, R., Dodis, Y., Fehr, S., Wichs, C.P.D.: Detection of Algebraic Manipulation with Applications to Robust Secret Sharing and Fuzzy Extractors. In: Smart, N. (ed.) EUROCRYPT 2008. LNCS, vol. 4965, pp. 471–488. Springer, Heidelberg (2008)

5. Dolev, D., Dwork, C., Waarts, O., Yung, M.: Perfectly secure message transmission. J. ACM 40(1), 17–47 (1993)
6. Fitzi, M., Franklin, M.K., Garay, J.A., Vardhan, S.H.: Towards Optimal and Efficient Perfectly Secure Message Transmission. In: Vadhan, S.P. (ed.) TCC 2007. LNCS, vol. 4392, pp. 311–322. Springer, Heidelberg (2007)
7. Kurosawa, K., Obana, S., Ogata, W.: t-Cheater Identifiable (k, n) Threshold Secret Sharing Schemes. In: Coppersmith, D. (ed.) CRYPTO 1995. LNCS, vol. 963, pp. 410–423. Springer, Heidelberg (1995)
8. Kurosawa, K., Suzuki, K.: Almost Secure (1-Round, n-Channel) Message Transmission Scheme. In: ICITS 2008 (2008)
9. McEliece, R.J., Sarwate, D.V.: On sharing secrets and Reed-Solomon codes. Com. Acm 24, 583–584 (1981)
10. Shamir, A.: How to Share a Secret. Communications of the ACM 22(11), 612–613 (1979)
11. Srinathan, K., Naraayanam, A., Pandu Rangan, C.: Optimal Perfectly Secure Message Transmission. In: Franklin, M. (ed.) CRYPTO 2004. LNCS, vol. 3152, pp. 545–561. Springer, Heidelberg (2004)
12. Obana, S.: Almost optimum t-Cheater Identifiable Secret Sharing Schemes. SCIS 2007 (in Japanese) (2007)
13. Rabin, T., Ben-Or, M.: Verifiable Secret Sharing and Multiparty Protocols with Honest Majority. Journal of the ACM 41(6), 1089–1109 (1994)

Interactive Hashing:
An Information Theoretic Tool
(Invited Talk)

Claude Crépeau[1,*], Joe Kilian[2,**], and George Savvides[3,***]

[1] McGill University, Montréal, QC, Canada
`crepeau@cs.mcgill.ca`
[2] Rutgers University, New Brunswick, NJ, USA
`jkilian@cs.rutgers.edu`
[3] European Patent Office, München, Germany
`gsavvides@gmail.com`

Abstract. Interactive Hashing has featured as an essential ingredient in protocols realizing a large variety of cryptographic tasks, notably Oblivious Transfer in the bounded memory model. In Interactive Hashing, a sender transfers a bit string to a receiver such that two strings are received, the original string and a second string that appears to be chosen at random among those distinct from the first.

This paper starts by formalizing the notion of Interactive Hashing as a cryptographic primitive, disentangling it from the specifics of its various implementations. To this end, we present an application-independent set of information theoretic conditions that all Interactive Hashing protocols must ideally satisfy. We then provide a standard implementation of Interactive Hashing and use it to reduce a very standard version of Oblivious Transfer to another one which appears much weaker.

1 Introduction

Interactive Hashing (IH) is a cryptographic primitive that allows a sender Alice to send a bit string w to a receiver Bob who receives two output strings, labeled w_0, w_1 according to lexicographic order. The primitive guarantees that one of the two outputs is equal to the original input. The other string is guaranteed to be effectively random, in the sense that it is chosen beyond Alice's control, even if she acts dishonestly. On the other hand, provided that from Bob's point of view w_0, w_1 are a priori equiprobable inputs for Alice, the primitive guarantees that Bob cannot guess which of the two was the original input with probability greater than $1/2$. We remark that typically both outputs are also available to Alice. See Figure 1.

In this article we provide a study of Interactive Hashing in the information theoretic setting and in isolation of any surrounding context. This modular approach

---

* Supported in part by NSERC, MITACS, CIFAR, and QuantumWorks.
** Some of this research was done while the author worked for NEC Research.
*** This research was done while the author was a student at McGill University.

R. Safavi-Naini (Ed.): ICITS 2008, LNCS 5155, pp. 14–28, 2008.
© Springer-Verlag Berlin Heidelberg 2008

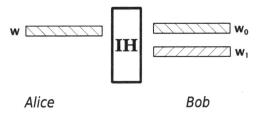

Fig. 1. Interactive Hashing: the sender Alice sends string w to Bob, who receives two strings w_0, w_1, labeled according to lexicographic order. One of the two (in our example, w_0) is equal to the input string while the other is effectively randomly chosen. Bob cannot distinguish which of the two was the original input.

allows specific implementations (protocols) of Interactive Hashing to be analyzed independently of any applications in which they appear as sub-protocols. It thus leads to a better appreciation of the power of Interactive Hashing as a *cryptographic primitive* in its own right.

To demonstrate the relevance of Interactive Hashing, we present an application to protocols for Oblivious Transfer (OT). Oblivious Transfer is an important primitive in modern cryptography. It was originally studied by Wiesner [Wie70] (under the name of "multiplexing"), in a paper that marked the birth of quantum cryptography and was later independently introduced to cryptography in several variations by Rabin [Rab81] and by Even, Goldreich and Lempel [EGL85]. Oblivious transfer has since become the basis for realizing a broad class of cryptographic protocols, such as bit commitment, zero-knowledge proofs, and general secure multiparty computation [Yao86, GMW87, Kil88, Gol04].

In a one-out-of-two Oblivious Transfer, denoted $\binom{2}{1}$-OT, a sender owns two secret bits b_0 and b_1, and a receiver wants to learn b_c for a secret bit c of his choice. The sender will only collaborate if the receiver can obtain information about exclusively one of b_0 or b_1. Likewise, the receiver will only participate provided that the sender cannot obtain any information about c.

1.1   Organization of the Paper

We present the previous work on Interactive Hashing in Section 2. In Section 3 we identify and formalize the information theoretic security properties of Interactive Hashing. Then, in Section 3.1 we turn our attention to the Interactive Hashing implementation that appeared as a sub-protocol in [OVY93] and refer the reader to recent work [Sav07, CCMS09] demonstrating that despite its simplicity, it meets all security properties set forth in Section 3. This new proof of security is an important improvement over the proof that appeared in [CCM98], where the authors demonstrate that a slight variant of the IH protocol of [OVY93] could be securely used in their specific scenario. The new proof is more general, as it is based on the security properties stated in Section 3. Moreover, the proof is significantly simpler and more intuitive. Lastly, it provides an easier to use and much tighter upper bound on the probability that the protocol fails to ensure that one of the two strings is sufficiently random. Section 4 defines our example problem: reducing $\binom{2}{1}$-OT to a very weak version of Oblivious Transfer. Section 5 exhibits the solution to our example problem using Interactive Hashing. Finally, we conclude in Section 6 and introduce a few open problems.

2   Previous Work

Various implementations of Interactive Hashing have appeared as sub-protocols in the cryptographic literature, first in computational contexts where at least one of the participants is polynomially bounded and later also in contexts where security is unconditional (information theoretic).

While reviewing the previous work, the reader should bear in mind that so far, Interactive Hashing has never been presented as an independent primitive. Instead, it only appears within the context of larger protocols achieving a variety of different cryptographic tasks. Not surprisingly, the properties it is expected to have can vary significantly from one application to the next, and thus the proof of security in each case depends on the specific setting.

2.1   Uses of Interactive Hashing in Computational Contexts

Interactive Hashing first appeared as a sub-protocol within a protocol achieving Oblivious Transfer from an unbounded sender to a polynomial-time bounded receiver [OVY93]. Soon thereafter, Interactive Hashing was deployed in various other scenarios, such as zero-knowledge proofs [OVY94] and bit commitment schemes [OVY92, NOVY98], where at least one of the participants was computationally bounded. For more recent applications of Interactive Hashing in this setting consult [HHK+05, NOV06, NV06, HR07].

2.2   Uses of Interactive Hashing in Information Theoretic Contexts

Beside the computational scenarios in which it was originally used, Interactive Hashing proved to be an important tool in information theoretic contexts as well. Its first such use was in protocols for Oblivious Transfer which are information-theoretically secure under the sole assumption that the receiver's memory is bounded [CCM98, Din01, DHRS07]. Interactive Hashing was later used to optimize reductions between Oblivious Transfer variants [CS06].

We remark that while some of the security properties required of Interactive Hashing in information theoretic settings bear a very close resemblance to their counterparts in computational settings, some other properties are substantially different. Moreover, the transition from computational to information theoretic settings requires a re-evaluation of *all* security properties of any protocol. For this reason, starting with [CCM98], the security properties of the underlying Interactive Hashing sub-protocol have been re-evaluated in the light of the specific, information theoretic context where it was used.

3   Information-Theoretic Secure Interactive Hashing

We now formalize the security properties that Interactive Hashing is expected to satisfy in information theoretic contexts. As these properties do not depend on any specific application, they allow us to define Interactive Hashing as an independent cryptographic primitive.

Definition 1. Interactive Hashing *is a cryptographic primitive between two players, the sender and the receiver. It takes as input a string* $w \in \{0,1\}^t$ *from the sender, and produces as output two* t–*bit strings one of which is* w *and the other* $w' \neq w$. *The output strings are available to both the sender and the receiver, and satisfy the following properties:*

1. The receiver cannot tell which of the two output strings was the original input. *Let the two output strings be* w_0, w_1, *labeled according to lexicographic order. Then if both strings were a priori equally likely to have been the sender's input* w, *then they are a posteriori equally likely as well[1].*

2. When both participants are honest, the input is equally likely to be paired with any of the other strings. *Let* w *be the sender's input and let* w' *be the second output of interactive hashing. Then provided that both participants follow the protocol,* w' *will be uniformly distributed among all* $2^t - 1$ *strings different from* w.

3. The sender cannot force both outputs to have a rare property. *Let* $\mathcal{G}$ *be a subset of* $\{0,1\}^t$ *representing the sender's "good set". Let* G *be the cardinality of* $\mathcal{G}$ *and let* $T = 2^t$. *Then if* G/T *is "small", the probability that a dishonest sender will succeed in having both outputs* w_0, w_1 *be in* $\mathcal{G}$ *is comparably "small".*

Remark 1. In the computational contexts of Section 2.1, similar properties to Properties 1 and 2 were also required. On the other hand, the computational counterpart to Property 3 is usually stated quite differently, as there is no predetermined good set $\mathcal{G}$. For instance, in [NOVY98] where the inputs and outputs of Interactive Hashing are interpreted as images under a one-way permutation π, one of the two outputs is required to be sufficiently random so that any polynomial-time algorithm that can compute pre-images to both outputs a significant fraction of the time can be used to efficiently invert π on a randomly chosen string with non-negligible probability.

We shall also point out that Property 3 is easy to satisfy when $G \in o(\sqrt{T})$ because of the so called Birthday paradox. If the receiver picks a random hash function h from $\{0,1\}^t \to \{0,1\}^{t-1}$ and announces it to the sender, only with very small probability will there exist a pair $w_0, w_1 \in \mathcal{G}$ such that $h(w_0) = h(w_1)$. The real challenge, met by Interactive Hashing, is to obtain Property 3 for sets $\mathcal{G}$ such that $G \in \Omega(\sqrt{T})$.

---

[1] Note that if we want this property to hold for all possible outputs, then w must be uniformly chosen. Otherwise, this property will only hold whenever w happens to be paired with a string w' having the same a priori probability as w.

3.1 A Secure Protocol for Interactive Hashing

We will be examining the implementation of Interactive Hashing given in Protocol 1. This standard implementation was originally introduced in a computational context by Ostrovsky, Venkatesan, and Yung [OVY93]. In Section 3.1 we will see that this very simple protocol actually meets all our information theoretic security requirements as well.

Protocol 1. Interactive Hashing

Let w be a t-bit string that the sender wishes to send to the receiver. All operations below take place in the binary field $\mathcal{F}_2$.

1. The receiver chooses a $(t - 1) \times t$ matrix Q uniformly at random among all binary matrices of rank $t - 1$. Let q_i be the ith query, consisting of the ith row of Q.
2. For $1 \leq i \leq t - 1$ do:
   (a) The receiver sends query q_i to the sender.
   (b) The sender responds with $c_i = q_i \cdot w$.
3. Given Q and c (the vector of Bob's responses), both parties compute the two values of w consistent with the linear system $Q \cdot w = c$. These solutions are labeled w_0, w_1 according to lexicographic order.

Remark 2. One way of choosing the matrix Q is to choose a $(t - 1) \times t$ binary matrix uniformly at random and test whether it has rank $t - 1$, repeating the process if necessary. Note that a later variation of the protocol [NOVY98] chose Q in a canonical way to guarantee that it has rank $t - 1$, which results in a somewhat more practical implementation. However, this appears to complicate the proof of security.

Theorem 1 establishes the security of Protocol 1.

Theorem 1. *[Sav07, CCMS09] Protocol 1 satisfies all three information theoretic security properties of Definition 1. Specifically, for Property 3, it ensures that a dishonest sender can succeed in causing both outputs to be in the "good set" $\mathcal{G}$ with probability at most $15.6805 \cdot {}^{G}/_{T}$.*

3.2 Proofs of Information Theoretic Security

Cachin, Crépeau, and Marcil [CCM98] proved a similar property to Property 3 for a slight variant of Protocol 1 in the context of memory-bounded Oblivious Transfer where again, the goal of a dishonest sender is to force both outputs of the protocol to be from a subset $\mathcal{G}$ of cardinality G (out of a total $T = 2^t$). While their approach relies on upper-bounding the number of the sender's remaining good strings during the various rounds of the protocol, the new proof of [Sav07, CCMS09] focuses instead on following the evolution of the number of *pairs* of good strings remaining after each round. This seems to be a more natural choice for this scenario, as there is exactly one such pair remaining at the end of the protocol if the sender succeeds in cheating and none otherwise (as opposed to two strings versus zero or one). Consequently, the probability of cheating is simply equal to the expected number of remaining pairs. Thanks to the nature of the protocol, it is relatively easy to establish an upper bound on the expected number of remaining pairs after each incoming query, and to keep track of its evolution through the protocol.

The new approach of [Sav07, CCMS09] not only leads to a simpler and more robust proof of security, but more importantly, it also allows to establish a more general and much tighter upper bound on a dishonest sender's probability of cheating. Specifically, it allows to show that any strategy a dishonest sender might employ can succeed with probability no larger than $15.6805 \cdot G/T$, for all fractions G/T of good strings. The corresponding upper bound in [CCM98] is $\sqrt{2} \cdot \sqrt[8]{G/T}$ and is only valid provided that $G/T < \left(16t^8\right)^{-1}$. It should be noted that the new upper bound is in fact tight up to a small constant. Indeed, the probability of succeeding in cheating using an optimal strategy is lower-bounded by the probability of getting two good output strings when the sender chooses $w \in \mathcal{G}$ as input and then acts honestly. By Property 2 of Interactive Hashing, w is equally likely to be paired with any of the remaining strings. It follows that the probability of w being paired with one of the other $G - 1$ good strings is exactly $G-1/T-1$. Assuming that $G \geq 50$, the new upper bound is larger than this lower bound by a factor of at most $15.6805 \cdot \left(\frac{G}{T}\right)\left(\frac{T-1}{G-1}\right) < 15.6805 \left(\frac{G}{G-1}\right) \leq 16$. This establishes that the new upper bound is tight up to a small constant in all cases where the possibility of cheating exists.

3.3 An Alternative Implementation

Ding *et al.* [DHRS07] make use of a new, constant-round Interactive Hashing protocol to achieve Oblivious Transfer with a memory-bounded receiver. The main idea behind their protocol, which requires only four rounds of interaction (compared to $t - 1$ rounds in Protocol 1), is that if the receiver sends a random permutation π to the sender (Round 1) who then applies it to his input string w and announces a certain number of bits of $\pi(w)$ (Round 2), then two more rounds suffice to transmit the remaining part of $\pi(w)$ so that only 1 bit remains undetermined: in Round 3, the receiver chooses a function g uniformly at random from a family of 2–wise independent 2–1 hash functions, and in Round 4 the sender announces the value of the function applied to the remaining bits of $\pi(w)$. The output of the Interactive Hashing protocol consists of the two possible inputs to the permutation π consistent with the values transmitted at rounds 2 and 4. The security of this scheme is based on the observation that the permutation π in the first round divides the (dishonest) sender's good set $\mathcal{G}$ into buckets (indexed by the bits transmitted at Round 2), so that with high probability, in each bucket the fraction of good strings is below the Birthday Paradox threshold. This allows regular 2–1 hashing to be used in Rounds 3 and 4 to complete the protocol.

It should be noted that since a random permutation would need exponential space to describe, the construction resorts to *almost t-wise independent permutations*, which can be efficiently constructed and compactly described.

Unfortunately, the protocol of [DHRS07] is less general than Protocol 1 for a variety of reasons: first, its implementation requires that the two parties know a priori an upper bound on the cardinality of the dishonest receiver's good set $\mathcal{G}$, as this will determine the number of bits of $\pi(w)$ announced in Round 2. Secondly, the upper bound for the probability that Property 3 is not met is, according to the authors' analysis, $\Omega\left(t \cdot {}^{\mathcal{G}}/_{T}\right)$ and only applies when $G \geq 4t$. Moreover, the protocol does not fully satisfy Property 2, but only a slight relaxation[2] of it. Lastly, the protocol is very involved, and probably prohibitively complicated to implement in practice. We leave it as an open problem to improve upon this construction.

4 Reducing OT to a Very Weak OT

We illustrate the power of Interactive Hashing in information theoretic contexts by considering the following straightforward scenario, originally suggested by the second author: suppose that a sender Alice and a receiver Bob wish to implement 1-out-of-k Bit Oblivious Transfer, which we will denote as $\binom{k}{1}$–Bit OT. For the purposes of our example, suffice it to say that Alice would like to make available k randomly chosen bits to Bob, who must be able to choose to learn any one of them, with all choices being equally likely from Alice's point of view. Alice is only willing to participate provided that (dishonest) Bob learns information about exclusively one bit, while Bob must receive the assurance that (dishonest) Alice cannot obtain any information about his choice. Suppose that all that is available to Alice and Bob is an insecure version of $\binom{k}{1}$–Bit OT, denoted $(k-1)$–faulty $\binom{k}{1}$–Bit OT, which allows honest Bob to receive (only) one bit of his choice but might allow a dishonest Bob to learn up to $k-1$ bits of his choice. The rest of this section focuses on the early work of the first two authors who had made repeated but unsuccessful attempts to find a satisfactory reduction of $\binom{k}{1}$–Bit OT to $(k-1)$–faulty $\binom{k}{1}$–Bit OT, whereas Protocol 4 shows how Interactive Hashing makes such a reduction almost trivial.

Remark 3. For simplicity, Protocol 2 and Protocol 4 reduce $\binom{2}{1}$–Bit OT to weaker versions of OT without any loss of generality since $\binom{k}{1}$–Bit OT can in turn be reduced to $\binom{2}{1}$–Bit OT using the well-known reduction in [BCR86]. We shall denote "$x +_k y$" to be "$x + y \bmod k$" except if $x + y \equiv 0 \pmod{k}$ in which case "$x +_k y = k$". More formally, $x +_k y = (x + y - 1 \bmod k) + 1$.

4.1 Reduction of $\binom{2}{1}$–Bit OT to $O(\sqrt{k})$–Faulty $\binom{k}{1}$–Bit OT

As a warm up exercise we exhibit a simple reduction of $\binom{2}{1}$–Bit OT to $O(\sqrt{k})$– faulty $\binom{k}{1}$–Bit OT, a faulty primitive, allowing a dishonest Bob to get at most $O(\sqrt{k})$ bits of Alice's input at his choosing.

---

[2] It approximates the uniform distribution over the remaining strings within some $\eta < 2^{-t}$.

Protocol 2. Reduction of $\binom{2}{1}$–Bit OT to $O(\sqrt{k})$–faulty $\binom{k}{1}$–Bit OT

Let $\overset{\circ}{b}_0, \overset{\circ}{b}_1$ and $\overset{\circ}{c}$ be the inputs of Alice and Bob, respectively, for $\binom{2}{1}$–Bit OT.

1. Alice and Bob agree on a security parameter n.
2. For $1 \leq i \leq n$ do:
   (a) Alice selects at random bits $r_{i1}, r_{i2}, \ldots, r_{ik}$ while Bob selects at random $c_i \in_R \{1, \ldots, k\}$.
   (b) Alice uses $O(\sqrt{k})$–faulty $\binom{k}{1}$–Bit OT to send her k bits to Bob, who chooses to learn r_{ic_i}.
   (c) Alice picks a random distance $\Delta_i \in_R \{1, \ldots, k/2\}$ and announces it to Bob.
   (d) Bob announces σ_i such that $c_i = \sigma_i +_k \overset{\circ}{c}\Delta_i$ to Alice.
3. Alice computes $R_0 = \bigoplus\limits_{i=1}^{n} r_{i\sigma_i}$ and $R_1 = \bigoplus\limits_{i=1}^{n} r_{i(\sigma_i +_k \Delta_i)}$.
4. Alice sends $e_0 = \overset{\circ}{b}_0 \oplus R_0$ and $e_1 = \overset{\circ}{b}_1 \oplus R_1$ to Bob.
5. Bob obtains $\overset{\circ}{b}_{\overset{\circ}{c}} = e_{\overset{\circ}{c}} \oplus R_{\overset{\circ}{c}} = e_{\overset{\circ}{c}} \oplus \bigoplus_{i=1}^{n} r_{ic_i}$.

It is relatively straightforward to see that when both participants are honest, Protocol 2 allows Bob to obtain the bit of his choice since he knows $R_{\overset{\circ}{c}} = \bigoplus_{i=1}^{n} r_{ic_i}$ and can thus decrypt $e_{\overset{\circ}{c}}$. In case Alice is dishonest, Bob's choice $\overset{\circ}{c}$ is perfectly hidden from her when she obtains σ_i at Step 2d. This is because at the beginning of the protocol, Bob is equally likely to make the choices σ_i or $\sigma_i +_k \Delta_i$.

Now consider what a dishonest Bob can do. At round i, upon learning Δ_i in Step 2c, the probability that there exists a pair of indices at distance Δ_i where Bob knows both bits is less than $\frac{\ell_i(\ell_i - 1)/2}{k/2}$ when Bob knows ℓ_i bits out of k. This is because the maximum number of distances possible between ℓ_i positions is $\ell_i(\ell_i - 1)/2$, while the total number of distances is $k/2$. Thus, for an appropriate choice of the hidden constant in the $O()$ notation we have $\frac{O(\sqrt{k}(\sqrt{k}-1)/2)}{k/2} < 1/2$. In consequence, the probability that in Step 2d Bob is able to claim a σ_i such that he knows both $r_{i\sigma_i}$ and $r_{i(\sigma_i +_k \Delta_i)}$ is less than $1/2$. See Figure 2 for an example. Therefore, the probability that after n rounds Bob may compute both R_0 and R_1 is less than $1/2^n$.

4.2 Reduction of $O(\sqrt{k})$–Faulty $\binom{k}{1}$–Bit OT to $(k/2)$–Faulty $\binom{k}{1}$–Bit OT

As a continuation of the previous exercise we reduce $O(\sqrt{k})$–faulty $\binom{k}{1}$–Bit OT to $(k/2)$–faulty $\binom{k}{1}$–Bit OT, a faulty primitive allowing a dishonest Bob to get at most $k/2$ bits of Alice's input at his choosing.

It is again relatively straightforward to see that when both participants are honest, Protocol 3 allows Bob to obtain the bit of his choice since he knows

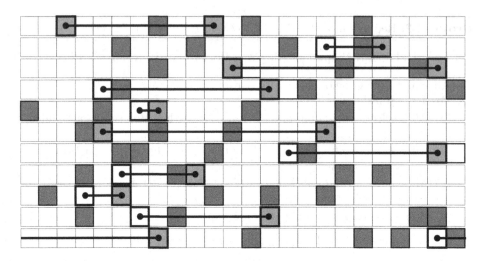

Fig. 2. $O(\sqrt{k})$-faulty $\binom{k}{1}$-Bit OT: Each row i corresponds to a round and in each row $O(\sqrt{k})$ grey squares indicate the positions obtained by a dishonest Bob. The bold lines indicate the distance Δ_i chosen by Alice. Bob can obtain both bits in the end if a pair of grey squares exists at the right distance in each row. We see that a few rows have such a pair but many don't.

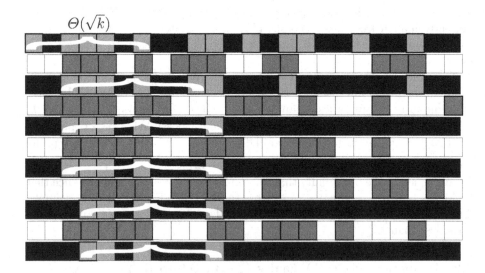

Fig. 3. $(k/2)$-faulty $\binom{k}{1}$-Bit OT: Each two rows $2i-1, 2i$ correspond to round i. Row $2i-1$ shows the number of bits known to dishonest Bob (in light grey). Each row $2i$, shows an execution of $(k/2)$-faulty $\binom{k}{1}$-Bit OT after mixing via π_i, and shifting via σ_i to align as many known bits (in darker grey) as possible in the first $\Theta(\sqrt{k})$ positions. Most of the times, it is not possible to save all the $\Theta(\sqrt{k})$ known bits.

Protocol 3. Reduction of $O(\sqrt{k})$–faulty $\binom{k}{1}$–Bit OT to $(k/2)$–faulty $\binom{k}{1}$–Bit OT

1. Alice and Bob agree on a security parameter n.
2. Bob selects at random $c \in_R \{1, \ldots, k\}$.
3. For $1 \leq i \leq 2n$ do:
   (a) Alice selects at random bits $r_{i1}, r_{i2}, \ldots, r_{ik}$ while Bob selects at random $c_i \in_R \{1, \ldots, k\}$.
   (b) Alice uses $(k/2)$–faulty $\binom{k}{1}$–Bit OT to send her k bits to Bob, who chooses to learn r_{ic_i}.
   (c) Alice picks a random permutation $\pi_i \in_R \{1, \ldots, k\} \to \{1, \ldots, k\}$ and announces it to Bob.
   (d) Bob computes a shift σ_i such that $\pi_i(c_i) = \sigma_i +_k c$ and announces it to Alice.
4. Alice computes For $1 \leq j \leq k$

$$R_j = \bigoplus_{i=1}^{2n} r_{i\pi_i^{-1}(\sigma_i + kj)}.$$

5. Bob outputs c and $R_c = \bigoplus_{i=1}^{2n} r_{ic_i}$.
6. Alice outputs $R_1, \ldots, R_k$.

$R_c = \bigoplus_{i=1}^{2n} r_{ic_i}$. In case Alice is dishonest, Bob's choice c is perfectly hidden from her when she obtains σ_i at Step 3d.

The rest of the reasoning is a bit more subtle. See Figure 3 for an example. Consider the first $\Theta(\sqrt{k})$ bits known by Bob. The number of sequences containing $k/2$ known bits that will have exactly those $\Theta(\sqrt{k})$ bits in the correct position is given by

$$\binom{k - \Theta(\sqrt{k})}{k/2} < \binom{k - \Theta(\sqrt{k})}{(k - \Theta(\sqrt{k}))/2} \approx \sqrt{\frac{2}{\pi}} \frac{2^{k - \Theta(\sqrt{k})}}{\sqrt{k - \Theta(\sqrt{k})}}.$$

All k shifts of these sequences are also successful for Bob because he can shift them to align them with the first $\Theta(\sqrt{k})$ bits known, thus a grand total of at most k times more or $\sqrt{\frac{2}{\pi}}\sqrt{k + \Theta(\sqrt{k})}2^{k-\Theta(\sqrt{k})}$. However, any new execution of $(k/2)$–faulty $\binom{k}{1}$–Bit OT combined with a random permutation π_i yields a completely random sequence with an equal number of bits known and unknown, or one out of $\binom{k}{k/2} \approx \sqrt{\frac{2}{\pi}} \frac{2^k}{\sqrt{k}}$. So the probability that a random sequence can be shifted to have the first $\Theta(\sqrt{k})$ known bits in the correct positions is at most the ratio of the two expressions:

$$\frac{k\binom{k-\Theta(\sqrt{k})}{k/2}}{\binom{k}{k/2}} < \frac{\sqrt{k + \Theta(\sqrt{k})}2^{k-\Theta(\sqrt{k})}}{2^k/\sqrt{k}} < O(k)2^{-\Theta(\sqrt{k})} \ll 1/2.$$

We assume that the number of bits known to Bob after the first i rounds is in $\Omega(\sqrt{k})$ (a position j is *known* to Bob if so far he obtained all the bits necessary to later compute R_j), otherwise we have already achieved our goal. For $n > k$, starting from $k/2$ known bits, and repeating the protocol $2n$ times, one of the following two options must hold:

1. At some round, Bob is left with less than $O(\sqrt{k})$ known bits
2. At all rounds, Bob has $\Omega(\sqrt{k})$ bits left, and has thus lost fewer than $k/2$ bits overall (unlikely since under these conditions, the expected number of bits lost is $n > k$)

This guarantees that the total number of bits still valid at the end of the protocol is definitely $O(\sqrt{k})$ except with exponentially small probability. Thus, this reduction can be used as a substitute for $O(\sqrt{k})$–faulty $\binom{k}{1}$–Bit OT in Protocol 2.

The combination of Protocol 2 and Protocol 3 is a $\Theta(n^2)$ time reduction from $\binom{2}{1}$–Bit OT to $(k/2)$–faulty $\binom{k}{1}$–Bit OT. However, it is easy to see that it will fail completely if we start with $(k-1)$–faulty $\binom{k}{1}$–Bit OT instead of $(k/2)$–faulty $\binom{k}{1}$–Bit OT. This is because in each execution of step 3c the resulting sequence will be a run of $k - 1$ known bits. In this situation Bob is able to choose a shift σ_i such that he *never* loses a single bit through the operations of Step 4.

We finally note that indeed for any $\epsilon < 1$, if dishonest Bob obtains ϵk bits per transfer, xoring two transfers, after permuting and shifting as in Protocol 3, transfers on average $\epsilon^2 k$ instead of ϵk. We may thus claim that the combined transfer produces at most $\epsilon' k$ known bits, for $\epsilon' = \frac{\epsilon^2 + \epsilon}{2} < \epsilon$, except with exponentially small probability. Repeating this idea at most a constant number of times produces a resulting $\epsilon' < 1/2$. Since the sequence $\epsilon > \epsilon' > \epsilon'' > ...$ converges to zero, using a constant extra amount of work we can extend the result established for $\epsilon = 1/2$ to any $\epsilon < 1$. This was the state of affairs until information theoretic Interactive Hashing was considered as a tool to solve this problem.

5   Reducing to $(k-1)$–Faulty $\binom{k}{1}$–Bit OT Using Interactive Hashing

Finally, we reduce $\binom{2}{1}$–Bit OT to $(k-1)$–faulty $\binom{k}{1}$–Bit OT, a faulty primitive allowing a dishonest Bob to get at most $k-1$ bits of Alice's input at his choosing. For simplicity, we will also assume that k is a power of 2.

It is relatively straightforward to see that when both participants are honest, Protocol 4 allows Bob to obtain the bit of his choice since he knows $R_d = \bigoplus_{i=1}^{n} r_{ic_i}$ and can thus decrypt $e_{\mathring{c}}$. In case Alice is dishonest, Bob's choice $\mathring{c}$ is perfectly hidden from her when she obtains f at Step 6. This is because at the beginning of the protocol, Bob is equally likely to make the choices encoded by w_0 as those encoded by w_1. Consequently, by Property 1 of Interactive Hashing, given the specific outputs, the probability of either of them having been the original input is exactly $1/2$. Hence d is uniformly distributed from Alice's point of view and so $f = d \oplus \mathring{c}$ carries no information about $\mathring{c}$.

Protocol 4. Reduction of $\binom{2}{1}$–Bit OT to $(k-1)$–faulty $\binom{k}{1}$–Bit OT

Let $\mathring{b}_0, \mathring{b}_1$ and $\mathring{c}$ be the inputs of Alice and Bob, respectively, for $\binom{2}{1}$–Bit OT.

1. Alice and Bob agree on a security parameter n.
2. For $1 \leq i \leq n$ do:
   (a) Alice selects at random bits $r_{i1}, r_{i2}, \ldots, r_{ik}$.
   (b) Alice uses $(k-1)$–faulty $\binom{k}{1}$–Bit OT to send her k bits to Bob, who chooses to learn r_{ic_i} for a randomly selected $c_i \in_R \{1, \ldots, k\}$. .
3. Bob encodes his choices during the n rounds of 2b as a bit string w of length $n \cdot \log(k)$ by concatenating the binary representations of $c_1, c_2, \ldots, c_n$.
4. Bob sends w to Alice using Interactive Hashing. Let w_0, w_1 be the output strings labeled according to lexicographic order, and let $d \in \{0,1\}$ be such that $w = w_d$.
5. Let $p_1, p_2, \ldots, p_n$ be the positions encoded in w_0 and let $q_1, q_2, \ldots, q_n$ be the positions encoded in w_1. Alice computes $R_0 = \bigoplus_{i=1}^{n} r_{ip_i}$ and $R_1 = \bigoplus_{i=1}^{n} r_{iq_i}$.
6. Bob sends $f = d \oplus \mathring{c}$ to Alice.
7. Alice sends $e_0 = \mathring{b}_0 \oplus R_f$ and $e_1 = \mathring{b}_1 \oplus R_{\bar{f}}$ to Bob.
8. Bob decodes $\mathring{b}_{\mathring{c}} = e_{\mathring{c}} \oplus R_{f \oplus \mathring{c}} = e_{\mathring{c}} \oplus R_d$.

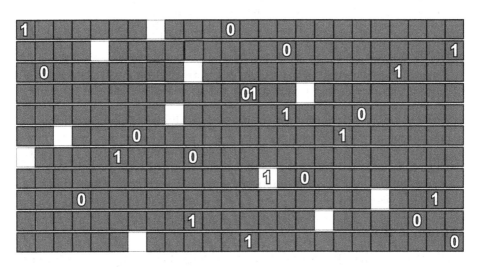

Fig. 4. $(k-1)$–faulty $\binom{k}{1}$–Bit OT: using Interactive Hashing Bob chooses two sequences of indices labelled with "zeros" and "ones". One of them corresponds to the sequence he knows (in the case where he is honest) while the second is the result of Interactive Hashing. Except with exponentially small probability, even if Bob is dishonest, one of the sequences will contain a missing (white) bit (a "one" in this example). Note that both "zero" and "one" may end up in the same location, once in a while, which is not a problem.

As for the case where Bob is dishonest, we can assume that he always avails himself of the possibility of cheating afforded by $(k-1)$–faulty $\binom{k}{1}$–Bit OT, and obtains $k-1$ out of k bits every time. Even so, though, by the end of Step 2, it is always the case that the fraction of all good encodings among all k^n possible encodings of positions is no larger than $f = \left(\frac{k-1}{k}\right)^n < e^{-n/k}$ (an encoding is "good" if all positions it encodes are known to Bob). Note that while f can be made arbitrarily small by an appropriate choice of n, the number of good strings $f * k^n$ always remains above the Birthday Paradox threshold. By Property 3 of Interactive Hashing, Bob cannot force both w_0 and w_1 to be among these "good" encodings except with probability no larger than $15.6805 \cdot e^{-n/k}$. This probability can be made arbitrarily small by an appropriate choice of the security parameter n. See Figure 4 for an example.

6   Conclusion and Open Problems

We have presented a rigorous definition of Interactive Hashing by distilling and formalizing its security properties in an information theoretic context, independently of any specific application. This opens the way to recognizing Interactive Hashing as a cryptographic primitive in its own right, and not simply as a subprotocol whose security properties, as well as their proof, depend on the specifics of the surrounding application. We have also demonstrated that there exists a simple implementation of Interactive Hashing (Protocol 1) that fully meets the above-mentioned security requirements, and cited a proof of correctness that significantly improves upon previous results in the literature.

Open problems. The interested reader is encouraged to consider the following open problems:

1. Devise a more appropriate name for Interactive Hashing which better captures its properties as a cryptographic primitive rather than the mechanics of its known implementations.
2. Investigate how much interaction, if any, is really necessary in principle to implement Interactive Hashing.
3. Explore ways to implement Interactive Hashing more efficiently. To this end, the constant-round Interactive Hashing protocol of [DHRS07] briefly described in Section 3.3 is an important step in the right direction. Improve on this construction so that it meets all the security requirements.

Acknowledgments

Claude thanks Simon Pierre Desrosiers for helping him clarify his mind while revising Section 4.

References

[BCR86]   Brassard, G., Crépeau, C., Robert, J.: Information theoretic reductions among disclosure problems. In: 27th Symp. of Found. of Computer Sci., pp. 168–173. IEEE, Los Alamitos (1986)

[CCM98]   Cachin, C., Crépeau, C., Marcil, J.: Oblivious transfer with a memory-bounded receiver. In: Proc. 39th IEEE Symposium on Foundations of Computer Science (FOCS), pp. 493–502 (1998)

[CCMS09]   Cachin, C., Crépeau, C., Marcil, J., Savvides, G.: Information-theoretic interactive hashing and oblivious transfer to a memory-bounded receiver. Journal of Cryptology (2009) (submitted for publication) (August 2007)

[CS06]   Crépeau, C., Savvides, G.: Optimal reductions between oblivious transfers using interactive hashing. In: Vaudenay, S. (ed.) EUROCRYPT 2006. LNCS, vol. 4004, pp. 201–221. Springer, Heidelberg (2006)

[DHRS07]   Ding, Y.Z., Harnik, D., Rosen, A., Shaltiel, R.: Constant-round oblivious transfer in the bounded storage model. Journal of Cryptology 20(2), 165–202 (2007)

[Din01]   Ding, Y.Z.: Oblivious transfer in the bounded storage model. In: Kilian, J. (ed.) CRYPTO 2001. LNCS, vol. 2139, pp. 155–170. Springer, Heidelberg (2001)

[EGL85]   Even, S., Goldreich, O., Lempel, A.: A randomized protocol for signing contracts. Communications of the ACM 28, 637–647 (1985)

[GMW87]   Goldreich, O., Micali, S., Wigderson, A.: How to play any mental game or a completeness theorem for protocols with honest majority. In: Proc. 19th Annual ACM Symposium on Theory of Computing (STOC), pp. 218–229 (1987)

[Gol04]   Goldreich, O.: Foundations of cryptography, vol. I & II. Cambridge University Press, Cambridge (2001–2004)

[HHK+05]   Haitner, I., Horvitz, O., Katz, J., Koo, C., Morselli, R., Shaltiel, R.: Reducing complexity assumptions for statistically-hiding commitment. In: Cramer, R.J.F. (ed.) EUROCRYPT 2005. LNCS, vol. 3494, pp. 58–77. Springer, Heidelberg (2005)

[HR07]   Haitner, I., Reingold, O.: A new interactive hashing theorem, Computational Complexity. In: Twenty-Second Annual IEEE Conference on CCC 2007, June 2007, pp. 319–332 (2007)

[Kil88]   Kilian, J.: Founding cryptography on oblivious transfer. In: Proc. 20th Annual ACM Symposium on Theory of Computing (STOC), pp. 20–31 (1988)

[NOV06]   Nguyen, M.-H., Ong, S.J., Vadhan, S.: Statistical zero-knowledge arguments for np from any one-way function, Foundations of Computer Science. In: 47th Annual IEEE Symposium on FOCS 2006, October 2006, pp. 3–14 (2006)

[NOVY98]   Naor, M., Ostrovsky, R., Venkatesan, R., Yung, M.: Perfect zero-knowledge arguments for NP using any one-way permutation. Journal of Cryptology 11(2), 87–108 (1998)

[NV06]   Nguyen, M.-H., Vadhan, S.: Zero knowledge with efficient provers. In: STOC 2006: Proceedings of the thirty-eighth annual ACM symposium on Theory of computing, pp. 287–295. ACM, New York (2006)

[OVY92]   Ostrovsky, R., Venkatesan, R., Yung, M.: Secure commitment against a powerful adversary. In: Finkel, A., Jantzen, M. (eds.) STACS 1992. LNCS, vol. 577, pp. 439–448. Springer, Heidelberg (1992)

[OVY93]   Ostrovsky, R., Venkatesan, R., Yung, M.: Fair games against an all-powerful adversary. In: Advances in Computational Complexity Theory. AMS, 1993, Initially presented at DIMACS workshop, vol. 13 (1990); Extended abstract in the proceedings of Sequences 1991, June 1991, Positano, Italy, pp. 155–169 (1991)

[OVY94]   Ostrovsky, R., Venkatesan, R., Yung, M.: Interactive hashing simplifies
           zero-knowledge protocol design. In: Helleseth, T. (ed.) EUROCRYPT
           1993. LNCS, vol. 765, pp. 267–273. Springer, Heidelberg (1994)
[Rab81]   Rabin, M.O.: How to exchange secrets by oblivious transfer, Tech. Report
           TR-81, Harvard (1981)
[Sav07]   Savvides, G.: Interactive hashing and reductions between oblivious trans-
           fer variants, Ph.D. thesis, McGill University (2007)
[Wie70]   Wiesner, S.: Conjugate coding, Reprinted in SIGACT News, vol. 15(1),
           original manuscript written ca. 1970 (1983)
[Yao86]   Yao, A.C.-C.: How to generate and exchange secrets. In: Proc. 27th IEEE
           Symposium on Foundations of Computer Science (FOCS), pp. 162–167
           (1986)

Distributed Relay Protocol for Probabilistic Information-Theoretic Security in a Randomly-Compromised Network

Travis R. Beals[1] and Barry C. Sanders[2]

[1] Department of Physics, University of California, Berkeley, California 94720, USA
[2] Institute for Quantum Information Science, University of Calgary, Alberta T2N 1N4, Canada

Abstract. We introduce a simple, practical approach with probabilistic information-theoretic security to mitigate one of quantum key distribution's major limitations: the short maximum transmission distance ($\sim$ 200 km) possible with present day technology. Our scheme uses classical secret sharing techniques to allow secure transmission over long distances through a network containing randomly-distributed compromised nodes. The protocol provides arbitrarily high confidence in the security of the protocol, and modest scaling of resource costs with improvement of the security parameter. Although some types of failure are undetectable, users can take preemptive measures to make the probability of such failures arbitrarily small.

Keywords: quantum key distribution; QKD; secret sharing; information theoretic security.

1 Introduction

Public key cryptography is a critical component of many widely-used cryptosystems, and forms the basis for much of our ecommerce transaction security infrastructure. Unfortunately, the most common public key schemes are known to be insecure against quantum computers. In 1994, Peter Shor developed a quantum algorithm for efficient factorization and discrete logarithms [1]; the (supposed) hardness of these two problems formed the basis for RSA and DSA, respectively. Sufficiently powerful quantum computers do not yet exist, but the possibility of their existence in the future already poses problems for those with significant forward security requirements.

A more secure replacement for public key cryptography is needed. Ideally, this replacement would offer information-theoretic security, and would possess most or all of the favorable qualities of public key cryptography. At present, no complete replacement exists, but quantum key distribution (QKD)—in conjunction with one-time pad (OTP) or other symmetric ciphers—appears promising.

QKD—first developed by Bennett and Brassard [2]—is a key distribution scheme that relies upon the uncertainty principle of quantum mechanics to guarantee that any eavesdropping attempts will be detected. In a typical QKD setup,

R. Safavi-Naini (Ed.): ICITS 2008, LNCS 5155, pp. 29–39, 2008.
© Springer-Verlag Berlin Heidelberg 2008

individual photons are sent through optical fiber or through free space from the sender to the receiver. The receiver performs measurements on the photons, and sender and receiver communicate via an authenticated (but not necessarily private) classical channel.

Optical attenuation of these single photon pulses limits the maximum transmission distance for a single QKD link to about 200 km over fiber with present technology [3], and significantly less through air. Unlike optically-encoded classical information, the "signal strength" of these photons cannot be amplified using a conventional optical amplifier; the No Cloning Theorem [4] prohibits this. We refer to this challenge as the *relay problem*.

Two classes of quantum repeaters have been proposed to resolve the distance limitations of QKD. The first makes use of quantum error correction to detect and rectify errors in specially-encoded pulses. Unfortunately, the extremely low error thresholds for such schemes ($\sim 10^{-4}$) make this impractical for use in a realistic quantum repeater. The second class of quantum repeaters uses entanglement swapping and distillation [5,6] to establish entanglement between the endpoints of a chain of quantum repeaters, which can then be used for QKD [7]. This method is much more tolerant of errors, and offers resource costs that scale only polynomially with the number of repeaters (i.e., polynomially with distance). However, such repeaters do have one major drawback: they require quantum memories with long decoherence times [6].

In order to be useful for practical operation, a quantum repeater must possess a quantum memory that meets the following three requirements:

1. Long coherence times: at a minimum, coherence times must be comparable to the transit distance for the entire repeater chain (e.g., ~ 10 ms for a trans-Atlantic link).
2. High storage density: the bandwidth for a quantum repeater is limited by the ratio of its quantum memory capacity to the transit time for the entire repeater chain [8].
3. Robustness in extreme environments: practical quantum repeaters must be able to operate in the range of environments to which telecom equipment is exposed (e.g., on the ocean floor, in the case of a trans-oceanic link).

These requirements are so demanding that it is possible that practical quantum repeaters will not be widely available until after large-scale quantum computers have been built—in other words, not until too late.

The distance limitations of QKD and the issues involved in developing practical quantum repeaters make it challenging to build secure QKD networks that span a large geographic area. The naïve solution of classical repeaters leads to exponentially decaying security with transmission distance if each repeater has some independent probability of being compromised. If large QKD networks are to be built in the near future (i.e., without quantum repeaters), an alternative method of addressing the single-hop distance limitation must be found. We refer to this as the *relay problem*.

Given an adversary that controls a randomly-determined subset of nodes in the network, we have developed a solution to the relay problem that involves encoding encryption keys into multiple pieces using a secret sharing protocol [9,10]. These shares are transmitted via multiple multi-hop paths through a QKD network, from origin to destination. Through the use of a distributed re-randomization protocol at each intermediate stage, privacy is maintained even if the attacker controls a large, randomly-selected subset of all the nodes.

We note that authenticated QKD is information-theoretic secure [11], as is OTP; in combination, these two cryptographic primitives provide information-theoretic security on the level of an individual link. Our protocol makes use of many such links as part of a network that provides information-theoretic security with very high probability. In particular, with some very small probability δ, the protocol fails in such a way as to allow a sufficiently powerful adversary to perform undetected man-in-the-middle (MITM) attacks. The failure probability δ can be made arbitrarily small by modest increases in resource usage. In all other cases, the network is secure. We describe the level of security of our protocol as *probabilistic information-theoretic*.

In analyzing our protocol, we consider a network composed of a chain of "cities", where each city contains several parties, all of whom are linked to all the other parties in that city. We assume intracity bandwidth is cheap, whereas intercity bandwidth is expensive; intercity bandwidth usage is the main resource considered in our scaling analysis. For the sake of simplicity, we consider communication between two parties (Alice and Bob) who are assumed to be at either end of the chain of cities. A similar analysis would apply to communication between parties at any intermediate points in the network.

2 Adversary and Network Model

It is convenient to model networks with properties similar to those described above by using undirected graphs, where each vertex represents a node or party participating in the network, and each edge represents a secure authenticated private channel. Such a channel could be generated by using QKD in conjunction with a shared secret key for authentication, or by any other means providing information-theoretic security.

We describe below an adversary and network model similar in some ways to one we proposed earlier[1] in the context of a protocol for authenticating mutual strangers in a very large QKD network, which we referred to as the *stranger authentication protocol*. In that protocol, edges represented shared secret keys, whereas here they represent physical QKD links. Network structure in the previous model was assumed to be random (possibly with a power law distribution, as is common in social networks), whereas here the network has a specific topology dictated by geographic constraints, the distance limitations of QKD, and the requirements of the protocol.

---

[1] Pre-print available at www.arXiv.org as arXiv:0803.2717.

2.1 Adversarial Capabilities and Limitations

We call the following adversary model the *sneaky supercomputer*:

(i) The adversary is computationally unbounded.
(ii) The adversary can listen to, intercept, and alter any message on any public channel.
(iii) The adversary can compromise a randomly-selected subset of the nodes in the network. Compromised nodes are assumed to be under the complete control of the adversary. The total fraction of compromised nodes is limited to $(1 - t)$ or less.

Such an adversary is very powerful, and can successfully perform MITM attacks against public key cryptosystems (using the first capability) and against unauthenticated QKD (using the second capability), but not against a QKD link between two uncompromised nodes that share a secret key for authentication (since quantum mechanics allows the eavesdropping to be detected) [11]. The adversary can always perform denial-of-service (DOS) attacks by simply destroying all transmitted information; since DOS attacks cannot be prevented in this adversarial scenario, we concern ourselves primarily with security against MITM attacks. Later, we will briefly consider variants of this adversarial model and limited DOS attacks.

The third capability in this adversarial model—the adversary's control of a random subset of nodes—simulates a network in which exploitable vulnerabilities are present on some nodes but not others. As a first approximation to modeling a real-world network, it is reasonable to assume the vulnerable nodes are randomly distributed throughout the network.

An essentially equivalent adversarial model is achieved if we replace the third capability as follows: suppose the adversary can attempt to compromise any node, but a compromise attempt succeeds only with probability $(1 - t)$, and the adversary can make no more than one attempt per node. In the worst case where the adversary attempts to compromise all nodes, the adversary will control a random subset of all nodes, with the fraction of compromised nodes being roughly $(1 - t)$.

2.2 The Network

For the relay problem, let us represent the network as a graph G, with $V(G)$ being the set of vertices (nodes participating in the network) and $E(G)$ being the set of edges (secure authenticated channels, e.g. QKD links between parties who share secret keys for authentication). $N = |V(G)|$ is the number of vertices (nodes). V_d is the set of compromised nodes, which are assumed to be under the adversary's control; $|V_d| \le N(1 - t)$. Furthermore, let us assume that the network has the following structure: nodes are grouped into m clusters—completely connected sub-graphs containing n nodes each. There are thus $N = mn$ nodes in the network. We label the nodes as $v_{i,j}$, $i \in \{1, \ldots, n\}$, $j \in \{1, \ldots, m\}$. Each node is connected to one node in the immediately preceding cluster and one node in the cluster immediately following it.

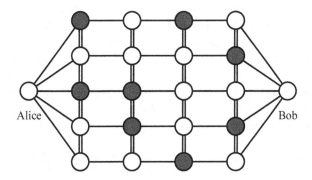

Fig. 1. White vertices represent honest parties, whereas shaded vertices represent dishonest parties. Double vertical lines represent secure communication links between all joined vertices (i.e., all parties within a given city can communicate securely). In the graph shown above, 40% of the parties in cities between Alice and Bob are dishonest, but Alice and Bob can still communicate securely using the method described in Sec. 3 and Fig. 2.

More formally, let $E_\ell(G) \equiv \{(v_{i,j}, v_{i,j+1}) : v_{i,j}, v_{i,j+1} \in V(G)\}$ and $E_\sigma(G) \equiv \{(v_{i,j}, v_{k,j}) : v_{i,j}, v_{k,j} \in V(G)\}$. Then, $E(G) \equiv E_\ell(G) \cup E_\sigma(G)$.

This network structure models a chain of m cities (a term which we use interchangeably with "cluster"), each containing n nodes. The cities are spaced such that the physical distance between cities allows QKD links only between adjacent cities. To realistically model the costs of communication bandwidth, we assume that use of long distance links (i.e., those represented by $E_\ell(G)$) is expensive, whereas intracity links (i.e., $E_\sigma(G)$) are cheap.

Next, we consider two additional nodes—a sender and a receiver. The sender (hereafter referred to as Alice or simply A) has direct links to all the nodes in city 1, while the receiver (Bob, or B) has a link to all nodes in city m. We assume Alice and Bob to be uncompromised. An example is shown in Fig. 1.

3   The Relay Protocol

In the relay problem, Alice wishes to communicate with Bob over a distance longer than that possible with a single QKD link, with quantum repeaters being unavailable. As described above, Alice and Bob are separated by m "cities", each containing n participating nodes. (In the case where different cities contain different numbers of participating nodes, we obtain a lower bound on security by taking n to be the minimum over all cities.)

To achieve both good security and low intercity bandwidth usage, we can employ a basic secret sharing scheme with a distributed re-randomization of the shares [12] performed by the parties in each city. This re-randomization procedure is similar to that used in the mobile adversary proactive secret sharing scheme [13,14]. Note that in the following protocol description, the second subscript labels the city, while the first subscript refers to the particular party within a city.

(i) Alice generates n random strings $r_{i,0}, i \in \{1, \ldots, n\}$ of length ℓ, $r \in \{0,1\}^{\ell}$. ℓ is chosen as described in Sec. 3.1.

(ii) Alice transmits the strings to the corresponding parties in the first city: $v_{i,1}$ receives $r_{i,0}$.

(iii) When a party $v_{i,j}$ receives a string $r_{i,j-1}$, it generates $n-1$ random strings $q_{i,j}^{(k)}, k \neq i$ of length ℓ, and transmits each string $q_{i,j}^{(k)}$ to party $v_{k,j}$ (i.e., transmission along the vertical double lines shown in Fig. 1).

(iv) Each party $v_{i,j}$ generates a string $r_{i,j}$ as follows:

$$r_{i,j} \equiv r_{i,j-1} \oplus \left(\bigoplus_{k, k \neq i} q_{i,j}^{(k)} \right) \oplus \left(\bigoplus_{k, k \neq i} q_{k,j}^{(i)} \right),$$

where the symbols ($\oplus$ and $\bigoplus$) are both understood to mean bitwise XOR. Note that the string $r_{i,j-1}$ is received from a party in the previous city, the strings $q_{i,j}^{(k)}$ are generated by the party $v_{i,j}$, and the strings $q_{k,j}^{(i)}$ are generated by other parties in the same city as $v_{i,j}$. The string $r_{i,j}$ is then transmitted to party $v_{i,j+1}$ (i.e., transmission along the horizontal lines shown in Fig. 1).

(v) Steps (iii) and (iv) are repeated until the strings reach the parties in city m. All the parties $v_{i,m}$ in city m forward the strings they receive to Bob.

(vi) Alice constructs $s \equiv \prod_i r_{i,0}$ and Bob constructs $s' \equiv \prod_i r_{i,j-1}$.

(vii) Alice and Bob use the protocol summarized in Fig. 2 and described in detail in Section 3.1 to determine if $s = s'$. If so, they are left with a portion of s (identified as s_3), which is their shared secret key. If $s \neq s'$, Alice and Bob discard s and s' and repeat the protocol.

3.1   Key Verification

In the last step of the protocol described above, Alice and Bob must verify that their respective keys, s and s', are the same and have not been tampered with. We note that there are many ways[2] to accomplish this; we present one possible method here (summarized in Fig. 2) for definiteness, but make no claims as to its efficiency.

We consider Alice's key s to be composed of three substrings, s_1, s_2, and s_3, with lengths ℓ_1, ℓ_2, and ℓ_3, respectively (typically, $\ell_3 \gg \ell_1, \ell_2$). Bob's key s' is similarly divided into s_1', s_2', and s_3'. If Alice and Bob successfully verify that $s_3' = s_3$, they can use s_3 as a shared secret key for OTP encryption or other cryptographic purposes.

The verification is accomplished as follows:

(i) Alice generates a random nonce r, and computes the hash $H[s_3]$ of $s3$. She then sends $(r, H[s_3]) \oplus s_1$ to Bob.

---

[2] See for example pp. 13–14 of the SECOQC technical report D-SEC-48, by L. Salvail [15].

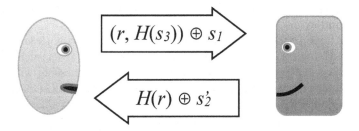

Fig. 2. Alice and Bob perform a verification sub-protocol to check that their respective secret keys, $s = (s_1, s_2, s_3)$ and $s' = (s_1', s_2', s_3')$, are in fact the same. Alice generates a random number r, concatenates it with the hash $H[s_3]$ of s_3, XORs this with s_1, and sends the result to Bob. Bob decodes with s_1', verifies that $H[s_3] = H[s_3']$, then sends back to Alice the result of bit-wise XORing the hash of r, $H[r]$, with s_2'. Finally, Alice decodes with s_2 and checks to see that the value Bob has computed for $H[r]$ is correct. Alice and Bob now know $s_3 = s_3'$ and can store s_3 for future use. Note that with this protocol, the adversary can fool Alice and Bob into accepting $s \neq s'$ with 100 % probability if the adversary knows s and s'.

(ii) Bob receives the message from Alice, decrypts by XORing with s_1', and verifies that the received value of $H[s_3]$ matches $H[s_3']$. If so, he accepts the key, and sends Alice the message $H[r] \oplus s_2'$. If not, Bob aborts.

(iii) Alice decrypts Bob's message by XORing with s_2, and verifies that the received value of $H[r]$ is correct. If so, Alice accepts the key, and verification is successful. If not, Alice aborts.

We now outline a proof of the security of this verification process, and discuss requirements for the hash function H. We begin with the assumption that Eve does not know s or s'; if she does, the relay protocol has failed, and Eve can perform MITM attacks without detection (conditions under which the relay protocol can fail are analyzed in Sec. 4). Our goal is to show that Alice and Bob will with very high probability detect any attempt by Eve to introduce errors in s_3' (i.e., any attempt by Eve to cause $s_3' \neq s_3$), and that the verification process will also not reveal any information about s_3 to Eve.

We note that any modification by Eve of the messages exchanged by Alice and Bob during the verification process is equivalent to Eve introducing errors in s_1' and s_2' during the main part of the relay protocol. If she controls at least one intermediate node, Eve can introduce such errors by modifying one or more of the strings transmitted by a node under her control. We can thus completely describe Eve's attack on the protocol by a string $e = (e_1, e_2, e_3)$, where $s' = s \oplus e$, and the three substrings e_1, e_2, and e_3 have lengths ℓ_1, ℓ_2, and ℓ_3, respectively (with $\ell = \ell_1 + \ell_2 + \ell_3$).

It is clear that Eve cannot gain any information about s_3 from the verification process, since the only information ever transmitted about s_3 (the hash $H[s_3]$) is encrypted by the OTP s_1, and s_1 is never re-used.

Before proceeding, let us further partition s_1 into two strings s_{1a} and s_{1b}, where s_{1a} is the portion of s_1 used to encrypt r, and s_{1b} is the portion used to encrypt $H[s_3]$. Let ℓ_{1a} and ℓ_{1b} be the lengths of s_{1a} and s_{1b}. We similarly partition s_1' and e_1.

Eve's only hope of fooling Bob into accepting a tampered-with key (i.e., accepting even though $s_3' \neq s_3$) is for her to choose e_{1b} and e_3 such that the expression $H[s_3] \oplus H[s_3 \oplus e_3] = e_{1b}$ is satisfied. Random guessing will give her a $\sim 2^{-\ell_{1b}}$ chance of tricking Bob into accepting; for Eve to do better, she must be able to exploit a weakness in the hash function H that gives her some information as to the correct value of e_{1b} for some choice of e_3. Note that Eve's best strategy for this attack is to choose e_{1a} and e_2 to be just strings of zeroes.

From this observation, we obtain the following condition on the hash function: for a random s_3 (unknown to Eve), there exists no choice of e_3 such that Eve has any information about the value of e_{1b} she should choose to satisfy $H[s_3] \oplus H[s_3 \oplus e_3] = e_{1b}$. In practice, it would be acceptable for Eve to gain a very small amount of information, as long as the information gained did not raise Eve's chances much beyond random guessing. This is a relatively weak requirement on H, and is likely satisfied by any reasonable choice of hash function.

To fool Alice into falsely accepting, Eve can either fool Bob via the aforementioned method, or Eve can attempt to impersonate Bob by sending Alice a random string of length ℓ_2, in the hopes that it happens to be equal to $s_2 \oplus H[r]$. Clearly, her chances for the latter method are no better than $2^{-\ell_2}$. The latter method of attack only fools Alice and not Bob; it is thus of limited use to Eve.

We note that the security of the verification protocol depends on the choice of ℓ_1 and ℓ_2 (as described above); these parameters should be chosen so as to provide whatever degree of security is required. Alice and Bob choose ℓ_3 so as to obtain whatever size key they desire. Since the security of the verification process does not depend on ℓ_3, the communication cost of key verification is negligible in the limit of large ℓ_3 (i.e., in the limit of large final key size).

4 Security of the Relay Protocol

In order for the secret to be compromised, there must be some $j \in \{1, \ldots, m-1\}$ such that, for all $i \in \{1, \ldots, n\}$, at least one of $v_{i,j}$ and $v_{i,j+1}$ is dishonest (i.e., such that, for some j, every string $r_{i,j}$ is either sent or received by a compromised party). If this happens, we say the protocol has been compromised at stage j. For a given j, the probability of compromise is $(1 - t^2)^n$, but the probability for j is not entirely independent of the probabilities for $j - 1$ and $j + 1$. Thus, we can bound from below the overall probability of the channel between Alice and Bob being secure, p_s, by (1):

$$p_s \geq \left[1 - (1 - t^2)^n\right]^{m-1}. \tag{1}$$

From this result, we see that, if we wish to ensure our probability of a secure channel between Alice and Bob is at least p_s, it is sufficient to choose $n = \log\left(1 - p_s^{1/(m-1)}\right) / \log\left(1 - t^2\right)$. Intercity bandwidth consumed is proportional to n, so we see that we have good scaling of resource consumption with communication distance. Alternatively, we can re-write the equation for choosing n in terms of a maximum allowed probability of compromise, $\delta = 1 - p_s$. For $\delta \ll 1$, we obtain the following relation:

$$n \simeq \frac{\log (m - 1) - \log \delta}{- \log (1 - t^2)}.$$

Total resource usage (intercity communication links required) scales as $\mathcal{O}(mn)$, or $\mathcal{O}(m \log m)$ for fixed δ, t. While intracity communication requirements scale faster (as $\mathcal{O}(mn^2)$), it is reasonable to ignore this because of the comparatively low cost of intracity communication and the finite size of the earth (which effectively limits m to a maximum of 100 or so for a QKD network with single link distances of ~ 100 km).

If each party in the network simultaneously wished to communicate with one other party (with that party assumed to be $m/2$ cities away on average), total intercity bandwidth would scale as $\mathcal{O}(m^2 n^2)$. By comparison, the bandwidth for a network of the same number of parties employing public key cryptography (and no secret sharing) would scale as $\mathcal{O}(m^2 n)$. Since n scales relatively slowly (i.e., with $\log m$), this is a reasonable penalty to pay for improved security.

5   Alternative Adversary Models

We now briefly consider a number of alternative adversary models. First, let us consider replacing adversary capability (iii) with the following alternative, which we term (iii'): the adversary can compromise up to $k - 1$ nodes of its choice. Compromised nodes are assumed to be under the complete control of the adversary, as before. In this scenario, the security analysis is trivial. If $k > n$, the adversary can compromise Alice and Bob's communications undetected. Otherwise, Alice and Bob can communicate securely.

We could also imagine an adversary controls some random subset of nodes in the network—as described by (iii)—and wishes to disrupt communications between Alice and Bob (i.e., perform a DOS attack), but does not have the capability to disrupt or modify public channels. Alice and Bob can modify the protocol to simultaneously protect against both this type of attack and also the adversary mentioned in Section 2.1. To do so, they replace the simple secret sharing scheme described above with a Proactive Verifiable Secret Sharing (PVSS) scheme [16]. In this scenario, nodes can check at each stage to see if any shares have been corrupted, and take corrective measures. This process is robust against up to $n/4 - 1$ corrupt shares, which implies that PVSS yields little protection against DOS attacks unless $t > t_{\text{thresh}} \approx \sqrt{3}/2$.

6   Conclusion

We have shown a protocol for solving the relay problem and building secure long-distance communication networks with present-day QKD technology. The protocol proposed employs secret sharing and multiple paths through a network of partially-trusted nodes. Through the choice of moderately large n in the relay problem, one can make the possibility of compromise vanishingly small. For fixed probability of compromise of each of the intermediate nodes, the number of nodes per stage required to maintain security scales only logarithmically with the number of stages (i.e., with distance).

Given that QKD systems are already commercially available, our methods could be implemented today.

Acknowledgments

We wish to thank Louis Salvail, Aidan Roy, Rei Safavi-Naini, Douglas Stebila, Hugh Williams, Kevin Hynes, and Renate Scheidler for valuable discussions. TRB acknowledges support from a US Department of Defense NDSEG Fellowship. BCS acknowledges support from iCORE and CIFAR.

References

1. Shor, P.W.: Algorithms for quantum computation: Discrete logarithms and factoring. In: Proc. of 35th Annual Symposium on Foundations of Computer Science, pp. 124–134 (1994)
2. Bennett, C.H., Brassard, G.: Quantum cryptography: Public key distribution and coin tossing. In: Proc. of IEEE International Conference on Computers, Systems, and Signal Processing, pp. 175–179 (1984)
3. Takesue, H., Nam, S.W., Zhang, Q., Hadfield, R.H., Honjo, T., Tamaki, K., Yamamoto, Y.: Quantum key distribution over a 40-db channel loss using superconducting single-photon detectors. Nature Photonics 1, 343–348 (2007)
4. Wootters, W.K., Zurek, W.H.: A single quantum cannot be cloned. Nature 299, 802–803 (1982)
5. Briegel, H.J., Dur, W., Cirac, J.I., Zoller, P.: Quantum repeaters: The role of imperfect local operations in quantum communication. Phys. Rev. Lett. 81, 5932–5935 (1998)
6. Duan, L.M., Lukin, M., Cirac, J.I., Zoller, P.: Long-distance quantum communication with atomic ensembles and linear optics. Nature 414, 413–418 (2001)
7. Ekert, A.K.: Quantum cryptography based on Bell's theorem. Phys. Rev. Lett. 67, 661–663 (1991)
8. Simon, C., de Riedmatten, H., Afzelius, M., Sangouard, N., Zbinden, H., Gisin, N.: Quantum repeaters with photon pair sources and multimode memories. Phys. Rev. Lett. 98, 190503 (2007)
9. Shamir, A.: How to share a secret. Comm.of the ACM 22, 612–613 (1979)
10. Blakley, G.R.: Safeguarding cryptographic keys. In: Proc. of the National Computer Conference, vol. 48, pp. 313–317 (1979)
11. Renner, R., Gisin, N., Kraus, B.: Information-theoretic security proof for quantum-key-distribution protocols. Physical Review A 72, 012332 (2005)
12. Ben-Or, M., Goldwasser, S., Wigderson, A.: Completeness theorems for non-cryptographic fault-tolerant distributed computation. In: Proc. of the 20th Annual ACM Symposium on Theory of Computing, pp. 1–10 (1988)

13. Ostrovsky, R., Yung, M.: How to withstand mobile virus attacks. In: Proc.of the 10th Annual ACM Symposium on Principles of Distributed Computing, pp. 51–59 (1991)
14. Herzberg, A., Jarecki, S., Krawczyk, H., Yung, M.: Proactive secret sharing, or how to cope with perpetual leakage. In: Coppersmith, D. (ed.) CRYPTO 1995. LNCS, vol. 963, pp. 339–352. Springer, Heidelberg (1995)
15. Salvail, L.: Security Architecture for SECOQC: Secret-key Privacy and Authenticity over QKD Networks. D-SEC-48, SECOQC (2007)
16. D'Arco, P., Stinson, D.R.: On unconditionally secure robust distributed key distribution centers. In: Zheng, Y. (ed.) ASIACRYPT 2002. LNCS, vol. 2501, pp. 346–363. Springer, Heidelberg (2002)

Strong Secrecy for Wireless Channels (Invited Talk)

João Barros[1] and Matthieu Bloch[2]

[1] Instituto de Telecomunicações, Faculdade de Ciências da Universidade do Porto,
Porto, Portugal
and MIT, Cambridge, MA
http://www.dcc.fc.up.pt~barros
[2] University of Notre Dame, Department of Electrical Engineering, Notre Dame, IN
http://www.prism.gatech.edu/~gtg578i/

Abstract. It is widely accepted by the information security community that a secrecy criterion based solely on minimizing the rate at which an eavesdropper extracts bits from a block of noisy channel outputs is too weak a concept to guarantee the confidentiality of the protected data. Even if this rate goes to zero asymptotically (i.e. for sufficiently large code-word length), vital information bits can easily be leaked to an illegitimate receiver. In contrast, many of the recent results in information-theoretic security for wireless channel models with continuous random variables rely on this weak notion of secrecy, even though previous work has shown that it is possible to determine the ultimate secrecy rates for discrete memoryless broadcast channels under a stronger secrecy criterion — namely one which bounds not the rate but the total number of bits obtained by the eavesdropper. Seeking to bridge the existing gap between fundamental cryptographic requirements and ongoing research in wireless security, we present a proof for the secrecy capacity of Gaussian broadcast channels under the strong secrecy criterion. As in the discrete memoryless case, the secrecy capacity is found to be the same as in the weaker formulation. The extension to fading channels is shown to be straightforward.

1 An Information-Theoretic Approach to Wireless Security

In contrast to their wireline counterparts, wireless links are exceptionally prone to eavesdropping attacks. As long as the eavesdropper (Eve, here with an antenna) is able to operate a suitable receiver at some location within the transmission range of the legitimate communication partners (Alice and Bob), information about the sent messages may be easily obtained from the transmitted signals and this eavesdropping activity is most likely to remain undetected. While the latter aspect is hard to prevent in wireless systems — in contrast to quantum systems which are known to have a no-cloning property — the former can be countered by (a) using strong end-to-end encryption to protect the confidential data (thus relying on computational security), (b) using secrecy attaining channel codes and signal processing at the physical-layer (exploiting the principles of

R. Safavi-Naini (Ed.): ICITS 2008, LNCS 5155, pp. 40–53, 2008.
© Springer-Verlag Berlin Heidelberg 2008

information-theoretic security), or (c) combining both solutions in an effective manner.

It is fair to state that cryptographic solutions based on the computational hardness of certain numerical problems have been the object of intense study for several decades, whereas information-theoretic security for wireless channels has only very recently caught the attention of the research community and is still very much at an infant stage. Building on Shannon's notion of *perfect* secrecy [16], the information-theoretic foundations for a physical-layer approach to security were first laid by Wyner [19] and later by Csiszár and Körner [4], who proved in seminal papers that there exist channel codes guaranteeing both robustness to transmission errors and a prescribed degree of data confidentiality. An extension to the Gaussian instance of the wiretap channel was promptly provided by Leung-Yan-Cheong and Hellman in [8]. Owing to the basic circumstances that (a) the legitimate receiver must have less noise than the attacker for the secrecy capacity to be strictly positive, (b) secrecy capacity achieving codes were not yet available, and (c) a viable security solution based on public-key cryptography was made available at the same time by Diffie and Hellman [5], these basic results in information-theoretic security were viewed by many as not more than a theoretical curiosity. In [11], Maurer offered a breakthrough by observing that legitimate users can always generate a secret key through public communication over an insecure yet authenticated channel, even when they have a worse channel than the eavesdropper.

It was not until a decade later that information-theoretic concepts found their way into wireless security research. Hero [7] introduced space-time signal processing techniques for secure communication over wireless links, and Negi and Goel [12] investigated achievable secret communication rates taking advantage of multiple-input multiple output communications. Parada and Blahut [14] established the secrecy capacity of various degraded fading channels. Barros and Rodrigues [1] provided a detailed characterization of the outage secrecy capacity of slow fading channels, and they showed that fading alone guarantees that information-theoretic security is achievable, even when the eavesdropper has a better average Signal-to-Noise Ratio (SNR) than the legitimate receiver – without the need for public communication over a feedback channel or the introduction of artificial noise. Practical secret key agreement schemes for this scenario are described by Bloch *et al.* in [2]. The ergodic secrecy capacity of fading channels was derived independently by Liang *et al.* [9] and Gopala *et al.* in [6] and power and rate allocation schemes for secret communication over fading channels were presented. Other recent directions include secure relays and the secrecy capacity of systems with multiple antennas.

No doubt the recent surge in research on information-theoretic security for wireless channels has produced a considerable number of non-trivial results. However, in order to increase their potential cryptographic value it is useful to revisit the most common underlying assumptions. Beyond the fact that code constructions capable of bridging the gap between theory and practice are still elusive, many of the aforementioned contributions have a non-obvious drawback, which is not necessarily related with the actual solutions but rather with subtle aspects of the problem formulation. Since they make use of the available secrecy results for Gaussian wiretap channels, a number of contributions in wireless information-theoretic security adopt the secrecy condition of the early work of Leung-Yan-Cheong and Helmann in [8] (and similarly [19,4]), which considers only the rate at which an eavesdropper is able to extract bits from a block of noisy channel outputs and not the total amount of information that he is able to obtain. As argued by Maurer and Wolf for discrete memoryless channels [10], the former is too weak a concept to guarantee the confidentiality of the protected data, because even if this rate goes to zero (in the limit of very large codeword length) vital information bits can easily be leaked to an illegitimate receiver. This motivates us to consider the secrecy capacity of wireless channels under the strong secrecy criterion.

1.1   A Case for Strong Secrecy

To underline the importance of a strong secrecy criterion, we now present two different examples. The first one shows a trivial (insecure) scheme that satisfies the weaker condition used in [8], whereas the second example highlights the fact that strong secrecy requires strong uniformity on what the eavesdropper sees.

Example 1. Suppose that Alice wants to send Bob a sequence of n bits, denoted u^n, which she wants to keep secret from Eve. For simplicity, we assume that all channels are noiseless, which means that both Bob and Eve observe noiseless versions of the cryptogram x^n sent by Alice. We consider two different (asymptotic) secrecy conditions:

Weak Secrecy: $\forall \epsilon > 0$ we have that $(1/n)H(U^n|X^n) \geq 1 - \epsilon$, for some n sufficiently large.
Strong Secrecy: $\forall \epsilon > 0$ we have that $H(U^n|X^n) \geq n - \epsilon$, for some n sufficiently large

Notice that the difference between these two measures of secrecy is that strong secrecy demands that the total uncertainty about u^n is arbitrarily close to n bits, whereas weak secrecy settles for the average uncertainty per bit to be arbitrarily close to 1. As we shall see this seemingly unimportant subtle issue can determine whether Eve is able to extract any information from the cryptogram x^n.

Suppose now that Alice produces the cryptogram x^n by computing the XOR of the first k bits $(u_1, u_2 \ldots u_k)$, $0 < k < n$, with a secret sequence of random bits s^k and appending the remaining $n - k$ bits $(u_{k+1}, u_{k+2}, \ldots, u_n)$ to the cryptogram. The sequence of secret bits s^k, which we assume to be shared via a private channel with Bob, is generated according to a uniform distribution and thus can be viewed as a one-time pad for the first k bits. Clearly, we have that $H(U^n|X^n) = n - k$, which proves unequivocally that this trivial scheme does not satisfy the strong secrecy criterion. However, this is no longer true when we accept the weak secrecy criterion. In fact, since $(1/n)H(U^n|X^n) = 1 - k/n$ Alice may actually disclose an extremely large number of bits, while satisfying the weak secrecy condition.

Example 2. Suppose once again that all channels are noiseless and Alice wants to send Bob a sequence of n bits, denoted u^n, which she wants to keep secret from Eve. Alice now produces the cryptogram x^n by computing the XOR of each bit u_i with a secret random bit s_i, such that $x^n = u^n \oplus s^n$. The sequence of secret bits s^n, which we assume to be shared via a private channel with Bob, is generated in a way such that the all-zero sequence has probability $1/n$ and all non-zero sequences are uniformly distributed. More formally, if $\mathcal{S}^n$ denotes the set of all binary sequences and $\underline{0}^n$ denotes a n-bit sequence with n zeros, then the probability distribution of the secret sequence can be written as

$$P(s^n) = \begin{cases} 1/n & \text{if } s^n = \underline{0} \\ \frac{(1-1/n)}{(2^n-1)} & \text{if } s^n \in \mathcal{S}^n \backslash \underline{0} \end{cases}$$

Clearly, since s^n is not uniformly distributed according to $P(\mathcal{S}^n) = 1/2^{-n}$, Alice's scheme cannot be classified as a one-time-pad and thus does not satisfy the perfect secrecy condition $H(U^n|X^n) = n$ established by Shannon. To verify that the aforementioned asymptotic condition for weak secrecy is met by this scheme, we introduce an oracle J which returns the following values

$$J = \begin{cases} 0 & \text{if } s^n = \underline{0} \\ 1 & \text{otherwise.} \end{cases}$$

Using this definition, we may write

$$(1/n)H(U^n|X^n) \geq (1/n)H(U^n|X^nJ)$$
$$= - \sum_{x^n,u^n} p(x^n, u^n, J = 0) \log p(x^n|u^n, J = 0)$$
$$- \sum_{x^n,u^n} p(x^n, u^n, J = 1) \log p(x^n|u^n, J = 1).$$

Since the first term is equal to zero, we can restrict our attention to the second term. Notice that

$$p(x^n, u^n, J = 1) = p(x^n|u^n, J = 1)p(u^n|J = 1)p(J = 1)$$

with

$$p(x^n|u^n, J = 1) = \begin{cases} 0 & \text{if } x^n = u^n \\ \frac{1}{2^n-1} & \text{otherwise,} \end{cases}$$

whereas $p(u^n|J = 1) = 1/2^n$ and $p(J = 1) = 1 - 1/n$. It follows that

$$(1/n)H(U^n|X^n) \geq - \sum_{x^n \neq u^n} \frac{1}{2^n - 1} \frac{1}{2^n} (1 - \frac{1}{n}) \log \frac{1}{2^n - 1}$$
$$= -(1 - \frac{1}{n}) \log \frac{1}{2^n - 1}$$
$$= \log 2^n - 1 - \frac{\log(2^n - 1)}{n}$$
$$\geq \log(2^n - 1) - 1.$$

Thus, we conclude that for any $\epsilon > 0$ there exists an n_0 such that $(1/n)H(U^n|X^n) \geq 1 - \epsilon$, and weak secrecy holds.

However, this does not at all imply that strong secrecy can be achieved by this scheme, in fact the following argument proves its failure:

$$\forall \epsilon > 0 \quad H(U^n|X^n) = H(X^n \oplus S^n|X^n)$$
$$= H(S^n|X^n)$$
$$\leq H(S^n)$$
$$= -\frac{1}{n}\log\frac{1}{n} - (2^n - 1) \cdot \frac{(1 - 1/n)}{(2^n - 1)}\log\frac{(1 - 1/n)}{(2^n - 1)}$$
$$= H_b(1/n) + (1 - 1/n)\log(2^n - 1)$$
$$\leq H_b(1/n) + n - 1$$
$$\leq n - 1 + \epsilon, \quad \text{for } n \text{ sufficiently large,}$$

where $H_b(\alpha) = -\alpha\log\alpha - (1/\alpha)\log(1/\alpha)$ is the binary entropy function. Although the weak secrecy condition would suggest that this scheme is secure, it follows from our analysis that the eavesdropper can acquire on average at least one bit of information from the cryptogram. A closer inspection reveals that there is actually a non negligible probability that the eavesdropper is able to obtain the entire information sequence. For example, if $n = 100$ bits, then the per letter entropy of the key becomes $(1/n)H(S^n) = 0.99$, which is very close to 1. However, the all-zero sequence occurs with probability $P(S^n = \underline{0}) = 0.01$, which implies that, because of the slight non-uniformity of the key, the eavesdropper has a one in one hundred chance of succeeding — even when the weak secrecy condition is met.

1.2 Contribution

Our contribution is a proof for the secrecy capacity of the Gaussian wiretap channel of [8] under the strong secrecy condition defined in [10]. As in the discrete memoryless case and using similar arguments as in [10], we are able to show that substituting the weak secrecy criterion by the stronger version does not alter the secrecy capacity. Based on this result, it is possible to re-evaluate the cryptographic validity of previous results on information-theoretic security for wireless channels. We believe that both this contribution and the work of Nitinawarat [13] on strong secret key agreement with Gaussian random variables and public discussion are important steps towards adding credibility to physical-layer security schemes based on information-theoretic reasoning (e.g. [18] and [3]).

The remainder of the paper is organized as follows. Section 2 provides a set of basic definitions and states the problem in a formal way. This is followed by a strong secrecy result for the Gaussian channel in Section 3. The paper concludes in Section 4 with a discussion of the implications of this result for the secrecy capacity of wireless fading channels.

2   Problem Statement

We assume that a legitimate user (Alice) wants to send messages to another user (Bob). Alice encodes the message $W \in \{1, \ldots, 2^{nR}\}$ into the codeword X^n. When Alice transmits her codeword, Bob observes the output of a discrete-time Gaussian channel (the *main* channel) given by

$$Y(i) = X(i) + Z_m(i),$$

where $Z_m(i)$ is a zero-mean Gaussian random variable that models the noise introduced by the channel at time i.

A third party (Eve) is also capable of eavesdropping Alice's transmissions. Eve observes the output of an independent Gaussian channel (the *eavesdropper* channel) given by

$$Z(i) = X(i) + Z_w(i),$$

where the random variable $Z_w(i)$ represents zero-mean Gaussian noise.

It is assumed that the channel input and the channel noise are independent. The codewords transmitted by Alice are subject to the average power constraint

$$\frac{1}{n} \sum_{i=1}^{n} \mathrm{E}\left[|X(i)|^2\right] \leq P,$$

and the average noise power in the main and the eavesdropper channels are denoted by N_m and N_w, respectively.

Let the transmission rate between Alice and Bob be R and the average error probability $P_e^n = P(W \neq \hat{W})$, where W denotes the sent message chosen uniformly at random and $\hat{W}$ denotes Bob's estimate of the sent message. We are interested in the following two notions of secrecy with respect to Eve.

Definition 1 (Weak Secrecy [19,4]). *We say that the rate R' is achievable with* weak secrecy *if $\forall \epsilon > 0$ for some n sufficiently large there exists an encoder-decoder pair satisfying $R \geq R' - \epsilon$, $P_e^n \leq \epsilon$ and*

$$(1/n)\,\mathrm{H}\left[W|Z^n\right] \geq 1 - \epsilon. \tag{1}$$

Definition 2 (Strong Secrecy [10]). *We say that the rate R' is achievable with* strong secrecy *if $\forall \epsilon > 0$ for some n_0 such that $n > n_0$ there exists an encoder-decoder pair satisfying $R \geq R' - \epsilon$, $P_e^n \leq \epsilon$ and*

$$\mathrm{H}\left[W|Z^n\right] \geq n - \epsilon. \tag{2}$$

The *weak secrecy capacity* C_s^w of the Gaussian channel corresponds to the maximum rate R that is achievable with weak secrecy. Its value was determined in [8] and can be computed according to

$$C_s^w = \begin{cases} C_m - C_w & \text{for } N_w > N_m \\ 0 & \text{otherwise.} \end{cases} \tag{3}$$

where

$$C_m = \frac{1}{2} \log \left(1 + \frac{P}{N_m}\right) \quad \text{and} \quad C_w = \frac{1}{2} \log \left(1 + \frac{P}{N_w}\right)$$

denote the capacity of the main and of the eavesdropper's channel, respectively.

Our goal is to determine the *strong secrecy capacity* C_s^s of the Gaussian channel, defined as the maximum transmission rate at which Bob and Alice can communicate with strong secrecy with respect to Eve.

3   Strong Secrecy Capacity for the Gaussian Channel

3.1   Proof Idea

The main results in information-theoretic security thus far can be roughly divided into two classes: (i) secrecy capacity (or rate-equivocation region) for channel models (e.g. [19]) and (ii) secret key capacity for source models (e.g. [11]). In the latter case, it is assumed that the legitimate partners may use the noisy channel to generate common randomness and communicate freely over a noiseless authenticated channel in order to agree on a common secret key. Although they are conceptually different, it is useful for our purposes to establish a clear connection between these two classes of problems. Specifically, we shall now show at an intuitive level that secure communication over a wiretap channel can be viewed as a special case of secret key agreement. These notions shall be made precise in the next Section, where we present the proof of our main theorem.

According to Shannon, "the fundamental problem of communication is that of reproducing at one point either exactly or approximately a message selected at another point" [16]. Suppose that communication in the source model occurs only in one direction, namely from Alice to Bob. In this case, Alice will know beforehand which secret key Bob will generate from the noisy channel outputs, because, knowing the side information sent by Alice, Bob is going to recover with overwhelming probability the exact same random sequence that is available to Alice at the start of the secret key agreement scheme. Thus, simply by carrying out the key generation process on her random sequence, Alice can construct the actual secret key before transmitting any data to Bob.

If we disregard complexity issues (which are of no importance in information-theoretic reasoning), then there is nothing preventing Alice from generating all possible secret keys beforehand. In other words, she can take all random sequences and run the key generation process. The set of secret keys that she can generate in this manner can be viewed as the set of messages that she can convey to Bob reliably and securely (in the Shannon sense on both counts).

3.2   Main Result

Our main result, whose proof follows [10] closely with the necessary adaptations for the Gaussian channel, is summarized in the following theorem.

Theorem 1. *For the Gaussian channel with power constraint P, we have that $C_s^s = C_s^w$.*

We will prove this result using a succession of lemmas.

Lemma 1 (adapted from [10]). *Let $\mathcal{Q}$ be a scalar quantizer, and let us assume that the eavesdropper observes $Z_\Delta = \mathcal{Q}(Z)$ instead of Z. Let X_Δ be a random variable with $\mathrm{E}\left[X_\Delta^2\right] \leq P$ taking only a finite number of (real) values, and let p_{X_Δ} denote its probability distribution. All rates R_s satisfying*

$$R_s \leq \max_{p_{X_\Delta}} [I(X_\Delta;Y) - I(X_\Delta;Z_\Delta)]$$

are achievable strong secrecy rates.

Proof. The key idea of this lemma is to analyze a simpler channel than the initial Gaussian wiretap channel illustrated in Fig. 1. The assumption that the eavesdropper observes a quantized version of the channel output is merely a mathematical convenience and shall be removed later.

We consider the conceptual channel illustrated in Fig. 2, where, in addition to the Gaussian wiretap channel, Alice has the option of sending messages to Bob over a public authenticated channel with infinite capacity. Furthermore, Alice's inputs X^n to the conceptual channel are restricted to discrete random variables, that is random variables whose support is a finite set of $\mathbb{R}$, and we assume that Eve observes a scalar quantized version Z_Δ^n of the continuous output Z^n of the channel.

Let $\epsilon > 0$ and let $p_{X_\Delta}(x)$ be a probability mass function on $\mathbb{R}$. We also define $R_s = I(X_\Delta;Y) - I(X_\Delta;Z_\Delta)$.

☐ Encoding and decoding procedures.
The coding scheme that we will use to communicate over the channel of Fig. 2 consists of three key ingredients.

1. a wiretap code $\mathcal{C}$ of blocklength n and rate R_s achieving an average probability error $P_e \leq \epsilon'$ over the main channel and ensuring an equivocation rate $(1/n)H(W|Z_\Delta^n) > R_s - \epsilon'$; for n sufficiently large; the existence of such a code for any $\epsilon' > 0$ follows from [19,4]; we let $\mathcal{C}^{\otimes m}$ denote the code obtained by the m-fold concatenation of $\mathcal{C}$;

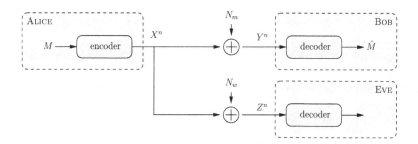

Fig. 1. Gaussian wiretap channel

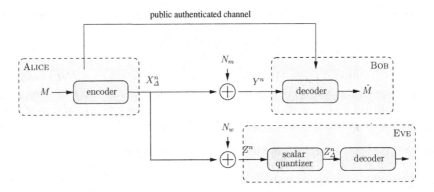

Fig. 2. Conceptual channel used in proof. Alice's inputs X_Δ^n to the Gaussian channels are restricted to discrete random variables and Eve observes a scalar quantized version Z_Δ^n of the continuous output Z^n of the channel.

2. a Slepian-Wolf encoder $f : \{0,1\}^{km} \to \{0,1\}^t$ (and its associated decoder $g : \{0,1\}^t \times \{0,1\}^{km} \to \{0,1\}^{km}$), whose parameters are to be determined later; the existence of such a code follows from [17];

3. an extractor $E : \{0,1\}^{km} \times \{0,1\}^d \to \{0,1\}^r$ whose parameters are to be determined later (extractors appear also in [10]); by enumerating all the values of E over $\{0,1\}^{km} \times \{0,1\}^d$, it is possible to associate to each sequence $w^r \in \{0,1\}^r$ a set $S(w^r) \subset \{0,1\}^{km} \times \{0,1\}^d$, such that

$$\forall w^{km}, w^d \in \{0,1\}^{km} \times \{0,1\}^d \quad E(w^{kr}, w^d) = w^r;$$

In order to transmit a sequence w^r, Alice performs the following encoding procedure.

1. select a pair (w^{km}, w^d) uniformly at random in $S(w^r)$;
2. transmit w^d over the public authenticated channel;
3. send $f(w^{km})$ obtained with the Slepian-Wolf encoder over the public authenticated channel;
4. encode w^{km} according to the code $\mathcal{C}^{\otimes m}$ and transmit the resulting codeword over the wiretap channel.

At the receiver, Bob decodes its information by performing the following operations.

1. retrieve w^d and $f(w^{km})$ from the public channel;
2. estimate $\hat{w}^{km}$ from the output of the wiretap channel according to the wiretap code $\mathcal{C}^{\otimes m}$;
3. decode $\tilde{w}^{km} = g(\hat{w}^{km}, f(w^{km}))$;
4. estimate $\hat{w}^r = E(\tilde{w}^{km}, w^r)$;

In the remainder of this section, the random variables corresponding to the sequences w^{km}, $\hat{w}^{km}$, w^r, $\hat{w}^r$, and w^d are denoted by W^{km}, $\hat{W}^{km}$, W^r, $\hat{W}^r$, and W^d, respectively.

□ Analysis of probability of error.

Letting $P_e^{\otimes m} = P\left[W^{km} \neq \hat{W}^{km}\right]$ denote the average probability of error of achieved by the code $\mathcal{C}^{\otimes m}$, we immediately have by the union bound:

$$P_e^{\otimes m} \leq mP_e \leq m\epsilon'.$$

From [17] (see also [10, Lemma 1]), for m large enough, there exist an encoding function $f : \{0,1\}^{km} \to \{0,1\}^t$ and a decoding function $g : \{0,1\}^{km} \times \{0,1\}^t \to \{0,1\}^{km}$ such that

$$t \leq H(\hat{W}^{km}|W^{km})(1+\epsilon')$$

and

$$P\left[\hat{W}^r \neq W^r\right] = P\left[W^{km} \neq g\left(f\left(W^{km}\right), \hat{W}^{km}\right)\right] < \epsilon.$$

Note that by Fano's inequality we have

$$t \leq \left(kP_e^{\otimes m} + 1\right)(1+\epsilon') = (mk\epsilon' + 1)(1+\epsilon').$$

□ Analysis of equivocation.

By definition of the wiretap code $\mathcal{C}$, we have that $H(W^k|Z_\Delta^n) > n(R_s - \epsilon')$. The following results states that if m is large enough, the inequality also holds for the min-entropy H_∞ [10]. Formally, let $\delta > 0$ and let $\mathcal{F}(\delta)$ denote the event that the sequences w^{km} and $\left(w^{km}, z_\Delta^{nm}\right)$ are δ-typical, and that z_Δ^{nm} is such that the probability taken over w'^{km} according to the distribution $p(w^{km}|Z_\Delta^{nm} = z^{nm})$ that (w'^{km}, z_Δ^{nm}) is δ-typical is at least $1 - \delta$. Then, from [10, Lemma 6] we have

$$m(1 - P[\mathcal{F}(\delta)]) \to 0 \quad \text{as } m \to \infty,$$

$$H_\infty(W^{km}|Z_\Delta^{nm}, \mathcal{F}(\delta)) \geq m\left(H(W^k|Z_\Delta^n) - 2\delta\right) + \log(1-\delta),$$

$$\geq mn\left(R_s - \epsilon' - \frac{2\delta}{n}\right) + \log(1-\delta).$$

Taking into account the messages disclosed over the public channel we have by [10, Lemma 10] that with probability at least $1 - 2^{-\log m}$

$$H_\infty(W^{km}|Z_\Delta^{nm}, f(W^{km}), \mathcal{F}(\delta)),$$

$$\geq mn\left(R_s - \epsilon' - \frac{2\delta}{n}\right) + \log(1-\delta) - (mk\epsilon'+1)(1+\epsilon') - \log m,$$

$$\overset{\Delta}{=} mnR_s(1-\eta) \quad \text{where} \quad \eta \to 0 \text{ as } n \to \infty.$$

From [10, Lemma 9], for any $\alpha, \eta' > 0$ and sufficiently large m, we can choose $E : \{0,1\}^{km} \to \{0,1\}^r$ with $d \leq \alpha km$ and $r \geq (R_s(1-\eta) - \eta')mn$ such that

$$H(E(W^{km}, W^d)|W^d, f(W^{km}), \mathcal{F}(\delta)) \geq r - 2^{-(mn)^{1/2-o(1)}}.$$

Hence, for m sufficiently large, the overall code achieves an equivocation

$$H\left(W^r|W^d, f(W^{km})\right) \geq H(E(W^{km}, W^d)|W^d, f(W^{km}), \mathcal{F}(\delta))(1-\delta) \geq r - \epsilon,$$

with a communication rate $R = r/(mn) \geq R_s - \epsilon$ over the wiretap channel, and the transmission of

$$\alpha km + (mk\epsilon' + 1)(1 + \epsilon') + \log m \triangleq \eta_3 mn$$

bits over the public channel, where $\eta_3 \to 0$ as $n \to \infty$. Notice that the public messages could be transmitted error-free over the wiretap channel itself (using for instance a capacity-approaching code) at a negligible cost in terms of overall transmission rate.

Therefore, $R_s = I(X_\Delta; Y) - I(X_\Delta; Z_\Delta)$ is an achievable strong secrecy rate.

The following lemma shows that restricting the eavesdropper's observations to quantized values is merely a mathematical convenience.

Lemma 2. *If the eavesdropper does not quantize his observations, all rates R_s satisfying*

$$R_s \leq \max_{p_{X_\Delta}} [I(X_\Delta; Y) - I(X_\Delta; Z)]$$

are achievable strong secrecy rates.

Proof. The proof relies heavily on the measure-theoretic definition of entropy, as described in [15]. We refer the reader to the above reference for a precise definition of entropy and information in this case.

Let us first introduce a family of scalar quantizers as follows. If $\mathcal{I}$ is an interval of $\mathbb{R}$, we denote its indicator function by $\mathbf{1}_\mathcal{I}$. For any $j \geq 1$, let $\left\{ \mathcal{I}_k^j : k \in \{1, \ldots, 2^j\} \right\}$ be the unique set of disjoint intervals of $\mathbb{R}$, symmetric around 0, such that for all k, $P_Z(\mathcal{I}_k^j) = \frac{1}{2^j}$. For each $\mathcal{I}_k^j$, define as x_k^j be the middle point of $\mathcal{I}_k^j$. The quantizer $\mathcal{Q}_j$ is defined as follows.

$$\mathcal{Q}_j : \mathbb{R} \to \mathbb{R} : z \longmapsto \sum_{k \in \{1, \ldots, 2^j\}} x_k^j \mathbf{1}_{\mathcal{I}_k^j}.$$

By construction, the knowledge of $\mathcal{Q}_n(z)$ allows to reconstruct the values of $\mathcal{Q}_j(z)$ for all $j \in \{0, \ldots, n\}$.

Let us now consider a suboptimal eavesdropper who would quantize the continuous output of the channel Z using the family of quantizers $\{\mathcal{Q}_j\}_{j \geq 0}$. The random variables $\mathcal{Q}_j(Z)$ resulting from the quantizations are denoted by Z_{Δ_j}. By construction, the sequence Z_{Δ_j} converges almost surely to the random variable Z as $j \to \infty$. Therefore, we have:

$$H(W|Z^n) \overset{(a)}{=} H(W|Z^n, \left\{ Z_{\Delta_j}^n \right\}_{j \geq 0}),$$

$$\overset{(b)}{=} H(W| \left\{ Z_{\Delta_j}^n \right\}_{j \geq 0}),$$

$$\overset{(c)}{=} \lim_{k \to \infty} H(W| \left\{ Z_{\Delta_j}^n \right\}_{0 \leq j \leq k}),$$

$$\overset{(d)}{=} \lim_{k \to \infty} H(W|Z_{\Delta_k}^n),$$

where (a) follows from [15, Corollary (b) p. 48], (b) follows from the almost sure convergence of $\left\{Z^n_{\Delta_j}\right\}$, (c) follows from [15, Theorem 3.10.1] and the fact that W takes only a finite number of values, and (d) follows from [15, Corollary (b) p. 48].

For any k, since $I(X_\Delta; Z_{\Delta_k}) \leq I(X_\Delta; Z)$, Lemma 1 guarantees that, for any p_{X_Δ}, there exists a code achieving a rate $R_s = I(X_\Delta; Y) - I(X_\Delta; Z)$ and ensuring an equivocation $H(W|Z_{\Delta_k})$ arbitrarily close to nR_s. As a consequence of the above equalities, for any $\epsilon > 0$, there exists k_0 sufficiently large and a code designed assuming that the eavesdropper quantizes his observations with $\mathcal{Q}_{k_0}$ such that

$$H(W|Z^n) \geq H(W|Z^n_{\Delta_{k_0}}) - \epsilon,$$

which concludes the proof.

Lemma 3. *The weak secrecy capacity is an achievable strong secrecy rate.*

Proof. Let G be a Gaussian random variable with zero mean and variance P. Let $\mathcal{Q}_j$ be the quantizer defined as in Lemma 2 (by replacing Z by G). Notice that we can always choose the quantized values in such a way that the random variable $G_{\Delta_j} = \mathcal{Q}_j(\Delta)$ satisfies the power constraint; hence, $I(G_{\Delta_j}; Y) - I(G_{\Delta_j}; Z)$ is an achievable strong secret key rate. Following the same approach as in the proof of Lemma 2, one can show that for any $\epsilon > 0$, there exists k_0 sufficiently large such that

$$I(G_{\Delta_{k_0}}; Y) \geq \frac{1}{2}\log(1 + \frac{P}{N_m}) - \epsilon \quad \text{and} \quad I(G_{\Delta_{k_0}}; Z) \leq \frac{1}{2}\log(1 + \frac{P}{N_w}).$$

Consequently, for any $\epsilon > 0$

$$R_s = \frac{1}{2}\log(1 + \frac{P}{N_m}) - \frac{1}{2}\log(1 + \frac{P}{N_w}) - \epsilon$$

is an achievable strong secrecy rate.

Lemma 4. *For the Gaussian wiretap channel, the strong secrecy capacity is equal to the weak secrecy capacity.*

Proof. By definition, the strong secrecy capacity cannot exceed the weak secrecy capacity; therefore all achievable strong secrecy rates are upper bounded by the weak secrecy capacity.

4   Implications for Fading Channels

Having established the strong secrecy capacity of the Gaussian Wiretap Channel, the next natural question is how this affects the fundamental security limits of wireless channels. More specifically, we consider the scenario in which Bob and Eve observe the outputs of a discrete-time Rayleigh fading channel (the *main channel*) given by

$$Y_m(i) = H_m(i)X(i) + Z_m(i),$$

and (the *eavesdropper*'s channel) given by

$$Y_w(i) = H_w(i)X(i) + Z_w(i),$$

respectively. Here, $H_m(i)$ and $H_w(i)$ are circularly symmetric complex Gaussian random variables with zero-mean and unit-variance representing the main channel and eavesdropper's channel fading coefficient, respectively. $Z_m(i)$ and $Z_w(i)$ denote zero-mean circularly symmetric complex Gaussian noise random variables. We further assume that the codewords transmitted by Alice are subject to the average power constraint

$$\frac{1}{n} \sum_{i=1}^{n} E\left[|X(i)|^2\right] \leq P,$$

and the average noise powers in the main channel and the eavesdropper's channel are denoted by N_m and N_w, respectively. The channel input, the channel fading coefficients, and the channel noises are all independent.

There are two cases of interest:

1. The main channel and the eavesdropper's channel are quasi-static fading channels, that is the fading coefficients, albeit random, are constant during the transmission of an entire codeword ($\forall i = 1, \ldots, n$ $H_m(i) = H_m$ and $H_w(i) = H_w$) and, moreover, independent from codeword to codeword. This corresponds to a situation where the coherence time of the channel is large [2];
2. The main channel and the eavesdropper's channel are ergodic fading channels, that is the fading coefficients are drawn randomly in an independent and identically distributed fashion for each transmitted symbol, which corresponds to a situation where the coherence time of the channel is short [9].

In both cases, the secrecy capacity is generically computed by assuming in the first case that every particular fading realization corresponds to one instance of the Gaussian wiretap channel, and in the second case that delay plays no role and so the encoder can wait as long as necessary to have enough identical fading realizations to be able to encode as if it was transmitting over the corresponding instance of the Gaussian wiretap channel.

Close inspection of the proofs shows that in both cases we can safely substitute the weak secrecy capacity achieving random code construction by the strong secrecy construction we presented in the previous section and obtain the strong secrecy capacity for both slow fading (as in [1,2]) and ergodic fading channels (as in [9]).

References

1. Barros, J., Rodrigues, M.R.D.: Secrecy capacity of wireless channels. In: Proceedings of the IEEE International Symposium on Information Theory, Seattle, WA (2006)

2. Bloch, M., Barros, J., Rodrigues, M.R.D., McLaughlin, S.W.: Wireless information-theoretic security. IEEE Transactions on Information Theory 54(6), 2515–2534 (2008)
3. Bloch, M., Thangaraj, A., McLaughlin, S.W., Merolla, J.-M.: LDPC-based Gaussian key reconciliation. In: Proc. of the IEEE International Workshop on Information Theory, Punta del Este, Uruguay (March 2006)
4. Csiszár, I., Korner, J.: Broadcast channels with confidential messages. IEEE Transactions on Information Theory 24(3), 339–348 (1978)
5. Diffie, W., Hellman, M.: New directions in cryptography. IEEE Transactions on Information Theory 22(6), 644–654 (1976)
6. Gopala, P.K., Lai, L., El-Gamal, H.: On the secrecy capacity of fading channels. In: Proceedings of IEEE International Symposium on Information Theory, Nice, France, eprint:cs.IT/0610103 (2007)
7. Hero, A.: Secure space-time communication. IEEE Transactions on Information 49(12), 3235–3249 (2003)
8. Leung-Yan-Cheong, S.K., Hellman, M.E.: The gaussian wiretap channel. IEEE Transactions on Information Theory 24(4), 451–456 (1978)
9. Liang, Y., Poor, H.V., Shamai, S.: Secure communication over fading channels. IEEE Transactions on Information Theory 54, 2470–2492 (2008)
10. Maurer, U., Wolf, S.: Information-theoretic key agreement: From weak to strong secrecy for free. In: Preneel, B. (ed.) EUROCRYPT 2000. LNCS, vol. 1807, p. 351. Springer, Heidelberg (2000)
11. Maurer, U.M.: Secret key agreement by public discussion from common information. IEEE Transactions on Information Theory 39(3), 733–742 (1993)
12. Negi, R., Goel, S.: Secret communication using artificial noise. In: Proceedings of the IEEE Vehicular Technology Conference, Dallas, TX (September 2005)
13. Nitinawarat, S.: Secret key generation for correlated gaussian sources. In: Proceedings of the Forty-Fifth Annual Allerton Conference, Monticello, IL (September 2007)
14. Parada, P., Blahut, R.: Secrecy capacity of SIMO and slow fading channels. In: Proceedings of the IEEE International Symposium on Information Theory, Adelaide, Australia (September 2005)
15. Pinsker, M.S.: Information and Information Stability of Random Variables and Processes. Holden Day (1964)
16. Shannon, C.E., et al.: A mathematical theory of communications. Bell System Technical Journal 27(7), 379–423 (1948)
17. Slepian, D., Wolf, J.K.: Noiseless Coding of Correlated Information Sources. IEEE Transactions on Information Theory 19(4), 471–480 (1973)
18. Thangaraj, A., Dihidar, S., Calderbank, A.R., McLaughlin, S.W., Merolla, J.-M.: Applications of LDPC codes to the wiretap channels. IEEE Transactions on Information Theory 53(8), 2933–2945 (2007)
19. Wyner, A.D.: The wire-tap channel. Bell System Technical Journal 54, 1355–1387 (1975)

Efficient Key Predistribution for Grid-Based Wireless Sensor Networks[*]

Simon R. Blackburn[1], Tuvi Etzion[2], Keith M. Martin[1],
and Maura B. Paterson[1,**]

[1] Department of Mathematics
Royal Holloway, University of London
Egham, Surrey, TW20 0EX, U.K.
{s.blackburn,keith.martin,m.b.paterson}@rhul.ac.uk
[2] Technion -Israel Institute of Technology
Department of Computer Science
Technion City, Haifa 32000, Israel
etzion@cs.technion.ac.il

Abstract. In this paper we propose a new key predistribution scheme for wireless sensor networks in which the sensors are arranged in a square grid. We describe how Costas arrays can be used for key predistribution in these networks, then define *distinct difference configurations*, a more general structure that provides a flexible choice of parameters in such schemes. We give examples of distinct difference configurations with good properties for key distribution, and demonstrate that the resulting schemes provide more efficient key predistribution on square grid networks than other schemes appearing in the literature.

Keywords: wireless sensor networks, key predistribution, costas arrays.

1   Introduction

Wireless sensors are small, battery-powered devices with the ability to take measurements of quantities such as temperature or pressure, and to engage in wireless communication. When a collection of sensors is deployed the sensors can communicate with each other and thus form an ad hoc network, known as a *wireless sensor network* (WSN), in order to facilitate the transmission and manipulation of data by the sensors. Such networks have a wide range of potential applications, including wildlife monitoring or pollution detection (see Römer and Mattern [33] for some examples of how they have been used in practice).

For many applications it is desirable to encrypt communications within the network, since wireless communication is highly vulnerable to interception. The limited memory and battery power of sensors means that for many purposes symmetric techniques are preferred to more computationally intensive public

---

[*] This research was partly carried out under EPSRC grant EP/E034632/1.
[**] This author was supported by EPSRC grant EP/D053285/1.

R. Safavi-Naini (Ed.): ICITS 2008, LNCS 5155, pp. 54–69, 2008.
© Springer-Verlag Berlin Heidelberg 2008

key operations. Thus sensors must share secret keys, in order to provide authentication, confidentiality, or data integrity. One method for enabling this is for the sensors' keys to be preloaded prior to deployment. This technique is known as *key predistribution*.

Much of the literature on key predistribution in wireless sensor networks deals with the case where the physical topology of the network is completely unknown prior to deployment [3,4,5,6,7,9,10,12,13,18,19,21,22,23,24,26,28,29,30,31,35]. In practice, however, many sensor network applications involve networks for which there is some degree of control (indeed, often complete control) over the sensors' locations. Key predistribution is particularly effective in such networks, as the location knowledge can be harnessed to develop more efficient schemes. For instance, it may be possible to reduce the number of keys shared by pairs of nodes that cannot physically communicate. Not only does this reduce the amount of keying material that must be stored, but it improves the resiliency of the network: an adversary learns fewer keys when capturing a given number of nodes, and those keys it does learn tend to be shared only by nodes in a restricted neighbourhood of those captured nodes. Also, a priori knowledge of location reduces the need for nodes to undergo location discovery or neighbour discovery; this may reduce or even eliminate any communication overheads in the key setup process, particularly in the case where there is some regularity or symmetry to the sensors' distribution.

While there are several examples of location-based schemes appearing in the literature [8,9,10,11,17,20,25,34], in the majority of cases the networks consist of randomly distributed nodes whose approximate location is known. In [27], Martin and Paterson give an indication of the types of networks that have been considered in the WSN key predistribution literature, and suggest that there is considerable scope for the development of schemes suited to specific network topologies, in situations where the topology is known before sensor deployment.

In this paper we consider the particular case of a network where the sensors are arranged in a square grid. There are many potential applications in which such a pattern may be useful: monitoring vines in a vineyard or trees in a commercial plantation or reforestation project, studying traffic or pollution levels on city streets, measuring humidity and temperature at regular intervals on library shelves, performing acoustic testing at each of the seats in a theatre, monitoring goods in a warehouse, indeed any application where the objects being studied are naturally distributed in a grid. For purposes of commercial confidentiality or for protecting the integrity of scientific data it is necessary to secure communication between sensors, and thus it is important to have efficient methods of distributing keying material in such networks. The goal of this paper is to provide some practical key predistribution schemes designed specifically for square grids. We show that the highly structured topology of these networks can be exploited to develop schemes that perform significantly better for this application than more general techniques, such as those of Eschenauer and Gligor [13]. Our schemes are designed for *homogeneous* networks in which all sensors have the same capabilities. We assume the nodes have no access to an external trusted authority (such as a base station) for the purposes of establishing keys once they have been deployed. We assume that the location of each node within the grid is known prior to deployment, and consider the problem of establishing pairwise keys between nodes within communication distance of one another. This setting can be described in the language of [27] as that of a locally 2-complete scheme for a network with fixed sensors and full location control.

In the following section, we discuss the desirable properties for key predistribution schemes based on square grids. In Sect. 4 we describe a key predistribution scheme based on *Costas arrays*, and we introduce the concept of *distinct-difference configurations* and use them to generalise our scheme. In Sect. 5 we discuss certain important properties of KPSs, and in Sect. 6 we compare the behaviour of our schemes to that of several schemes from the literature. We show that our schemes outperform these previously studied schemes under our network model.

2   The Network Model

We say that a wireless sensor network is *grid based* if it consists of a (potentially unbounded) number of identical sensors arranged in a square grid.

If each sensor has a maximum transmission range r then a sensor is able to communicate directly with all nodes within the circle of radius r that surrounds it. (We say that two squares occur at distance r if the Euclidean distance between the centres of the squares is r.) Without loss of generality we can scale our unit of distance so that adjacent nodes in the grid are at distance 1 from each other; we will adopt this convention throughout this paper as it removes unnecessary complications from our discussions.

We refer to nodes within the circle of radius r centred at some node Ψ as *r-neighbours* of Ψ. For most applications it is useful for any two neighbouring nodes in a sensor network to be able communicate securely. In designing a KPS, however, we are restricted by the limited storage capacity of the sensors: if a node has many neighbours, it may be unable to store enough keys to share a distinct key with each neighbour. We would like to design key predistribution schemes in which each node shares a key with as many of its r-neighbours as possible, while taking storage constraints into account. (Note that we only require keys to be shared by nodes that are r-neighbours, in contrast to a randomly distributed sensor network which potentially requires all pairs of nodes to share keys.) One way of achieving this is for each key to be shared by several different nodes; however, it is necessary to restrict the extent to which each key is shared, to protect the network against key compromise through node capture.

In Sect. 4 we propose a construction for KPSs that seek to balance the competing requirements discussed in this section. First, however, we describe a combinatorial structure that we will use in this construction.

3   Costas Arrays

Costas arrays were first introduced for use in the detection of sonar signals (see [16]), and have received much attention for this and other applications (an extensive bibliography can be found at [32]). To the best of our knowledge, the KPS we propose in Sect. 4 represents the first time these structures have been used for key distribution. In this section we provide basic definitions and properties of these arrays, and briefly describe some known constructions.

Definition 1. *A Costas array of order n is an $n \times n$ matrix with the following properties:*

- *each position is either blank or contains a dot,*
- *each row and each column contains exactly one dot,*
- *all $n(n-1)$ vectors connecting pairs of dots are distinct as vectors (any two vectors are different in either length or direction).*

Example 1

This is an example of a Costas array of order 3. It is easily seen that the six vectors connecting pairs of dots are distinct.

The application of Costas arrays in sonar or radar relies on the fact that if a translation is applied to a copy of a Costas array then at most one dot of the translated array coincides with a dot of the original array, unless the two are exactly superimposed. It is this property that motivates our use of Costas arrays in constructing KPSs. We formalise it as follows.

Lemma 1. *Let $S = \{\mathbf{d}_1, \mathbf{d}_2, \ldots, \mathbf{d}_n\}$ be the set of positions of the dots in a Costas array $\mathcal{A}$. Suppose the array $\mathcal{A}$ is translated by a vector $\mathbf{v}$ in the lattice $\mathbb{Z}^2$ and let $S' = \{\mathbf{d}_1 + \mathbf{v}, \mathbf{d}_2 + \mathbf{v}, \ldots, \mathbf{d}_n + \mathbf{v}\}$ be the set of positions of the dots in the translated array. Then if $\mathbf{v} \neq \mathbf{0}$, we have $|S \cap S'| \leq 1$.*

Proof. Suppose there exists a vector $\mathbf{v}$ and dot positions $\mathbf{d}_i, \mathbf{d}_j, \mathbf{d}_k, \mathbf{d}_l$ such that $\mathbf{d}_i = \mathbf{d}_j + \mathbf{v}$ and $\mathbf{d}_k = \mathbf{d}_l + \mathbf{v}$. Then $\mathbf{d}_i - \mathbf{d}_k = \mathbf{d}_j - \mathbf{d}_l$. As $\mathcal{A}$ is a Costas array, this implies that $\mathbf{d}_i = \mathbf{d}_j$ and $\mathbf{d}_k = \mathbf{d}_l$, and hence $\mathbf{v} = \mathbf{0}$.   □

Two main constructions for Costas arrays are known (see [14,15,16] for further discussion). Let p be an odd prime. An integer α is a *primitive root modulo p* if the powers $\alpha^1, \alpha^2, \ldots, \alpha^{p-1}$ are all distinct modulo p; such integers exist for all odd primes p.

The Welch Construction. Let α be a primitive root modulo p and let $\mathcal{A}$ be a $(p-1) \times (p-1)$ array. For $1 \leq i \leq p-1$ and $1 \leq j \leq p-1$ we put a dot in $\mathcal{A}(i,j)$ if and only if $\alpha^i \equiv j \pmod{p}$.

The Golomb Construction. Let q be a power of a prime and let α and β be two primitive elements in $\mathrm{GF}(q)$, i.e. elements that generate the multiplicative group of $\mathrm{GF}(q)$. We define $\mathcal{A}$ to be a $(q-2) \times (q-2)$ array. For $1 \leq i \leq q-2$ and $1 \leq j \leq q-2$ we put a dot in $\mathcal{A}(i,j)$ if and only if $\alpha^i + \beta^j = 1$. We remark that when $\alpha = \beta$ the construction is called the Lempel Construction.

There are several variants for these two constructions resulting in Costas arrays with orders slightly smaller (by 1, 2, 3, or 4) than the orders of these two constructions.

4 Construction of Key Predistribution Schemes for Grid-Based Networks

In this section we provide basic definitions relating to key predistribution, and examine certain properties that must be considered when designing such schemes, before proposing constructions of KPSs that are specifically adapted to grid-based networks.

Let $\mathcal{K}$ be a finite set whose elements we refer to as keys (whether they be either actual secret keys, or quantities from which such keys may be derived). We consider a set U of wireless sensors, each of which has sufficient memory to store m keys; after deployment the nodes U form a wireless sensor network W.

Definition 2. *A* key predistribution scheme (KPS) *for W is a map $U \to \mathcal{K}^m$ that assigns up to m keys from $\mathcal{K}$ to each node in U.*

Each node stores the keys assigned to it in its memory prior to deployment. Once the nodes are deployed we have the following possible situations.

– Two nodes that share one or more common elements of $\mathcal{K}$ can use them to derive a common key.
– Two nodes that do not share a key may rely on an intermediate node with which they both share a key in order to communicate securely; this is referred to as a *two-hop path.*

If each $k \in \mathcal{K}$ is assigned to a set $S_k \subset U$ of at most α nodes we refer to the KPS as an $[m, \alpha]$-*KPS*. As mentioned in Sect. 2, one of the goals when designing an $[m, \alpha]$-KPS is to enable each node to communicate directly with as many nodes as possible, hence we would like to maximise the expected number of neighbouring nodes that share at least one key with a given Ψ. We note that when evaluating properties of a grid-based network in which the network does not extend infinitely in all directions, complications may arise due to nodes on the edge of the network having a reduced number of neighbours. This can be avoided by restricting attention to properties of nodes on the *interior* of the network (nodes Ψ such that each grid position that is within range of Ψ contains a node of the network). This is a reasonable restriction to make as it greatly simplifies analysis and comparison of KPSs, especially since for a grid-based network of any size the edge nodes will only represent a small proportion of the network.

Theorem 1. *When an $[m, \alpha]$-KPS is used to distribute keys to nodes in a square grid network, the expected number of r-neighbours of a node ψ in the interior of the network that share at least one key with Ψ is at most $m(\alpha - 1)$. The value $m(\alpha - 1)$ is achieved precisely when the following conditions are met.*

1. *Each interior node stores exactly m keys, each of which are shared by exactly α nodes.*
2. *No pair of nodes shares two or more keys.*
3. *The distance between any two nodes sharing a key is at most r.*

Proof. The maximum number of keys allocated to an interior node Ψ by an $[m, \alpha]$-KPS is m; each of these keys is shared by at most α nodes (which may or may not be r-neighbours of Ψ). Hence a given interior node shares keys with at most $\alpha - 1$ of its r-neighbours, and this maximum value is achieved if and only if no two nodes share more than one key with Ψ, and every node with which Ψ shares a key is an r-neighbour of Ψ. The result follows directly. □

This result indicates that when distributing keys according to an $[m, \alpha]$-KPS, limiting the number of keys shared by each pair of nodes to at most one increases the number of pairs of neighbouring nodes that share keys, hence this is desirable from the point of view of efficiency. This restriction will be further exploited in the analysis of Sect. 5. In the following section we describe a method of constructing $[m, \alpha]$-KPSs with this property.

4.1 Key Predistribution Using Costas Arrays

We now propose a KPS for a grid-based network, in which the pattern of nodes that share a particular key is determined by a Costas array. The result is a $[n, n]$-KPS in which any two nodes have at most one key in common.

Construction 2. *Let $\mathcal{A}$ be a $n \times n$ Costas array. We can use $\mathcal{A}$ to distribute keys from a keypool $\mathcal{K}$ to a set U of nodes arranged in a grid-based network as follows.*

- *Arbitrarily choose one square of the grid to be the origin, and superimpose $\mathcal{A}$ on the grid, with its lower left-hand square over the origin. Select a key k_{00} from $\mathcal{K}$, and distribute it to nodes occurring in squares coinciding with a dot of $\mathcal{A}$ (so n nodes receive the key k_{00}).*
- *Similarly, for each square occurring at a position (i, j) in the grid, we place the lower left-hand square of $\mathcal{A}$ over that square, then assign a key $k_{ij} \in \mathcal{K}$ to the squares that are now covered by dots of $\mathcal{A}$.*

If the dots of the Costas array occur in squares $(0, a_0), (1, a_1), \ldots, (n-1, a_{n-1})$ of the array then the above scheme associates a key k_{ij} with the nodes in squares $(i, j + a_0), (i + 1, j + a_1), \ldots, (i + n - 1, j + a_{n-1})$ (where such nodes exist). We observe that the deterministic nature of this key allocation, together with the structured topology of a square grid, means that nodes can simply store the coordinates in the grid of those nodes with which they share keys, thus obviating the need for a shared-key discovery process with ensuing communication overheads.

Example 2. Consider the 3×3 Costas array of Example 1. If we use this array for key distribution as described above, each node stores three keys. Figure 1 illustrates this key distribution: each square in the grid represents a node, and each symbol contained in a square represents a key possessed by that node. The central square stores keys marked by the letters A, B and C; two further nodes share each of these keys, which are marked in bold. Letters in standard type represent keys used to connect the central node to one of its neighbours via a two-hop path, other keys are marked in grey. Note that we have only illustrated some of the keys; the pattern of key sharing extends in a similar manner throughout the entire network.

Fig. 1. Key distribution using a 3×3 Costas array

Theorem 3. *The key predistribution scheme in Construction 2 has the following properties:*

1. *Each sensor is assigned n different keys.*
2. *Each key is assigned to n sensors.*
3. *Any two sensors have at most one key in common.*
4. *The distance between two sensors which have a common key is at most $\sqrt{2}(n-1)$.*

Proof

1. There are n dots in $\mathcal{A}$. For each dot in turn, if we position $\mathcal{A}$ so that dot lies over a given node Ψ, this determines a positioning of $\mathcal{A}$ for which the corresponding key is allocated to Ψ. Hence Ψ stores n keys in total.
2. A key k_{ij} is assigned to n positions in the square grid, namely those that coincide with the n dots of a fixed shift of $\mathcal{A}$.

3. Suppose there exist two sensors A and B sharing (at least) two keys. These keys correspond to different translations of the array $\mathcal{A}$, hence there exist two translations of $\mathcal{A}$ in which dots occur at the positions of both A and B. However, by Lemma 1, two copies of $\mathcal{A}$ coincide in at most one dot, thus contradicting the original assumption.

4. The two most distant sensors which have a key in common must correspond to two dots in the same translation of $\mathcal{A}$. The largest distance between two dots in $\mathcal{A}$ occurs if they are in two opposite corners of the array, i.e. at distance $\sqrt{2}(n-1)$.

$\square$

Corollary 1. *When the $[n,n]$-KPS of Construction 2 is applied to a grid-based network then a node on the interior of the network shares keys with $n(n-1)$ other nodes, the maximum possible for a $[n,n]$-KPS.*

4.2   Distinct-Difference Configurations in Key Predistribution

The proof of Part 3 of Theorem 3 relies on the property that the vectors connecting pairs of dots in a Costas array are pairwise distinct. We do not, however, make use of the requirement that each row and column have exactly one dot. This suggests that we can relax this condition in order to explore other structures for use in key predistribution. This leads us to the following definition.

Definition 3. *A distinct-difference configuration $DD(m,r)$ consists of a set of m dots placed in a square grid such that*

- *any two of the dots in the configuration are at distance at most r apart,*
- *all $m(m-1)$ differences between pairs of dots are distinct as vectors (any two vectors differ either in length or direction).*

A Costas array is an example of a $DD(n,r)$, for some $r \leq \sqrt{2}(n-1)$. Like Costas arrays, a $DD(m,r)$ can be used for key predistribution:

Construction 4. *For a given $DD(m,r)$ we distribute keys as in Construction 2, using the $DD(m,r)$ in place of a Costas array.*

Theorem 5. *If a $DD(m,r)$ is used for key predistribution as described in Construction 4 the resulting KPS has the following properties:*

1. *Each sensor is assigned m different keys.*
2. *Each key is assigned to m sensors.*
3. *Any two sensors have at most one key in common.*
4. *The distance between two sensors which have a common key is at most r.*

Proof. As in the case of the Costas arrays, the fact that differences between pairs of dots are distinct imply that two nodes share at most one key. The limit on the distance between nodes sharing keys are a distance of at most r apart follows directly from the restriction on the distances between dots in the $DD(m,r)$. $\square$

Example 3

This is an example of a DD(3, 2). If used in a KPS each node stores 3 keys. Figure 2 illustrates (part of) the pattern of key sharing that results. As in Fig. 1, each square in the grid represents a node, and each letter represents a key possessed by that node. This key distribution has an advantage over that of Example 2

Fig. 2. Key predistribution using a DD(3, 2)

in that each node still shares keys with six other nodes, but these nodes are all 2-neighbours, rather than 3-neighbours.

This construction provides $[m, m]$-KPSs in which interior nodes share keys with an optimal number $m(m-1)$ of neighbouring nodes. We have greater flexibility than Construction 3.5 because we consider a more general class of configurations. So we are better able to choose a configuration whose properties match the application requirements. The use of a DD(m, r) enables the construction of a KPS suitable for the specific radius r and maximum storage m of a given network[1], whereas in the case of Costas arrays the number of dots and the maximal distance between them are directly linked.

We have noted that the use of a DD(m, r) maximises the number of r-neighbours that share keys with a given node. Additionally, it is desirable to maximise the number of r-neighbours that can communicate securely with a given node Ψ via a one-hop or two-hop path. We refer to this quantity as the *two-hop r-coverage* of a KPS. In the case of our scheme based on distinct-difference configurations we refer to the two-hop r-coverage of a DD(m, r) to indicate the two-hop r-coverage obtained by a KPS constructed from that configuration. Table 1 shows the maximum possible values for the two-hop r-coverage of a DD(m, r) for $r = 1, 2, \ldots, 12$. The empty positions in the table represent combinations of m and r for which no DD(m, r) exists. In Fig. 3 we illustrate DD(m, r) achieving the maximal two-hop r-coverage values shown in Table 1, for those cases where the corresponding two-hop r-coverage cannot be obtained

---

[1] provided a suitable DD(m, r) can be found. For a given r there is evidently an upper limit on the value of m for which a DD(m, r) exists. If the potential storage m exceeds this value a DD(m', r) could be employed with m' equal to the maximum number of dots possible in a distance r distinct-difference configuration.

Table 1. The maximum two-hop r-coverage of a DD(m,r)

$m \backslash r$	1	2	3	4	5	6	7	8	9	10	11	12
2	2	4	4	4	4	4	4	4	4	4	4	4
3	-	12	18	18	18	18	18	18	18	18	18	18
4	-	-	28	46	54	54	54	54	54	54	54	54
5	-	-	28	48	80	102	118	126	130	130	130	130
6	-	-	-	48	80	112	148	184	222	240	254	262
7	-	-	-	-	80	112	148	196	252	302	346	374
8	-	-	-	-	-	112	148	196	252	316	376	$\geq$432
9	-	-	-	-	-	-	148	196	252	316	376	440
10	-	-	-	-	-	-	-	196	252	316	376	440
11	-	-	-	-	-	-	-	-	252	316	376	440
12	-	-	-	-	-	-	-	-	-	316	376	440

by a configuration with smaller m (without increasing r) or smaller r (without increasing m). (For a given radius r the number of two-hop r-neighbours is evidently bounded by the total number of r-neighbours; these totals correspond to the numbers in bold in Fig. 3. Similarly, for a given m there is a maximum number of two-hop r-neighbours that can be achieved by a DD(m,r); these values appear in italics. Both trends are apparent in Table 1.) In the case of $m = 8, r = 12$ the best known two-hop r-coverage is 432.

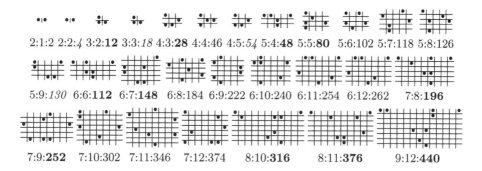

2:1:2 2:2:*4* 3:2:**12** 3:3:*18* 4:3:**28** 4:4:46 4:5:*54* 5:4:**48** 5:5:**80** 5:6:102 5:7:118 5:8:126

5:9:*130* 6:6:**112** 6:7:**148** 6:8:184 6:9:222 6:10:240 6:11:254 6:12:262 7:8:**196**

7:9:**252** 7:10:302 7:11:346 7:12:374 8:10:**316** 8:11:**376** 9:12:**440**

Fig. 3. Distinct-difference configurations with maximal two-hop r-coverage γ. The labels indicate the corresponding m:r:γ. The value of γ is given in bold if it is the maximum possible for the given r, and in italics if it is the maximum given m.

5 Evaluation of Key Predistribution Schemes for Grid-Based Networks

In Sect. 4 we indicated some desirable properties of key predistribution schemes in order to motivate our constructions. We now provide a wider analysis of the properties of these schemes. There are no standard metrics for evaluating KPSs, as desirable properties depend on the particular application environment; authors tend to devise their own metrics for evaluating the schemes they propose. Nevertheless the basic goals of these schemes remain the same: it is beneficial to restrict the amount of storage and communication overheads required, while maximising the number of secure communication links between nodes, even in the case when nodes are subject to adversarial compromise. In this section we consider each of these aspects, in the context of grid-based networks, and define the precise quantities we use in Sect. 6 to compare our schemes with previous schemes.

Table 2. A comparison of key predistribution schemes for a 100×100 grid-based network. (*Entries represent the mean over 10000 trials, with the sample standard deviation given in brackets.*)

Scheme	m	α	One-hop	Two-hop	Resilience		L. Resilience	
Costas	8	8	56	366	331	(86)	59	(53)
DD(8,11)	8	8	56	376	336	(86)	59	(53)
Liu & Ning	8	2	8	24	23.87	(1.48)	20.3	(7.0)
Eschenauer & Gligor	8	≈ 200	56.2 (7.0)	370.0 (3.8)	36	(38)	36	(38)
Ito *et al.*	8	≈ 8	36.2 (6.4)	319.6 (20.1)	259	(97)	52	(47)

Storage. There is no established consensus on the number of symmetric keys that a sensor can feasibly store in practice. Estimations in the literature range from "perhaps 30-50" [23] to more than 200 [6]. As sensor technology improves, the amount of memory available is increasing. However, there is always a tradeoff between the amount of memory used for cryptographic purposes and the amount available for the rest of the sensor's functionality. Also, the development of smaller, less power-hungry sensors will continue to place limits on memory capacity in the future. It is common for the storage requirement to be a parameter of a KPS, and for other properties to be described in terms of this parameter. When choosing parameters for the schemes we compare in Sect. 6, we fix an upper bound for the storage and consider only schemes whose storage requirements do not exceed this bound.

Cost of shared key discovery. The deterministic nature of our scheme means that no communication is required either for neighbour discovery, or for shared key discovery.

One-hop and two-hop coverage. As discussed in Sect. 4, our schemes ensure nodes have the maximum number $m(m-1)$ of one-hop r-neighbours that is possible for a $[m, m]$-KPS. Thus the number of secure communication links is maximised by choosing m to be as large as possible. Note that there are two factors constraining the size of m: the memory capacity of nodes, and the combinatorial limits on the size of m for a fixed value of r. In order to assess the connectivity of a scheme, it is also desirable to take into account the two-hop r-coverage. Table 1 illustrates that if the storage m is sufficient, it is possible to find distinct difference configurations for use in Construction 4 that ensure that every node on the interior of the network can communicate with each of its r-neighbours by either a one-hop or a two-hop path.

Resilience. Informally speaking, the resilience of a KPS is the extent to which secure communication can be maintained within the network when an adversary compromises a certain number of nodes and extracts the keys that they store. In Sect. 6 we will measure the resilience of a scheme by the expected number of r-neighbours of a node Ψ that can still communicate securely (i.e. by using keys unknown to the adversary) with Ψ by either a one-hop or two-hop path, after a fixed number of nodes have been compromised. We will consider both the case in which the compromised nodes are chosen uniformly throughout the network, and the case where the nodes are drawn uniformly from the r-neighbourhood of Ψ (we assume that Ψ itself is not compromised.) We refer to the quantity arising from the latter case as the *local resilience*.

6   Concrete Comparison of Existing Schemes

In order to illustrate the performance of the KPSs proposed in this paper we select some concrete values for the network parameters, which allows us to compare the performance of our schemes explicitly with other schemes appearing in the literature. Our schemes are shown to perform better than previously known schemes in our network model. We will consider a grid-based network with 10000 nodes arranged in a square, in which each node can store up to 8 keys and has a communication range $r = 11$. The results of our analysis of several schemes are summarised in Table 2. For each scheme we are interested in the values of m, α and the expected number of one-hop 11-neighbours *(One-hop)* and two-hop 11-neighbours *(Two-hop)*. We also measure the number of a node's two-hop links that remain secure after an adversary compromises five nodes, either uniformly throughout the network *(Resilience)*, or uniformly from among that node's 11-neighbours *(L. Resilience)*. These values for each scheme are displayed in Table 2, and represent the mean value over 10000 randomly generated instances. The corresponding sample standard deviation is given in brackets. In each case the parameters for the schemes have been chosen so that the storage requirement is at most 8 keys, and so that all schemes have (where possible) a similar number of one-hop 11-neighbours. We now give a brief description of the schemes we are considering, as well as an explanation of the parameter choices involved.

Construction 4. The 11-neighbourhood of a node contains 376 other nodes. If the storage limit is 8, then Construction 4 results in a KPS in which each node has 56 one-hop neighbours. Using the $DD(8, 11)$ shown in Fig. 3 means that all 376 11-neighbours of a given node can communicate with that node via a one-hop or two-hop path.

Construction 2. This construction also results in nodes having 56 one-hop neighbours, however the best two-hop 11-coverage that results from an 8×8 Costas array is 366, achieved by the following array.

Eschenauer and Gligor [13]. In Eschenauer and Gligor's KPS, each node is assigned m keys drawn uniformly without replacement from a key pool of a fixed size. By taking $m = 8$ and a keypool of size 400 for this network we obtain a KPS in which the number of one and two-hop 11-neighbours is similar to that of our schemes.

Liu and Ning [25]. Liu and Ning's 'closest pairwise scheme' is a location-based scheme in which each node shares keys with its c closest neighbours. Since we are working with a square grid, we can consider a scheme in which each node shares pairwise keys with the 8 nodes surrounding it.

Ito, Ohta, Matsuda and Yoneda [20]. The scheme of Ito et al. is a location-based, probabilistic scheme. They propose associating keys with points in the target area, then for each node they randomly choose m points that are expected to lie within its communication range after deployment, and assign the corresponding keys to that node. To deploy this scheme in our grid-based network we associate a key with each grid point, then for each node randomly choose 8 points within distance 11 of that node.

Other location based schemes. Most of the location-based KPSs in the literature do not assume a precise knowledge of sensor locations, but instead divide the target area into regions (square, rectangular, hexagonal and triangular regions have all been proposed) and suppose that the region in which each sensor will be deployed is known a priori. Schemes such as those in [9,10,17,34,25] involve all nodes in each region being given shares in a threshold key establishment scheme such as those of [1,2] with nodes receiving shares corresponding to each of the neighbouring regions. The storage constraints of the specific network environment we are considering mean that most of these scheme either cannot be employed, or else could only be employed with such low thresholds as to severely compromised their resilience.

The scheme of Du, Deng, Han, Chen and Varshney [11] similarly divides the target area into regions, and then modifies Eschenauer and Gligor's basic scheme by letting the pool from which nodes draw keys depend on the region in which they are to be deployed. However, Ito et al. argue that this does not provide sufficient granularity [20], as a rectangular region does not adequately model the circle throughout which a node is supposed to be able to communicate.

In Table 2 we compare our Costas array and DD(8, 11) schemes, Liu and Ning's closest pairwise scheme, Eschenauer and Gligor's scheme, and the scheme of Ito et al. for the choices of parameters discussed above. This data highlights several differences in the behaviour of the various schemes in this environment; in particular we note the following.

The local resilience of Eschenauer and Gligor's scheme is less than that of our schemes, and the resilience is substantially less (as their scheme does not take account of the nodes' locations, the resilience matches the local resilience). This is essentially due to the large value of α that is required in order for their scheme to give adequate one-hop or two-hop coverage. The use of location knowledge in the scheme of Ito et al. results in an improvement in resilience, although it is still significantly less than that of our schemes, and the one-hop and two-hop coverage is lower too. A change of parameters could increase the coverage, but at the cost of increasing α, so that any increase in resilience would be curtailed. Furthermore, even though [20] is location based, the fact that its key distribution is probabilistic means that it incurs the same shared-key-discovery cost as [13], whereas our deterministic schemes involve no key-discovery overheads.

The coverage of Liu and Ning's scheme is very low. The resilience is high in proportion to the coverage, in that most of the links are expected to remain unaffected after node compromise. However since the number of links existing prior to node compromise is small, then in absolute terms the resilience and local resilience are even lower than that of [13].

Thus we see that both Construction 2 and Construction 4 yield KPSs that provide good one-hop and two-hop coverage in grid-based networks with restricted storage, and that the resulting KPSs are demonstrably more resilient in the fact of node compromise than previously proposed schemes. They therefore represent a good solution whenever a very lightweight yet resilient KPS is required for a grid-based network.

References

1. Blom, R.: An Optimal Class of Symmetric Key Generation Systems. In: Beth, T., Cot, N., Ingemarsson, I. (eds.) EUROCRYPT 1984. LNCS, vol. 209, pp. 334–338. Springer, Heidelberg (1985)
2. Blundo, C., Santis, A.D., Herzberg, A., Kutten, S., Vaccaro, U., Yung, M.: Perfectly-Secure Key Distribution for Dynamic Conferences. In: Brickell, E.F. (ed.) CRYPTO 1992. LNCS, vol. 740, pp. 471–486. Springer, Heidelberg (1993)
3. Çamtepe, S.A., Yener, B.: Combinatorial Design of Key Distribution Mechanisms for Wireless Sensor Networks. In: Samarati, P., Ryan, P.Y.A., Gollmann, D., Molva, R. (eds.) ESORICS 2004. LNCS, vol. 3193, pp. 293–308. Springer, Heidelberg (2004)
4. Çamtepe, S.A., Yener, B., Yung, M.: Expander Graph Based Key Distribution Mechanisms in Wireless Sensor Networks. In: IEEE International Conference on Communications, vol. 5, pp. 2262–2267. IEEE press, New York (2006)
5. Chakrabarti, D., Maitra, S., Roy, B.K.: A Hybrid Design of Key Pre-distribution Scheme for Wireless Sensor Networks. In: Jajodia, S., Mazumdar, C. (eds.) ICISS 2005. LNCS, vol. 3803, pp. 228–238. Springer, Heidelberg (2005)
6. Chakrabarti, D., Maitra, S., Roy, B.K.: A Key Pre-distribution Scheme for Wireless Sensor Networks: Merging Blocks in Combinatorial Design. In: Zhou, J., López, J., Deng, R.H., Bao, F. (eds.) ISC 2005. LNCS, vol. 3650, pp. 89–103. Springer, Heidelberg (2005)
7. Chan, H., Perrig, A., Song, D.: Random Key Predistribution Schemes for Sensor Networks. In: IEEE Symposium on Security and Privacy, p. 197. IEEE press, New York (2003)
8. Chan, S.P., Poovendran, R., Sun, M.T.: A Key Management Scheme in Distributed Sensor Networks Using Attack Probabilities. In: IEEE GLOBECOM 2005, vol. 2 (2005)
9. Delgosha, F., Fekri, F.: Key Pre-distribution in Wireless Sensor Networks Using Multivariate Polynomials. In: IEEE Commun. Soc. Conf. Sensor and Ad Hoc Commun. and Networks - SECON 2005 (2005)

10. Delgosha, F., Fekri, F.: Threshold Key-Establishment in Distributed Sensor Networks Using a Multivariate Scheme. In: Infocom 2006 (2006)
11. Du, W., Deng, J., Han, Y.S., Chen, S., Varshney, P.K.: A Key Management Scheme for Wireless Sensor Networks Using Deployment Knowledge. In: INFOCOM (2004)
12. Du, W., Deng, J., Han, Y.S., Varshney, P.K.: A Pairwise Key Pre-distribution Scheme for Wireless Sensor Networks. In: Jajodia, S., Atluri, V., Jaeger, T. (eds.) CCS 2003, pp. 42–51. ACM Press, New York (2003)
13. Eschenauer, L., Gligor, V.D.: A Key-Management Scheme for Distributed Sensor Networks. In: Atluri, V. (ed.) CCS 2002, pp. 41–47. ACM Press, New York (2002)
14. Golomb, S.W.: Algebraic Constructions for Costas Arrays. J. Comb. Theory A. 37, 13–21 (1984)
15. Golomb, S.W., Taylor, H.: Constructions and Properties of Costas Arrays. P. IEEE. 72, 1143–1163 (1984)
16. Golomb, S.W., Taylor, H.: Two-Dimensional Synchronization Patterns for Minimum Ambiguity. IEEE T. Inform. Theory. 28, 600–604 (1982)
17. Huang, D., Mehta, M., Medhi, D., Harn, L.: Location-Aware Key Management Scheme for Wireless Sensor Networks. In: Setia, S., Swarup, V. (eds.) SASN 2004, pp. 29–42. ACM Press, New York (2004)
18. Hwang, D., Lai, B.C., Verbauwhede, I.: Energy-Memory-Security Tradeoffs in Distributed Sensor Networks. In: Nikolaidis, I., Barbeau, M., Kranakis, E. (eds.) ADHOC-NOW 2004. LNCS, vol. 3158, pp. 70–81. Springer, Heidelberg (2004)
19. Hwang, J., Kim, Y.: Revisiting Random Key Pre-distribution Schemes for Wireless Sensor Networks. In: Setia, S., Swarup, V. (eds.) SASN 2004, pp. 43–52. ACM Press, New York (2004)
20. Ito, T., Ohta, H., Matsuda, N., Yoneda, T.: A Key Pre-distribution Scheme for Secure Sensor Networks Using Probability Density Function of Node Deployment. In: Atluri, V., Ning, P., Du, W. (eds.) SASN 2005, pp. 69–75. ACM Press, New York (2005)
21. Lee, J., Stinson, D.R.: A Combinatorial Approach to Key Predistribution for Distributed Sensor Networks. In: IEEE Wireless Communications and Networking Conference, CD-ROM, 2005, paper PHY53-06, p. 6 (2005)
22. Lee, J., Stinson, D.R.: Deterministic Key Predistribution Schemes for Distributed Sensor Networks. In: Handschuh, H., Hasan, M.A. (eds.) SAC 2004. LNCS, vol. 3357, pp. 294–307. Springer, Heidelberg (2004)
23. Lee, J., Stinson, D.R.: On the Construction of Practical Key Predistribution Schemes for Distributed Sensor Networks Using Combinatorial Designs. ACM Trans. Inf. Syst. Secur. 11(2), 1–35 (2008)
24. Liu, D., Ning, P.: Establishing Pairwise Keys in Distributed Sensor Networks. In: Jajodia, S., Atluri, V., Jaeger, T. (eds.) CCS 2003, pp. 52–61. ACM Press, New York (2003)
25. Liu, D., Ning, P.: Location-Based Pairwise Key Establishments for Static Sensor Networks. In: Setia, S., Swarup, V. (eds.) SASN 2003, pp. 72–82. ACM Press, New York (2003)
26. Liu, D., Ning, P., Li, R.: Establishing Pairwise Keys in Distributed Sensor Networks. ACM Trans. Inf. Syst. Secur. 8(1), 41–77 (2005)
27. Martin, K.M., Paterson, M.B.: An Application-Oriented Framework for Wireless Sensor Network Key Establishment. In: WCAN 2007. ENTCS (to appear, 2007)
28. Mohaisen, A., Maeng, Y., Nyang, D.: On Grid-Based Key Pre-distribution: Toward a Better Connectivity in Wireless Sensor Network. In: SSDU 2007 (2007)

29. Mohaisen, A., Nyang, D.: Hierarchical Grid-Based Pairwise Key Predistribution Scheme for Wireless Sensor Networks. In: Römer, K., Karl, H., Mattern, F. (eds.) EWSN 2006. LNCS, vol. 3868, pp. 83–98. Springer, Heidelberg (2006)
30. Pietro, R.D., Mancini, L.V., Mei, A.: Random Key-Assignment for Secure Wireless Sensor Networks. In: Setia, S., Swarup, V. (eds.) SASN 2003, pp. 62–71. ACM Press, New York (2003)
31. Ramkumar, M., Memon, N.: An Efficient Key Predistribution Scheme for Ad Hoc Network Security. IEEE J. Sel. Area. Comm. 23, 611–621 (2005)
32. Rickard, S.: CostasArrays.org, http://www.costasarrays.org
33. Römer, K., Mattern, F.: The Design Space of Wireless Sensor Networks. Wirel. Commun. 11(6), 54–61 (2004)
34. Zhou, Y., Zhang, Y., Fang, Y.: Key Establishment in Sensor Networks Based on Triangle Grid Deployment Model. In: MILCOM 2005, vol. 3, pp. 1450–1455 (2005)
35. Zhu, S., Xu, S., Setia, S., Jajodia, S.: Establishing Pairwise Keys for Secure Communication in Ad Hoc Networks: A Probabilistic Approach. In: ICNP, pp. 326–335 (2003)

Does Physical Security of Cryptographic Devices Need a Formal Study? (Invited Talk)

François-Xavier Standaert[1], Tal G. Malkin[2], and Moti Yung[2,3]

[1] UCL Crypto Group, Université Catholique de Louvain
[2] Dept. of Computer Science, Columbia University, [3] Google Inc.
fstandae@uclouvain.be, {tal,moti}@cs.columbia.edu

Traditionally, cryptographic algorithms provide security against an adversary who has only black box access to cryptographic devices. That is, the only thing the adversary can do is to query the cryptographic algorithm on inputs of its choice and analyze the responses, which are always computed according to the correct original secret information. However, such a model does not always correspond to the realities of physical implementations.

During the last decade, significant attention has been paid to the physical security evaluation of cryptographic devices. In particular, it has been demonstrated that actual attackers may be much more powerful than what can be captured by the black box model. They can actually get a side-channel information, based on the device physical computational steps.

A large set of practical techniques for breaking and repairing (i.e., applying countermeasures) have been found in this area of physical security and further, the area is now an important part of "crypto-engineering." The issue that will be addressed is: Do we need more fundamental (perhaps more theoretical) study of the area?

In this talk, it will be argued that having a model and a more basic approach to formalizing the physical leakage can be useful and revealing. A model in this area relies on certain signals being communicated to the attacker, so it is (to some degree) of an Information Theory or Communication Theory nature. It will then be argued specifically that having a formal model and quantitative tools to measure the physical leakage, generalize specific instances, enables a more sound way to investigate aspects of device design and of attacks on devices, and sets up a fair ground for arguing about differences in approaches.

R. Safavi-Naini (Ed.): ICITS 2008, LNCS 5155, p. 70, 2008.
© Springer-Verlag Berlin Heidelberg 2008

A Single Initialization Server
for Multi-party Cryptography

Hugue Blier and Alain Tapp

Département d'informatique et de recherche opérationnelle
Université de Montréal, C.P. 6128, Succ. Centre-Ville
Montréal (QC), H3C 3J7, Canada

Abstract. We present information-theoretically secure bit commitment, zero-knowledge and multi-party computation based on the assistance of an initialization server. In the initialization phase, the players interact with the server to gather resources that are later used to perform useful protocols. This initialization phase does not depend on the input of the protocol it will later enable. Once the initialization is complete, the server's assistance is no longer required. This paper improves on previous work as there is only one server and it does not need to be trusted. If the server is honest, the protocols are secure against any coalition of dishonest players. If all players are honest, then there is an exponentially small probability that both the initialization phase succeeds and that later the protocol fails. That is, the server cannot create a situation in the initialization phase that would lead honest players to accuse each other. The protocols are built in a modular fashion and achieve linear complexity for the players in terms of the security parameter, number of players and the size of the circuit.

Keywords: two-party computation, multi-party computation, cryptography, zero-knowledge, initialization server.

1 Introduction

Two-party computation is a common scenario: Alice and Bob want to compute a function based on their inputs such that they get the correct output but also without revealing their respective input to the other participant. This situation can obviously be generalized to more than two participant. Multi-party computation was first introduced by [18, 24, 25]. It has been shown that without any computational assumptions, secure multi-party computation is possible if and only if a majority of participants are honest, in the presence of a broadcast channel [22]. If no broadcast channel is available, this proportion must be strictly more than 2/3 [3, 6]. Multi-party computation security can also be based on other assumptions: noisy channels [11, 14, 15], or using directly some primitives such as oblivious transfer (OT) [13, 19], trapdoor one-way permutations [18] or bounded memory [4, 5].

Beaver [1, 2] introduced in 1997 a model where a server is involved in the computation. This third party is said to be semi-trusted. It is trusted in the sense

R. Safavi-Naini (Ed.): ICITS 2008, LNCS 5155, pp. 71–85, 2008.
© Springer-Verlag Berlin Heidelberg 2008

that it doesn't collude with any participant and it follows the protocol correctly. But if the players are honest, a dishonest server cannot learn anything about the input and output of the protocol it enables. In some contexts, the qualifier *honest but curious* is also used. Beaver uses this server to distribute *commodities* to users prior to the calculation. Under these assumptions, he realizes a protocol for OT on which secure multi-party computation can be based. In the same model, Rivest [23] has also shown simple algorithms for bit commitment (BC) and OT. Many specific problems having practical applications have been solved using such a third party [10, 16, 17]. This model is very appealing since it is close to the Internet setting in which a server provides services. Since this server does not have to be fully trusted, it has practical applications.

Yet trust is an issue and this is the problem we address in this paper. In [1, 23], since the server has to follow the protocol, it is an issue to choose a server trusted by both parties. The way they addressed this problem was by using more than one server. The drawback is that the protocol is less practical. Here, our protocols deal with a dishonest server, as long as it doesn't collude with other participants. That is, the server could make the initialization phase fail, but will not be able to make honest players accuse each other of cheating. Once the initialization phase succeeds, the security of the primitives and protocols performed in the computation phase is unconditional.

Our protocols have the following properties. If the server does not collude with any player, the initialization phase enables protocols that achieve information theoretical privacy and correctness. That is, the protocols are resilient to both cheating players and a dishonest server at the same time under the no-collusion assumption. If all players are honest, the server will gain no information about the protocol realized after the initialization phase. Furthermore, whatever the server behaviour, the probability that both the initialization phase succeeds and the later protocol aborts is exponentially small. The last criteria is unusual in conventional multi-party computation but is reasonable in presence of two different types of actors.

An appealing aspect of our protocols is their simplicity and efficiency. As first said, the situation of multi-party computation has been studied for a long time and is well understood. An attentive reader will recognize flavours of known techniques. For example, our protocols are based on so-called commitment chips similar to two precomputed oblivious transfers and our bit commitments are constructed so that the Rudich technique [12, 13, 20] can be used and some noise can be tolerated.

It is worthwhile to mention that a simple but inefficient solution can easily be obtained from known techniques. For example the server, during the initialization phase, could distribute two random strings of n bits to Alice and Bob such that the Hamming distance between these two strings is ϵn. This could be probabilistically verified with some accuracy. Afterwards, Alice and Bob could use these two strings as one-time pads to communicate. This would result in a binary symmetric channel with error ϵ which is known to be sufficient for multi-party computation [13, 14] since it enables the participants to realize OT.

Another way would be to adapt ideas from [9] and [8]. It is not too hard to obtain similar results based these article for the two-party case, but for the multi-party case, the obtained protocol would be significantly less efficient than the one we present. Note also that [21] propose a elegant solution where the initialization server is fully trusted; in our protocol, the server does not have to be trusted and the solution we propose is also more efficient.

In the following sections, we present protocols for commitment (Sect. 2), committed circuit evaluation and zero-knowledge (Sect. 3) and multi-party secure computation (Sect. 4). Even though our protocols are intricate, the proofs are relatively straightforward are not particularly enlightening. We present proof sketches in the appendix.

2   Bit Commitment

BC is a cryptographic procedure composed of two phases. In the commitment phase, Alice commits to a bit value with Bob and in the opening phase, she reveals that bit. We say that the commitment is binding if, after the commitment phase, Alice can only open one unique value. We say that the commitment is concealing if, after the commitment phase, Bob has no information about the committed bit. Note that the opening phase is optional.

To accomplish BC (as well as all the following protocols), we rely on commitment chips (CCs). Our protocol begins by an initialization phase where the server creates enough CCs and gives them to the players. A CC i is a weak commitment to the value $v_i = x_1^i \oplus x_2^i \oplus x_3^i \oplus x_4^i$, the parity of four bits that the server privately transmits to Alice. Of these four bits, the server only transmits to Bob one of the first two and one of the last two. We will always suppose that communication between the players and the server is done in a private way. CCs can be seen as a combination of 2 $\binom{1}{2}$-OTs are constructed is such a way that the Rudich technique can be used. It is crucial that Alice doesn't know which bits Bob knows. The CCs created in the initialization phase are the resources shared by Alice and Bob to construct BCs and all other protocols.

In the protocols, we denote Alice by $\mathcal{A}$, Bob by $\mathcal{B}$ and the server by $\mathcal{S}$. Note that except if otherwise stated, the CCs and BCs are from Alice to Bob.

Protocol 1. CC Commit

Input: an index $i \in I$
Result: the CC indexed by i is created

$\mathcal{S}$ chooses $x_1^i, x_2^i, x_3^i, x_4^i \in_R \{0,1\}$ and sends them to $\mathcal{A}$
$\mathcal{S}$ chooses $\ell^i \in_R \{1,2\}$ and $r^i \in_R \{3,4\}$ and sends to $\mathcal{B}$ $(\ell^i, r^i, x_{\ell^i}, x_{r^i})$

To verify the honesty of the server (i.e. that the bits of Alice and Bob correspond), half of the CCs given by the server will be opened. In all our protocols, we say that a bit is *inconsistent* whenever Alice and Bob disagree on its value.

From the protocol **CC Preprocessing** we can already see the role of the two bits given to Bob: if Alice wants to change the value of one CC, she must

---

Protocol 2. CC Unveil

Input: an index $i \in I$
Result: the CC indexed by i is unveiled

$\mathcal{A}$ sends $x_1^i, x_2^i, x_3^i, x_4^i$ to $\mathcal{B}$
$\mathcal{B}$ outputs FAIL if $x_{\ell i}^i$ or $x_{r^i}^i$ are inconsistent

---

Protocol 3. CC Preprocessing

Result: I an index set of CCs

Let I be a set of indices
$\forall i \in I$, Call **CC Commit**(i)
$\mathcal{B}$ chooses $O \subset_R I$ such that $|O| = \frac{|I|}{2}$ and sends its description to $\mathcal{A}$
$\forall i \in O$, Call **CC Unveil**(i) and Bob outputs ABORT if the output is FAIL
$\mathcal{A}$ and $\mathcal{B}$ set I to $I \smallsetminus O$

---

change the value of at least one its four x_is. Since she is not aware of which bits Bob knows, she will change a bit Bob knows with probability one-half, and get caught. Note also that since Bob knows only two bits of each CC, he has no information about the parity of the four bits.

Since we would like Alice to only have an exponentially small probability of successfully cheating when committing, we define $s = 2k + 1$ (a odd security parameter), and a BC to the value b will be a group of $3s$ CCs to the value b. The choice of $3s$ instead of s is useful in the following section. Note that once the initialization phase is complete, the players do not need the server to realize BC.

After the initialization phase, a set of indices I corresponding to CCs is shared between Alice and Bob. To construct a BC (as well as other protocols), CCs are consumed and removed from this set.

Protocol 4. BC Commit

Input: $b \in \{0, 1\}$ and I an index set of CCs
Result: a BC B to the value b (I is updated)

$\mathcal{A}$ chooses $B \subset_R I$ such that $|B| = 3s$ and such that $\forall i \in B, v_i = b$
$\mathcal{A}$ sends a description of B to $\mathcal{B}$
$\mathcal{A}$ and $\mathcal{B}$ set I to $I \smallsetminus B$

To open the BC C, Alice only needs to reveal every bit of every CC. The condition for Bob to accept the opening is that no more than $\frac{1}{10}$ of the CCs aren't consistent with the bits he knows. Why? Because the server is not trusted. The verification done in the initialization phase assures the players that there is little inconsistency, but not that there is none.

If Alice is dishonest, she can choose to construct a BC in an *undefined* way by choosing CCs with two different values. In order to ensure that the BC value is always well-defined, we say that the value of a BC is the value of the majority of the values of the CCs of which it is made. This is why we choose s to be odd.

Protocol 5. BC Unveil

Input: a BC B
Result: B is opened

$\mathcal{A}$ sends b to $\mathcal{B}$
$\mathcal{B}$ sets e to 0
$\forall i \in B$
    Call **CC Unveil**(i)
    if **CC Unveil**(i) outputs FAIL or does not have value b, then set e to $e + 1$
If $e \geq \frac{|C|}{10}$, $\mathcal{B}$ outputs ABORT

Usually, in the analysis of a two-party protocol, we consider what happens when one of the participants is honest and the other is dishonest. Here, we also have to consider the fact that the server can be dishonest.

Lemma 1. (*BC Commit: concealing*) *As long as Bob and the server do not collude, after **BC Commit**(b), Bob has no information on b.*

Lemma 2. (*BC: binding*) *As long as Alice and the server do not collude, after **BC Commit**(B), **BC Unveil**(B = $\bar{b}$) has a chance exponentially small in s to succeed.*

Since we want to consider a cheating server, we also want to be sure that, if the server is dishonest, none of the honest players can be falsely incriminated.

Lemma 3. (*BC: robust*) *Given that Alice and Bob are honest, there is an exponentially small probability that both the preprocessing succeeds and that one of the later **BC Unveil** aborts.*

So, if Alice and Bob are honest and the server is dishonest, it cannot make the initialization phase succeed in such a way that later, a commitment phase or an opening phase will fail. Once the initialization phase has been done, the only way for the protocol to abort is if Alice or Bob misbehave. Thus, there is no way the server can cheat in a way that Alice or Bob will be accused wrongly (except with exponentially small probability).

A very useful characteristic of our BC protocol is the possibility for Alice to choose m BCs and prove to Bob that the parity of their committed values is p without revealing any other information. The parity of m CCs, each chosen from a different BC, must also be p. The protocol **CC Parity** verifies this fact, but has probability $1/2$ of failure in case Alice tries to cheat. **BC Parity** simply calls **CC Parity** s times to amplify this probability. This is the well-known technique introduced by Rudich. At the end of the **BC Parity** protocol, Bob will be convinced of the parity and all the BCs will remain valid, but s CCs contained in each BC will have been consumed.

Note that FAIL is an acceptable outcome for a sub-protocol but that when a sub-protocol outputs ABORT, it implies that the calling protocol also outputs ABORT and so on. Note that each BC is composed of $3s$ CCs. This implies that three operations (**BC Parity**, **BC Unveil**) can be performed on a single

---

Protocol 6. CC Parity

Input: a list of CC indices $i_1, i_2, \ldots, i_m$ and a parity p

Result: $\mathcal{B}$ learns if $p = v_{i_1} \oplus v_{i_2} \oplus \cdots \oplus v_{i_m}$

$\mathcal{A}$ sends p to $\mathcal{B}$

$\mathcal{A}$ computes $q = \bigoplus_{j=1}^{m} x_1^{i_j} \oplus x_2^{i_j}$ and sends it to $\mathcal{B}$

$\mathcal{B}$ sends $r \in_R \{0, 2\}$ to $\mathcal{A}$

For j from 1 to m, $\mathcal{A}$ sends to $\mathcal{B}$ $x_{1+r}^{i_j}$ and $x_{2+r}^{i_j}$

$\mathcal{B}$ checks that these values are consistent and:

If $r = 0$, $\mathcal{B}$ checks that $q = \bigoplus_{j=1}^{m} x_1^{i_j} \oplus x_2^{i_j}$

If $r = 2$, $\mathcal{B}$ checks that $p \oplus q = \bigoplus_{j=1}^{m} x_3^{i_j} \oplus x_4^{i_j}$

If an error is detected, the output of the protocol is FAIL

Protocol 7. BC Parity

Input: a list of BCs $B_1, B_2, \ldots, B_m$ and a bit p

Result: $\mathcal{B}$ learns if $p = b_1 \oplus b_2 \oplus \cdots \oplus b_m$

$\mathcal{A}$ computes $p = b_1 \oplus b_2 \oplus \cdots \oplus b_m$ and sends it to $\mathcal{B}$

$\mathcal{B}$ sets e to 0

Repeat s times

    For j from 1 to m

        $\mathcal{B}$ chooses $i_j \in_R B_j$ and send it to $\mathcal{A}$

        $\mathcal{A}$ and $\mathcal{B}$ sets B_j to $B_j \smallsetminus i_j$

    $\mathcal{A}$ and $\mathcal{B}$ call **CC Parity**$(i_1, i_2, \ldots, i_m, p)$

    If the protocol outputs FAIL, set e to $e + 1$

If $e > \frac{s}{10}$ then ABORT

BC before it becomes useless. This can be used to perform FAN-OUT and NOT gates in the obvious way.

Lemma 4. *(**BC Parity**: robust) Given that Alice and Bob are honest, the probability that both the initialization phase succeeds and that **BC Parity** outputs ABORT is exponentially small in s.*

Lemma 5. *(**BC Parity**: zero-knowledge) If Alice and the server are honest, after **BC Parity**$(B_1, B_2, \ldots, B_m)$, Bob cannot learn any information except $p = b_1 \oplus b_2 \oplus \cdots \oplus b_m$.*

Lemma 6. *(**BC Parity**: sound) Given that Alice and the server do not collude and that $p = b_1 \oplus b_2 \oplus \cdots \oplus b_m$, the probability that Parity BC$(B_1, B_2, \ldots, B_m, \bar{p})$ succeeds is exponentially small in s.*

3   Oblivious Circuit Evaluation and Zero-Knowledge

In this section, we discuss techniques called oblivious circuit evaluation (OCE) to compute functions on committed bits, producing committed bits with the right relationship without revealing any information whatsoever (i.e. in a zero-knowledge way). To do this, it is sufficient to be able to do a NOT gate and an AND gate on committed bits.

The NOT could be achieved using the **BC Parity** protocol from the previous section. One just has to observe that $x = y \Leftrightarrow x \oplus y = 0$. The implementation of the AND gate requires some preprocessing. This preprocessing step creates AND-Commitment-Chips (ACCs). An ACC is a triplet of commitment chips (V_1, V_2, V_3) such that $v_1 \wedge v_2 = v_3$. As you can se, we use uppercase letters for objects and lowercase letter for bit values. As usual, the preprocessing of the ACC is independent of the circuit to be evaluated later. Each AND gate requires the use of $10s$ ACCs. It is straightforward to see that with the tools to evaluate an arbitrary known circuit on committed values, it is easy to prove any statement in NP in a zero-knowledge way.

Suppose that Alice has commitments B_1 and B_2 and wants to commit herself to the AND of the two values. First, she creates ACCs to random values. Half of them are opened to ensure consistency. She then chooses a subset of the remaining ACCs with the appropriate value and then uses them to construct B_3 such that $b_1 \wedge b_2 = b_3$. In the protocol, the union of the third component of every ACC forms a BC to the desired value. For this to be secure, we have on one hand to manage potential errors but on the other hand to prevent Alice from using these to create a tweaked gate. Alice has therefore to group ACCs each time an AND gate is to be computed. The final protocol, **OCE** of a function F, can be realized using **BC Parity** to perform NOT and FAN-OUT gates and **OCE AND** for AND gates.

Protocol 8. OCE AND

Input: BCs B_1, B_2 and B_3
Result: $\mathcal{B}$ is convinced that $b_3 = b_1 \wedge b_2$

$\mathcal{A}$ chooses at random a set T of triplets of indices of CCs such that
$\quad \forall [i_1, i_2, i_3] \in T, v_{i_3} = v_{i_1} \wedge v_{i_2}$
$\quad |T| = 10s$
$\quad$ and sends it to $\mathcal{B}$
$\mathcal{B}$ sets e to 0
$\mathcal{B}$ creates $O \subset_R T$ such that $|O| = 5s$ and sends it to $\mathcal{A}$
$\forall [i_1, i_2, i_3] \in O$
$\quad \mathcal{A}$ opens i_1, i_2 and i_3 using **CC Unveil**
$\quad$ if any of the openings output FAIL or
$\quad$ if $v_{i_3} \neq v_{i_1} \wedge v_{i_2}$ $\mathcal{B}$ sets e to $e + 1$
If $e > \frac{5s}{10}$ then $\mathcal{B}$ outputs ABORT
$\mathcal{B}$ sets e to 0
$\mathcal{A}$ creates $S \subset T$ such that $|S| = s$ and $\forall [i_1, i_2, i_3] \in S, v_{i_1} = b_1$ and $v_{i_2} = b_2$
$\mathcal{A}$ sends a description of S to $\mathcal{B}$
$\mathcal{A}$ and $\mathcal{B}$ set T to $T \setminus S$
$\forall [i_1, i_2, i_3] \in S$
$\quad \mathcal{B}$ chooses $j_1 \in_R B_1, j_2 \in_R B_2$ and $j_3 \in_R B_3$
$\quad \mathcal{A}$ proves that $v_{i_1} = v_{j_1}, v_{i_2} = v_{j_2}$ and $v_{i_3} = v_{j_3}$ using **CC Parity**
$\quad$ If this FAILS then set e to $e + 1$
$\quad \mathcal{A}$ and $\mathcal{B}$ set B_1 to $B_1 \setminus j_1$, B_2 to $B_2 \setminus j_2$ and B_3 to $B_3 \setminus j_3$
If $e > \frac{s}{10}$ then $\mathcal{B}$ outputs ABORT

Lemma 7. *(**OCE**: robust) Given that Alice and Bob are honest, the probability that both the initialization phase succeeds and that the **OCE** protocol aborts is exponentially small in s.*

Lemma 8. *(**OCE**: sound) If Bob and the server are honest, the value of the commitments at the end of **OCE** protocol are correct except with exponentially small probability in s.*

Lemma 9. *(**OCE**: zero-knowledge) If Alice and the server are honest, Bob learns absolutely nothing while performing **OCE** with Alice.*

4   Secure Multi-party Computation

In this section, we deal with protocols that can involve more that two participants. Secure multi-party computation (MP) is a n player task where all players learn the output of a circuit evaluated on private inputs coming from each of them. This is a very general, useful and well-studied task. In this section, we present a protocol to implement information theoretically secure MP. As in our previous protocols, an initialization phase is required, but this phase does not depend on the function that is computed later. As usual in multi-party computation, all the input bits and the intermediate values are shared using secret sharing among all players. Since we have no bound on the number of dishonest players, the secret sharing scheme we choose is simply parity. In the first step, each player commits to his input. Then the circuit is evaluated gate by gate (AND gates and NOT gates), and the output is a committed secret shared value between all players. Finally, the answer bits are opened. Known techniques [7] could be used to reveal the result of the function gradually in order not to give an unfair advantage to any of the players. This process is called multi-party computation (MP).

We implement the inputs and all intermediate values by a distributed BC (DBC). A DBC B with value b is a set of n^2 BCs $B[i,j]$ (player i is committed to player j) with value $b[i,j]$ such that for all i, we have that for all j and j', $b[i,j] = b[i,j']$ and therefore we choose to denote that value by $b[i]$. In addition, $b = \bigoplus_{i=1}^{n} b[i]$. Of course, this is in the honest cases. Inconsistent DBCs will fail when used in an AND gate.

To begin the computation of the known circuit, each player i has to construct, with the help of the other players, a DBC to every b of his input bits. This is done by having player i commit to every other player to b ($\forall j, B[i,j] = b$) and all other players commit to 0 ($\forall k \neq i, j, B[k,j] = 0$). The consistency of the commitment of player i is not verified, but the fact that all other commitments are equal to zero is.

There is no way after **MP bit initialization** to be sure that player i is committed to the same value with all the players. If this is not the case, the first AND gate directly or indirectly involving this bit will fail, except with exponentially small probability.

Protocol 9. MP bit initialization

Input: a bit d from player i

Result: a DBC B with value b.

$\forall j \neq i$

>   Player i commits to b to Player j using **BC Commit**
>
> $\forall k \neq j$
>
>>   Player j commit to bit 0 to player k using **BC Commit**
>>
>>   Player k chooses s CCs in that commitment
>>
>>   Player j opens these CCs using **CC Unveil**
>>
>>   If more than $\frac{s}{10}$ are inconsistent or do not have value 0, Player k outputs

ABORT

Protocol 10. DACC

Result: a set D of DACC is created

Let D be a set of indices

For all $k \in D$

> S chooses uniformly at random $v[i], v'[i]$ and $v''[i]$ such that
>
> $\bigoplus_{i=1}^{n} v''[i] = \bigoplus_{i=1}^{n} v[i] \wedge \bigoplus_{i=1}^{n} v'[i]$
>
> $\forall i, j \neq i$, S creates CCs from i to j to the value $v[i], v'[i]$ and $v''[i]$ using **CC Commit**,
>
> $v[i], v'[i]$ and $v''[i]$ are associated with the index k

$\forall j$, player j chooses $1/2n$ indices in D and asks the other players to unveil all these CCs

>   If any of the unveiling FAILS or if $\bigoplus_{i=1}^{n} v''[i] \neq \bigoplus_{i=1}^{n} v[i] \wedge \bigoplus_{i=1}^{n} v'[i]$ then

ABORT

All players remove the opened value from D

In the preprocessing stage, the server creates random triplets of vectors of CCs, called Distributed AND CCs (DACCs). These triplets are such that the AND of the first two values equals the third one.

Note that there is an exponential number of different possible distinct DACCs. Therefore, the server cannot just choose groups of identical ones to form a Distributed AND BC (DABC). Actually the same kind of problem will also happen in the choice of DABC. In order to have an efficient algorithm, we have to use a trick, both in **DABC** and **MP AND**.

Once the DACCs are verified, they will be grouped by the server to create a DABC. The server does not group them such that the vectors are identical but only such that the parity of the vectors is identical. Note that by flipping an even number of bits, the parity of a vector does not change. Thus, to make an identical set, the participants have to modify the vector (in an even number of places) such that at the end they are identical. All this is accomplished without interaction with the server and without revealing information on the committed bit of the resulting triplet.

In order to process a NOT gate, one player (we arbitrarily choose player 1 here) commits to the opposite bit with every player. These new commitments replace his commitment in the DBC vector B.

Protocol 11. DABC

Input: D an index set of DACCs
Result: E a set of DABCs

The server chooses $C \subset_R D$ such that $|C| = s$ and
$\qquad \exists \alpha, \beta, \forall k \in C, \; \alpha = \bigoplus_{i=1}^{n} v_k[i]$ and $\beta = \bigoplus_{i=1}^{n} v'_k[i]$
Let $k' \in C$ be a specific index
The server broadcasts the index forming a description of C and the value k'
$\forall k \in C \smallsetminus k', \forall i$
$\qquad$ Player i broadcasts $t[i] = v_k[i] \oplus v_{k'}[i]$ and $t'[i] = v'_k[i] \oplus v'_{k'}[i]$
$\qquad$ For every 1 broadcasted,
$\qquad\qquad$ each player flips the first bit of the four-tuple constituting the CC
If $\bigoplus_{i=1}^{n} t[i] \neq 0$ or $\bigoplus_{i=1}^{n} t'[i] \neq 0$ then ABORT
D is set to $D \smallsetminus C$ and C is added to E
All the previous steps are repeated until there is are enough elements in D

Protocol 12. MP NOT

Input: a DBC B and a set E of DABCs
Result: a DBC B' such that $b \neq b'$

Let β be the value that player 1 is committed to in B
$\forall i \neq 1$
$\qquad$ Player 1 commits with $B'[1, i]$ to value $\overline{\beta}$ using **BC Commit**
$\qquad$ Player 1 proves to player i that $b'[1, i] \neq b[1, i]$ using **BC Parity**
$\qquad \forall j$ Player i and j rename $B[i, j]$ to $B'[i, j]$

In order to compute the AND, we will use the DABC. The idea is similar to the computation of an AND gate in the preceding section: choose a DABC such that the first two vectors are identical to those in the input of the gate and consider the third one as the output. Once again, an exponential number of DABCs would be needed to achieve a perfect matching. Fortunately, this is not required, we only need the number of differences to be even, which means the values are equal. This simple idea is very important in making the protocols efficient.

As mentioned, there is no way during the initialization phase to be sure the one player is committed to the same value with every other player. This problem is solved because of the properties of the **MP AND** protocol. In that protocol, every player must broadcast the parity of his values in B (and B') and his value in A (and A'). If he had committed to an opposite value in the initialization phase, he must now cheat the parity protocols. We must assume that every bit is involved directly or indirectly in at least one AND gate (possibly a dummy one).

Combining the protocols presented in this section, we obtain a protocol **MP**. FAN-OUT is done in the obvious way, the NOT and AND gates use protocols **MP NOT** and **MP AND** and initialization of input bits using protocol **MP bit initialization**. The **MP** protocol we obtain has the following nice properties.

Protocol 13. MP AND

Input: two DBCs B and B', E a DABC
Result: a DBC A'' such that $b \wedge b' = a''$

Repeat
      Player 1 chooses $C \in_R E$ ($C = (A, A', A'')$) and announces his choice
      $\forall i$
          Player i broadcasts $p[i] = b[i] \oplus a[i]$
          Player i broadcasts $p'[i] = b'[i] \oplus a'[i]$
Until $\bigoplus_i p[i] = 0$ and $\bigoplus_i p'[i] = 0$
$\forall i$
      $\forall j \neq i$
          Player i proves to player j that $p[i] = b[i] \oplus a[i]$ using **BC Parity**
          Player i proves to player j that $p'[i] = b'[i] \oplus a'[i]$ using **BC Parity**
The A'' is the resulting DBC

Lemma 10. *(MP: correct) If the server and all players are honest, the function is computed correctly with probability 1, in expected polynomial time.*

Lemma 11. *(MP: robust) Whatever the server does, if all players are honest, the probability that the preprocessing succeeds and MP fails is exponentially small in s.*

The previous lemma implies that if all players are honest it is almost impossible for the server to act in such a way that players will be led to believe that the protocols failed because of a dishonest player. Conversely, if a protocol fails after the initialization phase, this means that the most likely explanation is that a player cheated.

Lemma 12. *(MP: zero-knowledge) In MP, any group of dishonest players cannot learn anything else than the outcome of the function provided they do not collude with the server.*

5   Conclusion and Future Work

We have presented protocols for a server to provide resources to players so that they can perform at a later time protocols that implement bit commitment, zero-knowledge and secure multi-party computation. Our protocols and initialization phase are efficient, quite simple and their security is easy to verify. Table 1 summarizes the complexity, both in terms of communication and computation. The complexity of the protocols take into account the creation of necessary resources in the initialization phase. The complexity for the server in each of these protocols is obtained by multiplying by the number of players. We use n for the number of players, m for the size of the function and s for the security parameter.

Although we do not have any formal proof of the optimality of our protocols, the fact that they are linear in each parameter seems to indicate that except for

Table 1. Protocol Complexity

Protocol	Expected Amortized Complexity
BC Commit and **BC Unveil** $O(s)$	
BC Parity	$O(sm)$
OCE	$O(sm)$
MP bit initialization	$O(sn)$
DABC	$O(sn)$
MP NOT	$O(sn)$
MP AND	$O(sn)$
MP	$O(snm)$

the constants (which are already quite small), no further complexity improvement could be achieved.

Acknowledgements

Special thanks to Anne Broadbent for proof reading. We are also grateful to Jörn Müller-Quade for pointing out some interesting work. This research was made possible by generous funding from Canada's NSERC.

References

[1] Beaver, D.: Commodity-based cryptography (extended abstract). In: Proceedings of the 29th Annual ACM Symposium on Theory of Computing, pp. 446–455 (1997)

[2] Beaver, D.: Server-assisted cryptography. In: Proceedings of the New Security Paradigms Workshop, pp. 92–106 (1998)

[3] Ben-Or, M., Goldwasser, S., Wigderson, A.: Completeness theorems for noncryptographic fault-tolerant distributed computation (extended abstract). In: Proceedings of the 20th Annual ACM Symposium on Theory of Computing, pp. 1–10 (1988)

[4] Cachin, C., Crépeau, C., Marcil, S.: Oblivious transfer with a memory bounded receiver. In: Proceedings of IEEE Symposium on Foundations of Computer Science, pp. 493–502 (1998)

[5] Cachin, C., Maurer, U.: Unconditional security against memory-bounded adversaries. In: Kaliski Jr., B.S. (ed.) CRYPTO 1997. LNCS, vol. 1294, pp. 292–306. Springer, Heidelberg (1997)

[6] Chaum, D., Crépeau, C., Damgård, I.: Multiparty unconditionally secure protocols (extended abstract). In: Proceedings of the 20th Annual ACM Symposium on Theory of Computing, pp. 11–19 (1988)

[7] Cleve, R.: Controlled gradual disclosure schemes for random bits and their applications. In: Brassard, G. (ed.) CRYPTO 1989. LNCS, vol. 435, pp. 573–588. Springer, Heidelberg (1990)

[8] Cramer, R., Damgaard, I., Dziembowski, S., Hirt, M., Rabin, T.: Efficient multiparty computations with dishonest majority. In: Stern, J. (ed.) EUROCRYPT 1999. LNCS, vol. 1592, pp. 311–326. Springer, Heidelberg (1999)

[9] Cramer, R., Damgård, I., Maurer, U.: Efficient general secure multi-party computation from any linear secret-sharing scheme. In: Preneel, B. (ed.) EUROCRYPT 2000. LNCS, vol. 1807, pp. 316–334. Springer, Heidelberg (2000)

[10] Crescenzo, G.D., Ishai, Y., Ostrovsky, R.: Universal service-providers for database private information retrieval. In: Proceedings of the 17th Annual ACM Symposium on Principles of Distributed Computing, pp. 91–100 (1998)

[11] Crépeau, C.: Efficient cryptographic protocols based on noisy channels. In: Fumy, W. (ed.) EUROCRYPT 1997. LNCS, vol. 1233, pp. 306–317. Springer, Heidelberg (1997)

[12] Crépeau, C.: Commitment. In: van Tilborg, H.C. (ed.) Encyclopedia of Cryptography and Security, vol. 12, pp. 83–86 (2005)

[13] Crépeau, C., Graaf, J., Tapp, A.: Committed oblivious transfer and private multiparty computation. In: Coppersmith, D. (ed.) CRYPTO 1995. LNCS, vol. 963, pp. 110–123. Springer, Heidelberg (1995)

[14] Crépeau, C., Kilian, J.: Achieving oblivious transfer using weakened security assumptions. In: Proceedings of IEEE Symposium on Foundations of Computer Science, pp. 42–52 (1988)

[15] Crépeau, C., Morozov, K., Wolf, S.: Efficient unconditional oblivious transfer from almost any noisy channel. In: Proceedings of Fourth Conference on Security in Communication Networks, pp. 47–59 (2004)

[16] Du, W., Han, Y.S., Chen, S.: Privacy-preserving multivariate statistical analysis: Linear regression and classification. In: Proceedings of the 4th SIAM International Conference on Data Mining, pp. 222–233 (2004)

[17] Du, W., Zhan, Z.: Building decision tree classifier on private data. In: Proceedings of the IEEE ICDM Workshop on Privacy, Security and Data Mining, pp. 1–8 (2002)

[18] Goldreich, O., Micali, S., Wigderson, A.: How to play any mental game. In: Proceedings of the 19th Annual ACM Symposium on Theory of Computing, pp. 218–229 (1987)

[19] Kilian, J.: Founding cryptography on oblivious transfer. In: Proceedings of the 20th Annual ACM Symposium on Theory of Computing, pp. 20–31 (1988)

[20] Kilian, J.: A note on efficient zero-knowledge proofs and arguments. In: Proceedings of the 24th Annual ACM Symposium on Theory of Computing, pp. 723–732 (1992)

[21] Nascimento, A.C.A., Müller-Quade, J., Otsuka, A., Hanaoka, G., Imai, H.: Unconditionally non-interactive verifiable secret sharing secure against faulty majorities in the commodity based model. In: Jakobsson, M., Yung, M., Zhou, J. (eds.) ACNS 2004. LNCS, vol. 3089, Springer, Heidelberg (2004)

[22] Rabin, T., Ben-Or, M.: Verifiable secret sharing and multiparty protocols with honest majority. In: Proceedings of the 21th Annual ACM Symposium on Theory of Computing, pp. 73–85 (1989)

[23] Rivest, R.: Unconditionally secure commitment and oblivious transfer schemes using private channels and a trusted initializer (unpublished manuscript) (1999)

[24] Yao, A.: Protocols for secure computations. In: Proceedings of IEEE Symposium on Foundations of Computer Science, pp. 160–164 (1982)

[25] Yao, A.: How to generate and exchange secrets. In: Proceedings of IEEE Symposium on Foundations of Computer Science, pp. 162–167 (1986)

Appendix

The protocols we presented are built in a modular fashion and relatively simple, so their security is not to hard to see. Here we only give brief sketches of proofs. We mostly use the following two ideas: the fact that the parity of a random string is unknown when one of its bits is unknown, and Chernoff bound arguments.

Proof (Lemma 1). If Bob and the server do not collude, it is easy to see that after the preprocessing phase, Bob has no information about the CCs that have been created. The fact that **BC Commit** is concealing follows directly from this.

Proof (Lemma 2). If Alice and the server do not collude, for each CC, Alice ignores which two bits Bob knows. If the BC has value b (the value of the majority of CCs) then to open $\bar{b}$, Alice must lie on at least $s/2$ CCs in the protocol **CC Unveil**. Each time there is a probability $\frac{1}{2}$ that Bob will see some inconsistency. It is clear that the probability that more than $1/10$ of the executions of **CC Unveil** fail is exponentially close to 1 in the security parameter s (Chernoff).

Proof (Lemma 3). During the initialization phase, if the CCs created by the server are such that $\frac{1}{20}$ of them are inconsistent (i.e. for at least one bit, Bob and Alice have opposite values), then the probability that the protocol **CC Preprocessing** succeeds is exponentially small in s (Chernoff). Now, if the fraction of incoherent CCs is less than $\frac{1}{20}$ and if the initialization succeeded, the probability for Alice to choose $3s$ CCs such that at least $\frac{1}{10}$ of them are inconsistent is exponentially small in s (Chernoff).

Proof (Lemma 4). Same argument as in Lemma 3.

Proof (Lemma 5). If Bob and the server do not collude, in each CC, $v = x_1 \oplus x_2 \oplus x_3 \oplus x_4$. Bob ignores either x_1 or x_2 as well as either x_3 or x_4. Since each CC is independent and because only (x_1 and x_2) or (x_3 and x_4) are revealed, Bob does not learn any information on v. It is important that each time a BC is involved in a BC Parity, CCs are not reused.

Proof (Lemma 6). Every time the protocol **CC Parity** is used, if the parity of the CCs selected is not p, there is a probability $1/4$ that Bob will find some inconsistency. If the parity of the BCs is $\bar{p}$, because the indices i_j are chosen at random, there is a probability at least $1/2$ that the parity of the selected CCs will also be $\bar{p}$. Thus, each time the protocol **CC Parity** is used, there is a probability $1/8$ that Bob will see some inconsistencies. Remember that that if Alice is dishonest the BCs used in the protocol might be composed of inconsistent CCs.

Proof (Lemma 7). Using the same argument as in Lemma 3, one can show that the evaluation of NOT and AND gates is robust. From this we conclude that **OCE** is robust.

Proof (Lemma 8). Again, the soundness of **OCE** relies on the soundness of the AND and NOT gates. The soundness of the NOT gate follows from Lemma 6. For the soundness of the AND gate, note that because of the way the ACCs are created, the probability that Alice could insert more than $\frac{s}{10}$ incorrect ACCs (the AND relation is not true) is exponentially small. When choosing the subset S, Alice could gather all these ACCs but this does not suffice to succeed in proving a false relation in the rest of the **OCE AND** protocol which also relies on the **BC Parity** protocol.

Proof (Lemma 9). The zero-knowledgeless of **OCE** easily derives from the zero-knowledgeless of the NOT and AND gates, which itself follows from Lemma 5.

Proof (Lemma 10). If all players are honest, if the protocol MP terminates then the value obtained at the end of the protocol is correct. Note that the protocols **DACC** and **MP AND** have a probabilistic part which makes their running time an expected value. In both protocols, each trial has a probability of success of $1/2$.

Proof (Lemma 11). This is because of the way the protocol **DACC** tests for inconsistencies and because of the fact that BC and **BC Parity** are robust themselves.

Proof (Lemma 12). This follows from the fact that the preprocessing stage does not depend on the function to be evaluated and from the fact that BCs are concealing, **BC Parity** is zero-knowledge and DBCs are distributed using a secret sharing scheme that is secure against any coalition of $n - 1$ players.

Statistical Security Conditions for
Two-Party Secure Function Evaluation

Claude Crépeau[1] and Jürg Wullschleger[2]

[1] McGill University, Montréal, QC, Canada
crepeau@cs.mcgill.ca
[2] University of Bristol, Bristol, United Kingdom
j.wullschleger@bristol.ac.uk

Abstract. To simplify proofs in information-theoretic security, the standard security definition of two-party secure function evaluation based on the real/ideal model paradigm is often replaced by an information-theoretic security definition. At EUROCRYPT 2006, we showed that most of these definitions had some weaknesses, and presented new information-theoretic conditions that were equivalent to a simulation-based definition in the real/ideal model. However, there we only considered the perfect case, where the protocol is not allowed to make any error, which has only limited applications.

We generalize these results to the statistical case, where the protocol is allowed to make errors with a small probability. Our results are based on a new measure of information that we call the *statistical information*, which may be of independent interest.

Keywords: Secure function evaluation, information-theoretic security, security definition, oblivious transfer.

1 Introduction

Secure function evaluation [1] allows two (or more) parties to jointly compute a function in a secure way, which means that no player may get additional information about the other players' inputs or outputs, other than what may be deduced from their own input and output. A computationally secure solution to this problem has been given in [2]. Schemes ensuring unconditional security were subsequently provided in [3] and independently in [4].

Oblivious transfer [5,6,7] is a simple primitive of central interest in secure function evaluation. It allows a sender to send one of n binary strings of length k to a receiver. The primitive allows the receiver to receive the string of his choice while concealing this choice from a (possibly dishonest) sender. On the other hand, a dishonest receiver cannot obtain information about more than one of the strings, including partial joint information on two or more strings. It has since been proved that oblivious transfer is in fact sufficient by itself to securely compute any function [8,9]. More completeness results followed in [10,11,12,13].

R. Safavi-Naini (Ed.): ICITS 2008, LNCS 5155, pp. 86–99, 2008.
© Springer-Verlag Berlin Heidelberg 2008

1.1   Security Definitions

Formal security definitions for secure function evaluation have been proposed in [14] and [15]. Both definitions were inspired by the *simulation paradigm* used in [16] to define zero-knowledge proofs of knowledge. These definitions require that for any adversary, there exists a simulated adversary in an ideal setting (which is secure by definition) that achieves the same. That protocols which satisfy these definitions are *sequentially composable* has been proved in [17]. See also [18].

Later, a stronger notion of security, called *universal composability*, has been defined in [19] and independently in [20]. It guarantees that protocols are securely composable in any way.

Even though simulation-based security definitions are widely accepted as being the right definition of security today, ad-hoc definitions are still widely used due to their simplicity. Unfortunately, as we showed in [21], many of these definitions proposed for various specific scenarios have turned out to be deficient. We proposed in [21] simple information-theoretic conditions for the security of function evaluation, and proved that they are equivalent to the standard definition in the real/ideal model. However, these conditions could only be applied in the perfect case, when the protocol does not have any failure probability and does not leak any information, and therefore had only a very limited range of applications. For the special case of *randomized oblivious transfer*, these conditions have been generalized in [22] to the statistical case, where the protocol is allowed to make errors with a small probability.

1.2   Information Measures

The *Shannon mutual information* has been introduced in [23], and is one of the most important tools in information theory, as a measure of *how many bits of information* one random variable has over the other. The mutual information tells us for example how many bits can be transmitted over a noisy channel.

In information-theoretic cryptography, the mutual information has also been used in security definitions, to express that an adversary obtains almost no information about some secret, i.e., that two random variables are *almost independent*. But since in cryptography we are not interested in *how many bits* the adversary gets, but in the *probability* that he gets *any* information at all, the mutual information is not a good measure for that task.

1.3   Contribution

First, we propose a new measure of information that we call the *statistical information*, which is better suited to express security conditions than the mutual information. The difference between the statistical and the mutual information is the distance measure they are based on: while the mutual information is based on the relative entropy, the statistical information is based on the statistical distance.

Then we will generalize the results from [21] and [22]. We present necessary and sufficient information theoretic conditions for any two-party secure function evaluation in the statistical case, and apply them to oblivious transfer. The statistical information plays a very important role to state these conditions.

1.4 Related Work

Recently, Fehr and Schaffner showed in [24] that similar results also hold in the quantum setting. They presented security conditions for quantum protocols where the honest players have classical input and output, and showed that any quantum protocol that satisfies these conditions can be used as a sub-protocol in a classical protocol.

1.5 Preliminaries

For a random variable X, we denote its distribution by P_X and its domain by $\mathcal{X}$. $P_{Y|X} = P_{XY}/P_X$ denotes a conditional probability distribution, which models a probabilistic function that takes x as input and outputs y, distributed according to $P_{Y|X=x}$.

Definition 1. *The* statistical distance *between two distributions P_X and $P_{X'}$ over $\mathcal{X}$ is defined as $\delta(P_X, P_{X'}) = \frac{1}{2} \sum_{x \in \mathcal{X}} |P_X(x) - P_{X'}(x)|$.*

If $\delta(P_X, P_{X'}) \leq \varepsilon$, we may also write $P_X \equiv_\varepsilon P_{X'}$ or $X \equiv_\varepsilon X'$. We will need the following basic properties of δ.

Lemma 1 (Triangle Inequality). *For any distributions P_X, $P_{X'}$ and $P_{X''}$, we have*
$$\delta(P_X, P_{X''}) \leq \delta(P_X, P_{X'}) + \delta(P_{X'}, P_{X''}) .$$

Lemma 2 (Data Processing). *For any distributions P_{XY} and $P_{X'Y'}$, we have*
$$\delta(P_X, P_{X'}) \leq \delta(P_{XY}, P_{X'Y'}) .$$

Lemma 3. *For any distributions P_X and $P_{X'}$, and any conditional distribution $P_{Y|X}$, we have*
$$\delta(P_X, P_{X'}) = \delta(P_X P_{Y|X}, P_{X'} P_{Y|X}) .$$

Lemma 4. *For any distributions P_X and $P_{X'}$ we have $\delta(P_X, P_Y) \leq \varepsilon$, if and only if there exist events $\mathcal{E}_X$ and $\mathcal{E}_Y$ with $\Pr[\mathcal{E}_X] = \Pr[\mathcal{E}_Y] = 1 - \varepsilon$ and $P_{X|\mathcal{E}_X} = P_{Y|\mathcal{E}_Y}$.*

2   Statistical Information

In this section, we introduce the *statistical information* I_S. While the mutual information uses relative entropy as the underlying distance measure, we will use the statistical distance. Its value tells us how close the distribution of three random variables X, Y and Z is to a *Markov-chain*.

Definition 2. *The* statistical information *of X and Y given Z is defined as*
$$I_S(X; Y \mid Z) := \delta(P_{XYZ}, P_Z P_{X|Z} P_{Y|Z}) .$$

Obviously, this measure is non-negative and symmetric in X and Y. We will now show more properties of I_S, which are related to similar properties of the mutual information.

Lemma 5 (Chain rule). *For all P_{WXYZ}, we have*

$$I_S(WX; Y \mid Z) \leq I_S(W; Y \mid Z) + I_S(X; Y \mid WZ)$$

Proof. We have

$$I_S(X; Y \mid WZ) = \delta(P_{WXYZ}, P_{WYZ}P_{X|WZ}) \, .$$

From Lemma 3 follows that

$$\delta(P_{WYZ}P_{X|WZ}, P_Z P_{W|Z} P_{Y|Z} P_{X|WZ}) = \delta(P_{WYZ}, P_Z P_{W|Z} P_{Y|Z})$$
$$= I_S(W; Y \mid Z) \, .$$

Using Lemma 1 and $P_{WX|Z} = P_{W|Z}P_{X|WZ}$, we get

$$\delta(P_{WXYZ}, P_Z P_{WX|Z} P_{Y|Z}) \leq I_S(W; Y \mid Z) + I_S(X; Y \mid WZ) \, . \qquad \square$$

Lemma 6 (Monotonicity). *For all P_{WXYZ}, we have*

$$I_S(W; Y \mid Z) \leq I_S(WX; Y \mid Z) \, .$$

Proof. Using Lemma 2, we get

$$I_S(WX; Y \mid Z) = \delta(P_{WXYZ}, P_Z P_{W|Z} P_{X|WZ} P_{Y|Z})$$
$$\geq \delta(P_{WYZ}, P_Z P_{W|Z} P_{Y|Z})$$
$$= I_S(W; Y \mid Z) \, . \qquad \square$$

Note that there exist P_{XYZ} and $Q_{ZX}Q_{Y|Z}$, where

$$\delta(P_{XYZ}, Q_{ZX}Q_{Y|Z}) < \delta(P_{XYZ}, P_Z P_{X|Z} P_{Y|Z}),$$

so $P_Z P_{X|Z} P_{Y|Z}$ is not always the closest Markov-chain to P_{XYZ}. Luckily, as the following two lemmas show, $P_Z P_{X|Z} P_{Y|Z}$ is only by a factor of 4 away from the optimal Markov-chain, which is sufficient for our applications[1].

Lemma 7. *For all probability distributions P_{XYZ}, we have*

$$I_S(X; Y \mid Z) \leq 2 \cdot \min_{Q_{Y|Z}} \delta(P_{XYZ}, P_{XZ}Q_{Y|Z}) \, .$$

---

[1] An alternative definition for I_S would be to take the distance to the closest Markov-chain. However, we think that this would make the definition much more complicated, at almost no benefit.

Proof. Let $Q_{Y|Z}$ be the conditional probability distribution that minimizes the expression, and let $\varepsilon := \delta(P_{XYZ}, P_{XZ}Q_{Y|Z})$. We have

$$P_{XZ}Q_{Y|Z} = P_Z Q_{Y|Z} P_{X|Z} \ .$$

Let $Q'_{YZ} := P_Z Q_{Y|Z}$. From Lemma 2 follows that $\delta(P_{YZ}, Q'_{YZ}) \leq \varepsilon$ and from Lemma 3 that $\delta(P_{YZ}P_{X|Z}, Q'_{YZ}P_{X|Z}) \leq \varepsilon$. From Lemma 1 follows then that

$$\delta(P_{XYZ}, P_{XZ}P_{Y|Z}) \leq 2\varepsilon \ . \qquad \square$$

Lemma 8. *For all probability distributions P_{XYZ}, we have*

$$\mathrm{I_S}(X;Y \mid Z) \leq 4 \cdot \min_{Q_{XZ}, Q_{Y|Z}} \delta(P_{XYZ}, Q_{XZ}Q_{Y|Z}) \ .$$

Proof. Let Q_{XZ} and $Q_{Y|Z}$ be the conditional probability distributions that minimize the expression, and let $\varepsilon := \delta(P_{XYZ}, Q_{XZ}Q_{Y|Z})$. From Lemma 2 follows that $\delta(P_{XZ}, Q_{XZ}) \leq \varepsilon$ and from Lemma 3 that $\delta(P_{XZ}Q_{Y|Z}, Q_{XZ}Q_{Y|Z}) \leq \varepsilon$. From Lemma 1 follows that $\delta(P_{XYZ}, P_{XZ}Q_{Y|Z}) \leq 2\varepsilon$. The statement follows by applying Lemma 7. $\qquad \square$

Lemma 9. *For all P_{WXYZ}, we have*

$$\mathrm{I_S}(X;Y \mid WZ) \leq 2 \cdot \mathrm{I_S}(WX;Y \mid Z) \ .$$

Proof. From Lemma 7 follows that

$$
\begin{aligned}
\mathrm{I_S}(X;Y \mid WZ) &\leq 2 \cdot \min_{Q_{Y|WZ}} \delta(P_{WXYZ}, P_{WXZ}Q_{Y|WZ}) \\
&\leq 2 \cdot \delta(P_{WXYZ}, P_{WXZ}P_{Y|Z}) \\
&= 2 \cdot \mathrm{I_S}(WX;Y \mid Z) \ . \qquad \square
\end{aligned}
$$

2.1 Relation between I and $\mathrm{I_S}$

Since we would like to use $\mathrm{I_S}$ in situations where previously the Shannon mutual information I has been used, it is important to know how these two measures relate to each other. Using Pinsker's inequality (see, for example, Lemma 16.3.1 in [25]) and Jensen's inequality, it is easy to show that

$$\mathrm{I_S}(X;Y \mid Z) \leq \sqrt{\mathrm{I}(X;Y \mid Z)} \ .$$

The other direction can be shown using Lemma 12.6.1 from [25]. We get that for $\mathrm{I_S}(X;Y \mid Z) \leq \frac{1}{4}$,

$$\mathrm{I}(X;Y \mid Z) \leq -2 \cdot \mathrm{I_S}(X;Y \mid Z) \log \frac{2 \cdot \mathrm{I_S}(X;Y \mid Z)}{|\mathcal{X}| \cdot |\mathcal{Y}| \cdot |\mathcal{Z}|} \ .$$

3   Two-Party Secure Function Evaluation

3.1   Definition of Security in the Real/Ideal Paradigm

We will now give a definition of secure function evaluation based on the real/ideal model paradigm. We use the same definitions as [21], which are based on Definition 7.2.10 of [18] (see also [17]).

Let $x \in \mathcal{X}$ denote the input of the first party, $y \in \mathcal{Y}$ the input of the second party and $z \in \{0,1\}^*$ an additional auxiliary input available to both parties, that is ignored by all honest parties. A *g-hybrid protocol* is a pair of (randomized) algorithms $\Pi = (A_1, A_2)$ which can interact by exchanging messages and which additionally have access to the functionality g. A pair of algorithms $\overline{A} = (\overline{A}_1, \overline{A}_2)$ is called *admissible* for protocol Π if either $\overline{A}_1 = A_1$ or $\overline{A}_2 = A_2$, i.e., if at least one of the parties is honest and uses the algorithm defined by the protocol Π. The joint execution of Π under $\overline{A}$ on input pair $(x, y) \in \mathcal{X} \times \mathcal{Y}$ and auxiliary input $z \in \{0,1\}^*$ in the real model, denoted by

$$\mathrm{REAL}^g_{\Pi, \overline{A}(z)}(x, y) ,$$

is defined as the output pair resulting from the interaction between $\overline{A}_1(x, z)$ and $\overline{A}_2(y, z)$ using the functionality g.

The *ideal model* defines the optimal setting where the players have access to an ideal functionality f they wish to compute. The trivial f-hybrid protocol $B = (B_1, B_2)$ is defined as the protocol where both parties send their inputs x and y unchanged to the functionality f and output the values u and v received from f unchanged. Let $\overline{B} = (\overline{B}_1, \overline{B}_2)$ be an admissible pair of algorithms for B. The joint execution of f under $\overline{B}$ in the ideal model on input pair $(x, y) \in \mathcal{X} \times \mathcal{Y}$ and auxiliary input $z \in \{0,1\}^*$, denoted by

$$\mathrm{IDEAL}_{f, \overline{B}(z)}(x, y) ,$$

is defined as the output pair resulting from the interaction between $\overline{B}_1(x, z)$ and $\overline{B}_2(y, z)$ using the functionality f.

We say that a protocol securely computes a functionality, if anything an adversary can do in the real model can be simulated in the ideal model.

Definition 3 (Statistical Security). *A g-hybrid protocol Π securely computes f with an error of at most ε if for every pair of algorithms $\overline{A} = (\overline{A}_1, \overline{A}_2)$ that is admissible in the real model for the protocol Π, there exists a pair of algorithms $\overline{B} = (\overline{B}_1, \overline{B}_2)$ that is admissible in the ideal model for protocol B (and where the same players are honest), such that for all $x \in \mathcal{X}$, $y \in \mathcal{Y}$, and $z \in \{0,1\}^*$, we have*

$$\mathrm{IDEAL}_{f, \overline{B}(z)}(x, y) \equiv_\varepsilon \mathrm{REAL}^g_{\Pi, \overline{A}(z)}(x, y) .$$

A very important property of the above definition is that it implies *sequential composition*, see [17]. Note that in contrast to [17] or [18], we do not require the simulation to be efficiently computable.

The following lemma formalizes the idea already mentioned in [21], namely that if a protocol is secure against adversaries without auxiliary input, then it is also secure against adversaries with auxiliary input. To avoid that the ideal adversary with auxiliary input gets infinitely big, we have to additionally require that there exists an explicit construction of the ideal adversary without auxiliary input.

Lemma 10. *If a g-hybrid protocol Π securely computes f with an error ε against adversaries with constant auxiliary input and the construction of the ideal adversary is explicit, then it securely computes f with an error of at most ε.*

Proof. If both players are honest the auxiliary input is ignored and the lemma holds. Let player i be malicious and denote by $\overline{A}_i$ the algorithm used. For a fixed $z \in \{0,1\}^*$, let $\overline{A}_i^z$ be equal to $\overline{A}_i$, but with the auxiliary input z hard-wired into it. Since Π securely computes f with an error ε against adversaries with constant auxiliary input, there exists an algorithm $\overline{B}_i^z$, such that for all $x \in \mathcal{X}$ and $y \in \mathcal{Y}$, we have

$$\mathrm{IDEAL}_{f,\overline{B}^z}(x,y) \equiv_\varepsilon \mathrm{REAL}^g_{\Pi,\overline{A}^z}(x,y) \ .$$

Now, we let $\overline{B}_i$ be the concatenation of all $\overline{B}_i^z$, i.e., on auxiliary input z the adversary $\overline{B}_i$ behaves as $\overline{B}_i^z$. Note that since we have an explicit construction of $\overline{B}_i^z$, $\overline{B}_i$ has a finite description. Obviously, we have for all $x \in \mathcal{X}$, $y \in \mathcal{Y}$, and $z \in \{0,1\}^*$ that

$$\mathrm{IDEAL}_{f,\overline{B}(z)}(x,y) \equiv_\varepsilon \mathrm{REAL}^g_{\Pi,\overline{A}(z)}(x,y) \ .$$

Hence, Π securely computes f with an error of at most ε. $\square$

Therefore, to show the security of a protocol in our model, the auxiliary input can be omitted, which we will do for the rest of this paper.

3.2   Information-Theoretic Conditions for Security

We will now state our main results, which are information-theoretic conditions for the *statistical* security of a protocol *without the use of an ideal model*.

First of all, we will slightly change our notation. Let X and Y be random variables denoting the player's inputs, distributed according to a distribution P_{XY} unknown to the players, and let U and V be random variables denoting the outputs of the two parties, i.e., for specific inputs (x,y) we have

$$(U,V) = \mathrm{REAL}^g_{\Pi,\overline{A}}(x,y) \ , \quad (\underline{U},\underline{V}) = \mathrm{IDEAL}_{f,\overline{B}}(x,y) \ .$$

The security condition of Definition 3 can be expressed as

$$P_{\underline{UV}|X=x,Y=y} \equiv_\varepsilon P_{UV|X=x,Y=y} \ .$$

To simplify the statement of the following theorem, we will assume that the ideal functionality f is deterministic. It can be generalized to probabilistic functionalities without any problems.

The conditions for the security for player 1 must ensure that there exists an ideal adversary that achieves almost the same as the real adversary. We achieve this by requiring that there exists a virtual input value Y' that the adversary could have created (this is ensured by $I_S(X; Y' \mid Y) \approx 0$), and a virtual output value V' that, together with U, could be the output of the ideal functionality, given X and Y' as input (this is ensured by $\Pr[(U, V') = f(X, Y')] \approx 1$). The protocol is secure if the adversary's output V could have been calculated by him from Y, Y' and V', which is ensured by $I_S(UX; V \mid YY'V') \approx 0$.

Theorem 1. *A protocol Π securely computes the deterministic functionality f with an error of at most 3ε, if for every pair of algorithms $\overline{A} = (\overline{A}_1, \overline{A}_2)$ that is admissible in the real model for the protocol Π and for any input (X, Y) distributed according to P_{XY} over $\mathcal{X} \times \mathcal{Y}$, $\overline{A}$ produces outputs (U, V) distributed according to $P_{UV|XY}$, such that the following conditions are satisfied:*

- (Correctness) *If both players are honest, we have*

$$\Pr[(U, V) = f(X, Y)] \geq 1 - \varepsilon \, .$$

- (Security for Player 1) *If player 1 is honest then there exist random variables Y' and V' distributed according to $P_{Y'V'|XYUV}$ such that*

$$\Pr[(U, V') = f(X, Y')] \geq 1 - \varepsilon \, ,$$

$$I_S(X; Y' \mid Y) \leq \varepsilon$$

and

$$I_S(UX; V \mid YY'V') \leq \varepsilon \, .$$

- (Security for Player 2) *If player 2 is honest then there exist random variables X' and U' distributed according to $P_{X'U'|XYUV}$ such that*

$$\Pr[(U', V) = f(X', Y)] \geq 1 - \varepsilon \, ,$$

$$I_S(Y; X' \mid X) \leq \varepsilon$$

and

$$I_S(VY; U \mid XX'U') \leq \varepsilon \, .$$

Both $P_{Y'V'|XYUV}$ and $P_{X'U'|XYUV}$ should have explicit constructions.

Proof. If both players are honest, the correctness condition implies

$$P_{UV|X=x, Y=y} \equiv_\varepsilon P_{\underline{UV}|X=x, Y=y} \, ,$$

for all x and y. If both players are malicious nothing needs to be shown.

Without loss of generality, let player 1 be honest and player 2 be malicious. Let us for the moment assume that the input distribution P_{XY} is fixed and known to the adversary, so the joint distribution in the real model is

$$P_{XYUV} = P_{XY} P_{UV|XY} \, .$$

We will define an admissible protocol $\overline{B} = (B_1, \overline{B}_2)$ in the ideal model that produces almost the same output distribution as the protocol Π in the real model. On input y, let $\overline{B}_2$ choose his input y' according to $P_{Y'|Y=y}$, which we model by the channel $P_{\underline{Y}'|Y}$. After receiving $\underline{v}'$ from the ideal functionality f, let $\overline{B}_2$ choose his output $\underline{v}$ according to $P_{V|Y=y,Y'=y',V'=\underline{v}'}$, which we model by the channel $P_{\underline{V}|Y\underline{Y}'\underline{V}'}$. The distribution of the input/output in the ideal model is given by

$$P_{XY\underline{U}\underline{V}} = P_{XY} \sum_{\underline{y}',\underline{v}'} P_{\underline{Y}'|Y} P_{\underline{U}\underline{V}'|X\underline{Y}'} P_{\underline{V}|Y\underline{Y}'\underline{V}'} \, ,$$

where $(\underline{U}, \underline{V}') = f(X, \underline{Y}')$.

In the real model, it follows from $\mathrm{I_S}(X; Y' \mid Y) \leq \varepsilon$ that

$$P_{XY} P_{Y'|XY} \equiv_\varepsilon P_{XY} P_{Y'|Y} \, ,$$

from $\mathrm{I_S}(UX; V \mid YY'V') \leq \varepsilon$ that

$$P_{XY} P_{UY'V'|XY} P_{V|XYUY'V'} \equiv_\varepsilon P_{XY} P_{UY'V'|XY} P_{V|YY'V'} \, ,$$

and from $\Pr[(U, V') = f(X, Y')] \geq 1 - \varepsilon$ and Lemma 4 that

$$P_{XY} P_{Y'|XY} P_{\underline{U}\underline{V}'|X\underline{Y}'} \equiv_\varepsilon P_{XY} P_{Y'|XY} P_{UV'|XYY'} \, .$$

We have

$$P_{XY\underline{U}\underline{V}} = P_{XY} \sum_{\underline{y}',\underline{v}'} P_{\underline{Y}'|Y} P_{\underline{U}\underline{V}'|X\underline{Y}'} P_{\underline{V}|Y\underline{Y}'\underline{V}'}$$

$$\equiv_\varepsilon P_{XY} \sum_{\underline{y}',\underline{v}'} P_{Y'|XY} P_{\underline{U}\underline{V}'|X\underline{Y}'} P_{\underline{V}|Y\underline{Y}'\underline{V}'}$$

$$\equiv_\varepsilon P_{XY} \sum_{\underline{y}',\underline{v}'} P_{Y'|XY} P_{UV'|XYY'} P_{\underline{V}|Y\underline{Y}'\underline{V}'}$$

$$\equiv_\varepsilon P_{XY} \sum_{\underline{y}',\underline{v}'} P_{Y'|XY} P_{UV'|XYY'} P_{V|XYUY'V'}$$

$$= P_{XYUV} \, .$$

Therefore, given P_{XY}, we are able to construct an adversary in the ideal model that simulates the output of the real protocol with an error of at most 3ε. However, we have to show that a *fixed* adversary in the ideal model works for *every* input $(x, y) \in \mathcal{X} \times \mathcal{Y}$.[2]

Given P_{XY}, let e be the average error of the simulation, and let e_{xy} be the error if the input is (x, y). We have $e = \sum_{x,y} P_{XY}(x, y) \cdot e_{xy}$. Let $h(P_{XY}) \to P'_{XY}$ a function that maps from the space of all distribution over $\mathcal{X} \times \mathcal{Y}$ to itself, where

$$P'_{XY}(x, y) := P_{XY}(x, y) \cdot \frac{e_{xy} + 1}{e + 1} \, .$$

[2] This part is missing in [21], but there the problem can be solved easily by fixing P_{XY} to the uniform distribution. But in our case, this would give us an error bound that would depend on the dimension of the input, which would be quite weak.

h is a continuous[3] function from a non-empty, compact, convex set $S \subset \mathbb{R}^{|\mathcal{X} \times \mathcal{Y}|}$ into itself, so by Brouwer's Fixed Point Theorem h must have a fixed point distribution Q_{XY}. (A constructive proof of Brower's Fixed Point Theorem can be found in [26].) So we have for all (x, y) that

$$Q_{XY}(x, y) = Q_{XY}(x, y) \cdot \frac{e_{xy} + 1}{e + 1}$$

and $Q_{XY}(x, y) > 0$, and hence $e_{xy} = e$. Therefore, by taking the adversary in the ideal model for the input distribution Q_{XY}, the output will have the same error e for all inputs. Since $e \leq 3\varepsilon$, we get for all x and y

$$P_{\underline{UV}|X=x,Y=y} \equiv_{3\varepsilon} P_{UV|X=x,Y=y} ,$$

which implies that the protocol is secure with an error of at most 3ε.   □

Theorem 2 now shows that our conditions are not only sufficient but also necessary.

Theorem 2. *If a protocol Π securely computes the deterministic functionality f with an error of at most ε, then for every pair of algorithms $\overline{A} = (\overline{A}_1, \overline{A}_2)$ that is admissible in the real model for the protocol Π and for any input (X, Y) distributed according to P_{XY} over $\mathcal{X} \times \mathcal{Y}$, $\overline{A}$ produces outputs (U, V) distributed according to $P_{UV|XY}$, such that the following conditions are satisfied:*

- (Correctness) *If both players are honest, we have*

$$\Pr[(U, V) = f(X, Y)] \geq 1 - \varepsilon .$$

- (Security for Player 1) *If player 1 is honest then there exist random variables Y' and V' distributed according to $P_{Y'V'|UVXY}$ such that*

$$\Pr[(U, V') = f(X, Y')] \geq 1 - \varepsilon ,$$

$$I_S(X; Y' \mid Y) = 0$$

and

$$I_S(UX; V \mid YY'V') \leq 4\varepsilon .$$

- (Security for Player 2) *If player 2 is honest then there exist random variables X' and U' distributed according to $P_{X'U'|UVXY}$ such that*

$$\Pr[(U', V) = f(X', Y)] \geq 1 - \varepsilon ,$$

$$I_S(Y; X' \mid X) = 0$$

and

$$I_S(VY; U \mid XX'U') \leq 4\varepsilon .$$

---

[3] We can assume that $P_{Y'V'|XYUV}$ is a continuous function of P_{XY}.

Proof. There exists an admissible pair of algorithms $\overline{B} = (\overline{B}_1, \overline{B}_2)$ for the ideal model such that for all $x \in \mathcal{X}$ and $y \in \mathcal{Y}$, we have

$$P_{\underline{UV}|X=x,Y=y} =_\varepsilon P_{UV|X=x,Y=y} \ .$$

If both players are honest we have $\overline{B} = B$. B_1 and B_2 forward their inputs (X, Y) unchanged to the trusted third party, get back $(\underline{U}', \underline{V}') := f(X, Y)$ and output $(\underline{U}, \underline{V}) = (\underline{U}', \underline{V}') = f(X, Y)$. It follows that $\Pr[(U, V) = f(X, Y)] \geq 1 - \varepsilon$.

Without loss of generality, let player 1 be honest and player 2 be malicious. Let us look at the execution of $\overline{B} = (B_1, \overline{B}_2)$, and let P_{XY} be an arbitrary input distribution. The malicious $\overline{B}_2$ can be modeled by the two conditional probability distributions $P_{\underline{Y}'\underline{S}|Y}$ computing the input to the ideal functionality f and some internal data $\underline{S}$, and $P_{\underline{V}|\underline{V}'\underline{S}}$ computing the output. We get

$$P_{XY\underline{UV}\underline{Y}'\underline{V}'} = \sum_s P_{XY} P_{\underline{Y}'\underline{S}|Y} P_{\underline{UV}'|X\underline{Y}'} P_{\underline{V}|\underline{V}'\underline{S}} \tag{1}$$

$$= P_{XY} P_{\underline{Y}'|Y} P_{\underline{UV}'|X\underline{Y}'} \sum_s P_{\underline{S}|Y\underline{Y}'} P_{\underline{V}|\underline{V}'\underline{S}} \tag{2}$$

$$= P_{XY} P_{\underline{Y}'|Y} P_{\underline{UV}'|X\underline{Y}'} P_{\underline{V}|Y\underline{V}'\underline{Y}'} \ , \tag{3}$$

where $(\underline{U}, \underline{V}') = f(X, \underline{Y}')$.

Let $P_{\underline{Y}'\underline{V}'|\underline{UV}XY} := P_{\underline{Y}'\underline{V}'|\underline{UV}XY}$. From $P_{\underline{Y}'\underline{V}'|\underline{UV}XY} = P_{\underline{Y}'|Y} P_{\underline{V}'|\underline{UV}XY\underline{Y}'}$ follows that

$$\mathrm{I_S}(X; \underline{Y}' \mid Y) = 0 \ .$$

From $P_{\underline{UV}XY} \equiv_\varepsilon P_{UVXY}$ and Lemma 3 follows that

$$P_{XYUV\underline{Y}'\underline{V}'} \equiv_\varepsilon P_{XY\underline{UV}\underline{Y}'\underline{V}'} \ .$$

Since $P_{XY\underline{UV}\underline{Y}'\underline{V}'} = P_{XY\underline{UV}'\underline{Y}'} P_{\underline{V}|Y\underline{V}'\underline{Y}'}$, it follows from Lemma 8 that

$$\mathrm{I_S}(UX; \underline{V} \mid YY'\underline{V}') \leq 4\varepsilon \ ,$$

and from Lemma 2 follows $P_{XY'UV'} \equiv_\varepsilon P_{X\underline{Y}'UV'}$, and therefore

$$\Pr[(U, V') = f(X, Y')] \geq 1 - \varepsilon \ . \qquad \square$$

3.3   Oblivious Transfer

We now apply Theorem 1 to 1-out-of-n string oblivious transfer, or $\binom{n}{1}$-OT^k for short. The ideal functionality f_{OT} is defined as $f_{\mathrm{OT}}(X, C) := (\bot, X_C)$, where $\bot$ denotes a constant random variable, $X = (X_0, \ldots, X_{n-1})$, $X_i \in \{0,1\}^k$ for $i \in \{0, \ldots, n-1\}$, and $C \in \{0, \ldots, n-1\}$.

Theorem 3. *A protocol Π securely computes $\binom{n}{1}$-OT^k with an error of at most 6ε if for every pair of algorithms $\overline{A} = (\overline{A}_1, \overline{A}_2)$ that is admissible for protocol Π and for any input (X, C), $\overline{A}$ produces outputs (U, V) such that the following conditions are satisfied:*

- (Correctness) *If both players are honest, then $U = \bot$ and*

$$\Pr[V = X_C] \geq 1 - \varepsilon \,.$$

- (Security for Player 1) *If player 1 is honest, then we have $U = \bot$ and there exists a random variable C' distributed according to $P_{C'|XCV}$, such that*

$$\mathrm{I_S}(X; C' \mid C) \leq \varepsilon, \text{ and } \mathrm{I_S}(X; V \mid CC'X_{C'}) \leq \varepsilon \,.$$

- (Security for Player 2) *If player 2 is honest, we have $V \in \{0,1\}^k$ and*

$$\mathrm{I_S}(C; U \mid X) \leq \varepsilon \,.$$

Proof. We need to show that these conditions imply the conditions of Theorem 1 for $\varepsilon' := 2\varepsilon$. For correctness and the security for player 1 this is trivial.

For the security for player 2, we choose $X' = (X'_0, \ldots, X'_{n-1})$ as follows: for all values i, let X'_i be chosen according to the distribution $P_{V|XU,C=i}$ except for X'_C. We set $X'_C = V$. Note that all X'_i, $0 \leq i \leq n-1$, have distribution $P_{V|XU,C=i}$. Thus X' does not depend on C given XU, and we have $\mathrm{I_S}(C; X' \mid XU) = 0$. From Lemma 5 follows that

$$\mathrm{I_S}(C; X'U \mid X) \leq \mathrm{I_S}(C; U \mid X) + \mathrm{I_S}(C; X' \mid XU) \leq \varepsilon \,.$$

Lemmas 6 implies that $\mathrm{I_S}(C; X' \mid X) \leq \varepsilon$ and, since V is a function of X' and C, it follows from Lemma 9 that

$$\mathrm{I_S}(VC; U \mid XX') = \mathrm{I_S}(C; U \mid XX') \leq 2 \cdot \mathrm{I_S}(C; X'U \mid X) \leq 2\varepsilon \,.$$

The statements follows by applying Theorem 1.   □

Furthermore, note that using Lemmas 5 and 6, we get

$$\begin{aligned}
\mathrm{I_S}(C; U \mid X) &\leq \mathrm{I_S}(C; X'U \mid X) \\
&\leq \mathrm{I_S}(C; X' \mid X) + \mathrm{I_S}(C; U \mid XX') \\
&\leq \mathrm{I_S}(C; X' \mid X) + \mathrm{I_S}(VC; U \mid XX') \,,
\end{aligned}$$

from which it is easy to show that the conditions of Theorem 1 also imply the conditions in Theorem 3.

References

1. Yao, A.C.: Protocols for secure computations. In: Proceedings of the 23rd Annual IEEE Symposium on Foundations of Computer Science (FOCS 1982), pp. 160–164 (1982)
2. Goldreich, O., Micali, S., Wigderson, A.: How to play any mental game. In: Proceedings of the 21st Annual ACM Symposium on Theory of Computing (STOC 1987), pp. 218–229. ACM Press, New York (1987)

3. Ben-Or, M., Goldwasser, S., Wigderson, A.: Completeness theorems for non-cryptographic fault-tolerant distributed computation. In: Proceedings of the 21st Annual ACM Symposium on Theory of Computing (STOC 1988), pp. 1–10. ACM Press, New York (1988)
4. Chaum, D., Crépeau, C., Damgård, I.: Multiparty unconditionally secure protocols (extended abstract). In: Proceedings of the 21st Annual ACM Symposium on Theory of Computing (STOC 1988), pp. 11–19. ACM Press, New York (1988)
5. Wiesner, S.: Conjugate coding. SIGACT News 15(1), 78–88 (1983)
6. Rabin, M.O.: How to exchange secrets by oblivious transfer. Technical Report TR-81, Harvard Aiken Computation Laboratory (1981)
7. Even, S., Goldreich, O., Lempel, A.: A randomized protocol for signing contracts. Commun. ACM 28(6), 637–647 (1985)
8. Goldreich, O., Vainish, R.: How to solve any protocol problem - an efficiency improvement. In: Pomerance, C. (ed.) CRYPTO 1987. LNCS, vol. 293, pp. 73–86. Springer, Heidelberg (1988)
9. Kilian, J.: Founding cryptography on oblivious transfer. In: Proceedings of the 20th Annual ACM Symposium on Theory of Computing (STOC 1988), pp. 20–31. ACM Press, New York (1988)
10. Crépeau, C.: Verifiable disclosure of secrets and applications. In: Quisquater, J.-J., Vandewalle, J. (eds.) EUROCRYPT 1989. LNCS, vol. 434, pp. 181–191. Springer, Heidelberg (1990)
11. Goldwasser, S., Levin, L.A.: Fair computation of general functions in presence of immoral majority. In: Menezes, A., Vanstone, S.A. (eds.) CRYPTO 1990. LNCS, vol. 537, pp. 77–93. Springer, Heidelberg (1991)
12. Crépeau, C., van de Graaf, J., Tapp, A.: Committed oblivious transfer and private multi-party computation. In: Coppersmith, D. (ed.) CRYPTO 1995. LNCS, vol. 963, pp. 110–123. Springer, Heidelberg (1995)
13. Kilian, J.: More general completeness theorems for secure two-party computation. In: Proceedings of the 32th Annual ACM Symposium on Theory of Computing (STOC 2000), pp. 316–324. ACM Press, New York (2000)
14. Micali, S., Rogaway, P.: Secure computation (abstract). In: Feigenbaum, J. (ed.) CRYPTO 1991. LNCS, vol. 576, pp. 392–404. Springer, Heidelberg (1992)
15. Beaver, D.: Foundations of secure interactive computing. In: Feigenbaum, J. (ed.) CRYPTO 1991. LNCS, vol. 576, pp. 377–391. Springer, Heidelberg (1992)
16. Goldwasser, S., Micali, S., Rackoff, C.: The knowledge complexity of interactive proof systems. SIAM J. Comput. 18(1), 186–208 (1989)
17. Canetti, R.: Security and composition of multiparty cryptographic protocols. Journal of Cryptology 13(1), 143–202 (2000)
18. Goldreich, O.: Foundations of Cryptography. Basic Applications, vol. II. Cambridge University Press, Cambridge (2004)
19. Canetti, R.: Universally composable security: A new paradigm for cryptographic protocols. In: Proceedings of the 42th Annual IEEE Symposium on Foundations of Computer Science (FOCS 2001), pp. 136–145 (2001), http://eprint.iacr.org/2000/067
20. Backes, M., Pfitzmann, B., Waidner, M.: A universally composable cryptographic library (2003), http://eprint.iacr.org/2003/015
21. Crépeau, C., Savvides, G., Schaffner, C., Wullschleger, J.: Information-theoretic conditions for two-party secure function evaluation. In: Vaudenay, S. (ed.) EUROCRYPT 2006. LNCS, vol. 4004, pp. 538–554. Springer, Heidelberg (2006), http://eprint.iacr.org/2006/183

22. Wullschleger, J.: Oblivious-Transfer Amplification. PhD thesis, ETH Zurich, Switzerland (2007)
23. Shannon, C.E.: A mathematical theory of communication. Bell System Tech. Journal 27, 379–423 (1948)
24. Fehr, S., Schaffner, C.: Composing quantum protocols in a classical environment (2008), http://arxiv.org/abs/0804.1059
25. Cover, T.M., Thomas, J.A.: Elements of Information Theory. Wiley-Interscience, Chichester (1991)
26. Kellogg, R.B., Li, T.Y., Yorke, J.: A constructive proof of the brouwer fixed-point theorem and computational results. SIAM Journal on Numerical Analysis 13(4), 473–483 (1976)

Upper Bounds for Set Systems with the Identifiable Parent Property

Michael J. Collins

Sandia National Laboratories[*]
Albuquerque, NM USA 87185
mjcolli@sandia.gov

Abstract. We derive upper bounds on the size of set systems having the c-identifiable parent property (c-IPP) and the c-traceability property (c-TA).

1 Introduction

A combinatorial model for traitor tracing in broadcast encryption was introduced in [3] and [5]. In this model a data supplier gives each user a different set of k keys, drawn from a base set V of v keys (a set of size k will be called a k-set). Any k-subset of V can be used to decrypt a message: for each new broadcast, the data supplier generates a new encryption key $s \notin V$ and distributes s using a k-out-of-v threshold secret sharing scheme. Each share of s is encrypted with a different key from V, and these encrypted shares are broadcast.

A coalition of c users may collude, combining some of their keys to produce a new, unauthorized k-set T. If such a "traitor" set is confiscated, we would like to be able to identify at least one of the users who contributed to T. This motivates the following definitions:

Definition 1. *Let $\mathcal{F}$ be a collection of k-subsets of V, and let $T \subset V$. The c-parent sets of T are*

$$P_c(T) = \{\mathcal{P} \subset \mathcal{F} : |\mathcal{P}| \leq c \text{ and } T \subset \cup_{U \in \mathcal{P}} U\}$$

Definition 2. *A collection $\mathcal{F}$ of k-subsets of V has the c-Identifiable Parent Property if, for all k-subsets $T \subset V$, either $P_c(T)$ is empty, or*

$$\bigcap_{\mathcal{P} \in P_c(T)} \mathcal{P} \neq \emptyset$$

Such a collection is called a c-IPP(k, $|\mathcal{F}|$, $|V|$) set system.

It is natural to consider the special case in which we can identify parents of T by finding those $S \in \mathcal{F}$ which maximize $|S \cap T|$:

---

[*] Sandia is a multiprogram laboratory operated by Sandia Corporation, a Lockheed Martin Company, for the United States Department of Energy's National Nuclear Security Administration under contract DE-AC04-94AL85000.

R. Safavi-Naini (Ed.): ICITS 2008, LNCS 5155, pp. 100–106, 2008.
© Springer-Verlag Berlin Heidelberg 2008

Definition 3. *A collection $\mathcal{F}$ of k-subsets of V has the c-Traceability Property if, for all k-subsets $T \subset V$, either $P_c(T)$ is empty, or*

$$\bigcap_{P \in P_c(T)} \mathcal{P} \supset \{U \in \mathcal{F} : |U \cap T| = \max_{S \in \mathcal{F}} |S \cap T|\}$$

Such a collection of sets is called a c-TA$(k, |\mathcal{F}|, |V|)$ set system.

Erdős, Frankl, and Füredi [4] proved that if $\mathcal{F}$ is a family of k-subsets of a v-set such that no member of $\mathcal{F}$ is contained in the union of c others, then

$$|\mathcal{F}| \leq \frac{\binom{v}{\lceil k/c \rceil}}{\binom{k-1}{\lceil k/c \rceil - 1}} \tag{1}$$

Clearly a c-IPP(k, b, v) set system satisfies these conditions (since no coalition of c users can produce the keyset of some other user); we are not aware of any previous work stating a better bound than (1). Alon and Stav [1] and Blackburn [2] show that a c-IPP *code* of length k over an alphabet of size v has size at most

$$(\lfloor (c/2+1)^2 \rfloor - 1) v^{\lceil k/(\lfloor (c/2+1)^2 \rfloor - 1) \rceil} \tag{2}$$

and our bounds on c-IPP set systems are similar. A code is a collection of codewords $u = (u_1, u_2, \cdots u_k)$ from V^k; each user has one codeword, and if a coalition of users produces an unauthorized word T, only keys from position i can be used to produce T_i. So in a code the parent sets are defined as follows.

Definition 4. *Let $\mathcal{F}$ be a code of length k over V, and let $T \in V^k$. The c-parent sets of T are*

$$P_c(T) = \{\mathcal{P} \subset \mathcal{F} : |\mathcal{P}| \leq c \text{ and } T_i \in \{U_i : U \in \mathcal{P}\} \text{ for all } 1 \leq i \leq k \}$$

2   c-IPP Set Systems

We first prove the following

Lemma 1. *Let $\mathcal{F}$ be a c-IPP(k, b, v) set system. Then there is some $X \in \mathcal{F}$ and some $\lceil \frac{k}{1 + \lfloor c/2 \rfloor} \rceil$-subset $Y \subset X$ such that Y is not contained in the union of any $\lceil c/2 \rceil$ sets from $\mathcal{F} \backslash \{X\}$.*

Proof. Suppose on the contrary that, for any $\lceil \frac{k}{1 + \lfloor c/2 \rfloor} \rceil$-subset Y of any $X \in \mathcal{F}$, there exist $Y_1, \cdots Y_{\lceil c/2 \rceil}$ (all different from X) such that $Y \subset \cup_{i=1}^{\lceil c/2 \rceil} Y_i$. We will show that $\mathcal{F}$ is not c-IPP.

Let $X_1, \cdots X_{1 + \lfloor c/2 \rfloor}$ be distinct members of $\mathcal{F}$; by our assumption there exist $Y_{1,1}, \cdots Y_{1, \lceil c/2 \rceil} \in \mathcal{F}$ (none of them equal to X_1) such that

$$\left| \bigcup_{1 \leq j \leq \lceil c/2 \rceil} Y_{1,j} \cap X_1 \right| \geq \left\lceil \frac{k}{1 + \lfloor c/2 \rfloor} \right\rceil . \tag{3}$$

Now for each $2 \leq i' \leq 1 + \lfloor c/2 \rfloor$ similarly choose $Y_{i',1}, \cdots Y_{i',\lceil c/2 \rceil}$ such that

$$\left| \bigcup_{i \leq i'} \bigcup_{1 \leq j \leq \lceil c/2 \rceil} Y_{i,j} \cap X_i \right| \geq i' \frac{k}{1 + \lfloor c/2 \rfloor} . \tag{4}$$

Our supposition guarantees the existence of these sets; for each i' select a subset $Y_{i'} \subset X_{i'}$ of size at most $\lceil \frac{k}{1+\lfloor c/2 \rfloor} \rceil$ that is disjoint from what has been covered already with $i < i'$, and choose sets $Y_{i',j}$ to contain $Y_{i'}$.

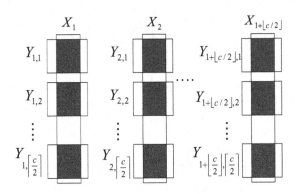

Fig. 1. Proof of Lemma 1

Figure 1 illustrates these sets; the shaded intersections represent a set T of size at least k. Now

$$T \subset \bigcup_i X_i \tag{5}$$

and also for each i'

$$T \subset \bigcup_{i \neq i'} X_i \cup \bigcup_j Y_{i',j} . \tag{6}$$

Note that the intersection of all these coalitions must be disjoint, even though it is not necessarily the case that all of the X_i and $Y_{i,j}$ are distinct. If $X_{i'} = Y_{i'',j}$ then this set will be excluded from (6) because $i' \neq i''$; while if $Y_{1,j_1} = Y_{2,j_2} = \cdots = Y_{c,j_c}$ this set will be excluded from (5). These are the only possibilities since all the X_i are distinct. Thus it is impossible to identify a parent of T, and this proves the lemma. □

Now define a *unique* subset of X (with respect to collection $\mathcal{F}$) to be a subset which is not contained in any $Z \in \mathcal{F}\backslash\{X\}$. If we consider the proof of (1) given in [4], we find that it can be restated in the following way:

Lemma 2. *Let $\mathcal{F}$ be a collection of sets; suppose $|S| = k$ and S is not contained in the union of any c members of $\mathcal{F}\backslash\{S\}$. Then S has at least $\binom{k-1}{\lceil \frac{k}{c} \rceil - 1}$ unique $\lceil \frac{k}{c} \rceil$-subsets.*

We can now prove

Theorem 1. *Let $\mathcal{F}$ be a c-IPP(k, b, v) set system. Then*

$$b \le \frac{\left(\begin{array}{c} v \\ \left\lceil \frac{k}{\lfloor c^2/4 \rfloor + \lceil c/2 \rceil} \right\rceil \end{array} \right)}{\left(\begin{array}{c} \left\lceil \frac{k}{1+\lfloor c/2 \rfloor} \right\rceil - 1 \\ \left\lceil \frac{k}{\lfloor c^2/4 \rfloor + \lceil c/2 \rceil} \right\rceil - 1 \end{array} \right)}.$$

Proof. Let X and Y be as in the statement of Lemma 1. Then by Lemma 2 Y (and hence X) contains at least

$$\left(\begin{array}{c} \left\lceil \frac{k}{1+\lfloor c/2 \rfloor} \right\rceil - 1 \\ \left\lceil \frac{\left\lceil \frac{k}{1+\lfloor c/2 \rfloor} \right\rceil}{\lceil c/2 \rceil} \right\rceil - 1 \end{array} \right) = \left(\begin{array}{c} \left\lceil \frac{k}{1+\lfloor c/2 \rfloor} \right\rceil - 1 \\ \left\lceil \frac{k}{\lfloor c^2/4 \rfloor + \lceil c/2 \rceil} \right\rceil - 1 \end{array} \right)$$

unique $\left\lceil \frac{k}{\lfloor c^2/4 \rfloor + \lceil c/2 \rceil} \right\rceil$-subsets; here we make use of the fact that $\left\lceil \frac{\lceil k/a \rceil}{b} \right\rceil = \left\lceil \frac{k}{ab} \right\rceil$ (for any integers a, b) and that $\lceil c/2 \rceil \lfloor c/2 \rfloor = \lfloor c^2/4 \rfloor$. Now remove X from $\mathcal{F}$; the resulting family is obviously still c-IPP so we can repeatedly apply Lemma 1, removing this many unique sets of keys for each member of $\mathcal{F}$. Clearly no set of keys can be removed more than once, and the theorem follows. $\qquad\square$

Theorem 1 can be strengthened when $c=2$:

Theorem 2. *Let $\mathcal{F}$ be a 2-IPP(k, b, v) set system. Then*

$$b \le \frac{\left(\begin{array}{c} v \\ \lceil k/3 \rceil \end{array} \right)}{\left(\begin{array}{c} \lceil 2k/3 \rceil - 1 \\ \lceil k/3 \rceil - 1 \end{array} \right)}.$$

Proof. We show that some member of such a set system must contain a $\lceil \frac{2k}{3} \rceil$-subset which is not covered by any two other users. The upper bound will then follow as in the proof of Theorem 1.

Suppose on the contrary that, for any $\lceil \frac{2k}{3} \rceil$-subset Y of any $X \in \mathcal{F}$, there exist $Y_1, Y_2 \ne X$ such that $Y \subset Y_1 \cup Y_2$. We will show that $\mathcal{F}$ is not 2-IPP. Given $X \in \mathcal{F}$ there must (by our assumption) exist $Y \ne X$ such that $|X \cap Y| = \tau + \frac{k}{3}$ with $\tau \ge 0$. Now $Y \backslash X$ must be covered by 2 other sets; thus there must exist a set Z with $|Z \cap Y \backslash X| \ge \frac{2k/3-\tau}{2}$, and similarly there must exist Z' with $|Z' \cap X \backslash Y| \ge \frac{2k/3-\tau}{2}$. Thus there is a set T of k keys contained in both $X \cup Z$ and $Y \cup Z'$; if $Z = Z'$ then note that T is also contained in $X \cup Y$ (see Fig. 2). Thus it is impossible to identify a parent of T. $\qquad\square$

Theorems 1 and 2 can be improved slightly by the following observation. Let $t = \left\lceil \frac{k}{\lfloor c^2/4 \rfloor + \lceil c/2 \rceil} \right\rceil$. We know that no set is contained in the union of c others;

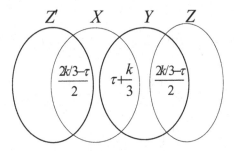

Fig. 2. Proof of Theorem 2

thus once we have removed all but $c + 1$ sets, each remaining set must have at least one key not contained in any other remaining set; thus each remaining set has at least $\binom{k-1}{t-1}$ unique t-subsets (of which $\binom{\lceil \frac{k}{1+\lfloor c/2 \rfloor} \rceil - 1}{t-1}$ are already counted), and similarly the final remaining set has $\binom{k}{t}$ unique t-subsets. Thus

$$
b \le \frac{\binom{v}{t}}{\binom{\lceil \frac{k}{1+\lfloor c/2 \rfloor} \rceil - 1}{t-1}} - c \left(\frac{\binom{k-1}{t-1}}{\binom{\lceil \frac{k}{1+\lfloor c/2 \rfloor} \rceil - 1}{t-1}} - 1 \right) - \frac{\binom{k}{t}}{\binom{\lceil \frac{k}{1+\lfloor c/2 \rfloor} \rceil - 1}{t-1}} + 1 .
$$

3 c-TA Set Systems

The following is proved in [5]:

Theorem 3. *If $\mathcal{F}$ is a family of k-sets in which every t-subset of every set is unique, then $\mathcal{F}$ is $\left\lfloor \sqrt{\frac{k-1}{t-1}} \right\rfloor$-TA.*

It is easy to verify that this implies the following sufficient condition for a set system to be c-TA:

Corollary 1. *If $\mathcal{F}$ is a family of k-sets in which every $\lceil \frac{k}{c^2} \rceil$-subset of every set is unique, then $\mathcal{F}$ is c-TA.*

We prove

Theorem 4. *Let $\mathcal{F}$ be a c-TA(k, b, v) set system. Then every member of $\mathcal{F}$ contains at least one unique $\lceil \frac{k}{c^2} \rceil$-subset, and*

$$
b \le \binom{v}{\lceil \frac{k}{c^2} \rceil} .
$$

Proof. Suppose on the contrary that some $A \in \mathcal{F}$ does not contain any unique $\lceil \frac{k}{c^2} \rceil$-subsets; we will show that $\mathcal{F}$ is not c-TA. Select $B_1 \in \mathcal{F} \backslash \{A\}$ to maximize

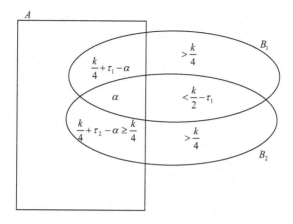

Fig. 3. Proof of Theorem 4 with $c = 2$

$|A \cap B_1|$; by assumption $|A \cap B_1| = \tau_1 + k/c^2$ with $\tau_1 \geq 0$. Now for each $2 \leq i \leq c$ we may assume that there exist $B_i \in \mathcal{F} \backslash \{A\}$ such that

$$|A \cap (B_1 \cup \cdots \cup B_i)| \geq |A \cap (B_1 \cup \cdots \cup B_{i-1})| + \frac{k}{c^2} \qquad (7)$$

i.e. B_i contains at least $\lceil \frac{k}{c^2} \rceil$ elements of A which are not contained in $B_1 \cup \cdots \cup B_{i-1}$. If $|A \backslash (B_1 \cup \cdots \cup B_{i-1})| > \frac{k}{c^2}$ then our assumption implies (7); otherwise it implies that A is contained in the union of c or fewer other sets, in which case $\mathcal{F}$ would not even be c-IPP.

For each i we have $|B_i \cap A| = \tau_i + k/c^2$ with $\tau_1 \geq \tau_i \geq 0$. Now let

$$T' = A \cap \bigcup_i B_i \ .$$

From (7) we have $|T'| \geq \lceil \tau_1 + k/c \rceil$. We will exhibit a traitor set T of size k, such that $T \subset \cup_i B_i$ and yet $|T \cap A| \geq |T \cap B_i|$ for all i (see Fig. 3 for an illustration of the case $c = 2$). This set will contain T', along with some keys from each $B_i \backslash A$. We may assume that

$$\left| \left(\bigcup_{1 \leq i < j \leq c} B_i \cap B_j \right) \backslash A \right| < k - |T'| \leq \frac{c-1}{c} k - \tau_1$$

for if this were not the case, then there would be at least k keys which are contained in two or more of the sets $A, B_1, \cdots B_c$; then any c of these users could produce the same traitor set, so $\mathcal{F}$ would not even be c-IPP. Therefore each B_i contains more than

$$k - (\tau_i + k/c^2) - (\frac{c-1}{c} k - \tau_1) \geq \frac{c-1}{c^2} k$$

keys which are not in A and not in any other B_j. So let T contain $\lceil \frac{c-1}{c^2} k \rceil$ such keys from each B_i. Then we have $|T| \geq k$ and $T \subset \cup_i B_i$, and also for each i

$$|B_i \cap T| = \tau_i + k/c^2 + \left\lceil \frac{c-1}{c^2} k \right\rceil \leq \lceil \tau_1 + k/c \rceil \leq |T \cap A|$$

as required.

The upper bound on $|\mathcal{F}|$ follows immediately from the fact that each $A \in \mathcal{F}$ contains a unique $\lceil \frac{k}{c^2} \rceil$-subset. $\square$

References

1. Alon, N., Stav, U.: New bounds on parent-identifying codes: The case of multiple parents. Comb. Probab. Comput. 13(6), 795–807 (2004)
2. Blackburn, S.R.: An upper bound on the size of a code with the k-identifiable parent property. J. Comb. Theory, Ser. A 102(1), 179–185 (2003)
3. Chor, B., Fiat, A., Naor, M., Pinkas, B.: Tracing traitors. IEEE Transactions on Information Theory 46(3), 893–910 (2000)
4. Füredi, Z., Erdős, P., Frankl, P.: Families of finite sets in which no set is covered by the union of r others. Israel J. Math. 51(1), 79–89 (1985)
5. Stinson, D.R., Wei, R.: Combinatorial properties and constructions of traceability schemes and frameproof codes. SIAM J. Discr. Math. 11, 41–53 (1998)

Oblivious Transfer Based on the McEliece Assumptions

Rafael Dowsley[1], Jeroen van de Graaf[2], Jörn Müller-Quade[3], and Anderson C.A. Nascimento[1]

[1] Department of Electrical Engineering, University of Brasilia,
Campus Universitario Darcy Ribeiro, Brasilia, CEP: 70910-900, Brazil
`rafaeldowsley@redes.unb.br, andclay@ene.unb.br`
[2] Laboratrio de Computação Científica, Universidade Federal de Minas Gerais,
CEP 31270-901, Brazil
`jvdg@ufmg.br`
[3] Universität Karlsruhe, Institut fuer Algorithmen und Kognitive Systeme
Am Fasanengarten 5, 76128 Karlsruhe, Germany
`muellerq@ira.uka.de`

Abstract. We implement one-out-of-two bit oblivious transfer (OT) based on the assumptions used in the McEliece cryptosystem: the hardness of decoding random binary linear codes, and the difficulty of distinguishing a permuted generating matrix of Goppa codes from a random matrix. To our knowledge this is the first OT reduction to these problems only.

1 Introduction

Oblivious transfer [31,27,11] is a primitive of central importance in modern cryptography as it implies two-party secure computation [16,20] and multi-party computation [9]. There exist several flavors of OT, but they are all equivalent [8]. In this work, we focus on the so-called one-out-of-two oblivious transfer (OT). This is a two-party primitive where a sender (Alice) inputs two bits b_0, b_1 and a receiver (Bob) inputs a bit c called the *choice bit*. Bob receives b_c and remains ignorant about b_{1-c}, while Alice only receives a confirmation message from Bob after he completed his part of the protocol successfully. In particular, Alice cannot learn Bob's choice.

OT can be constructed based on computational assumptions, both generic such as enhanced trapdoor permutations [11,14,17] and specific such as factoring [27], Diffie-Hellman [3,25,1], Quadratic or Higher-Order Residuosity, or from the Extended Riemann Hypothesis [18].

Our result: We build OT based on the two assumptions used in the McEliece cryptosystem [23]: (1) hardness of decoding of a random linear code (known to be NP-complete [4], and known to be equivalent to the learning parity with noise (LPN) problem [28]); and (2) indistinguishability of the scrambled generating matrix of the Goppa code [22] from a random one. It is noteworthy that there

R. Safavi-Naini (Ed.): ICITS 2008, LNCS 5155, pp. 107–117, 2008.
© Springer-Verlag Berlin Heidelberg 2008

exists no black box reduction from Public Key Cryptography to OT [13]. However, by exploiting some algebraic properties of cyphertexts geenrated by the McElice Cryptosystem we bypass the negative results of [13].

Comparison to other work: To our knowledge, this is the first oblivious transfer protocol based on the McEliece assumptions only and, concurrently with [19], the first computationally secure oblivious transfer protocol not known to be broken by a quantum computer. However, for obtaining a protocol of equivalent complexity, [19] uses additional assumptions: the random oracle assumption and permuted kernels. Also, [19] needs Shamir's zero knowledge proofs [30] which are avoided in our simpler construction. Our protocol is unconditionally secure for Bob and computationally secure for Alice.

In this work, we consider only *static* adversaries, i.e., we assume that either Alice or Bob is corrupted *before* the protocol begins.

2 Preliminaries

In this section, we establish our notation and provide some facts from coding theory and formal definitions of security for oblivious transfer and bit commitment. Then, for the sake of completeness, we describe the McEliece cryptosystem and introduce the assumptions on which its security, and also the security of our protocol is based.

Henceforth, we will denote by $x \in_R D$ a uniformly random choice of element x from its domain D; and by $\oplus$ a bit-wise exclusive OR of strings. All logarithms are to the base 2.

Two sequences $\{X_n\}_{n \in \mathbb{N}}$ and $\{Y_n\}_{n \in \mathbb{N}}$ of random variables are called *computationally indistinguishable*, denoted $X \stackrel{c}{=} Y$, if for every non-uniform probabilistic polynomial-time distinguisher D there exists a negligible function $\epsilon(\cdot)$ such that for every $n \in \mathbb{N}$,

$$|Pr[D(X_n) = 1] - Pr[D(Y_n) = 1]| < \epsilon(n)$$

2.1 Security Definition of Oblivious Transfer

Let us denote by $View_{\widetilde{A}}(\widetilde{A}(z), B(c))$ and $View_{\widetilde{B}}(A(b_0, b_1), \widetilde{B}(z))$ the *views* of dishonest Alice and Bob, respectively, which represent their inputs z, results of all local computations, and messages exchanged. Our definition of security is based on the one shown in [18] (conveniently adapted to protocols with more than two messages).

Definition 1. *A protocol $[A, B](b_0, b_1; c)$ is said to* securely implement oblivious transfer, *if at the end of its execution by the sender Alice and the receiver Bob which are modelled as probabilistic polynomial time (PPT) Turing machines having as their input a security parameter N, the following properties hold:*

- *Completeness: when the players honestly follow the protocol, Bob outputs b_c while Alice has no output.*

- Security for Alice: *For every PPT adversary $\tilde{B}$, every input z, and a (sufficiently long) random tape R_B chosen at random, there exists a choice bit c such that for $b_c \in \{0,1\}$ the distribution (taken over Alice's randomness) of runs of $\tilde{B}(z)$ using randomness R_B with Alice having input b_c and $b_{\bar{c}} = 0$ is computationally indistinguishable from the distribution of runs with Alice having input b_c and $b_{\bar{c}} = 1$.*
- Security for Bob: *For any PPT adversary $\tilde{A}$, any security parameter N and any input z of size polynomial in N, the view that $\tilde{A}(z)$ obtains when Bob inputs $c = 0$ is computationally indistinguishable from that of when Bob inputs $c = 1$, denoted:*

$$View_{\tilde{A}}(\tilde{A}(z), B(0))|_z \overset{c}{=} View_{\tilde{A}}(\tilde{A}(z), B(1))|_z.$$

A protocol is said to be secure against honest-but-curious players, if the previous definition holds in the case Alice and Bob follow the protocol. An oblivious-transfer protocol is unconditionally secure against a player if the given properties hold even when this player is not computationally bounded.

2.2   Security Definition of String Commitment

We also need commitment schemes in our constructions. A string commitment protocol consists of two stages. In the first one, called *Commit*, the sender (Alice) provides the receiver (Bob) with evidence about her input bit-string b. Bob cannot learn it before the second stage, called *Open*, where Alice reveals her commitment to Bob, such that she cannot open a value different from b without being caught with high probability. Let us denote by $View_{\tilde{A}}(\tilde{A}(z), B(a))$ and $View_{\tilde{B}}(A(b), \tilde{B}(z))$ the *views* of dishonest Alice and Bob, respectively, which represent their inputs z, results of all local computations, and messages exchanged. Our definition is based on [24].

Definition 2. *A protocol $[A, B](b)$ is said to securely implement string commitment, if at the end of its execution by the sender Alice and the receiver Bob, which are represented as PPT Turing machines having as their input a security parameter N, the following properties hold:*

- Completeness: *when the players honestly follow the protocol, Bob accepts b.*
- Hiding: *For any PPT adversary $\tilde{B}$, any security parameter N, any input z of size polynomial in N, and any $k \in \mathbb{N}$, after the Commit stage, but before the Open stage, the view of $\tilde{B}(z)$ when Alice inputs $b \in \{0,1\}^k$ is computationally indistinguishable from the view where Alice inputs any other $b' \in \{0,1\}^k$, $b' \neq b$:*

$$View_{\tilde{B}}(A(b), \tilde{B}(z))|_z \overset{c}{=} View_{\tilde{B}}(A(b'), \tilde{B}(z))|_z$$

- Binding: *For any PPT adversary $\tilde{A}$, any security parameter N and any input z of size polynomial in N, any $k \in \mathbb{N}$, there exists $b \in \{0,1\}^k$ which can be computed by Alice after the Commit stage, such that the probability that $\tilde{A}(b')$, $b' \neq b$ is accepted by Bob in the Open stage is negligible in N.*

A string commitment protocol is unconditionally secure against a player if the properties in Definition 2 hold even when this player is not computationally bounded.

2.3 McEliece Cryptosystem

The folowing definition was taken from [19]. The McEliece cryptosystem [23] consists of a triplet of probabilistic algorithms $ME = (Gen_{ME}, Enc_{ME}, Dec_{ME})$ and $M = \{0, 1\}^k$.

- Key generation algorithm: The PPT key generation algorithm Gen_{ME} works as follows:
  1. Generate a $k \times n$ generator matrix $\mathbf{G}$ of a Goppa code, where we assume that there is an efficient error-correction algorithm Correct which can always correct up to t errors.
  2. Generate a $k \times k$ random non-singular matrix $\mathbf{S}$.
  3. Generate a $n \times n$ random permutation matrix $\mathbf{T}$.
  4. Set $\mathbf{P} = \mathbf{SGT}$, and output $pk = (\mathbf{P}, t)$ and $sk = (\mathbf{S}, \mathbf{G}, \mathbf{T})$.
- Encryption algorithm: Enc_{ME} takes a plaintext $m \in \{0, 1\}^k$ and the public-key pk as input and outputs ciphertext $c = m\mathbf{P} \oplus e$, where $e \in \{0, 1\}^n$ is a random vector of Hamming weight t.
- Decryption algorithm: Dec_{ME} works as follows:
  1. Compute $c\mathbf{T}^{-1}(= (m\mathbf{S})\mathbf{G} \oplus e\mathbf{T}^{-1})$, where $\mathbf{T}^{-1}$ denotes the inverse matrix of $\mathbf{T}$.
  2. Compute $m\mathbf{S} = \mathsf{Correct}(c\mathbf{T}^{-1})$.
  3. Output $m = (m\mathbf{S})\mathbf{S}^{-1}$.

2.4 Security Assumptions

In this subsection, we briefly introduce and discuss the McEliece assumptions used in this work. First, we assume that there is no efficient algorithm which can distinguish the scrambled (according to the description in the previous Subsection) generating matrix of the Goppa code P and a random matrix of the same size. Currently, the best algorithm by Courtois et al. [7] works as follows: enumerate each Goppa polynomial and verify whether the corresponding code and the generator matrix $\mathbf{G}$ are "permutation equivalent" or not by using the *support splitting algorithm* [29], which is $n^t(1 + o(1))$-time algorithm, with n and t as defined in the previous subsection.

Assumption 3. *There is no PPT algorithm which can distinguish the public-key matrix P of the McEliece cryptosystem from a random matrix of the same size with non-negligible probability.*

We note that this assumption was utilized in [7] to construct a digital signature scheme.

The underlying assumption on which McEliece is the hardness of decoding random linear codes. This problem is known to be NP-complete [4], and all currently known algorithms to solve this problem are exponential. In particular, for small number of errors, the best one was presented by Canteaut and Chabaud [6].

Assumption 4. *The Syndrome Decoding Problem problem is hard for every PPT algorithm.*

We will also need a bit commitment scheme based on the same assumption. Of course we could use a modification of the McEliece system which is semantical secure, see [26]. However, we can do better.

According to a well-known result by Naor [24], bit commitment scheme can be constructed using a pseudorandom generator. The latter primitive can be built efficiently using the Syndrome Decoding problem as described by Fischer and Stern [12]. Naor's scheme is unconditionally binding, computationally hiding and meets the completeness property. So using this construction we are using only one of the McEliece assumption. In addition, for *string* commitment Naor's construction is very efficient.

3   Passively Secure Protocol for OT

For now, assume Alice and Bob to be honest-but-curious. We first sketch the intuition behind this protocol. We construct it according to the paradigm presented in [3]. Bob sends to Alice an object which is either a public key or a randomized public key for which the decoding problem is difficult. To randomize a public key, we use bitwise-XOR with a random matrix. Alice, in turn, computes the bitwise-XOR of the received entity with the same random matrix, hereby obtaining the second "key". She encrypts b_0 and b_1 with the received and computed keys, respectively, and sends the encryptions to Bob. The protocol is secure for Bob because Alice cannot distinguish a public key from a random matrix. The protocol is complete because Bob can always decrypt b_c. At the same time, it is also secure for Alice, because Bob is unable to decrypt the second bit as he cannot decode the random code.

Recall that Alice's inputs are the bits b_0 and b_1 while Bob inputs the bit c wishing to receive b_c. Denote the Hamming weight of a vector z by $w_H(z)$.

Protocol 5

1. Alice chooses a $k \times n$ random binary matrix Q and sends it to Bob.
2. Bob generates a secret key (S, G, T) following the procedures of the McEliece algorithm, sets $P_c = SGT$ and $P_{1-c} = P_c \oplus Q$ and sends P_0, t to Alice.
3. Alice computes $P_1 = P_0 \oplus Q$, then encrypts two random bit strings $r_0, r_1 \in_R \{0,1\}^k$ with P_0 and P_1, respectively, i.e., for $i = 0, 1 : y_i = r_i P_i \oplus z_i$, where $z_i \in \{0,1\}^n$, $w_H(z_i) = t$, computes for $i = 0, 1$: $m_i \in_R \{0,1\}^k$, encrypts b_0 and b_1 as follows: for $i = 0, 1 : \hat{b}_i = b_i \oplus \langle r_i, m_i \rangle$ where "$\langle \cdot, \cdot \rangle$" denotes a scalar product modulo 2 and finally sends for $i = 0, 1 : y_i, m_i, \hat{b}_i$ to Bob.
4. Bob decrypts r_c and computes $b_c = \hat{b}_c \oplus \langle r_c, m_c \rangle$.

The next theorem formally states the security of the above protocol.

Theorem 1. *Protocol 5 is complete and secure for both Alice and Bob against passive attacks according to Definition 1 under Assumptions 3 and 4.*

Proof. Given that under passive attacks, the players always follow the protocol, we argue the properties listed in Definition 1.

Completeness: This follows by observing that Bob always receives a valid encryption of r_c that allows him to compute b_c in Step 4.

Security for Alice: Let $\widetilde{B}$ be any PPT passively cheating receiver. Let c be the bit such that $\hat{b}_{1-c} = b_{1-c} \oplus \langle r_{1-c}, m_{1-c} \rangle$ and $y_{1-c} = r_{1-c}(P_c \oplus Q) \oplus z_{1-c}$. Note that Q is chosen randomly and independently from P_c, so from $\widetilde{B}$'s point of view, learning r_{1-c} is equivalent to decoding a random linear code with generating matrix $P_c \oplus Q$. This is known to be hard [4]. It was proven in [15] that $\langle r, m \rangle$ is a hard-core predicate for any one-way function f given $f(r)$ and m. Hence, by Assumption 4, the distribution (taken over Alice's randomness) of runs of $\widetilde{B}(z)$ using randomness R with Alice having input b_c and $b_{\overline{c}} = 0$ is computationally indistinguishable from the distribution of runs with Alice having input b_c and $b_{\overline{c}} = 1$.

Security for Bob: This follows directly from Assumption 3. Honest-but-curious Alice is unable to distinguish between $P = SGT$ and a random $k \times n$ matrix, and hence she is also unable to tell $P_c = SGT$ from $P_{1-c} = SGT \oplus Q$ for any $c \in \{0, 1\}$. This implies computational indistinguishability of the protocol views for Alice.

Unfortunately, Protocol 5 is not secure if the parties cheat actively. One problem is that, given a random matrix Q, Bob can come up with two matrices P', P'', where $P' \oplus P'' = Q$, such that they are the generating matrices of the codes with some reasonably good decoding properties. It is clear that in this case, Bob will be able to partially decode *both* b_0 and b_1.

4 Fully Secure Protocol

In order to arm the passive protocol with security against malicious parties one could use a general *compiler* as the one in [14]. However, we present a direct and more efficient aproach:

1. Implement a randomized oblivious transfer in which Bob is forced to choose his the public key **before** and therefore **independent** of Q, if not he will be detected with probability at least $\frac{1}{2}$.
2. Convert the randomized oblivious transfer into an oblivious transfer for specific inputs with the same characteristics of security;
3. Reduce the probability that a malicious Bob learns simultaneously information on *both* b_0 and b_1.

4.1 Random OT with High Probability of B Cheating

First, we implement a protocol that outputs two random bits a_0, a_1 to Alice and outputs a random bit d and a_d to Bob. In this protocol, Alice detects with probability at least $\frac{1}{2} - \epsilon$ a malicious Bob that chooses the public key *depending* of Q.

To achieve this, Bob generates two different McEliece keys by following the same procedures of protocol 5 and by using two random bits c_0, c_1. He commits to P_{0,c_0} and P_{1,c_1}. Then, Bob receives two random matrices Q_0 and Q_1 from Alice, computes $P_{0,1-c_0} = P_{0,c_0} \oplus Q_0$ and $P_{1,1-c_1} = P_{1,c_1} \oplus Q_1$ and sends $P_{0,0}, P_{1,0}, t$ to her. Alice chooses one of the commitments for Bob to open and checks if the opened information is consistent with an honest procedure; otherwise, she stops the protocol. Finally, she encrypts a_0 and a_1 using the matrices associated to the commitment that was not opened.

Protocol 6

1. Bob generates two McEliece secret keys (S_0, G_0, T_0) and (S_1, G_1, T_1). He chooses $c_0, c_1 \in_R \{0, 1\}$ and sets $P_{0,c_0} = S_0 G_0 T_0$ and $P_{1,c_1} = S_1 G_1 T_1$. He commits to P_{0,c_0} and P_{1,c_1}.
2. Alice chooses Q_0 and Q_1 uniformly at random and sends them to Bob.
3. Bob computes $P_{0,1-c_0} = P_{0,c_0} \oplus Q_0$ and $P_{1,1-c_1} = P_{1,c_1} \oplus Q_1$. He sends $P_{0,0}, P_{1,0}, t$ to Alice.
4. Alice computes $P_{0,1} = P_{0,0} \oplus Q_0$ and $P_{1,1} = P_{1,0} \oplus Q_1$. Then she chooses the challenge $j \in_R \{0, 1\}$ and sends it to Bob.
5. Bob opens his commitment to $P_{1-j,c_{1-j}}$ and sets $d = c_j$
6. Alice checks the following: $P_{1-j,c_{1-j}}$ must be equal to $P_{1-j,0}$ or $P_{1-j,1}$, otherwise she stops the protocol.
7. Alice encrypts two random bit strings $r_0, r_1 \in_R \{0, 1\}^k$ with $P_{j,0}$ and $P_{j,1}$, respectively, i.e., for $i = 0, 1 : y_i = r_i P_{j,i} \oplus z_i$, where $z_i \in \{0, 1\}^n$, $w_H(z_i) = t$, computes for $i = 0, 1$: $m_i \in_R \{0, 1\}^k$, encrypts $a_0, a_1 \in_R \{0, 1\}$ as follows: for $i = 0, 1 : \hat{a}_i = a_i \oplus \langle r_i, m_i \rangle$ where "$\langle \cdot, \cdot \rangle$" denotes a scalar product and finally sends for $i = 0, 1 : y_i, m_i, \hat{a}_i$ to Bob.
8. Bob decrypts r_d and computes $a_d = \hat{a}_d \oplus \langle r_d, m_d \rangle$. If Bob encounters a decoding error while decrypting r_d, then he outputs $a_d = 0$.

Theorem 2. *Assuming the used bit commitment scheme secure, protocol 6 implements a randomized oblivious transfer that is complete and secure for Bob against active attacks according to Definition 1 under Assumptions 3 and 4. Additionally, the probability that a malicious Bob learns both a_0 and a_1 is at most $\frac{1}{2} + \epsilon(n)$ where $\epsilon(n)$ is a negligible function.*

Proof. **Completeness:** An honest Bob always passes the test of Step 6 and receives a valid encryption of r_d, so he can compute a_d.

Security for Alice: In order to obtain simultaneously information on a_0 and a_1, Bob must learn r_0 and r_1. The encryptions of r_0 and r_1 only depend on $P_{j,0}$ and $P_{j,1}$, respectively.

If Bob sends both $P_{0,0}$ and $P_{1,0}$ chosen according to the protocol (honest procedure), then the probability that he learns both inputs of Alice is the same as in the passive protocol, i.e., it is negligible. If Bob chooses in a malicious way both $P_{0,0}$ and $P_{1,0}$, then with overwhelming probability Alice will stop the protocol in step 6 and Bob will learn neither r_0 nor r_1.

The best strategy for Bob is to choose honestly one of the matrices and choose the other in a malicious way, thus he can cheat and partially decode *both* r_0 and r_1 in case Alice asks him to open the matrix correctly chosen. However, note that with probability $\frac{1}{2}$, Alice asks him to open the matrix maliciously chosen. In this case, Bob will be able to open the commitment with the value that Alice expects in step 6 only with negligible probability. Thus, the probability that a malicious Bob learns both a_0 and a_1 is at most $\frac{1}{2} + \epsilon(n)$ where $\epsilon(n)$ is a negligible function.

Security for Bob: The commitment to $P_{j,c_j} = P_{j,d}$ is not opened, so the security for Bob follows from Assumption 3 as in the protocol 5.

As long as the commitment is secure, possible differences from the passive scenario are the following ones:

- Alice could cheat by sending a specially chosen matrix Q, however by Assumption 3, she cannot tell P_{j,c_j} from random, hence her choice of Q will not affect her ability to learn d;
- For some $i \in \{0, 1\}$, Alice may use a different matrix instead of $P_{j,i}$ for encrypting r_i in Step 7 hoping that $i = d$ so that Bob will encounter the decoding error and then complain, hereby disclosing his choice. However, the last instruction of Step 8 thwarts such attack by forcing Bob to accept with a fixed output "0". Sending a "wrong" syndrome is then equivalent to the situation when Alice sets his input $a_i = 0$.

Thus, it follows that the protocol is secure against Alice.

4.2   Derandomizing the Previous Protocol

Subsequently, we use the method of [2] to transform the randomized oblivious transfer into an (ordinary) oblivious transfer with the same characteristics of security.

Protocol 7

1. Bob and Alice execute the protocol 6. Alice receives a_0, a_1 and Bob receives d, a_d.
2. Bob chooses c, sets $e = c \oplus d$ and sends e to Alice.
3. Alices chooses $b_0, b_1 \in \{0, 1\}$, computes $f_0 = b_0 \oplus a_e$ and $f_1 = b_1 \oplus a_{1 \oplus e}$ and sends f_0, f_1 to Bob.
4. Bob computes $b_c = f_c \oplus a_d$.

Theorem 3. *Protocol 7 implements an oblivious transfer with the same characteristics of security of the protocol 6.*

Proof. **Completeness:** $f_c = b_c \oplus a_{c \oplus e} = b_c \oplus a_d$, so an honest Bob can recover b_c because he knows a_d.

Security for Alice: $f_{1 \oplus c} = b_{1 \oplus c} \oplus a_{1 \oplus c \oplus e} = b_{1 \oplus c} \oplus a_{1 \oplus d}$, so Bob can recover both b_0 and b_1 only if he knows a_0 and a_1.

Security for Bob: Alice has to discover d in order to compute c, thus the security for Bob follows from the protocol 6.

4.3 Reducing the Probability of B Cheating

Finally, we use the reduction of [10] to minimize the probability that a malicious Bob learns both inputs of Alice. In this reduction, protocol 7 is executed s times in parallel, where s is a security parameter. The inputs in each execution are chosen in such way that Bob must learn both bits in all executions to be able to compute both inputs of Alice in protocol 8.

Protocol 8

1. Alice chooses $b_0, b_1 \in \{0,1\}$ and $b_{0,1}, b_{0,2}, \ldots, b_{0,s}, b_{1,1}, b_{1,2}, \ldots, b_{1,s} \in_R \{0,1\}$ such that $b_0 = b_{0,1} \oplus b_{0,2} \oplus \ldots \oplus b_{0,s}$ and $b_1 = b_{1,1} \oplus b_{1,2} \oplus \ldots \oplus b_{1,s}$.
2. Bob chooses $c \in \{0,1\}$.
3. Protocol 7 is executed s times, with inputs $b_{0,i}, b_{1,i}$ from Alice and $c_i = c$ from Bob for $i = 1 \ldots s$.
4. Bob computes $b_c = b_{c,1} \oplus b_{c,2} \oplus \ldots \oplus b_{c,s}$.

Theorem 4. *Assuming that the bit commitment scheme used in protocol 6 is secure, protocol 8 is complete and secure for both Alice and Bob against active attacks according to Definition 1 under Assumptions 3 and 4.*

Proof. **Completeness:** An honest Bob learns all $b_{c,i}$ for $i = 1 \ldots s$ in the s executions of protocol 7 and therefore he can compute b_c.

Security for Alice: Bob must discover both bits in all executions of protocol 7 in order to learn something simultaneously on b_0 and b_1. The probability that a malicious Bob learns both bits in an execution of protocol 7 is at most $\frac{1}{2} + \epsilon(n)$, where $\epsilon(n)$ is a negligible function. There exists an n_0 such that $\epsilon(n) < \frac{1}{4}$ for any $n > n_0$. We can choose $n > n_0$, so $\beta = \frac{1}{2} + \epsilon(n) < \frac{3}{4}$ and the probability that a malicious Bob learns both b_0 and b_1 is less than $(\frac{3}{4})^s$, which is negligible in s. Thus, the protocol is secure for Alice.

Security for Bob: Alice discovers c if she learns any c_i, but this probability is negligible because the probability that she learns a specific c_i in the respective execution of the protocol 7 is negligible and the number of executions of the protocol 7 is polynomial.

Acknowledgements. The authors acknowledge previous discussions with Kirill Morozov and Hideki Imai.

References

1. Aiello, W., Ishai, Y., Reingold, O.: Priced Oblivious Transfer: How to Sell Digital Goods. In: Pfitzmann, B. (ed.) EUROCRYPT 2001. LNCS, vol. 2045, pp. 119–135. Springer, Heidelberg (2001)
2. Beaver, D.: Precomputing Oblivious Transfer. In: Coppersmith, D. (ed.) CRYPTO 1995. LNCS, vol. 963, pp. 97–109. Springer, Heidelberg (1995)

3. Bellare, M., Micali, S.: Non-Interactive Oblivious Transfer and Applications. In: Brassard, G. (ed.) CRYPTO 1989. LNCS, vol. 435, pp. 547–557. Springer, Heidelberg (1990)
4. Berlekamp, E.R., McEliece, R.J., Avan Tilborg, H.C.: On the Inherent Intractability of Certain Coding Problems. IEEE Trans. Inf. Theory 24, 384–386 (1978)
5. Blum, A., Furst, M., Kearns, M., Lipton, R.J.: Cryptographic primitives based on hard learning problems. In: Stinson, D.R. (ed.) CRYPTO 1993. LNCS, vol. 773, pp. 278–291. Springer, Heidelberg (1994)
6. Canteaut, A., Chabaud, F.: A new algorithm for finding minimum-weight words in a linear code: application to primitive narrow-sense BCH codes of length 511. IEEE Trans. Inf. Theory 44(1), 367–378 (1998)
7. Courtois, N., Finiasz, M., Sendrier, N.: How to Achieve a McEliece Digital Signature Scheme. In: Boyd, C. (ed.) ASIACRYPT 2001. LNCS, vol. 2248, pp. 157–174. Springer, Heidelberg (2001)
8. Crépeau, C.: Equivalence between two flavors of oblivious transfers. In: Pomerance, C. (ed.) CRYPTO 1987. LNCS, vol. 293, pp. 350–354. Springer, Heidelberg (1988)
9. Crépeau, C., van de Graaf, J., Tapp, A.: Committed Oblivious Transfer and Private Multi-Party Computations. In: Coppersmith, D. (ed.) CRYPTO 1995. LNCS, vol. 963, p. 110. Springer, Heidelberg (1995)
10. Damgård, I., Kilian, J., Salvail, L.: On the (Im)possibility of Basing Oblivious Transfer and Bit Commitment on Weakened Security Assumptions. In: Stern, J. (ed.) EUROCRYPT 1999. LNCS, vol. 1592, pp. 56–73. Springer, Heidelberg (1999)
11. Even, S., Goldreich, O., Lempel, A.: A randomized protocol for signing contracts. In: Proceedings CRYPTO 1982, pp. 205–210. Plenum Press (1983)
12. Fischer, J., Stern, J.: An Efficient Pseudo-Random Generator Provably as Secure as Syndrome Decoding. In: Maurer, U.M. (ed.) EUROCRYPT 1996. LNCS, vol. 1070, pp. 245–255. Springer, Heidelberg (1996)
13. Gertner, Y., Kannan, S., Malkin, T., Reingold, O., Viswanathan, M.: The Relationship between Public Key Encryption and Oblivious Transfer. In: FOCS 2000, pp. 325–335 (2000)
14. Goldreich, O.: Foundations of Cryptography (Basic Applications), vol. 2. Cambridge University Press, Cambridge (2004)
15. Goldreich, O., Levin, L.A.: Hard-Core Predicates for Any One-Way Function. In: 21st ACM Symposium on the Theory of Computing, pp. 25–32 (1989)
16. Goldreich, O., Micali, S., Wigderson, A.: How to Play Any Mental Game, or: A completeness theorem for protocols with honest majority. In: Proc. 19th ACM STOC, pp. 218–229. ACM Press, New York (1987)
17. Haitner, I.: implementing Oblivious Transfer Using Collection of Dense Trapdoor Permutations. In: Naor, M. (ed.) TCC 2004. LNCS, vol. 2951, pp. 394–409. Springer, Heidelberg (2004)
18. Kalai, Y.: Smooth Projective Hashing and Two-Message Oblivious Transfer. In: Cramer, R.J.F. (ed.) EUROCRYPT 2005. LNCS, vol. 3494, pp. 78–95. Springer, Heidelberg (2005)
19. Kobara, K., Morozov, K., Overbeck, R.: Oblivious Transfer via McEliece's PKC and Permuted Kernels, Cryptology ePrint Archive 2007/382 (2007)
20. Kilian, J.: Founding Cryptography on Oblivious Transfer. In: 20th ACM STOC, pp. 20–31. ACM Press, New York (1988)
21. Kobara, K., Imai, H.: Semantically Secure McEliece Cryptosystems – Conversions for McEliece PKC. In: Kim, K.-c. (ed.) PKC 2001. LNCS, vol. 1992, pp. 19–35. Springer, Heidelberg (2001)

22. McEliece, R.J.: The Theory of Information and Coding. The Encyclopedia of Mathematics and Its Applications, vol. 3. Addison-Wesley, Reading (1977)
23. McEliece, R.J.: A Public-Key Cryptosystem Based on Algebraic Coding Theory. In: Deep Space Network progress Report (1978)
24. Naor, M.: Bit Commitment using Pseudo-Randomness. In: Brassard, G. (ed.) CRYPTO 1989. LNCS, vol. 435, pp. 128–136. Springer, Heidelberg (1990)
25. Naor, M., Pinkas, B.: Efficient Oblivious Transfer Protocols. In: SODA 2001 (SIAM Symposium on Discrete Algorithms) (2001)
26. Nojima, R., Imai, H., Kobara, K., Morozov, K.: Semantic Security for the McEliece Cryptosystem without Random Oracles. WCC 2007, Versailles, France (April 2007)
27. Rabin, M.O.: How to Exchange Secrets by Oblivious Transfer. Technical Memo TR-81, Aiken Computation Laboratory, Harvard University (1981)
28. Regev, O.: On Lattices, Learning with Errors, Random Linear Codes, and Cryptography. In: Proc. 37th STOC, pp. 84–93 (2005)
29. Sendrier, N.: Finding the Permutation Between Equivalent Linear Codes: The Support Splitting Algorithm. IEEE Trans. Inf. Theory 46(4), 1193–1203 (2000)
30. Shamir, A.: An efficient identification scheme based on permuted kernels. In: Brassard, G. (ed.) CRYPTO 1989. LNCS, vol. 435, pp. 606–609. Springer, Heidelberg (1990)
31. Wiesner, S.: Conjugate coding. Sigact News 15(1), 78–88 (1983) (original manuscript written circa 1970)

List Error-Correction with Optimal Information Rate
(Invited Talk)

Venkatesan Guruswami[*]

Department of Computer Science and Engineering
University of Washington
Seattle, WA
venkat@cs.washington.edu

Abstract. The construction of error-correcting codes that achieve the best possible trade-off between information rate and the amount of errors that can be corrected has been a long sought-after goal. This talk will survey some of the work on list error-correction algorithms for algebraic codes [8,5], culminating in the construction of codes with the *optimal* information rate for any desired error-correction radius [7,4]. Specifically, these codes can correct a fraction p of worst-case errors (for any desired $0 < p < 1$) with rate $1 - p - \epsilon$ for any constant $\epsilon > 0$. We will describe these codes, which are called folded Reed-Solomon codes, and give a peek into the algebraic ideas underlying their list decoding.

Over the years, list-decodable codes have also found applications extraneous to coding theory [3, Chap. 12], including several elegant ones in cryptography. The problem of decoding Reed-Solomon codes (also known as polynomial reconstruction) and its variants from a large number of errors has been suggested as an intractability assumption to base the security of protocols on [6]. Progress on list decoding algorithms for algebraic codes has led to cryptanalysis of some of these schemes. It is interesting to note that the line of research that eventually led to the above-mentioned result for folded Reed-Solomon codes can be traced back to a cryptographic assumption concerning simultaneous polynomial reconstruction and algorithms for decoding "interleaved" Reed-Solomon codes that it inspired [1,2]. Given the cryptographic theme of the ICITS conference, we will also briefly allude to the above connection in the talk.

References

1. Bleichenbacher, D., Kiayias, A., Yung, M.: Decoding of interleaved Reed Solomon codes over noisy data. In: Baeten, J.C.M., Lenstra, J.K., Parrow, J., Woeginger, G.J. (eds.) ICALP 2003. LNCS, vol. 2719, pp. 97–108. Springer, Heidelberg (2003)
2. Coppersmith, D., Sudan, M.: Reconstructing curves in three (and higher) dimensional spaces from noisy data. In: Proceedings of the 35th Annual ACM Symposium on Theory of Computing, June 2003, pp. 136–142 (2003)

[*] Supported by NSF CCF-0343672 and a David and Lucile Packard Foundation Fellowship.

R. Safavi-Naini (Ed.): ICITS 2008, LNCS 5155, pp. 118–119, 2008.
© Springer-Verlag Berlin Heidelberg 2008

3. Guruswami, V.: List Decoding of Error-Correcting Codes. LNCS, vol. 3282. Springer, Heidelberg (2004) (published in ACM Distinguished Theses series)
4. Guruswami, V., Rudra, A.: Explicit codes achieving list decoding capacity: Error-correction with optimal redundancy. IEEE Transactions on Information Theory 54(1), 135–150 (2008)
5. Guruswami, V., Sudan, M.: Improved decoding of Reed-Solomon and algebraic-geometric codes. IEEE Transactions on Information Theory 45, 1757–1767 (1999)
6. Kiayias, A., Yung, M.: Directions in polynomial reconstruction based cryptography. IEICE Transactions E87-A(5), 978–985 (2004)
7. Parvaresh, F., Vardy, A.: Correcting errors beyond the Guruswami-Sudan radius in polynomial time. In: Proceedings of the 46th Annual IEEE Symposium on Foundations of Computer Science, pp. 285–294 (2005)
8. Sudan, M.: Decoding of Reed-Solomon codes beyond the error-correction bound. Journal of Complexity 13(1), 180–193 (1997)

Theory of Quantum Key Distribution: The Road Ahead (Invited Talk)

Norbert Lütkenhaus[1]

Institute for Quantum Computing, University of Waterloo, Waterloo, Canada
nlutkenhaus@iqc.ca
http://www.iqc.ca/people/person.php?id=48

Quantum Key Distribution (QKD) has been an area with lots of research activity. So nearly 25 years after the publication of the Bennett-Brassard 1984 protocol, what is left to do? As a basis of my talk, I will present the ideas of quantum key distribution in a language that emphasizes the common basis with information theoretic secure key distribution schemes that are based on independent noise assumptions in channels. As I will show, the role quantum theory plays is to verify the nature of correlations between sender, receiver and eavesdropper based only on the observations of sender and receiver. For reviews of practical QKD and issues addressed in this presentation, see [1,2,3].

Current research directions concentrate on the theoretic side on the optimal method of extracting secret key out of given observed correlations between sender and receiver. As it is the case in the classical scenario, different protocols using for example one-way or two-way communication over an authenticated public channel can have different maximum thresholds for error rates, and can yield different key rates. Other research directions deal with side channels and imperfections that are unavoidable in the implementation of the QKD protocols. After all, in implementations we are not sending 'qubits', the quantum equivalent of classical bits, but real optical signals that have a rich internal structure.

As for applications, it is desirable to go beyond the simple point-to-point QKD connection and I will present research done within the European Consortium SEC-OQC [4] that builds a network demonstrator using trusted repeater stations in Vienna. This demonstrator involves the development of optical technology for the QKD implementation, but also the development of key management structures and routing protocols that are compatible with high-security application scenarios.

References

1. Lütkenhaus, N.: Secret keys from quantum correlations. Informatik - Forschung und Entwicklung 21, 29–37 (2006)
2. Lo, H.K., Lütkenhaus, N.: Quantum cryptography: from theory to practice. Physics in Canada 63, 191–196 (2007)
3. Scarani, V., Bechmann-Pasquinucci, H., Cerf, N.J., Dušek, M., Lütkenhaus, N., Peev, M.: A framework for practical quantum cryptography,
http://arxiv.org/abs/quant-ph/0802.4155
4. http://www.secoqc.net

R. Safavi-Naini (Ed.): ICITS 2008, LNCS 5155, p. 120, 2008.
© Springer-Verlag Berlin Heidelberg 2008

Susceptible Two-Party Quantum Computations

Andreas Jakoby[1,*], Maciej Liśkiewicz[1,**], and Aleksander Mądry[2]

[1] Institute of Theoretical Computer Science, University of Lübeck, Germany
liskiewi@tcs.uni-luebeck.de
[2] Massachusetts Institute of Technology, Cambridge, MA, USA

Abstract. In secure two-party function evaluation Alice holding initially a secret input x and Bob having a secret input y communicate to determine a prescribed function $f(x, y)$ in such a way that after the computation Bob learns $f(x, y)$ but nothing more about x other than he could deduce from y and $f(x, y)$ alone, and Alice learns nothing. Unconditionally secure function evaluation is known to be essentially impossible even in the quantum world. In this paper we introduce a new, weakened, model for security in two-party quantum computations. In our model – we call it susceptible function computation – if one party learns something about the input of the other one with advantage ε then the probability that the correct value $f(x, y)$ is computed, when the protocol completes, is at most $1 - \delta(\varepsilon)$, for some function δ of ε. Thus, this model allows to measure the trade-off between the advantage of a dishonest party and the error induced by its attack. Furthermore, we present a protocol for computing the one-out-of-two oblivious transfer function that achieves a quadratic trade-off i.e. $\delta = \Omega(\varepsilon^2)$.

1 Introduction

In two-party computation, Alice holding initially a private (i.e., secret) input $x \in \{0, 1\}^n$ and Bob having a private input $y \in \{0, 1\}^m$ communicate to determine a given function $f(x, y) \in \{0, 1\}^p$. In the standard *one-sided* setting the computation is secure if the, possible malicious, parties with unbounded computing power perform a communication protocol in such a way that (1) at the end of an honest execution of the protocol Bob learns the value $f(x, y)$ unambiguously (2) no matter what Bob does he cannot learn anything more about x other than what follows from the values of y and $f(x, y)$, and (3) no matter what Alice does, she learns nothing.

In [6] Beimel, Malkin, and Micali have given a combinatorial characterization of all securely computable functions in classical setting. It is proved there that f can be computed securely if and only if there do not exist inputs x_0, x_1, y_0, y_1 such that $f(x_0, y_0) = f(x_1, y_0)$ and $f(x_0, y_1) \neq f(x_1, y_1)$. Unfortunately, almost all useful functions fail to satisfy this criterion.

---

* Part of this work was done during the stay of the first author at the University of Freiburg, Germany.
** On leave from Instytut Informatyki, Uniwersytet Wrocławski, Poland.

R. Safavi-Naini (Ed.): ICITS 2008, LNCS 5155, pp. 121–136, 2008.
© Springer-Verlag Berlin Heidelberg 2008

An important example of a function that cannot be computed in such way is the one-out-of-two oblivious transfer function OT defined as follows: let Alice hold initially two secret bits a_0, a_1 and let Bob have a secret selection bit i. Then we define $OT((a_0, a_1), i) = a_i$. The problem has been proposed in [16,15,12] as a generalization of Rabin's notion for oblivious transfer [22]. Oblivious transfer is a primitive of central importance particularly in secure two-party and multi-party computations. It is well known ([18,9]) that OT can be used as a basic component to construct protocols solving more sophisticated tasks of secure computations such as two-party oblivious circuit evaluation.

The impossibility of (unconditionally) secure function computations in the *classical* setting rises a question whether, and if so - in which way, *quantum* cryptography can ensure the security. Indeed, much interest has been devoted to develop quantum two-party protocols [3,4,8,14,13,10,7,23], some of which were claimed to be unconditionally secure [10,7,23]. However, in his paper [21] Lo proved that such (unconditionally) secure computations of all non-trivial functions are impossible even in quantum setting. As a corollary, a possibility of a secure quantum computation of the one-out-of-two oblivious transfer function OT is ruled out.

Moreover, Lo [21] generalized his impossibility result to non-ideal protocols, being ones that may violate the security constraints (1)-(3) slightly. In his 'non-ideal' model the requirements are relaxed as follows:

(1') The density matrix that Bob has at the end of the protocol can be slightly different from an eigenstate of the measurement operator that he is supposed to use (thus, the correctness with probability 1 is not guaranteed any more, even if parties follow the protocol honestly).

(2') There is allowed a small probability of Alice's distinguishing between different Bob's inputs.

(3') There is allowed also a small probability of Bob's distinguishing between different Alice's inputs.

So, intuitively, the result of Lo states that there is no quantum protocol for computing any non-trivial function such that its correctness is high and the information leakage is small.

In this paper we consider a slightly different relaxation of ideal case of the security requirements for the one-sided two-party computation. Our model, we call it *susceptible function computation*, requires the constraint (1) (i.e. an honest execution of the protocol computes $f(x, y)$ correctly) but it allows, even huge information gain by a cheater. However, it requires that if the leakage is big then the probability that Bob computes the correct value $f(x, y)$ is proportionally small. In other words (precise definition will be given in Section 2), for a function $\delta(\cdot)$ we require that for all inputs x and y

(a) If both parties follow the protocol then at the end of the computation Bob learns the value $f(x, y)$ unambiguously.

(b) If Alice learns y with advantage ε then the probability that Bob computes the correct value $f(x,y)$ at the end of the protocol, is at most $1 - \delta(\varepsilon)$, for some function δ of ε.

(c) If Bob with advantage ε learns about x more than what follows from the values of y and $f(x,y)$ then the probability that Bob is able to compute correctly the value $f(x,y)$ is at most $1 - \delta(\varepsilon)$.

Particularly, if both Alice and Bob honestly perform a $\delta(\varepsilon)$-susceptible protocol, for an appropriate function δ, then Bob learns the value $f(x,y)$ correctly and he gains no additional information about x and Alice learns nothing about y. Note, that in our model Bob cannot get full knowledge about x; otherwise he would be able to compute $f(x,y)$ correctly, what contradicts requirement (c).

Intuitively, our model investigates the security of two-party computations when, for some external reasons, the correct computation of $f(x,y)$ is desired by both parties that are, nevertheless, curious to acquire additional knowledge about the input of the other party. To get this additional information a cheating party may arbitrarily deviate from the protocol.[1] But, the key feature of our model is that it imposes a trade-off between the addition knowledge that a cheating party can infer and the correctness of the value $f(x,y)$ computed by Bob. Particularly, if for given Alice's input x and Bob's input y the parties need to compute the correct value $f(x,y)$ with probability 1 then for any strategy used by a cheating party he or she is not able to gain any additional information. However, if for some external reasons, it is sufficient that the protocol may compute the correct value with probability (at least) $1 - \varepsilon$ then a cheater may get some (limited) additional information, and the amount of information is bounded by $\delta(\varepsilon)$.

The main result of this paper states that for the OT function there exists a susceptible protocol with $\delta(\varepsilon) = \Omega(\varepsilon^2)$. Hence, we show that a non-trivial function can be computed $\Omega(\varepsilon^2)$-susceptible. That is, we give an OT protocol which, speaking informally (precise definitions are presented in Section 3), fulfills the following properties.

- If both Alice having initially bits a_0, a_1 and Bob having bit i are honest then Bob learns the selected bit a_i, but he gains no further information about the other bit and Alice learns nothing.
- If Bob is honest and has a bit i and Alice learns i with advantage ε then for all input bits $a_0, a_1 \in \{0,1\}$ the probability that Bob computes the correct value a_i, when the protocol completes, is at most $1 - \Omega(\varepsilon^2)$.
- If Alice is honest and has bits a_0, a_1 then for every input bit $i \in \{0,1\}$ it is true that if Bob can predict the value a_{1-i} with advantage ε then the probability that Bob learns correctly a_i is at most $1 - \Omega(\varepsilon^2)$.

Such a model of function evaluation is new and there exists no *classical* counterpart of such susceptible two-party computations. This follows from a

---

[1] This is in contrast to honest-but-curious model, where parties have to follow the protocol faithfully.

combinatorial characterization of functions securely computable in the honest-but-curious model given by Beaver [5] and Kushilevitz [20] as well as from the characterization theorem of privately computable functions in a weak sense by Chor and Kushilevitz [11].

Though these papers study the so called *two-sided* setting, in which both parties learn the result of the function when the protocol is completed, we can apply them for the one-sided model for slightly modified functions: we replace the original function $f(x, y)$ by $r \oplus f(x, y)$ where r is an additional Bob's input and $\oplus$ denotes the bitwise xor-function. Now, using this modification one can conclude from [5,20] that if a classical (one-sided) protocol computes OT correctly with probability 1 then its information leakage is strictly greater than 0.

Moreover, from [11] we get that if a classical protocol computes OT correctly with probability $1 - \varepsilon$, then one of the parties can learn something about the input of the other one with advantage at least $\frac{1}{2} - \varepsilon$. The characterization from [11] holds for honest-but-curious players, but we can apply it also to the malicious setting: we just make the malicious party to use the honest-but-curious strategy to cheat. Thus, the theorem by Chor and Kushilevitz can also be used to analyze even malicious attacks. Clearly, the above assertions invalidate existence of any susceptible two-party protocols in classical setting.

Comparison to Previous Work. For secure two-party computations two models are considered in the literature. In the first one, the *honest-but-curious* model, we assume that the players never deviate from the given protocol but try to acquire knowledge about the input of the other player only by observing the communication. In the second setting, the *malicious* model, Alice or Bob may arbitrarily deviate from the protocol to defeat the security constraints. Moreover, depending on the computational power of the players we distinguish between computationally security and information theoretically security. In the first case we assume that any player is computationally bounded and in the second case we do not restrict the computational power of the players.

Recall, that in the classical malicious model, only few (trivial) functions can be computed securely in the information theoretic setting ([6]). The similar holds also for the honest-but-curious model. This follows from the characterization by Beaver [5] and Kushilevitz [20]. In [19] Klauck shows that in the honest-but-curious model quantum computations do not help. He proves that every function that can be computed securely using a quantum protocol can also be computed securely by a deterministic protocol.[2] On the other hand, he shows that allowing a small leakage, quantum communication allows us to compute Boolean functions which are not securely computable in the classical honest-but-curious model.

As we already mentioned, [21] proved that for quantum protocols in malicious setting it is impossible to compute securely any non-trivial function. In the light of this fact, Hardy and Kent [17] and independently Aharonov et al. [2], have introduced the notion of cheat sensitive protocols which, instead of unconditional

---

[2] In the literature one calls secure computations in the honest-but-curious model also private computations.

security, give only a guarantee that if one party cheats then the other has a proportional probability of detecting the mistrustful party. The result of Aharonov
et al. [2] presents a protocol for quantum bit commitment they call it quantum
bit escrow that ensures that whenever one party cheats with advantage ε then,
at the end of the protocol, there exists a test that can be performed by the other
party that detects the cheating with probability $\Omega(\varepsilon^2)$. However, the drawback
of this protocol is that only one party can perform the test i.e. only one party can
check whether the other cheated, and there is no mechanism that would allow
fair resolving of this conflict. The authors state finding a protocol without this
drawback as an open problem. Also the protocol presented by Hardy and Kent
[17] is a weak variant of cheat sensitive quantim bit commitment in the sense that
either Alice or Bob can detect a cheating party with non-zero probability. From
this perspective, our result can be seen as a cheat sensitive protocol for oblivious
transfer (which subsumes bit commitment) with $\Omega(\varepsilon^2)$ trade-off, provided there
is some way of allowing the party to test whether Bob computed correct value.
Unfortunately, since we do not know how to implement such mechanism, the
open problem is still unsettled.

2   Preliminaries

We assume that the reader is already familiar with the basics of quantum cryptography (see [2] for a description of the model and results that will be helpful).
The model of quantum two-party computation we use in this paper is essentially
the same as defined in [2].

For a mixed quantum state ρ and a measurement $\mathcal{O}$ on ρ, let $\rho^{\mathcal{O}}$ denote the
classical distribution on the possible results obtained by measuring ρ accord-
ing to $\mathcal{O} = \{O_j\}_j$, i.e. $\rho^{\mathcal{O}}$ is some distribution $p_1, \ldots, p_t$ where p_j denotes the
probability that we get result j and O_j are projections on the orthonormal sub-
spaces corresponding to j. We use L_1-norm to measure distance between two
probability distributions $p = (p_1, \ldots, p_t)$ and $q = (q_1, \ldots, q_t)$ over $\{1, 2, \ldots, t\}$:
$|p - q|_1 = \frac{1}{2} \sum_{i=1}^{t} |p_i - q_i|$.

In the following we investigate one sided two party quantum protocols $F =
(A, B)$, i.e. let x denote the input of Alice and y denote the input of Bob then at
the end of the protocol Bob knows the result $F(x, y)$ of the protocol. By purifica-
tion we can assume that each protocol consists of two phases. In the first phase,
called quantum phase, both parties perform only unitary transformations on the
quantum states. In the second phase both parties only perform a measurement
and maybe some computations on classical bits.

We say that a quantum protocol $F = (A, B)$ for computing the function f is
$\delta(\varepsilon)$-susceptible with respect to Alice, if for every strategy A' used by Alice the
protocol $F' = (A', B)$ fulfills the following condition: *Let $\rho_A^{x,y}$ denote a reduced
density matrix in Alice's hand at the end of the quantum phase of Alice and let
$\mathcal{O}$ be the measurement of y by Alice. Then for all x and y it is true: if for some*

y' with $y \neq y'$ it holds that $|(\rho_A^{x,y})^{\mathcal{O}} - (\rho_A^{x,y'})^{\mathcal{O}}|_1 \geq \varepsilon$ then the probability that Bob computes the correct value of $f(x,y)$ is at most $1 - \delta(\varepsilon)$, i.e. $\Pr[F'(x,y) = f(x,y)] \leq 1 - \delta(\varepsilon)$.

We say that $F = (A, B)$ is $\delta(\varepsilon)$-susceptible with respect to Bob, if for every strategy B' used by Bob the protocol $F' = (A, B')$ fulfills the following condition: Let $\rho_B^{x,y}$ denote a reduced density matrix in Bob's hand at the end of the quantum phase of Bob and let $\mathcal{O}$ be the measurement of x by Bob. Then for all y and for all x it is true: if for some $x' \neq x$ with $f(x,y) = f(x',y)$ it holds that $|(\rho_B^{x,y})^{\mathcal{O}} - (\rho_B^{x',y})^{\mathcal{O}}|_1 \geq \varepsilon$ then the probability that Bob computes the correct value of $f(x,y)$ is at most $1 - \delta(\varepsilon)$.

Both probabilities are taken over the random inputs of all the parties.

Definition 1. *Let $\delta(\varepsilon)$ be a function in ε. A quantum protocol F for computing f is $\delta(\varepsilon)$-susceptible if the following conditions hold:*

1. *If both parties follow F then Bob computes f correctly, i.e. $\Pr[F(x,y) = f(x,y)] = 1$ for all x and y,*

2. *F is $\delta(\varepsilon)$-susceptible with respect to Alice, and*

3. *F is $\delta(\varepsilon)$-susceptible with respect to Bob.*

We recall that we are interested in unconditional security, so in particular the above definition does not restrict the computational power of adversaries.

Let $|0\rangle, |1\rangle$ be an encoding of classical bits in our computational (perpendicular) basis. Let $|0_\times\rangle = \frac{1}{\sqrt{2}}(|0\rangle - |1\rangle)$, $|1_\times\rangle = \frac{1}{\sqrt{2}}(|0\rangle + |1\rangle)$ be an encoding of classical bits in diagonal basis. By R_α, $\alpha \in \{0, \frac{1}{2}, 1\}$, we denote the unitary operation of rotation by an angle of $\alpha \cdot \pi/2$. More formally:

$$R_\alpha := \begin{pmatrix} \cos(\alpha \cdot \frac{\pi}{2}) & \sin(\alpha \cdot \frac{\pi}{2}) \\ -\sin(\alpha \cdot \frac{\pi}{2}) & \cos(\alpha \cdot \frac{\pi}{2}) \end{pmatrix}$$

We should note that this operation allows us to exchange between the bit encoding in perpendicular and in diagonal basis. Moreover, by applying R_1 we can flip the value of the bit encoded in any of those two bases.

Let $||A||_t = \mathrm{tr}(\sqrt{A^\dagger A})$, where $\mathrm{tr}(A)$ denotes trace of matrix A. A fundamental theorem gives us a bound on L_1-norm for the probability distributions on the measurement results:

Theorem 1 (see [1]). *Let ρ_0, ρ_1 be two density matrices on the same Hilbert space $\mathcal{H}$. Then for any generalized measurement $\mathcal{O}$ $|\rho_0^{\mathcal{O}} - \rho_1^{\mathcal{O}}|_1 \leq \frac{1}{2}||\rho_0 - \rho_1||_t$. This bound is tight and the orthogonal measurement $\mathcal{O}$ that projects a state on the eigenvectors of $\rho_0 - \rho_1$ achieves it.*

A well-known result states that if $|\phi_1\rangle$, $|\phi_2\rangle$ are pure states, then $|| \, |\phi_1\rangle\langle\phi_1| - |\phi_2\rangle\langle\phi_2| \, ||_t = 2\sqrt{1 - |\langle\phi_1|\phi_2\rangle|^2}$.

3 $\Omega(\varepsilon^2)$-Susceptible Oblivious Transfer

In this section we present a $\Omega(\varepsilon^2)$-susceptible protocol for OT.

Protocol 1 (Susceptible QOT). Input $A : a_0, a_1 \in \{0,1\}, B : i \in \{0,1\}$;
Output $B : a_i$.

1. A chooses randomly $\alpha \in_R \{0, \frac{1}{2}\}$ and $h \in_R \{0,1\}$ and sends to B:
$$R_\alpha |a_1 \oplus h\rangle \otimes R_\alpha |a_0 \oplus h\rangle$$
2. B receives $|\Phi_1\rangle \otimes |\Phi_0\rangle$, chooses randomly $\beta \in_R \{0,1\}$ and sends $R_\beta |\Phi_i\rangle$ back to A.
3. A receives $|\Phi\rangle$, computes $R_\alpha^{-1}|\Phi\rangle$, measures the state in computational basis obtaining the result n and sends $m = n \oplus h$ to B.
4. B receives m and computes $a_i = m \oplus \beta$.

Here, as usually, $\oplus$ denotes xor. To see that this protocol computes OT correctly if both parties are honest we remind that the operator $R_\alpha R_\beta$ commutes with R_α^{-1} (this is not true in general, although it is true in two dimensions) and that R_β is (up to a phase) a NOT-gate conditioned on β. We will now focus on the question whether Protocol 1 still retains security if we use it against malicious parties. The following theorem follows from Lemma 1 and 2 which will be proven in the remaining part of this section:

Theorem 2. Protocol 1 is a $\Omega(\varepsilon^2)$-susceptible protocol for OT.

3.1   Malicious Alice

Lemma 1. Let Alice and Bob perform Protocol 1 and assume Bob is honest and deposits a bit i, with $\Pr[i = 0] = 1/2$. Then for every strategy used by Alice, every value a' Bob learns at the end of the computation it holds that for all $a_0, a_1 \in \{0,1\}$ and for any generalized measurement $\mathcal{O}$

$$\text{if } |(\rho_A^0)^{\mathcal{O}} - (\rho_A^1)^{\mathcal{O}}|_1 \geq \varepsilon \text{ then } \Pr_{i\in_R\{0,1\}}[a' = a_i] \leq 1 - c_A \cdot \varepsilon^2 .$$

where ρ_A^j denotes a reduced density matrix in Alice hand at the end of the protocol if Bob's input bit is given by $i := j$ and $c_A > 0$ is a constant independent of Alice's strategy.

Proof: Any cheating strategy $\mathcal{A}$ of Alice corresponding to her input a_0, a_1 can be described as preparing some state $|\Phi\rangle = \sum_{x\in\{0,1\}^2} |v_x, x\rangle$, sending the two right-most qubits to Bob and performing some measurement $\mathcal{O} = \{H_0, H_1, H_2, H_3\}$ on this what she gets back after Bob's round, where H_0, H_1, H_2, H_3 are four pairwise orthogonal subspaces being a division of whole Hilbert space that comes into play, such that, for $l, k = 0, 1$, if our measurement indicates the outcome corresponding to H_{2k+l} then it reflects Alice's belief that $i = l$ and that the message $m = k$ should be sent to Bob. We emphasis that we allow Alice's strategy to depend on her input.

The outline of the proof is the following. We first bond the fact that $\mathcal{A}$ achieves some advantage ε to a certain relation between $\mathcal{H}$ and $|\Phi\rangle$. Then we show that this relation implies at least $c_A \cdot \varepsilon^2$ of noise in the value of a' computed by Bob.

We first consider the case when $a_0 \oplus a_1 = 0$. Clearly, in this case $m \oplus a_0 = m \oplus a_1 = \beta$. So if Alice manages to compute m that is correct i.e. $a' = m \oplus \beta = a_i$ then she also knows the value of β. Thus, we can compute the probability of $\mathcal{A}$ computing the correct result, by computing the the probability that she can indicate the value of β correctly.

Let $\rho_{a,b}$ be a density matrix of Alice's system after Bob's round, corresponding to $i = a$ and $\beta = b$. After some calculations we get:

$$\rho_{0,0} = \sum_{x=(x_1,x_2)\in\{0,1\}^2} |v_x x_1\rangle\langle v_x x_1|$$
$$+ |v_{00}0\rangle\langle v_{10}1| + |v_{10}1\rangle\langle v_{00}0| + |v_{11}1\rangle\langle v_{01}0| + |v_{01}0\rangle\langle v_{11}1|$$
$$\rho_{0,1} = \sum_{x=(x_1,x_2)\in\{0,1\}^2} |v_x \overline{x_1}\rangle\langle v_x \overline{x_1}|$$
$$- |v_{00}1\rangle\langle v_{10}0| - |v_{10}0\rangle\langle v_{00}1| - |v_{11}0\rangle\langle v_{01}1| - |v_{01}1\rangle\langle v_{11}0|$$
$$\rho_{1,0} = \sum_{x=(x_1,x_2)\in\{0,1\}^2} |v_x x_2\rangle\langle v_x x_2|$$
$$+ |v_{00}0\rangle\langle v_{01}1| + |v_{01}1\rangle\langle v_{00}0| + |v_{11}1\rangle\langle v_{10}0| + |v_{10}0\rangle\langle v_{11}1|$$
$$\rho_{1,1} = \sum_{x=(x_1,x_2)\in\{0,1\}^2} |v_x \overline{x_2}\rangle\langle v_x \overline{x_2}|$$
$$- |v_{00}1\rangle\langle v_{01}0| - |v_{01}0\rangle\langle v_{00}1| - |v_{11}0\rangle\langle v_{10}1| - |v_{10}1\rangle\langle v_{11}0| .$$

where $\overline{x_t}$ means flipping bit x_t, i.e. $\overline{x_t} = 1 - x_t$.

We look first onto Alice's advantage that she can achieve. In order to cheat, Alice has to distinguish between two density matrices $\gamma_l = \frac{1}{2}\rho_{l,0} + \frac{1}{2}\rho_{l,1}$ for $l \in \{0,1\}$, where γ_l corresponds to $i = l$. By examination of the difference of those matrices we get, after some calculations, that:

$$\gamma_0 - \gamma_1 = \frac{1}{2}|V_S 0\rangle\langle V_A 1| + \frac{1}{2}|V_A 1\rangle\langle V_S 0| - \frac{1}{2}|V_S 1\rangle\langle V_A 0| - \frac{1}{2}|V_A 0\rangle\langle V_S 1|$$

where $|V_S\rangle = |v_{00}\rangle + |v_{11}\rangle$ and $|V_A\rangle = |v_{10}\rangle - |v_{01}\rangle$. One can easily show that the advantage $\varepsilon := |(\rho_A^0)^{\mathcal{O}} - (\rho_A^1)^{\mathcal{O}}|_1$ of Alice is at most $\sum_{l=0}^{3} \sigma_l$ where

$$\sigma_l = |\mathrm{tr}(H_l(\gamma_0 - \gamma_1)H_l^\dagger)|$$
$$\leq \sum_{j\in\{0,1\}} \tfrac{1}{2}|tr(H_l(|V_S(j-1)\rangle\langle V_A j| + |V_A j\rangle\langle V_S(j-1)|)H_l^\dagger)|$$
$$\leq \sum_{j\in\{0,1\}} (|\langle O_j^l|V_A j\rangle| \cdot |\langle V_S(1-j)|O_j^l\rangle|)$$
$$\leq \sum_{j\in\{0,1\}} |\langle O_j^l|V_A j\rangle|$$

and $|O_j^l\rangle$ is an orthogonal, normalized projection of $|V_A j\rangle$ onto subspace H_l. The second inequality is true because we have $\mathrm{tr}(H_l|V_A j\rangle\langle\psi|H_l^\dagger) = \langle O_j^l|V_A j\rangle\langle\psi|O_j^l\rangle$ for every state $|\psi\rangle$.

Let j_l be the index for which $|\langle O_{j_l}^l|V_A j_l\rangle| \geq |\langle O_{1-j_l}^l|V_A(1-j_l)\rangle|$. Clearly, $\sigma_l \leq 2|\langle O_{j_l}^l|V_A j_l\rangle|$. Moreover, we assume that $\sigma_0 + \sigma_1 \geq \sigma_2 + \sigma_3$. If this is not the case we could satisfy this condition by altering the strategy $\mathcal{A}$ of Alice (by appropriate rotation of her basis) in such a way that the definitions of H_k and H_{k+2} would swap leaving everything else unchanged.

We look now on the probability of obtaining the correct result by Alice. The probability p_0 of Alice getting outcome that convinces her that $\beta = 0$ in case when actually $\beta = 1$ is at least

$$p_0 \geq \tfrac{1}{2}\langle O^0_{j_0}|\rho_{0,1}|O^0_{j_0}\rangle + \tfrac{1}{2}\langle O^0_{j_0}|\rho_{1,1}|O^0_{j_0}\rangle =$$
$$\tfrac{1}{2}|\langle O^0_{j_0}|v_{00}1\rangle - \langle O^0_{j_0}|v_{01}0\rangle|^2 + \tfrac{1}{2}|\langle O^0_{j_0}|v_{00}1\rangle - \langle O^0_{j_0}|v_{10}0\rangle|^2$$
$$+ \tfrac{1}{2}|\langle O^0_{j_0}|v_{11}0\rangle - \langle O^0_{j_0}|v_{01}1\rangle|^2 + \tfrac{1}{2}|\langle O^0_{j_0}|v_{11}0\rangle - \langle O^0_{j_0}|v_{10}1\rangle|^2 .$$

So, by inequality $|a - b|^2 + |a - c|^2 \geq \tfrac{1}{2}|b - c|^2$ we get that

$$p_0 \geq \tfrac{1}{4}|\langle O^0_{j_0}|v_{01}0\rangle - \langle O^0_{j_0}|v_{10}0\rangle|^2 + \tfrac{1}{4}|\langle O^0_{j_0}|v_{01}1\rangle - \langle O^0_{j_0}|v_{10}1\rangle|^2$$
$$= \tfrac{1}{4}|\langle O^0_{j_0}|V_A0\rangle|^2 + \tfrac{1}{4}|\langle O^0_{j_0}|V_A1\rangle|^2 \geq \tfrac{1}{16}\sigma_0^2.$$

Similar calculation of the probability p_1 of getting outcome convincing Alice that $\beta = 1$ when actually $\beta = 0$ yields that the probability of computing wrong result is at least

$$\Pr[a' \neq a_i] = \Pr[\beta \oplus m \neq a_i] \geq \frac{1}{16}(\sigma_0^2 + \sigma_1^2) \geq \frac{1}{256}(\textstyle\sum_{l=0}^{3}\sigma_l)^2.$$

Hence, the lemma holds for the case $a_0 \oplus a_1 = 0$.

Since in case of $a_0 \oplus a_1 = 1$ the reasoning is completely analogous - we exchange only the roles of $|V_S\rangle$ and $|V_A\rangle$ and Alice has to know the value of $\beta \oplus i$, instead of β in order to give the correct answer to Bob, the proof is concluded. ∎

In fact, the above lemma is asymptotically tight since we can design a strategy of Alice which allows her to meet the quadratical bound imposed by the above lemma. To see this, consider $|\Phi\rangle = \sqrt{1 - \Delta}|000\rangle + \sqrt{\Delta}|110\rangle$. Intuitively, we label the symmetric and anti-symmetric part of $|\Phi\rangle$ with 0 and 1. Let $H_2 = |01\rangle\langle 01|$, $H_3 = 0$. One can easily calculate that

$$\rho_{0,0} = (1 - \Delta)|00\rangle\langle 00| + \sqrt{\Delta(1 - \Delta)}(|00\rangle\langle 11| + |11\rangle\langle 00|) + \Delta|11\rangle\langle 11|$$

$$\rho_{1,0} = (1 - \Delta)|00\rangle\langle 00| + \Delta|10\rangle\langle 10|$$

and therefore $||\rho_{0,0} - \rho_{1,0}||_t \geq \sqrt{\Delta(1 - \Delta)} - 2\Delta$. So, by Theorem 1 there exists a measurement $\{H_0, H_1\}$ allowing us to distinguish between those two density matrices with $\sqrt{\Delta(1 - \Delta)} - 2\Delta$ accuracy and moreover $H_2, H_3 \perp H_0, H_1$ since $\text{tr}(H_2\rho_{0,0}H_2^\dagger) = \text{tr}(H_2\rho_{1,0}H_2^\dagger) = 0$. Now, let $M = \{H_0, H_1, H_2, H_3\}$ be Alice's measurement. To cheat, we use the following strategy $\mathcal{A}$ corresponding to her input $a_0 = a_1 = 0$. Alice sends the last two qubits of $|\Phi\rangle$ to Bob, after receiving the qubit back she applies the measurement M. If the outcome is H_2 then she answers $m = a_0 \oplus \beta = 1$ to Bob and sets $i' = 0$ with probability $\tfrac{1}{2}$, in the other case she sends $m = a_0 \oplus \beta = 0$ to Bob and according to the outcome being 0 or 1 she sets $i' = 0$ ($i' = 1$).

To see that this strategy gives correct result with probability greater than $1 - \frac{\Delta}{2}$ we should note that probability of outcome H_2 in case of $\beta = 0$ is 0 and in case of $\beta = 1$ is $1 - \Delta$. On the other hand, since $\beta = 0$ with probability $\frac{1}{2}$, Alice's advantage in determining the input of Bob is greater than $\frac{1}{2}\sqrt{\Delta} - \frac{3}{2}\Delta$. So, by setting $\varepsilon = \frac{1}{2}\sqrt{\Delta} - \frac{3}{2}\Delta$, we get that the presented strategy proves that the Protocol 1 cannot be $\delta(\varepsilon)$ susceptible for $\delta(\varepsilon) \geq 2\varepsilon^2$.

3.2 Malicious Bob

Now, we analyze Bob's possibility of cheating. Our goal is to show:

Lemma 2. *Let Alice and Bob perform Protocol 1. Assume Alice is honest and deposits bits a_0, a_1, with $\Pr[a_0 = 0] = \Pr[a_1 = 0] = 1/2$. Let i denote Bob's input bit. Then for every strategy $\mathcal{B}$ used by Bob and any value a_i' computed by Bob it holds that for $i = 0$*

$$\text{if } |(\rho_B^{a_0 a_1, 0})^{\mathcal{O}} - (\rho_B^{a_0 \bar{a}_1, 0})^{\mathcal{O}}|_1 \geq \varepsilon \text{ then } \Pr_{a_0, a_1 \in_R \{0,1\}}[a_0' = a_0] \leq 1 - c_B \varepsilon^2$$

and for $i = 1$

$$\text{if } |(\rho_B^{a_0 a_1, 1})^{\mathcal{O}} - (\rho_B^{\bar{a}_0 a_1, 1})^{\mathcal{O}}|_1 \leq \varepsilon \text{ then } \Pr_{a_0, a_1 \in_R \{0,1\}}[a_1' = a_1] \geq 1 - c_B \varepsilon^2.$$

where $\rho_B^{a_0 a_1, i}$ denotes a reduced density matrix in Bob's hand at the end of the protocol and $c_B > 0$ is a constant independent of Bob's strategy.

Proof: Consider some malicious strategy $\mathcal{B}$ of Bob. Wlog we may assume that $i = 0$ - the case of $i = 1$ is completely symmetric. In the following we skip the superscript i, i.e. let $\rho_B^{a_0 a_1}$ denote $\rho_B^{a_0 a_1, i}$, for short. Our aim is to show that

$$\text{if } |(\rho_B^{a_0 a_1})^{\mathcal{O}} - (\rho_B^{\bar{a}_0 a_1})^{\mathcal{O}}|_1 \leq \varepsilon \text{ then } \Pr_{a_0, a_1 \in_R \{0,1\}}[a' \neq a_0] \leq c_B \varepsilon^2.$$

Strategy $\mathcal{B}$ can be think of as a two step process. First a unitary transformation U is acting on $|\Phi_{a_0, a_1, h}\rangle = |v\rangle \otimes R_\alpha |a_1 \oplus h\rangle \otimes R_\alpha |a_0 \oplus h\rangle$, where v is an ancillary state[3]. Next the last qubit of $U(|\Phi_{a_0, a_1, h}\rangle)$ is sent to Alice[4], she performs step 3 of Protocol 1 on these qubit and sends the classical bit m back to Bob. Upon receiving m, Bob executes the second part of his attack: he performs some arbitrary measurement $\mathcal{O} = \{H_0, H_1, H_2, H_3\}$, where outcome corresponding to subspace H_{2l+k} implies Bob's believe that $a_0' = l$ and $a_1' = k$.

The unitary transformation U can be described by a set of vectors $\{V_k^{l,j}\}$ such that $U(|v\rangle \otimes |l, j\rangle) = |V_0^{l,j}\rangle \otimes |0\rangle + |V_1^{l,j}\rangle \otimes |1\rangle$. Or alternatively in diagonal basis, by a set of vectors $\{W_k^{l,j}\}$ such that $U(|v\rangle \otimes |l_\times, j_\times\rangle) = |W_0^{l,j}\rangle \otimes |0_\times\rangle + |W_1^{l,j}\rangle \otimes |1_\times\rangle$.

---

[3] Note that this does not restrict Bob's power. Particularly, when Bob tries to make a measurement in the first step then using standard techniques we can move this measurement to the second step.

[4] We can assume wlog that the last qubit is sent since U is arbitrary.

We present now, an intuitive, brief summary of the proof. Informally, we can think of U as about some kind of disturbance of the qubit $R_\alpha|a_0 \oplus h\rangle$ being sent back to Alice. First, we will show that in order to cheat Bob's U has to accumulate after Step 2, till the end of the protocol, some information about the value of $a_0 \oplus h$ hidden in this qubit. On the other hand, to get the proper result i.e. the value of a_0, this qubit (which is sent back to Alice) has to still contain actual information about encoded value being disturbed at the smallest possible degree. That implies for Bob a necessity of some sort of partial cloning of that qubit, which turns out to impose the desired bounds on possible cheating. We show this by first reducing the task of cloning to one where no additional hint in the form of $R_\alpha|a_1 \oplus h\rangle$ is provided and then we analyze this simplified process. In this way, this proof gives us a sort of quantitative non-cloning theorem. Although, it seems to concern only our particular implementation of the protocol, we believe that this scenario is useful enough to be of independent interests.

We analyze first Bob's advantage i.e. his information gain about a_1. Wlog we may assume that Bob can distinguish better between two values of a_1 if $a_0 = 0$. That is

$$|(\rho_B^{00})^{\mathcal{O}} - (\rho_B^{01})^{\mathcal{O}}|_1 \geq |(\rho_B^{10})^{\mathcal{O}} - (\rho_B^{11})^{\mathcal{O}}|_1 .$$

Let now $\rho_{j,k,l}$ be a density matrix of the system before Bob's final measurement, corresponding to $\alpha = j \cdot \frac{1}{2}$, $h = k$, $a_1 = l$ and $a_0 = 0$. The advantage $\varepsilon = |(\rho_B^{00})^{\mathcal{O}} - (\rho_B^{01})^{\mathcal{O}}|_1$ of Bob in this case can be estimated by Bob's ability to distinguish between the following density matrices:

$$\frac{1}{4}(\rho_{0,0,0} + \rho_{1,0,0} + \rho_{0,1,0} + \rho_{1,1,0}) \quad \text{(case } a_1 = 0\text{), and}$$

$$\frac{1}{4}(\rho_{0,0,1} + \rho_{1,0,1} + \rho_{0,1,1} + \rho_{1,1,1}) \quad \text{(case } a_1 = 1\text{).}$$

Using the triangle inequality we get that for the measurement $\mathcal{O}$ performed by Bob

$$\varepsilon \leq \frac{1}{8}(|\rho_{0,0,0}^{\mathcal{O}} - \rho_{0,1,1}^{\mathcal{O}}|_1 + |\rho_{1,1,0}^{\mathcal{O}} - \rho_{1,0,1}^{\mathcal{O}}|_1 + |\rho_{0,1,0}^{\mathcal{O}} - \rho_{0,0,1}^{\mathcal{O}}|_1 + |\rho_{1,0,0}^{\mathcal{O}} - \rho_{1,1,1}^{\mathcal{O}}|_1). \quad (1)$$

Each component corresponds to different values of α and $h \oplus a_1$. And each component is symmetric to the other in such a way that there exists a straight-forward local transformation for Bob (i.e. appropriate rotation of the computational basis on one or both qubits) which transform any of above components onto another. So, we can assume wlog that the advantage in distinguishing between $\rho_{0,0,0}$ and $\rho_{0,1,1}$, $\varepsilon_0 = |\rho_{0,0,0}^{\mathcal{O}} - \rho_{0,1,1}^{\mathcal{O}}|_1$ is the maximum component in the right-hand side of the inequality (1) and therefore we have $\varepsilon \leq \frac{1}{2}\varepsilon_0$. Let, for short, $\gamma_0 = \rho_{0,0,0}$ and $\gamma_1 = \rho_{0,1,1}$. One can easily calculate that

$$\gamma_0 = |0\rangle\langle 0| \otimes |V_0^{00}\rangle\langle V_0^{00}| + |1\rangle\langle 1| \otimes |V_1^{00}\rangle\langle V_1^{00}| \quad (2)$$

$$\gamma_1 = |0\rangle\langle 0| \otimes |V_1^{01}\rangle\langle V_1^{01}| + |1\rangle\langle 1| \otimes |V_0^{01}\rangle\langle V_0^{01}|. \quad (3)$$

As we can see to each value of m in above density matrices corresponds a pair of vectors which are critical for Bob's cheating. I.e. the better they can be distinguishable by his measurement the greater is his advantage. But, as we will see later, this fact introduces perturbation of the indication of the value of a_0.

First, we take a look on the measurements H_0, H_1 performed by Bob. Let us define σ_{2m+p} for $p, m \in \{0, 1\}$ as follows

$$\sigma_{2m+p} = \begin{cases} |\mathrm{tr}(H_p|0V_p^{0p}\rangle\langle 0V_p^{0p}|H_p^\dagger) - \mathrm{tr}(H_p|0V_{1-p}^{0(1-p)}\rangle\langle 0V_{1-p}^{0(1-p)}|H_p^\dagger)| & \text{if } m = 0, \\ |\mathrm{tr}(H_p|1V_{1-p}^{0p}\rangle\langle 1V_{1-p}^{0p}|H_p^\dagger) - \mathrm{tr}(H_p|1V_p^{0(1-p)}\rangle\langle 1V_p^{0(1-p)}|H_p^\dagger)| & \text{if } m = 1. \end{cases}$$

Let for $m = 0$, $p_0 \in \{0, 1\}$ be such that $\sigma_{p_0} \geq \sigma_{1-p_0}$ and similarly, for $m = 1$ let $p_1 \in \{0, 1\}$ be such that $\sigma_{2+p_1} \geq \sigma_{2+(1-p_1)}$. Then we get

$$|\gamma_0^{\mathcal{O}} - \gamma_1^{\mathcal{O}}|_1 = \sum_{t=0}^3 |\mathrm{tr}(H_t\gamma_0 H_t^\dagger) - \mathrm{tr}(H_t\gamma_1 H_t^\dagger)|$$
$$\leq 2(\sigma_{p_0} + \sigma_{2+p_1}) + \sum_{t=2}^3 |\mathrm{tr}(H_t\gamma_0 H_t^\dagger) - \mathrm{tr}(H_t\gamma_1 H_t^\dagger)|.$$

We should see first that the second term in the above sum corresponds to advantage in distinguishing between two values of a_1 by measurement H_2, H_3 in case of $a_0 = 0$. But those subspaces reflect Bob's belief that $a_0 = 1$. Therefore, we have that

$$\sum_{t=2}^3 |\mathrm{tr}(H_t\gamma_0 H_t^\dagger) - \mathrm{tr}(H_t\gamma_1 H_t^\dagger)| \leq \Pr_{a_0, a_1 \in_R \{0,1\}}[a_0' \neq a_0 | a_0 = 0].$$

So, we can neglect this term because it is of the order of the square of the advantage (if not then our lemma would be proved). We get: $\frac{\varepsilon_0}{2} \leq \sigma_{p_0} + \sigma_{2+p_1}$.

Now, we define projection O_m as follows. For $m = 0$ let O_0 be the normalized orthogonal projection of $|0V_{p_0}^{0p_0}\rangle$ onto the subspace H_{p_0} if

$$\mathrm{tr}(H_{p_0}|0V_{p_0}^{0p_0}\rangle\langle 0V_{p_0}^{0p_0}|H_{p_0}^\dagger) \geq \mathrm{tr}(H_{p_0}|0V_{1-p_0}^{0(1-p_0)}\rangle\langle 0V_{1-p_0}^{0(1-p_0)}|H_{p_0}^\dagger).$$

Otherwise, let O_0 be the normalized orthogonal projection of $|0V_{1-p_0}^{0(1-p_0)}\rangle$ onto H_{p_0}. Analogously, we define O_1 as a normalized orthogonal projection of $|1V_{1-p_1}^{0p_1}\rangle$ onto the subspace H_{p_1} if

$$\mathrm{tr}(H_{p_1}|1V_{1-p_1}^{0p_1}\rangle\langle 1V_{1-p_1}^{0p}|H_{p_1}^\dagger) \geq \mathrm{tr}(H_{p_1}|1V_{p_1}^{0(1-p_1)}\rangle\langle 1V_{p_1}^{0(1-p_1)}|H_{p_1}^\dagger)$$

else O_1 is a normalized orthogonal projection of $|1V_{p_1}^{0(1-p_1)}\rangle$ onto H_{p_1}. Hence we get

$$\sigma_{p_0} \leq ||\langle 0V_{p_0}^{0p_0}|O_0\rangle|^2 - |\langle 0V_{1-p_0}^{0(1-p_0)}|O_0\rangle|^2|,$$
$$\sigma_{2+p_1} \leq ||\langle 1V_{1-p_1}^{0p_1}|O_1\rangle|^2 - |\langle 1V_{p_1}^{0(1-p_1)}|O_1\rangle|^2|.$$

We proceed now, to investigation of the probability of obtaining the correct result i.e. the correct value of a_0. Recall that $\Pr[a_1 = 0] = \frac{1}{2}$ so the density matrices corresponding to initial configuration of the second qubit - $R_\alpha|a_1 \oplus h\rangle$ is now exactly $\frac{1}{2}|0\rangle\langle 0| + \frac{1}{2}|1\rangle\langle 1|$ even if we know h and α. So, from the point of view of the protocol, as perceived by Bob, those two density matrices are indistinguishable. Therefore, we can substitute the second qubit from the initial configuration with a density matrix $\frac{1}{2}|0\rangle\langle 0| + \frac{1}{2}|1\rangle\langle 1|$ of a random bit r

encoded in perpendicular basis and the probability of obtaining proper result is unchanged.

We analyze now the probability of computing the correct result in case of $r = 0$. Note, that the vectors $\{V_k^{0,j}\}_{k,j}$ still describe U, but vectors $\{W_k^{0j}\}_{k,j}$ are different, they are defined by U acting now on initial configuration $|v\rangle \otimes |0\rangle \otimes R_\alpha|j\rangle$, with $\alpha = \frac{1}{2}$. We investigate the correspondence between $\{V_k^{0j}\}_{k,j}$ and the new vectors. For $j = 0$ we have:

$$U(|v00_\times\rangle) = \tfrac{1}{\sqrt{2}}U(|v00\rangle - |v01\rangle) = \tfrac{1}{\sqrt{2}}(V_0^{00}|0\rangle + V_1^{00}|1\rangle - V_0^{01}|0\rangle - V_1^{01}|1\rangle)$$
$$= \tfrac{1}{2}((V_0^{00} - V_1^{00} - V_0^{01} + V_1^{01})|0_\times\rangle + (V_0^{00} + V_1^{00} - V_0^{01} - V_1^{01})|1_\times\rangle)).$$

Similarly, for $j = 1$ we have:

$$U(|v01_\times\rangle) = \tfrac{1}{\sqrt{2}}U(|v00\rangle + |v01\rangle) = \tfrac{1}{\sqrt{2}}(V_0^{00}|0\rangle + V_1^{00}|1\rangle + V_0^{01}|0\rangle + V_1^{01}|1\rangle)$$
$$= \tfrac{1}{2}((V_0^{00} - V_1^{00} + V_0^{01} - V_1^{01})|0_\times\rangle + (V_0^{00} + V_1^{00} + V_0^{01} + V_1^{01})|1_\times\rangle)).$$

Thus, let us denote these vectors by

$$\widetilde{W}_0^{00} = \frac{1}{2}((V_0^{00} + V_1^{01}) - (V_0^{01} + V_1^{00})), \quad \widetilde{W}_1^{00} = \frac{1}{2}((V_0^{00} - V_1^{01}) - (V_0^{01} - V_1^{00})),$$

$$\widetilde{W}_0^{01} = \frac{1}{2}((V_0^{00} - V_1^{01}) + (V_0^{01} - V_1^{00})), \quad \widetilde{W}_1^{01} = \frac{1}{2}((V_0^{00} + V_1^{01}) + (V_0^{01} + V_1^{00})).$$

In order to obtain the correct result Bob has to distinguish between the density matrices corresponding to two values of a_0. In particular, he has to distinguish between density matrices γ_0', γ_1' corresponding to two possible values of a_0 knowing that $m = 0$. These density matrices are:

$$\gamma_0' = \frac{1}{4}|0\rangle\langle 0| \otimes (|V_0^{00}\rangle\langle V_0^{00}| + |V_1^{01}\rangle\langle V_1^{01}| + |\widetilde{W}_0^{00}\rangle\langle\widetilde{W}_0^{00}| + |\widetilde{W}_1^{01}\rangle\langle\widetilde{W}_1^{01}|), \quad (4)$$

$$\gamma_1' = \frac{1}{4}|0\rangle\langle 0| \otimes (|V_0^{01}\rangle\langle V_0^{01}| + |V_1^{00}\rangle\langle V_1^{00}| + |\widetilde{W}_0^{01}\rangle\langle\widetilde{W}_0^{01}| + |\widetilde{W}_1^{00}\rangle\langle\widetilde{W}_1^{00}|). \quad (5)$$

Now, the probability of failure i.e. the probability that in case of $m = 0$ Bob's measurement indicates that $a_0 = 0$ if in fact it is $a_0 = 1$, is at least

$$\mathrm{tr}(H_{p_0}\gamma_1' H_{p_0}^\dagger) \geq \mathrm{tr}(|O_0\rangle\langle O_0|\gamma_1')$$
$$= \tfrac{1}{4}(|\langle 0V_0^{01}|O_0\rangle|^2 + |\langle 0V_1^{00}|O_0\rangle|^2 + |\langle 0\widetilde{W}_0^{01}|O_0\rangle|^2 + |\langle 0\widetilde{W}_1^{00}|O_0\rangle|^2).$$

But since the fact that $\widetilde{W}_0^{01} = \frac{1}{2}((V_0^{00} - V_1^{01}) + (V_0^{01} - V_1^{00}))$, $\widetilde{W}_1^{00} = \frac{1}{2}((V_0^{00} - V_1^{01}) - (V_0^{01} - V_1^{00}))$, and the parallelogram law ($|a+b|^2 + |a-b|^2 = 2|a|^2 + 2|b|^2$), we have that this probability is at least

$$\tfrac{1}{4}(|\langle 0\widetilde{W}_0^{01}|O_0\rangle|^2 + |\langle 0\widetilde{W}_1^{00}|O_0\rangle|^2) \geq \tfrac{1}{8}|\langle 0V_0^{00}|O_0\rangle - \langle 0V_1^{01}|O_0\rangle|^2$$

$$\geq \tfrac{1}{32}(|\langle 0V_0^{00}|O_0\rangle| - |\langle 0V_1^{01}|O_0\rangle|)^2(|\langle 0V_0^{00}|O_0\rangle| + |\langle 0V_1^{01}|O_0\rangle|)^2$$

$$\geq \tfrac{1}{32}(|\langle 0V_0^{00}|O_0\rangle|^2 - |\langle 0V_1^{01}|O_0\rangle|^2)^2 \geq \tfrac{\sigma_{p_0}^2}{32}.$$

Similarly we analyze density matrices γ_0'', γ_1'' corresponding to two possible values of a_0 knowing that $m = 1$. These density matrices are equal to resp. γ_1' and γ_0' after changing $|0\rangle\langle 0|$ to $|1\rangle\langle 1|$. Now, by repeating completely analogous estimation of failure's probability with usage of vectors $|V_0^{01}\rangle$, $|V_1^{00}\rangle$, $|\widetilde{W}_0^{00}\rangle$, and $|\widetilde{W}_1^{01}\rangle$, we get that this probability is at least $\frac{\sigma_{2+p_1}^2}{32}$. Therefore, since the vectors involved in imposing failure in both cases are distinct, we conclude that $\Pr_{a_1 \in_R \{0,1\}}[a_0' \neq a_0 | r = 0] \geq \frac{\sigma_{p_0}^2 + \sigma_{2+p_1}^2}{32}$. Hence we have

$$\Pr_{a_1 \in_R \{0,1\}}[a_0' \neq a_0]$$
$$= \tfrac{1}{2}\Pr_{a_1 \in_R \{0,1\}}[a_0' \neq a_0 | r = 0] + \tfrac{1}{2}\Pr_{a_1 \in_R \{0,1\}}[a_0' \neq a_0 | r = 1]$$
$$\geq \frac{\sigma_{p_0}^2 + \sigma_{2+p_1}^2}{64} \geq \frac{\varepsilon^2}{128}$$

and the lemma is proved.

Finally, it is worth mentioning that the value of m doesn't need to be correlated in any way with value of a_i. That is, Bob by using entanglement (for instance, straightforward use of Bell states) can make the value of m independent of a_i and still acquire perfect knowledge about a_i. He uses simple error-correction to know whether $m = a_i$ or $m = 1 - a_i$. His problems with determining whether flip has occurred, start only when he wants additionally to accumulate some information about the value of $a_i \oplus h$.   ∎

Once again, it turns out that the quadratic susceptibility is asymptotically optimal. To see that this quadratical bound imposed by the above lemma can be achieved consider the following cheating strategy. Let U^* be such that $U^*(|v\rangle \otimes |l, j\rangle) = |v_j\rangle \otimes |l, j\rangle$. So, $|V_j^{l,j}\rangle = |v_j\rangle \otimes |l\rangle$ and $|V_{1-j}^{l,j}\rangle = 0$. Moreover, let $\langle v_0 | v_1 \rangle = \sqrt{1 - \Delta}$. As we can see, usage of U^* accumulates some information about value of $j = a_0 \oplus h$ by marking it with two non-parallel (therefore possible to distinguish) vectors in Bob's system. We do now the following. We use U^* on $|v\rangle \otimes R_\alpha |a_1 \oplus h\rangle \oplus R_\alpha |a_0 \oplus h\rangle$ and send the last qubit to Alice. When we get the message m which is exactly a_0 with probability[5] of order $1 - \Delta$, we make an optimal measurement to distinguish between v_0 and v_1. By Theorem 1 this optimal measurement has advantage of order $\sqrt{\Delta}$. So, after getting the outcome j', we know that $\Pr[j' = a_0 \oplus h] \geq \frac{1}{2} + \Omega(\sqrt{\Delta})$ and we can simply compute the value of $h' = m \oplus j'$. Having such knowledge about the value of h' we can distinguish between values of a_1 encoded in the second qubit $R_\alpha |a_1 \oplus h\rangle$ with the advantage proportional to $\Omega(\sqrt{\Delta})$. So, our claim follows.

4 Concluding Remark

In this paper we have presented a $\Omega(\varepsilon^2)$-susceptible protocol for OT. An interesting question is whether we can find $\delta(\varepsilon)$-susceptible protocols for other nontrivial functions and a reasonable δ and whether there exists a combinatorial characterization for such functions.

---

[5] This can be easily computed - the perturbation arises when $\alpha = \frac{1}{2}$.

The next natural question to ask is whether there exists a $\delta(\varepsilon)$-susceptible protocol for OT such that $\delta(\varepsilon)$ is asymptotically greater than $\Omega(\varepsilon^2)$. In fact, looking at the quadratic trade-off of the expression $||\ |\phi_1\rangle\langle\phi_1| - |\phi_2\rangle\langle\phi_2|\ ||_t$ in the case of $\langle\phi_1|\phi_2\rangle = 1 - \varepsilon$ and the case of $\langle\phi_1|\phi_2\rangle = \varepsilon$ might suggest that the quadratic trade-off (which similarly arises in [2]) is inherent for all non-trivial susceptible computable functions.

It is also interesting to know, whether our protocol could be transformed into one that does not need external reasons to make the correct computation of $OT((a_1, a_2), i)$ desirable for both parties i.e. a protocol in which failure to compute $OT((a_1, a_2), i)$ correctly would immediately lead to detection of cheating.

Finally, even if our protocol is very simple - thus may be relatively easy to implement - the constants hidden in $\Omega(\varepsilon^2)$ are rather impractical. Thus, trying to come up with a different protocol with better constants or some way of amplifying the trade-off of our protocol can be worthwhile.

References

1. Aharonov, D., Kitaev, A., Nisan, N.: Quantum circuits with mixed states. In: Proc. STOC 1998, pp. 20–30 (1998)
2. Aharonov, D., Ta-Shma, A., Vazirani, U., Yao, A.: Quantum bit escrow. In: Proc. STOC 2000, pp. 705–714 (2000)
3. Ardehali, M.: A perfectly secure quantum bit commitment protocol, Los Alamos preprint archive quant-ph/9505019
4. Ardehali, M.: A simple quantum oblivious transfer protocols, Los Alamos preprint archive quant-ph/9512026
5. Beaver, D.: Perfect Privacy for Two Party Protocols, Technical Report TR-11-89, Harvard University (1989)
6. Beimel, A., Malkin, T., Micali, S.: The All-or-Nothing Nature of Two-Party Secure Computation. In: Wiener, M.J. (ed.) CRYPTO 1999. LNCS, vol. 1666, pp. 80–97. Springer, Heidelberg (1999)
7. Bennet, C., Brassard, G., Crépau, C., Skubiszewska, M.-H.: Practical quantum oblivious transfer. In: Feigenbaum, J. (ed.) CRYPTO 1991. LNCS, vol. 576, pp. 351–366. Springer, Heidelberg (1992)
8. Brassard, G., Crépau, C.: Quantum bit commitment and coin tossing protocols. In: Menezes, A., Vanstone, S.A. (eds.) CRYPTO 1990. LNCS, vol. 537, pp. 49–61. Springer, Heidelberg (1991)
9. Brassard, G., Crépau, C., Robert, J.-M.: Information Theoretic Reductions Among Disclosure Problems. In: Proc. FOCS, pp. 168–173 (1986)
10. Brassard, G., Crépau, C., Jozsa, R., Langlois, D.: A quantum bit commitment scheme provably unbreakable by both parties. In: Proc. FOCS, pp. 362–371 (1993)
11. Chor, B., Kushilevitz, E.: A Zero-One Law for Boolean Privacy. SIAM Journal on Discrete Mathematics 4(1), 36–47 (1991)
12. Crépeau, C.: Equivalence between two flavors of oblivious transfers. In: Pomerance, C. (ed.) CRYPTO 1987. LNCS, vol. 293, pp. 350–354. Springer, Heidelberg (1988)
13. Crépeau, C.: Quantum oblivious transfer. Journal of Modern Optics 41(12), 2445–2454 (1994)
14. Crépeau, C., Salvail, L.: Quantum Oblivious Mutual Identification. In: Guillou, L.C., Quisquater, J.-J. (eds.) EUROCRYPT 1995. LNCS, vol. 921, pp. 133–146. Springer, Heidelberg (1995)

15. Even, S., Goldreich, O., Lempel, A.: A randomized protocol for signing contracts. Comm. ACM 28, 637–647 (1985)
16. Fischer, M.J., Micali, S., Rackoff, C.: A secure protocol for the oblivious transfer. In: Proc. EUROCRYPT 1984 (1984); Printed version in J. of Cryptology, 9(3), 191-195 (1996)
17. Hardy, L., Kent, A.: Cheat Sensitive Quantum Bit Commitment. Phys. Rev. Lett. 92, 157901 (2004)
18. Kilian, J.: Founding cryptography on oblivious transfer. In: Proc. STOC, pp. 20–31 (1988)
19. Klauck, H.: Quantum and approximate privacy. Theory of Computing Systems 37(1), 221–246 (2004)
20. Kushilevitz, E.: Privacy and Communication Complexity. SIAM J. on Disc. Math. 5(2), 273–284 (1992)
21. Lo, H.K.: Insecurity of quantum secure computations. Phys. Rev. A 56, 1154–1162 (1997)
22. Rabin, M.O.: How to exchange secrets by oblivious transfer, Tech. Memo TR-81, Aiken Computation Laboratory (1981)
23. Yao, A.C.: Security of quantum protocols against coherent measurements. In: Proc. STOC, pp. 67–75 (1995)

Perfectly Reliable and Secure Communication Tolerating Static and Mobile Mixed Adversary

Ashish Choudhary[1,*], Arpita Patra[1], Ashwinkumar B.V.[1], K. Srinathan[2], and C. Pandu Rangan[1]

[1] Dept. of Computer Science and Engineering
IIT Madras, Chennai, India 600036
{ashishc,arpita,ashwin}@cse.iitm.ernet.in, rangan@iitm.ernet.in
[2] Center for Security, Theory and Algorithmic Research
International Institute of Information Technology,
Hyderabad, India 500032
srinathan@iiit.ac.in

Abstract. In this paper, we study the problem of *perfectly reliable message transmission* (PRMT) and *perfectly secure message transmission* (PSMT) between a sender **S** and a receiver **R** in an undirected synchronous network, tolerating a mixed adversary, where the adversary can be either static or mobile. The *connectivity requirement, phase complexity* and *communication complexity* are three important parameters of any interactive PRMT/PSMT protocol and are well studied in the literature in the presence of a static/mobile Byzantine adversary. However, in the presence of a mixed adversary, we encounter several surprising consequences. In this paper, we prove that even though the connectivity requirement for PRMT is same against both static and mobile mixed adversary, the lower bound on communication complexity for PRMT tolerating a mobile mixed adversary is more than its static mixed counterpart. This is interesting because against a "Byzantine adversary", the connectivity requirement and the lower bound on the communication complexity of PRMT protocols are same for both static and mobile case. Thus our result shows that for PRMT, a mobile mixed adversary is more powerful than its static counterpart. As our second contribution, we design a four phase communication optimal PSMT protocol tolerating a "static mixed adversary". Comparing this with the existing three phase communication optimal PSMT protocol against a "static Byzantine adversary", we find that additional one phase is enough to design communication optimal protocol against a static mixed adversary. Finally, we show that the connectivity requirement and lower bound on communication complexity of any PSMT protocol is same against both static and mobile mixed adversary, thus proving that mobility of the adversary has no effect on PSMT. To show that our bound is tight, we also present a worst case nine phase communication optimal PSMT protocol tolerating a mobile mixed adversary which is first of it's kind. This also shows that

---

* Work Supported by Project No. CSE/05-06/076/DITX/CPAN on Protocols for Secure Communication and Computation Sponsored by Department of Information Technology, Government of India.

R. Safavi-Naini (Ed.): ICITS 2008, LNCS 5155, pp. 137–155, 2008.
© Springer-Verlag Berlin Heidelberg 2008

the mobility of the adversary does not hinder to design constant phase communication optimal PSMT protocol. In our protocols, we have used new techniques which can be effectively used against both static and mobile mixed adversary and are of independent interest.

1   Introduction

In *perfectly reliable message transmission* (PRMT) problem, a sender **S** is connected to a receiver **R** in an unreliable network by n node disjoint paths called wires; **S** wishes to send a message m, chosen from a finite field $\mathbb{F}$, reliably to **R**, in a *guaranteed* manner (without any error), in spite of the presence of several kinds of faults in the network. The *perfectly secure message transmission* (PSMT) problem has an additional constraint that the adversary should get *no* information about m. The faults in the network is modeled by an *adversary* who controls the actions of nodes in the network in a variety of ways and have *unbounded computing power*. Security against such an adversary is called *information theoretic security*, which is also known as *perfect security*. The PRMT and PSMT problem was first studied and solved by Dolev et.al [5] against static Byzantine adversary. The PRMT and PSMT problems are very important primitives in various reliable and secure distributed protocols. If **S** and **R** are directly connected (which is generally assumed in generic secure multiparty protocols [2,7,13,21]), then reliable and secure communication is trivially guaranteed. However, in reality, it is not economical to directly connect every two nodes in the network. Therefore such a complete network can only be virtually realized by simulating the missing links using PRMT and PSMT protocols as primitives.

Existing Results: There are various settings in which PRMT and PSMT problem has been studied extensively in the past (see [5,4,6,14,8,19,16,12]). The most natural and interesting questions posed in the context of PRMT/PSMT are: (a) POSSIBILITY: What is the necessary and sufficient condition that a given network should satisfy for the possibility of PRMT/PSMT from **S** to **R**? (b) OPTIMALITY: Once the POSSIBILITY of a protocol is ensured in a given network, what is the communication complexity lower bound for any reliable/secure protocol to send a message of specific length. Moreover, how to design *communication optimal* PRMT/PSMT protocols which satisfies the lower bound? The above questions can be examined in various settings. The questions in (a) and (b) have been completely answered against **static Byzantine** adversarial model in [12,16,1,18,9]) and against **mobile Byzantine** adversarial model in [19,11]. In [15], the authors have partially answered the questions (a) and (b) against **static mixed** adversarial model. However, nothing is known in **mobile mixed** adversarial model. Also in spite of being a very practical adversarial model, **mobile mixed** adversary have got no exposure in context of PRMT/PSMT.

Why to Study Mixed Mobile Adversary?: In a typical large network, certain nodes may be strongly protected and few others may be moderately/weakly protected. An adversary may only be able to failstop(/eavesdrop in) a strongly

Table 1. Connectivity requirement and lower bound on communication complexity for PRMT and PSMT problems; Results with "*" are provided in this paper. Moreover, all the bounds are tight. Here ℓ is the number of field elements in the message. The communication complexity is in terms of field elements.

	Byzantine Adversary		Mixed Adversary	
	Static	Mobile	Static	Mobile
PRMT; Connectivity (n)	$2t_b + 1$ [5]	$2t_b + 1$ [19]	$2t_b + t_f + 1$ [15]	$2t_b + t_f + 1$*
PRMT; Lower Bound	$\Omega(\ell)$ [18,12]	$\Omega(\ell)$ [11]	$\Omega\left(\frac{(n-t_f)\ell}{n-(t_b+t_f)}\right)$ [15]	$\Omega(\frac{n\ell}{n-(t_b+t_f)})$*
PSMT; Connectivity (n)	$2t_b + 1$ [5]	$2t_b + 1$ [19]	$2t_b + t_f + t_p + 1$ [15]	$2t_b + t_f + t_p + 1$*
PSMT; Lower Bound	$\Omega(\frac{n\ell}{n-2t_b})$ [16]	$\Omega(\frac{n\ell}{n-2t_b})$ [16]	$\Omega(\frac{n\ell}{n-(2t_b+t_f+t_p)})$ [15]*	$\Omega(\frac{n\ell}{n-(2t_b+t_f+t_p)})$*

protected node, while he may affect a weakly protected node in Byzantine fashion. Thus, we may capture the abilities of an adversary in a more realistic manner using three parameters t_b, t_f, t_p where t_b, t_f, t_p are the number of nodes under the influence of adversary in Byzantine, failstop and passive fashion respectively. Also it is better to grade different kinds of disruption done by adversary and consider them separately, rather than treating every kind of fault as Byzantine fault, as this is an "overkill". Also we stress that a mobile adversary may capture practical scenarios better than a static adversary. For example when **S** and **R** are engaged in interaction for a long time, then some faults in initial phases can be fixed and in the mean time, a hacker may attack some other nodes.

Recently in [17], the authors have studied the issues related to the POSSIBILITY and OPTIMALITY of *almost perfectly reliable and secure message transmission*[1] against static mixed adversary, where **R** may output an incorrect message with very negligible probability. However, our protocols have zero error probability. We stress that the techniques used in [17] cannot be used to design PRMT/PSMT protocols against mixed adversary, as there is a negligible (but non-zero) probability involved in the techniques of [17].

Our Contribution: In this work, we focus our attention on PRMT/PSMT in undirected synchronous networks against static and mobile mixed adversary. Table 1 tabulates both the existing and proposed (in this paper) connectivity requirement and communication complexity lower bound results.

1: We provide a four phase communication optimal PSMT protocol tolerating a static mixed adversary, which is a first protocol of its kind. Comparing this with the existing three phase communication optimal PSMT protocol against a static Byzantine adversary [12], we find that one additional phase is enough for a communication optimal PSMT protocol against a static mixed adversary.
2: We show that PRMT tolerating a mobile mixed adversary is possible iff PRMT is possible against a static mixed adversary. We prove the lower bound on the communication complexity of any PRMT protocol against a mobile mixed adversary and show that it is tight by designing a three phase communication

---

[1] In [17], the authors have termed it as *probabilistic perfectly reliable and secure message transmission*.

optimal PRMT protocol, whose communication complexity matches this bound. Comparing these results with existing results for PRMT against a static mixed adversary, we find that though mobility of mixed adversary has no affect on POSSIBILITY of PRMT protocols, it significantly affects its OPTIMALITY. This is surprising because **mobile Byzantine** and **static Byzantine** adversary has same effect in PRMT in terms of POSSIBILITY [19] and OPTIMALITY [11].

3: We show that mobility of the adversary does not affect the POSSIBILITY and OPTIMALITY of PSMT protocols tolerating mixed adversary. We also present a worst case nine phase communication optimal PSMT protocol tolerating a mobile mixed adversary, which is first of it's kind. Comparing this with the first contribution, we conclude that mobility of adversary does not hinder the possibility of designing **constant phase** communication optimal PSMT protocol against mixed adversary, even though it requires slightly more number of phases.

To design our protocols, we propose new techniques, which can be effectively used against both static and mobile mixed adversary. We stress that our results on mixed adversary are not simple and trivial extensions of the existing results on Byzantine adversary.

2 Definitions, Network Settings and Adversarial Model

The underlying network is a synchronous network represented by an undirected graph where **S** and **R** are two nodes. A *mixed adversary*, with *unbounded* computing power, controls at most t_b, t_f and t_p nodes (excluding **S, R**) in Byzantine, fail-stop and passive fashion respectively. Following the approach of [5], we abstract the network and concentrate on solving PRMT/PSMT problem for a single pair of processors (**S, R**), connected by n vertex disjoint paths $w_1, w_2, \ldots, w_n$, also known as wires. In the worst case, if adversary controls a single node on a wire, then out of n wires, at most t_b, t_f and t_p wires can be under the control of the adversary in Byzantine, failstop and passive fashion respectively.

A wire which is controlled in a failstop fashion may fail to deliver any information, but if it delivers the information then it will be correct. However, the adversary will have no idea about the information that passed through a wire which is controlled in failstop fashion. A wire which is passively controlled will always deliver correct information. However, the adversary will also completely know the information, which passed through a passively controlled wire. A Byzantine corrupted wire may deliver correct information or it may deliver incorrect information. However, in any case, the adversary will completely know the information, which passed through a Byzantine corrupted wire. The mixed adversary can be static or mobile. We denote the static and mobile mixed adversary by $\mathcal{A}^{static}_{(t_b,t_f,t_p)}$ and $\mathcal{A}^{mobile}_{(t_b,t_f,t_p)}$ respectively.

Scope of $\mathcal{A}^{static}_{(t_b,t_f,t_p)}$: $\mathcal{A}^{static}_{(t_b,t_f,t_p)}$ controls the **same** set of t_b, t_f and t_p wires among the n wires, in Byzantine, fail-stop and passive fashion respectively, in different phases of any PRMT/PSMT protocol. A wire which is under the control of $\mathcal{A}^{static}_{(t_b,t_f,t_p)}$, will remain so throughout the protocol.

Scope of $\mathcal{A}^{mobile}_{(t_b,t_f,t_p)}$: $\mathcal{A}^{mobile}_{(t_b,t_f,t_p)}$ may control **different** set of t_b, t_f and t_p wires among n wires, in Byzantine, fail-stop and passive fashion respectively, in different phases of any PRMT/PSMT protocol. A wire controlled by $\mathcal{A}^{mobile}_{(t_b,t_f,t_p)}$ in some phase, may become free in subsequent phase. Though $\mathcal{A}^{mobile}_{(t_b,t_f,t_p)}$ can control different set of wires in different phases of the protocol, it does not allow the adversary to gain any information which has previously passed (in earlier phases of the protocol) through the wires under its control in current phase. This is because the wires (and hence the nodes along these wires) erase all the local information from its memory at the end of each phase. Also any wire which is not under the control of the adversary in current phase will behave correctly, irrespective of the way it behaved in earlier phases of a protocol. The adversary can gain information from the wires in a cumulative fashion.

Throughout the paper we use m to denote the message that **S** wants to send to **R**, where m is a sequence of $\ell \geq 1$ field elements from a finite field $\mathbb{F}$. The only restriction on $\mathbb{F}$ is that $|\mathbb{F}| \geq n$. We use $|m|$ to denote the number of field elements in m. Any information which is sent through all the wires is said to be "broadcast". If x is "broadcast" over at least $2t_b + t_f + 1$ wires, then receiver will be able to correctly receive x by taking the majority among the received values. The communication complexity of any protocol is the total number of field elements communicated by **S** and **R** in the protocol. We say that a wire is **corrupted**, if the information sent over the wire is changed. A wire which is not under the control of the adversary is said to be **honest**.

Definition 1 (Optimal PRMT/PSMT (OPRMT/OPSMT) Protocol).
Let $\mathcal{N}$ be a network, under the influence of $\mathcal{A}^{static}_{(t_b,t_f,t_p)}$ or $\mathcal{A}^{mobile}_{(t_b,t_f,t_p)}$ and Π be a PRMT/PSMT protocol, which sends m by communicating $O(b)$ field elements. Then Π is called an OPRMT/OPSMT protocol if the lower bound on the communication complexity of any PRMT/PSMT protocol in $\mathcal{N}$ to send m is $\Omega(b)$ field elements.

3   Coding Theory Preliminaries

In our protocols, we have used Reed-Solomon (RS) codes. Let $Ch_{(t_b,t_f)}$ be a noisy channel, where at most t_f and t_b locations of a codeword can be arbitrarily erased and changed respectively during the transmission. We call the later type of errors as Byzantine errors.

Definition 2 ([10]). *For a message block $M = (m_1 \ m_2 \ \dots \ m_k)$ over $\mathbb{F}$, define Reed-Solomon polynomial as $P_M(x) = m_1 + m_2 x + m_3 x^2 + \dots + m_k x^{k-1}$. Let $\alpha_1, \alpha_2, ..., \alpha_n, n > k$, denote a sequence of distinct and fixed elements from $\mathbb{F}$. Then vector $C = (c_1 \ c_2 \ \dots \ c_n)$ where $c_i = P_M(\alpha_i), 1 \leq i \leq n$ is called the Reed-Solomon (RS) codeword of size n for the message block M.*

The next theorem summarizes a known result related to Reed-Solomon (RS) codes.

Theorem 1 (Singleton Bound [10]). *Suppose a sender generates a RS codeword C of size $|C| = N$, for a message block M of size k and sends the codeword C through $Ch_{(t_b, t_f)}$. Let the received codeword be C' of size $|C'| \geq N - t_f$ and different from C in at most t_b locations. Then the receiver can reconstruct the message M from C' iff $N \geq 2t_b + t_f + k$.*

Theorem 2 gives the number of errors which can be corrected and detected by RS codes.

Theorem 2 ([10,4]). *Let C denotes the RS codeword for a message block of size k, where $|C| = n$ and let C be sent over $Ch_{(t_b, t_f)}$. Let n' denotes the size of the received codeword C', where $n' \geq n - t_f$. Then RS decoding can correct up to c Byzantine errors in C' and simultaneously detect additional d Byzantine errors in C' iff $n' - k \geq 2c + d$.*

RS-DECODING ALGORITHM[10]: Berlekamp Welch algorithm is one of the most simple and efficient RS decoding algorithms existing in the literature. In general, we denote the RS decoding algorithm by $RS - DEC(n', c, d, k)$. The algorithm takes an n' length codeword C' received through $Ch_{(t_b, t_f)}$, where C' corresponds to a codeword which was encoded using a polynomial of degree $k - 1$ (so the message block size is k). Let $t'_b \leq t_b$ denotes the **actual** number of Byzantine errors that are present in C'. The only information receiver knows about t'_b is that $t'_b \leq t_b$. The variables c and d are passed as parameters to the algorithm, where c represents the number of Byzantine errors that receiver wants to correct in C' and d represents the number of additional Byzantine errors that receiver wants to detect in C'. The variables c and d should satisfy the relation given in Theorem 2. In addition, $c + d \leq t_b$. The algorithm tries to correct at most c Byzantine errors in C'. In addition to this, it tries to detect at most d additional Byzantine errors (if they are present) in C'. The algorithm either (a) outputs a polynomial of degree $k - 1$, along with an error list or (b) fails to output any polynomial of degree $k - 1$. The error list (if it is produced) contains at most c entries, where each entry is a pair, indicating an error location in C' along with the value received at that location in C'.

Definition 3. *We call an error list generated by $RS - DEC$ algorithm as "good" if each of the values in the error list, pointed as corrupted/modified value, is indeed corrupted. Otherwise we call the error list as "bad".* **When an error list is "bad", it must point a correct value in C' as corrupted.**

We now design a single phase PRMT protocol called **PRMT-Mixed** using RS codes tolerating $\mathcal{A}^{static}_{(t_b, t_f, t_p)}$. In the protocol, **S** and **R** are connected by $N \geq 2t_b + t_f + 1$ wires, $w_i, 1 \leq i \leq N$.

Lemma 1. *Protocol **PRMT-Mixed** correctly sends m by communicating $O\left(\frac{N\ell}{N - 2t_b - t_f}\right)$ field elements.*

Proof: Follows from the working of the protocol and Theorem 1.   □

Protocol **PRMT-Mixed** has the following important property.

Theorem 3. *If* **R** *in advance knows the identity of* $\alpha \leq t_b$ *wires which are Byzantine corrupted, then protocol* **PRMT-Mixed** *can reliably send* m *using block size* $k \leq (N - 2t_b - t_f) + \alpha$.

Proof: Since **R** knows α wires which are Byzantine corrupted, it simply ignores these wires and therefore the connectivity (set of active wires) reduces to $N - \alpha$. Also among the values received by **R** along these $N - \alpha$ wires, at most $t_b - \alpha$ could be Byzantine corrupted. Substituting these values in Theorem 1, we get $k \leq N - \alpha - 2(t_b - \alpha) - t_f \leq (N - 2t_b - t_f) + \alpha$. Hence **PRMT-Mixed**$(m, \ell, N, t_b, t_f, k)$ will work correctly with $k \leq (N - 2t_b - t_f) + \alpha$.

Protocol PRMT-Mixed$(m, \ell, N, t_b, t_f, k)$: Single Phase PRMT Tolerating $\mathcal{A}^{static}_{(t_b, t_f, t_p)}$

- **S** breaks m into blocks $\mathbf{B_1}, \mathbf{B_2}, \ldots, \mathbf{B_{\ell/k}}$, each consisting of k field elements, where $k = N - 2t_b - t_f$. If ℓ is not an exact multiple of k, a default padding can be used.
- For each block $\mathbf{B_j}$, $1 \leq j \leq \ell/k$ of size k, **S** computes n length RS codeword of $\mathbf{B_j}$ denoted by $(c_{j1}c_{j2} \ldots c_{jN})$. **S** sends c_{ji}, $1 \leq j \leq \ell/k$ along the wire w_i, $1 \leq i \leq N$.
- **R** parallely receives the (possibly corrupted/erased) c_{ji}'s for all $\mathbf{B_j}$'s and applies the RS decoding algorithm to each of them and reconstructs all $\mathbf{B_j}$'s. **R** then concatenates the $\mathbf{B_j}$'s to recover the message m.

---

4   OPSMT Tolerating $\mathcal{A}^{static}_{t_b}$ and Its Limitations

The existing OPSMT protocol against a t_b active static Byzantine adversary $\mathcal{A}^{static}_{t_b}$ works as follows [12]: **S** and **R** are connected by $n = 2t_b + 1$ wires, of which at most t_b can be under the control of $\mathcal{A}^{static}_{t_b}$. Essentially, **S** sends one random t_b degree polynomial over each of the n wires and their n values distributed over n wires. After a sequence of interaction between **S** and **R** according to the protocol, the constant coefficients of the $t_b + 1$ polynomials which are not under the control of the adversary, are established as an *information theoretic secure* "one time pad" between **S** and **R**. Moreover the communication complexity of the interaction is $O(n^2)$. Now using this one time pad, **S** securely sends $t_b + 1 = \Theta(n)$ field elements to **R** by communicating $O(n^2)$ field elements [12].

For tolerating $\mathcal{A}^{static}_{(t_b, t_f, t_p)}$, **S** and **R** must be connected by at least $n = 2t_b + t_f + t_p + 1$ wires (see Theorem 4). Now if we use the same technique of sending polynomials as well as their values (as used in OPSMT protocol against $\mathcal{A}^{static}_{t_b}$), **S** and **R** ends up in establishing a secure "one time pad" of length $t_b + 1$ after communicating $O(n^2)$ field elements. The reason is that adversary can failstop t_f wires and passively listen the polynomials over $(t_b + t_p)$ wires. Therefore only $n - t_f - t_b - t_p = t_b + 1$ polynomials will be unknown to the adversary. Since $n = 2t_b + t_f + t_p + 1$, t_b may not be $\Theta(n)$ and can even be a constant. Thus the resulting PSMT protocol may send a message of very small size with very high communication complexity of $O(n^2)$, which may not be an OPSMT protocol against $\mathcal{A}^{static}_{(t_b,t_f,t_p)}$. In the next section, we propose certain new protocols based on some new techniques, using which we can design OPSMT protocols tolerating both $\mathcal{A}^{static}_{(t_b,t_f,t_p)}$ and $\mathcal{A}^{mobile}_{(t_b,t_f,t_p)}$.

5   OPSMT Tolerating Static Mixed Adversary $\mathcal{A}^{static}_{(t_b,t_f,t_p)}$

We first recall the characterization for the possibility and the lower bound on communication complexity of any multiphase PSMT protocol tolerating $\mathcal{A}^{static}_{(t_b,t_f,t_p)}$.

Theorem 4 ([15]). *Any r-phase ($r \geq 2$) PSMT protocol between* **S** *and* **R** *in an undirected network* $\mathcal{N}$ *tolerating* $\mathcal{A}^{static}_{(t_b,t_f,t_p)}$ *is possible iff* $\mathcal{N}$ *is* $(2t_b + t_f + t_p + 1)$-*(**S,R**)-connected.*

Theorem 5 ([15]). *Any r-phase ($r \geq 2$) PSMT protocol which securely sends ℓ field elements in the presence of* $\mathcal{A}^{static}_{(t_b,t_f,t_p)}$ *needs to communicate* $\Omega\left(\frac{n\ell}{n-(2t_b+t_f+t_p)}\right)$ *field elements, where $n \geq 2t_b + t_f + t_p + 1$.*

Let **S** and **R** be connected by $n = 2t_b + t_f + t_p + 1$ wires $w_i, 1 \leq i \leq n$. We design a four phase OPSMT protocol $OPSMT\_\Pi^{static}_{(t_b,t_f,t_p)}$ which securely sends n field elements by communicating $O(n^2)$ field elements, tolerating $\mathcal{A}^{static}_{(t_b,t_f,t_p)}$. We first design few sub-protocols and finally combine them to get $OPSMT\_\Pi^{static}_{(t_b,t_f,t_p)}$.

Assumption 1. *In our protocols, we assume that whenever sender sends some information to receiver through n wires, then the receiver receives information over first N' ($n - t_f \leq N' \leq n$) wires and the last $n - N'$ fails to deliver any information to the receiver.*

5.1 $Pad\_Establishment\_\Pi^{static}_{(t_b,t_f,t_p)}$- A Conditional Single Phase PSMT Protocol

Let **A** and **B** be connected by $n = 2t_b + t_f + t_p + 1$ wires under the influence of $\mathcal{A}^{static}_{(t_b,t_f,t_p)}$. Also **A** in advance knows the identity of at least $\frac{t_b}{2}$ Byzantine corrupted wires. We then design a single phase sub-protocol $Pad\_Establishment\_\Pi^{static}_{(t_b,t_f,t_p)}$, given in Table 2, which securely establishes an information theoretically secure, random one time pad of length n between **A** and **B**.

Theorem 6. $Pad\_Establishment\_\Pi^{static}_{(t_b,t_f,t_p)}$ *establishes the information theoretic secure n tuple $q = [q_1(0) \ \ldots \ q_n(0)]$ between* **A** *and* **B** *against* $\mathcal{A}^{static}_{(t_b,t_f,t_p)}$ *in single phase by communicating $O(n^2)$ field elements.*

Proof: From L_{fault}, **B** identifies $|L_{fault}| \geq \frac{t_b}{2}$ Byzantine corrupted wires and neglects them. Among the remaining wires, at most t_f can fail to deliver any information. So in the worst case $n' = 2t_b + t_p + 1 - |L_{fault}|$. The codeword $Q'_j, 1 \leq j \leq n$ received by **B**, represents a RS codeword, which is RS encoded using a polynomial of degree $k - 1 = t_b - |L_{fault}| + t_p$. Also **B** knows that in Q'_j, at most $t_b - |L_{fault}|$ values could be corrupted and tries to correct these errors by applying $RS - DEC$ with $c = t_b - |L_{fault}|$ and $d = 0$. Substituting the values of n', c, d and k in the inequality of Theorem 2, we find that $RS - DEC(n', t_b - |L_{fault}|, 0, t_b - |L_{fault}| + t_p + 1)$ will be able to correct all the $t_b - |L_{fault}| \leq \frac{t_b}{2}$ errors in Q'_j and outputs $q_j(x)$ correctly.

The adversary gets at most $t_b - |L_{fault}| + t_p$ distinct points on each $t_b - |L_{fault}| + t_p$ degree polynomial $q_j(x)$, implying information theoretic security for each $q_j(0)$. For each $q_j(x), 1 \leq j \leq n$, **A** sends $n - |L_{fault}| = O(n)$ values which incurs a total communication complexity of $O(n^2)$. Also communication complexity of broadcasting L_{fault} is $O(n^2)$. □

Table 2. Conditional Single Phase Protocol to Establish an One Time Pad

Protocol $Pad\_Establishment\_\Pi^{static}_{(t_b, t_f, t_p)}$
Computation and Communication by A
• **A** saves the identity of the known faulty wires in a list L_{fault}. According to the problem specification, $\frac{t_b}{2} \leq |L_{fault}| \leq t_b$. **A** selects n random polynomials $q_j(x), 1 \leq j \leq n$, over $\mathbb{F}$, each of degree $t_b - |L_{fault}| + t_p$. For each $q_j(x), 1 \leq j \leq n$, **A** computes a RS codeword $[q_{j1} \ q_{j2} \ \cdots \ q_{jn}]$ of size n. For $1 \leq i \leq n$, if wire $w_i \notin L_{fault}$, then **A** sends to **B** the values q_{ji} over w_i. Finally **A** broadcasts L_{fault} to **B**.
Computation by B
• **B** receives L_{fault} and neglects any information received over $w_i \in L_{fault}$. Among the remaining wires, at most t_f wires can fail to deliver any information. Suppose **B** receives values over the first $n' \geq n - |L_{fault}| - t_f$ wires. Let **B** receives q'_{ji} over $w_i, 1 \leq i \leq n'$. Let $Q'_j = [q'_{j1} \ q'_{j2} \ \cdots \ q'_{jn'}], 1 \leq j \leq n$ denote the jth received codeword. **B** applies $RS - DEC(n', t_b - |L_{fault}|, 0, t_b - |L_{fault}| + t_p + 1)$ algorithm to Q'_j, recovers $q_j(x)$ and hence $q_j(0)$. The n tuple $q = [q_1(0) \ q_2(0) \ \cdots \ q_n(0)]$ is established correctly and securely between **A** and **B**.

5.2 $Error\_Identification\_\Pi^{static}_{(t_b, t_f, t_p)}$ - A Three Phase Protocol to Identify at Least $\frac{t_b}{2}$ Byzantine Corrupted Wires

As before **A** and **B** are connected by $n = 2t_b + t_f + t_p + 1$ wires. We now design a *novel* three phase protocol $Error\_Identification\_\Pi^{static}_{(t_b, t_f, t_p)}$, given in Table 3, tolerating $\mathcal{A}^{static}_{(t_b, t_f, t_p)}$, which has the following properties: (a) If at most $\frac{t_b}{2}$ wires get Byzantine corrupted during first phase then **A** securely establishes an one time pad of length n with **B** at the end of second phase. (b) If more than $\frac{t_b}{2}$ wires get Byzantine corrupted during first phase, then the pad will not be established. However, either **A** comes to know the identity of at least $\frac{t_b}{2}$ Byzantine corrupted wires at the end of second phase or **B** comes to know the identity of at least $\frac{t_b}{2}$ Byzantine corrupted wires at the end of third phase.

Table 3. A three phase protocol

Protocol $Error\_Identification\_\Pi^{static}_{(t_b,t_f,t_p)}$

Phase I: (A to B): **A** randomly selects n polynomials $p_1(x), p_2(x), \ldots, p_n(x)$ over $\mathbb{F}$, each of degree $t_b + t_p$. For each $p_j(x), 1 \leq j \leq n$, **A** computes a RS codeword $[p_{j1}\ p_{j2}\ \ldots\ p_{jn}]$ of size n. Over wire $w_i, 1 \leq i \leq n$, **A** sends the values p_{ji}.

Phase II: (B to A): Let **B** receives information over first n' wires where $n - t_f \leq n' \leq n$. Let **B** receives $p'_{ji}, 1 \leq j \leq n$ over wire $w_i, 1 \leq i \leq n'$. **B** then forms the received codewords $P'_j = [p'_{j1}\ p'_{j2}\ \ldots\ p'_{jn'}], 1 \leq j \leq n$.

• In each $P'_j, 1 \leq j \leq n$, **B** assumes at most $\frac{t_b}{2}$ values to be corrupted, applies $RS - DEC(n', \frac{t_b}{2}, 0, t_b + t_p + 1)$ algorithm to each P'_j and tries to reconstruct some polynomial $\bar{p}_j(x)$ of degree $t_b + t_p$.

• If there exists some $j \in \{1, 2, \ldots, n\}$, such that **B** fails to recover a $t_b + t_p$ degree polynomial after applying $RS - DEC(n', \frac{t_b}{2}, 0, t_b + t_p + 1)$ to codeword P'_j, then **B** broadcasts to **A**, "ERROR-R" signal and received codeword P'_j, along with its index j. /* At least $t_b/2 + 1$ Byzantine errors are present in P'_j. */

• If some polynomial of degree $t_b + t_p$ is reconstructed after applying RS decoding algorithm to each of n received codewords, then **B** proceeds as follows:

Let $Error\_List_j$ denotes the error list obtained by applying RS decoding algorithm to P'_j. Also let L_j be the number of pairs in $Error\_List_j$. Since RS decoding is applied to P'_j, assuming the number of errors in P'_j to be at most $\frac{t_b}{2}$, $L_j \leq \frac{t_b}{2}$. For $1 \leq j \leq n$, **B** broadcasts $Error\_List_j$ to **A**.

Computation by A

• If **A** receives "ERROR-R" signal and index j along with P'_j, then **A** locally compares P'_j with P_j (the original j^{th} codeword restricted to first n' locations), finds the identity of at least $\frac{t_b}{2} + 1$ faulty wires which delivered incorrect components of P_j during first phase and TERMINATES the protocol.

• If **A** receives n error-lists and all the n error lists are "good", then **A** concludes that **B** has recovered each $p_j(x), 1 \leq j \leq n$ correctly and the protocol terminates. Otherwise, **A** finds at least one $j \in \{1, 2, \ldots, n\}$, such that $Error\_List_j$ is "bad". If there are multiple such j's, **A** randomly selects one. In this case, **A** concludes that **B** reconstructed $\bar{p}_j(x) \neq p_j(x)$ and initiates **Phase III**.

Conditional Phase III: A to B: If **A** has identified a j such that **B** has reconstructed $\bar{p}_j(x) \neq p_j(x)$, then **A** broadcasts to **B** the tuple $[p_{j1}\ p_{j2}\ \ldots\ p_{jn}]$, which is the original codeword corresponding to $p_j(x)$ (which **A** had sent during **Phase I**). In this case, **B** correctly receives the actual codeword corresponding to $p_j(x)$, compares it with the codeword P'_j (corresponding to $p_j(x)$) which it has received during **Phase I**, identifies more than $\frac{t_b}{2}$ faulty wires and terminates the protocol.

We now formally prove the properties of protocol $Error\_Identification\_\Pi^{static}_{(t_b,t_f,t_p)}$.

Theorem 7. *1. If at most $\frac{t_b}{2}$ wires are Byzantine corrupted during* **Phase I**, *then an n length information theoretically secure pad $p = [p_1(0)\ p_2(0)\ \ldots\ p_n(0)]$ is established between* **A** *and* **B** *at the end of* **Phase II**.
   2. If more than $\frac{t_b}{2}$ Byzantine errors occurred during **Phase I**, *then either* **A** *or* **B** *comes to know the identity of more than $\frac{t_b}{2}$ corrupted wires at the end of* **Phase II** *or* **Phase III** *respectively.*

Proof. See the full version of this paper [3]. □

Theorem 8. *Communication complexity of $Error\_Identification\_\Pi^{static}_{(t_b,t_f,t_p)}$ is $O(n^2 t_b)$.*

5.3 Reducing the Communication Complexity of Protocol $Error\_Identification\_\Pi^{static}_{(t_b,t_f,t_p)}$

We now present a nice trick to reduce the communication complexity of sending n error-lists from $O(n^2 t_b)$ to $O(n^2)$ in **Phase II** of protocol $Error\_Identification\_\Pi^{static}_{(t_b,t_f,t_p)}$ (previously, it has been broadcast). Let $ERROR\_List_J$ be the error-list with maximum number of pairs L_J, where $J \in \{1, 2, \ldots, n\}$. If there are several error-lists with L_J pairs, then **B** arbitrarily selects one. **B** then broadcasts *only* $Error\_List_J$ and sends the remaining error-lists after concatenating them into a list Y and executing the protocol **PRMT-Mixed**$(Y, |Y|, n, t_b, t_f, L_J)$. **A** correctly receives $Error\_List_J$ and verifies whether it is "good". If it is, then **A** concludes that **B** has correctly recovered $p_J(x)$. In this case, **A** also identifies L_J faulty wires from $Error\_List_J$. Thus from Theorem 3, protocol **PRMT-Mixed** will correctly deliver the list Y containing the remaining error-lists. On the other hand, if **A** finds that $Error\_List_J$ is "bad", then **A** concludes that **B** has not recovered $p_J(x)$ correctly. In this case, **A** fails to know L_J faults from $Error\_List_J$ and hence can not recover list Y delivered using **PRMT-Mixed**. But still **A** identifies one polynomial $(p_J(x))$ which is not received correctly by **B** (due to more than $\frac{t_b}{2}$ errors during **Phase I**). *Note that while the properties of protocol $Error\_Identification\_\Pi^{static}_{(t_b,t_f,t_p)}$ (Theorem 7) remain intact by incorporating these changes, the communication complexity reduces to $O(n^2)$.* For complete formal details, see the full version of the paper [3].

Lemma 2. *The above steps when incorporated in* **Phase II** *of protocol $Error\_Identification\_\Pi^{static}_{(t_b,t_f,t_p)}$, reduces its communication complexity to $O(n^2)$.*

Proof. Broadcasting L_J incurs a communication overhead of $O(n^2)$. From Lemma 1 and Theorem 3, **PRMT-Mixed**$(Y, |Y|, n, t_b, t_f, L_J)$ incurs a communication overhead of $O\left(\frac{|Y|}{L_J} * n\right) = O(n^2)$ because $|Y| \leq (n-1) * (2L_J)$. □

5.4   Designing Four Phase OPSMT Protocol $OPSMT\_\Pi^{static}_{(t_b,t_f,t_p)}$

We now combine $Error\_Identification\_\Pi^{static}_{(t_b,t_f,t_p)}$ and $Pad\_Establishment\_\Pi^{static}_{(t_b,t_f,t_p)}$ to design a four phase OPSMT protocol called $OPSMT\_\Pi^{static}_{(t_b,t_f,t_p)}$, given in Table 4, tolerating $\mathcal{A}^{static}_{(t_b,t_f,t_p)}$. In the protocol, we show, how an one time pad is established between **S** and **R**. Once **S** knows that the pad is going to be established, **S** can blind the message by XORing it with the pad and broadcasts the blinded message to **R** in the last phase of the protocol. On receiving the blinded message, **R** extracts the message by XORing the blinded message with the pad. We now prove the correctness and security of protocol $OPSMT\_\Pi^{static}_{(t_b,t_f,t_p)}$.

Theorem 9. *In* $OPSMT\_\Pi^{static}_{(t_b,t_f,t_p)}$, **S** *correctly establishes a random, information theoretically secure one time pad of length n with* **R** *in four phases.*

Proof: In $OPSMT\_\Pi^{static}_{(t_b,t_f,t_p)}$, the sub-protocol $Error\_Identification\_\Pi^{static}_{(t_b,t_f,t_p)}$ terminates in either two phases or three phases. If it terminates in two phases, then there are two possibilities: If at the end of second phase, **R** concludes that the pad p is *securely* established with **S**, then **R** terminates the protocol in third phase by broadcasting "SUCCESS-R" signal. Otherwise at the end of **Phase II**, **R** will know the identity of at least $\frac{t_b}{2} + 1$ faulty wires (see Theorem 7). With this knowledge, **R** *securely* establishes the pad q with **S** during **phase III** using sub-protocol $Pad\_Establishment\_\Pi^{static}_{(t_b,t_f,t_p)}$ (Theorem 6).

If $Error\_Identification$ terminates in three phases, then at the end of **Phase III**, **S** identifies at least $\frac{t_b}{2} + 1$ faulty wires (Theorem 7). Now **S** establishes the pad q with **R** during fourth phase, using $Pad\_Establishment$ (see Theorem 6). The security of pad p (q) follows from Theorem 7 (Theorem 6). □

Table 4. A Four Phase OPSMT Protocol Tolerating $\mathcal{A}^{static}_{(t_b,t_f,t_p)}$

Protocol $OPSMT\_\Pi^{static}_{(t_b,t_f,t_p)}$
• **R** and **S** starts executing protocol $Error\_Identification\_\Pi^{static}_{(t_b,t_f,t_p)}$, where **Phase I** is initiated by **R**. IF at the end of **Phase II** of protocol $Error\_Identification\_\Pi^{static}_{(t_b,t_f,t_p)}$, pad $p = [p_1(0)\ p_2(0)\ \ldots\ p_n(0)]$ is established securely between **R** and **S**, then **R** terminates the protocol by broadcasting "SUCCESS-R" signal to **S**.
• IF at the end of **Phase II** of $Error\_Identification\_\Pi^{static}_{(t_b,t_f,t_p)}$, **R** identifies $\frac{t_b}{2} + 1$ faulty wires, then **R** securely establishes an one time pad $q = [q_1(0)\ q_2(0)\ \ldots\ q_n(0)]$ with **S** by executing $Pad\_Establishment\_\Pi^{static}_{(t_b,t_f,t_p)}$.
• IF at the end of **Phase III** of protocol $Error\_Identification\_\Pi^{static}_{(t_b,t_f,t_p)}$, **S** identifies at least $\frac{t_b}{2} + 1$ faulty wires, then **S** securely establishes an one time pad $q = [q_1(0)\ q_2(0)\ \ldots\ q_n(0)]$ with **R** by executing protocol $Pad\_Establishment\_\Pi^{static}_{(t_b,t_f,t_p)}$ and terminates the protocol.

Theorem 10. *Protocol $OPSMT\_\Pi^{static}_{(t_b, t_f, t_p)}$ is an OPSMT protocol communicating $O(n^2)$ field elements.*

Proof. The communication complexity follows from Lemma 2, Theorem 6 and working of the protocol. From Theorem 5, in an $n = 2t_b + t_f + t_p + 1$ connected network, any four phase PSMT protocol has to communicate $\Omega(n^2)$ field elements to securely send n field elements against $\mathcal{A}^{static}_{(t_b, t_f, t_p)}$. Since communication complexity of $OPSMT\_\Pi^{static}_{(t_b, t_f, t_p)}$ is $O(n^2)$, it is an OPSMT protocol. $\square$

Remark 1. Noticeably $OPSMT\_\Pi^{static}_{(t_b, t_f, t_p)}$ sends only codeword of polynomials, in contrast to the existing protocol summarized in section 4, which sends both polynomial and its codeword. The advantage that we get by sending only codeword is that we obtain one information theoretic secure value per codeword (after some intermediate information exchanges and then applying RS decoding), thus establishing a secure one time pad of size $\Theta(n)$ between **S** and **R**. Soon, we will show that this technique can be used to design OPRMT and OPSMT protocols even against mobile mixed adversary.

6   OPRMT Tolerating Mobile Mixed Adversary $\mathcal{A}^{mobile}_{(t_b, t_f, t_p)}$

We first recall that for the existence of any PRMT protocol tolerating $\mathcal{A}^{static}_{(t_b, t_f, t_p)}$, the network should be $(2t_b + t_f + 1)$-(**S**, **R**)-connected [15]. The next theorem gives the characterization of PRMT tolerating $\mathcal{A}^{mobile}_{(t_b, t_f, t_p)}$.

Theorem 11. *PRMT between **S** and **R** in an undirected network $\mathcal{N}$, tolerating $\mathcal{A}^{mobile}_{(t_b, t_f, t_p)}$ is possible iff $\mathcal{N}$ is $(2t_b + t_f + 1)$-(**S,R**)-connected.*

PROOF: $(2t_b + t_f + 1)$-(**S,R**)-connected network is required for the existence of PRMT against a weaker adversary $\mathcal{A}^{static}_{(t_b, t_f, t_p)}$ [15]. Hence it is required against more stronger $\mathcal{A}^{mobile}_{(t_b, t_f, t_p)}$. On the other hand, if $\mathcal{N}$ is $(2t_b + t_f + 1)$-(**S**, **R**)-connected, then **S** can reliably send a message by broadcasting it to **R**. $\square$

As a sufficiency proof, we specified broadcasting which is a naive protocol. It communicates $n\ell$ field elements for transmitting ℓ elements reliably. So it is not an efficient PRMT protocol against $\mathcal{A}^{mobile}_{(t_b, t_f, t_p)}$. So, the important question here is: can we reliably send a message containing ℓ field elements by communicating less than $O(n\ell)$ field elements against $\mathcal{A}^{mobile}_{(t_b, t_f, t_p)}$? We answer this question by proving the lower bound on communication complexity of PRMT protocols tolerating $\mathcal{A}^{mobile}_{(t_b, t_f, t_p)}$ and show that it is more than the existing lower bound against $\mathcal{A}^{static}_{(t_b, t_f, t_p)}$. This shows that as far as lower bound on communication complexity of PRMT is concerned, $\mathcal{A}^{mobile}_{(t_b, t_f, t_p)}$ is more powerful than $\mathcal{A}^{static}_{(t_b, t_f, t_p)}$.

Remark 2. In [15], it is shown that any PRMT protocol in a n-(**S**, **R**)-connected network $(n \geq 2t_b + t_f + 1)$, communicates $\Omega\left(\frac{(n - t_f)\ell}{n - (t_b + t_f)}\right)$ field elements in order to reliably send ℓ field elements against $\mathcal{A}^{static}_{(t_b, t_f, t_p)}$. If $n = 2t_b + t_f + 1$, then this it implies that any PRMT protocol has to communicate $\Omega(\ell)$ field elements to reliably send a message containing ℓ field elements against $\mathcal{A}^{static}_{(t_b,t_f,t_p)}$. Moreover, in [20], the authors have shown that this bound is tight by designing an $O\left(\log(\frac{t_f}{n-t_f})\right)$ phase OPRMT protocol.

Theorem 12. *Any PRMT protocol between* **S** *and* **R** *connected by* $n \geq 2t_b + t_f + 1$ *wires under the influence of* $\mathcal{A}^{mobile}_{(t_b,t_f,t_p)}$ *must communicate* $\Omega(\frac{n\ell}{n-(t_b+t_f)})$ *field elements in order to transmit a message containing* ℓ *field elements.*

PROOF (SKETCH): The proof of the theorem is inspired by entropy based argument, used to prove the lower bound on the communication complexity of PRMT/PSMT protocols against $\mathcal{A}^{static}_{t_b}$ [18]. The complete formal proof is available in the full

Table 5. Three Phase OPRMT Protocol Tolerating $\mathcal{A}^{mobile}_{(t_b,t_f,t_p)}$

Protocol $OPRMT\_\Pi^{mobile}_{(t_b,t_f,t_p)}$
Phase I: S to R: **S** divides m into blocks $B_1, B_2, \ldots, B_z$, each containing $1 + \frac{t_b}{2}$ field elements. For each $B_j, 1 \leq j \leq z$, **S** computes a RS codeword of size n denoted by $[c_{j1}\ c_{j2}\ \ldots\ c_{jn}]$ and sends c_{ji} through w_i.
Phase II: R to S: **R** receives information over the first $n - t_f \leq n' \leq n$ wires. Through these n' wires, **R** receives the values $c'_{ji}, 1 \leq j \leq z, 1 \leq i \leq n'$. Let $C'_j, 1 \leq j \leq z$ denotes j^{th} received codeword where $C'_j = [c'_{j1}\ c'_{j2}\ \ldots\ c'_{jn'}]$. **R** applies $RS - DEC(n', \frac{t_b}{2}, \frac{t_b}{2}, \frac{t_b}{2} + 1)$ algorithm to each C'_j and tries to correct $\frac{t_b}{2}$ errors and simultaneously detect additional $\frac{t_b}{2}$ errors in C'_j.
– If $RS - DEC$ does not detect additional errors ($\leq \frac{t_b}{2}$) in any C'_j, after correcting at most $\frac{t_b}{2}$ errors, then $RS - DEC$ recovers each block B_j of m correctly. **R** recovers m by concatenating all B_j's and broadcasts "TERMINATE" signal to **S**.   – If $\exists J \in \{1, 2, \ldots, z\}$, such that $RS - DEC$ detects additional errors in C'_J, after correcting at most $\frac{t_b}{2}$ errors, then **R** broadcasts C'_J and index J.
Phase III: S to R: If **S** receives "TERMINATE" signal, then he terminates the protocol. Else **S** does the following:
– **S** receives C'_J and index J. After locally comparing C'_J with its corresponding original codeword C_J, **S** identifies at least $\frac{t_b}{2} + 1$ wires which were Byzantine corrupted during **Phase I** and broadcasts their identity to **R**.
Local Computation by R: If during second phase, **R** has broadcasted C'_J, then **R** correctly receives the identity of at least $\frac{t_b}{2} + 1$ wires, which delivered incorrect values during **Phase I**. From each codeword C'_j received during first phase, **R** removes the c'_{ji}'s received over these corrupted wires. **R** applies $RS - DEC$ to the new C'_j's, assuming the number of errors c (to be corrected) to be at most $\frac{t_b}{2}$ and the number of additional errors d (to be detected) to 0 and correctly recovers all B_j's and hence m.

version of this paper [3]. Rather, here we try to quantify the reason behind different lower bound for static and mobile mixed adversary. In static case, the lower bound is derived by assuming that both $\mathbf{S}$ and $\mathbf{R}$ knows the set of wires which are fail-stop corrupted in *advance*. Hence the term $(n - t_f)$ appears in the numerator of the lower bound expression against $\mathcal{A}^{static}_{(t_b,t_f,t_p)}$ (see Remark 2). This is a reasonable assumption because against static adversary, we can always strategies protocols to remember faults caught in earlier phases and use that knowledge to amortize the overall communication complexity and message size in later phases (the OPRMT protocol of [20] is based on this important principle). However, protocols tolerating mobile mixed adversary is memoryless because adversary corrupts different set of wires in different phases of the protocol. Hence, the protocols against mobile mixed adversary cannot use the knowledge of the faults, which occurred in previous phases, to amortize the communication complexity and message size in later phases.   □

We now design a three phase OPRMT protocol $OPRMT\_\Pi^{mobile}_{(t_b,t_f,t_p)}$, given in Table 5, which reliably sends a message m containing $n(t_b + 1)$ field elements by communicating $O(n^2)$ field elements, where $n = 2t_b + t_f + 1$.

Theorem 13. $OPRMT\_\Pi^{mobile}_{(t_b,t_f,t_p)}$ *reliably sends* $n(t_b + 1)$ *field elements by communicating* $O(n^2)$ *field elements in three phases tolerating* $\mathcal{A}^{mobile}_{(t_b,t_f,t_p)}$.

Proof. See the full version of this paper [3].   □

7   OPSMT Tolerating Mobile Mixed Adversary $\mathcal{A}^{mobile}_{(t_b,t_f,t_p)}$

The characterization for the possibility of any multiphase PSMT protocol tolerating $\mathcal{A}^{mobile}_{(t_b,t_f,t_p)}$ is same as the characterization for PSMT against $\mathcal{A}^{static}_{(t_b,t_f,t_p)}$ (see Theorem 4). The fact that $\mathcal{A}^{mobile}_{(t_b,t_f,t_p)}$ is more powerful than $\mathcal{A}^{static}_{(t_b,t_f,t_p)}$ proves the necessity of the characterization. To prove the sufficiency, we present an OPSMT protocol in the sequel tolerating $\mathcal{A}^{mobile}_{(t_b,t_f,t_p)}$. Before that we note that the lower bound on communication complexity of PSMT protocols against $\mathcal{A}^{static}_{(t_b,t_f,t_p)}$ (specified in Theorem 5) holds good in case of PSMT protocols tolerating $\mathcal{A}^{mobile}_{(t_b,t_f,t_p)}$. Since $\mathcal{A}^{mobile}_{(t_b,t_f,t_p)}$ is more powerful than $\mathcal{A}^{static}_{(t_b,t_f,t_p)}$, any lower bound against $\mathcal{A}^{static}_{(t_b,t_f,t_p)}$ is a trivial lower bound against $\mathcal{A}^{mobile}_{(t_b,t_f,t_p)}$. We now show that this bound is *tight*. We present a *constant* phase OPSMT protocol $OPSMT\_\Pi^{mobile}_{(t_b,t_f,t_p)}$, given in Table 6, 7 and 8, which securely sends $\Theta(n)$ field elements by communicating $O(n^2)$ field elements against $\mathcal{A}^{mobile}_{(t_b,t_f,t_p)}$, where $\mathbf{S}$ and $\mathbf{R}$ are connected by $n = 2t_b + t_f + t_p + 1$ wires. The protocol terminates in at most nine phases and establishes an information theoretically secure one time pad of length either $n - 1$ or $\frac{n}{2}$ between $\mathbf{S}$ and $\mathbf{R}$.

Notice that the technique proposed in section 5.3 for sending n error lists in a single phase incurring $O(n^2)$ communication complexity, can not be adopted against mobile adversary. This is so because the technique used the knowledge of the Byzantine corruption done in earlier phases. However, mobile adversary

Table 6. A Constant Phase OPSMT Protocol Tolerating $\mathcal{A}^{mobile}_{(t_b, t_f, t_p)}$

Protocol $OPSMT\_\Pi^{mobile}_{(t_b, t_f, t_p)}$

Phase I: S to R: **S** selects n random polynomials $p_j(x), 1 \leq j \leq n$ over $\mathbb{F}$, each of degree $t_b + t_p$, such that $p_j(0) = s_j$. For each $p_j(x)$, **S** forms a RS codeword $[c_{j1}\ c_{j2}\ \ldots\ c_{jn}]$ of size n and sends c_{ji} over wire w_i.

Phase II: R to S: **R** receives c'_{ji}'s over the first $n - t_f \leq n' \leq n$ wires. **R** applies $RS-DEC(n', \frac{t_b}{2}, 0, t_b + t_p + 1)$ to the $j^{th}, 1 \leq j \leq n$ received codeword $C'_j = [c'_{j1}\ c'_{j2}\ \ldots\ c'_{jn'}]$. There are two possible cases:

1. Corresponding to each $C'_j, 1 \leq j \leq n$, $RS-DEC$ outputs some polynomial $\bar{p}_j(x)$ of degree $t_b + t_p$, along with error list $Error\_List_j$ containing at most $\frac{t_b}{2}$ pairs. **R** then combines **only the first** $\frac{n}{2}$ error lists and reliably sends them to **S** using three phase PRMT protocol $OPRMT\_\Pi^{mobile}_{(t_b, t_f, t_p)}$.

2. There exists at least one $J \in \{1, 2, \ldots, n\}$, such that $RS-DEC$, when applied to C'_J, fails to output any $t_b + t_p$ degree polynomial. In this case, **R** broadcasts C'_J and its index J.

Table 7. Remaining Execution of $OPSMT\_\Pi^{mobile}_{(t_b, t_f, t_p)}$, when step 2 of Phase II has been executed

---

Execution I

Phase III: S to R

- **S** correctly receives index J and codeword C'_J. After locally comparing C'_J with its corresponding actual codeword C_J, **S** identifies at least $\frac{t_b}{2} + 1$ wires which delivered incorrect values to **R** during **Phase I**. **S** saves the identity of these wires in a list L_{fault} and broadcasts L_{fault} to **R**.

- **S** also lists all c_{ji}'s, $j \in \{1, 2, \ldots, n\} - \{J\}$, sent during **Phase I**, over $w_i \in L_{fault}$. **S** then re-sends these $(n-1) \times |L_{fault}| = O(nt_b)$ values by executing the three phase PRMT protocol $OPRMT\_\Pi^{mobile}_{(t_b, t_f, t_p)}$. This will occupy the next three phases. /* The re-send values are already known to $\mathcal{A}^{mobile}_{(t_b, t_f, t_p)}$ because the wires in L_{fault} were under the control of $\mathcal{A}^{mobile}_{(t_b, t_f, t_p)}$ during **Phase I**. */

Local Computation by R (At the end of Phase V)

• After receiving list L_{fault}, **R** identifies $|L_{fault}| > \frac{t_b}{2}$ wires which has delivered incorrect information during **Phase I**. **R** removes from the $n - 1$ codewords C'_j's, $j \in \{1, 2, \ldots, n\} - \{J\}$ (received during **Phase I**), the values c'_{ji}'s, which **R** has received along $w_i \in L_{fault}$ during **Phase I**. **R** replaces them with the corresponding actual c_{ji}'s, which **S** has re-send through PRMT protocol $PRMT\_\Pi^{mobile}_{(t_b, t_f, t_p)}$.

• After replacement, **R** knows that out of the n' values in each $C'_j, j \in \{1, 2, \ldots, n\} - \{J\}$, at most $t_b - |L_{fault}|$ could be corrupted. **R** applies $RS-DEC(n', t_b - |L_{fault}|, 0, t_b + t_p + 1)$ algorithm to these $n - 1$ C'_j's and correctly recovers $p_j(x)$'s. The constant term of these $n-1$ polynomials constitute an $n-1$ length information theoretically secure pad established between **S** and **R** and the protocol terminates here.

Table 8. Remaining Execution of $OPSMT\_\Pi_{(t_b,t_f,t_p)}^{mobile}$, when step 1 of Phase II has been executed

---

Execution II

/* **R** has initiated three phase $OPRMT - \Pi_{(t_b,t_f,t_p)}^{mobile}$ to reliably send first $\frac{n}{2}$ error lists during **Phase II**. The $OPRMT$ protocol will be over at the end of **Phase IV**.*/

Local Computation by S (At the end of Phase IV): S reliably receives first $\frac{n}{2}$ error lists through $OPRMT\_\Pi_{(t_b,t_f,t_p)}^{mobile}$ and checks the status of these error lists.

- If all error lists are "good", then **S** concludes that **R** has correctly recovered $p_j(x), 1 \leq j \leq \frac{n}{2}$ correctly and an information theoretically secure pad $[p_1(0) \; p_2(0) \; p_{n/2}(0)]$ is established with **R**. **S** terminates the protocol by broadcasting terminating signal to **R**. Accordingly **R** terminates the protocol.
- If $\exists J \in \{1, 2, \ldots, \frac{n}{2}\}$, such that $Error\_List_J$ is "bad", then **S** concludes that more than $\frac{t_b}{2}$ values has been changed in J^{th} codeword during **Phase I**.

Phase V: S to R (If second case happens in the above computation)

S asks **R** to broadcast the Jth codeword as received by **R** during **Phase I**. **S** does this by broadcasting index J along with "ERROR" signal.

Phase VI: R to S

On receiving "ERROR" signal and index J during **Phase V**, **R** broadcasts C'_J, received during **Phase I**.

Phase VII: S to R

On receiving C'_J, **S** identifies more than $\frac{t_b}{2}$ wires which were Byzantine corrupted during **Phase I** and saves them in a list L_{fault}. From here onwards the execution is similar as in **Execution I**. We specify only the small differences:

- If $w_i \in L_{fault}$, then **S** lists the ith component of the codewords corresponding to the last $\frac{n}{2}$ polynomials $p_j(x), n/2 + 1 \leq j \leq n$. **S** reliably re-sends these components by executing $OPRMT\_\Pi_{(t_b,t_f,t_p)}^{mobile}$. Recall that in this execution sequence, **R** had not sent the last $\frac{n}{2}$ error lists during **Phase II** (step 1). The re-send values are already known to the adversary and does not give any extra information about $p_j(x), n/2 + 1 \leq j \leq n$.
- $OPRMT\_\Pi_{(t_b,t_f,t_p)}^{mobile}$ terminates in **Phase IX** (since it takes 3 phases) and therefore at the end of **phase IX**, **R** performs the same local computation as done in **Execution I** to correctly recover the polynomials $p_j(x), n/2 + 1 \leq j \leq n$ to establish a pad of size $\frac{n}{2}$. The $\frac{n}{2}$ size pad constitutes the constant term of the recovered polynomials $p_j(x), n/2 + 1 \leq j \leq n$.

---

can corrupt different set of wires in different phases. So, here we use the three phase reliable protocol $OPRMT\_\Pi_{(t_b,t_f,t_p)}^{mobile}$ to send the error lists in three phases with same communication complexity of $O(n^2)$. Also note that while executing $OPRMT\_\Pi_{(t_b,t_f,t_p)}^{mobile}$, **S** and **R** can neglect a pre-determined set of t_p wires and run the protocol on the remaining $2t_b + t_f + 1$ wires (the PRMT protocol requires only $2t_b + t_f + 1$ wires between **S** and **R**). This does not affect the correctness and working of the protocol.

Theorem 14. *Protocol $OPSMT\_\Pi_{(t_b,t_f,t_p)}^{mobile}$ correctly and securely establishes an one time pad of length $\Theta(n)$ between* **S** *and* **R** *in at most nine phases by communicating $O(n^2)$ field elements tolerating $\mathcal{A}_{(t_b,t_f,t_p)}^{mobile}$.*

Proof. See the full version of this paper [3]. □

8   Conclusion

In this paper we have contributed significantly to the progress of the state of the art in the problem of PRMT and PSMT. We presented a number of constant phase protocols which are first of their kind and enjoys the property of being communication optimal against static and mobile mixed adversary . One can try to reduce the phase complexity of our OPRMT and OPSMT protocols tolerating static and mobile mixed adversary.

References

1. Agarwal, S., Cramer, R., de Haan, R.: Asymptotically optimal two-round perfectly secure message transmission. In: Dwork, C. (ed.) CRYPTO 2006. LNCS, vol. 4117, pp. 394–408. Springer, Heidelberg (2006)
2. Ben-Or, M., Goldwasser, S., Wigderson, A.: Completeness theorems for non-cryptographic fault-tolerant distributed computation. In: Proc. of 20th ACM STOC, pp. 1–10 (1988)
3. Choudhary, A., Patra, A., Ashwinkumar, B.V., Srinathan, K., Pandu Rangan, C.: Perfectly reliable and secure communication tolerating static and mobile mixed adversary. Cryptology ePrint Archive, Report 2008/232 (2008)
4. Desmedt, Y., Wang, Y.: Perfectly secure message transmission revisited. In: Knudsen, L.R. (ed.) EUROCRYPT 2002. LNCS, vol. 2332, pp. 502–517. Springer, Heidelberg (2002)
5. Dolev, D., Dwork, C., Waarts, O., Yung, M.: Perfectly secure message transmission. JACM 40(1), 17–47 (1993)
6. Franklin, M., Wright, R.: Secure communication in minimal connectivity models. Journal of Cryptology 13(1), 9–30 (2000)
7. Goldreich, O., Micali, S., Wigderson, A.: How to play any mental game. In: Proc. of 19th ACM STOC, pp. 218–229 (1987)
8. Kumar, M.V.N.A., Goundan, P.R., Srinathan, K., Rangan, C.P.: On perfectly secure communication over arbitrary networks. In: Proc. of 21st PODC, pp. 193–202. ACM Press, New York (2002)
9. Kurosawa, K., Suzuki, K.: Truly efficient 2-round perfectly secure message transmission scheme. In: Smart, N. (ed.) EUROCRYPT 2008. LNCS, vol. 4965, pp. 324–340. Springer, Heidelberg (2008)
10. MacWilliams, F.J., Sloane, N.J.A.: The Theory of Error Correcting Codes. North-Holland Publishing Company, Amsterdam (1978)
11. Patra, A., Choudhary, A., Gayatri, M., Pandu Rangan, C.: Efficient perfectly reliable and secure communication tolerating mobile adversary. In: Proc. of ACISP 2008. Cryptology ePrint Archive, Report 2008/086 (to appear, 2008)

12. Patra, A., Choudhary, A., Srinathan, K., Rangan, C.P.: Constant phase bit optimal protocols for perfectly reliable and secure message transmission. In: Barua, R., Lange, T. (eds.) INDOCRYPT 2006. LNCS, vol. 4329, pp. 221–235. Springer, Heidelberg (2006)
13. Rabin, T., Ben-Or, M.: Verifiable secret sharing and multiparty protocols with honest majority. In: Proc. of 21st ACM STOC, pp. 73–85 (1989)
14. Sayeed, H., Abu-Amara, H.: Efficient perfectly secure message transmission in synchronous networks. Information and Computation 126(1), 53–61 (1996)
15. Srinathan, K.: Secure distributed communication. PhD Thesis, IIT Madras (2006)
16. Srinathan, K., Narayanan, A., Pandu Rangan, C.: Optimal perfectly secure message transmission. In: Franklin, M. (ed.) CRYPTO 2004. LNCS, vol. 3152, pp. 545–561. Springer, Heidelberg (2004)
17. Srinathan, K., Patra, A., Choudhary, A., Rangan, C.P.: Probabilistic perfectly reliable and secure message transmission - possibility, feasibility and optimality. In: Srinathan, K., Rangan, C.P., Yung, M. (eds.) INDOCRYPT 2007. LNCS, vol. 4859, pp. 101–122. Springer, Heidelberg (2007)
18. Srinathan, K., Prasad, N.R., Pandu Rangan, C.: On the optimal communication complexity of multiphase protocols for perfect communication. In: IEEE Symposium on Security and Privacy, pp. 311–320 (2007)
19. Srinathan, K., Raghavendra, P., Pandu Rangan, C.: On proactive perfectly secure message transmission. In: Pieprzyk, J., Ghodosi, H., Dawson, E. (eds.) ACISP 2007. LNCS, vol. 4586, pp. 461–473. Springer, Heidelberg (2007)
20. AshwinKumar, B.V., Patra, A., Choudhary, A., Srinathan, K., Pandu Rangan, C.: On tradeoff between network connectivity, phase complexity and communication complexity of reliable communication tolerating mixed adversary. In: Proc. of ACM PODC (to appear, 2008)
21. Yao, A.C.: Protocols for secure computations. In: Proc. of 23rd IEEE FOCS, pp. 160–164 (1982)

Key Refreshing in Wireless Sensor Networks

Simon R. Blackburn[1], Keith M. Martin[1], Maura B. Paterson[1,*],
and Douglas R. Stinson[2,**]

[1] Department of Mathematics
Royal Holloway, University of London
Egham, Surrey, TW20 0EX, U.K.
{s.blackburn,keith.martin,m.b.paterson}@rhul.ac.uk
[2] David R. Cheriton School of Computer Science
University of Waterloo
Waterloo, Ontario, Canada N2L 3G1
dstinson@uwaterloo.ca

Abstract. The problem of establishing symmetric keys in wireless sensor networks has been extensively studied, but other aspects of key management have received comparatively little attention. In this paper we consider the problem of refreshing keys that are shared among several nodes in a WSN, in order to provide forward security. We discuss several applications that lead to sensor networks with very different properties, and we propose key refreshing schemes that are useful in each of these environments, together with resynchronisation methods that allow nodes possessing different versions of a key to arrive at a common version.

Keywords: key refreshing, wireless sensor networks, forward security.

1 Introduction

A wireless sensor network (WSN) consists of a number of small, battery-powered sensing devices (known as sensor nodes) that employ wireless communication to form a network in order to distribute and manipulate the sensed data. As public-key cryptographic techniques are regarded as being undesirably costly for these highly constrained devices it is necessary for nodes to share symmetric keys for the purposes of providing authentication, data integrity or confidentiality. Much research has been done on the problem of establishing shared keys in such networks (see [3,8,14] for surveys of this area); less attention has been paid to the ongoing key management requirements that arise after a network has been deployed. One such requirement, recognised in the cryptographic community since the 1980s (see [5]), is *forward security*: if a node is captured and its secret material compromised, an adversary should not be able to decrypt messages that were intercepted by the adversary in the past. In a network environment, we may weaken this requirement to insisting that the adversary cannot decrypt

* Research supported by EPSRC grant EP/D053285/1.
** Research supported by NSERC grant 203114-06.

R. Safavi-Naini (Ed.): ICITS 2008, LNCS 5155, pp. 156–170, 2008.
© Springer-Verlag Berlin Heidelberg 2008

messages that were broadcast more than a very short time ago. Forward security is of particular significance in a WSN, as the nodes operate in an uncontrolled environment and lack tamper proof hardware, and hence are vulnerable to adversarial compromise. Moreover, the difficulty of distinguishing node compromise from routine node failure adds to the security challenges of such an environment.

Schemes for *refreshing* keys (updating keys using a one-way function) in order to provide forward security in a WSN setting have so far been restricted to networks in which there are no group keys and where nodes are capable of storing a separate key for each of their neighbours (this is the case for the schemes proposed by Klonowski et al. [6] and Mauw et al. [9]). But these restrictions are often not valid: group keys (which could be shared by many nodes) are needed in many applications; even when keys are only used to secure pairwise links, a node might use the same key to communicate with more than one of its neighbours because of limited storage capabilities. (For example, this will often be the case if key predistribution techniques such as those of Eschenauer and Gligor [4] or Lee and Stinson [7] are used.) Indeed, when a network is dense, the number of secure links a node might want to establish might exceed the number of keys it is able to store.

This paper is the first to examine how to provide forward security by key refreshing in networks with these more general patterns of key sharing. We consider five network environments that require different methods of key refreshing. We propose three different key refreshing solutions: the *synchronous* techniques of event-driven refreshing (Scheme 1) and flooded refreshing (Scheme 2), and the *asynchronous* message-driven refreshing (Scheme 3). In addition, we propose two methods of resynchronising the versions of each key in the asynchronous case: by means of a flood, or through the use of a leader election algorithm.

In Sect. 2 we consider definitions of forward security appearing in the literature, and examine standard techniques for refreshing pairwise keys, as well as those that have been proposed for use in sensor networks.

In Sect. 3 we discuss several applications for sensor networks that give rise to five distinct categories of networks with differing properties. As suggested by the examples given in [13] by Römer and Mattern, the properties of sensors and their communication patterns can vary much more widely than is acknowledged in much of the sensor network literature. The network environments we describe encompass a wide range of possible WSNs: sensors may be fixed or mobile, the network may be dense or sparse, the amount of communication within the network may be steady, or it may fluctuate. In fact, the schemes we propose are not restricted to sensor networks, but may find application in any network in which symmetric keys are shared by more than two entities. We assume that each node stores a number of symmetric keys from some key pool, and that each key is potentially stored by a number of different nodes. We further suppose that a node is able to determine its *neighbours:* nodes with which it shares at least one key, and which are within its communication range.

In Sect. 4 we propose schemes for updating keys to provide forward security in the first two environments we have identified.

In Sect. 5 we discuss a scheme appropriate for the remaining three environments, and provide schemes for resynchronising the versions of keys possessed by nodes in cases where the nodes hold differing versions of the same key. We conclude with a discussion of some further issues relating to key refreshing in WSNs.

2   Forward Security through Pairwise Key Refreshing

In this section we describe standard techniques for achieving forward security for a single pairwise key, as well as two schemes that have been proposed in a sensor network context. We then point out the problems of extending pairwise schemes to the setting where a key is shared by more than one node in a network.

2.1   Notions of Forward Security

Provably Secure Refreshing. In [1], Bellare and Yee describe how symmetric keys can be refreshed using a *stateful generator:* a pseudorandom bit generator that takes a state as input, then produces an output block and a new state, which is used as the input for the next iteration of the generator. Such a generator is defined to be *forward secure* if an adversary who is given access to the state of the generator at a time of its choice cannot feasibly distinguish the sequence of bits previously output by the generator from a random sequence. A stateful generator can be used for key refreshing in the following manner. Let $g : \{0,1\}^s \to \{0,1\}^{b+s}$ be a pseudorandom generator (such as the Blum-Blum-Shub generator [2], for example) and let s_0 be a randomly chosen s-bit initial state. The first b bits of $g(s_0)$ are output as an initial key k_1, and the remaining s bits are stored as the state s_1. A sequence of keys k_i can then be produced by applying g to the state s_{i-1}, updating the state using the output of g each time. Bellare and Yee prove that this stateful generator is forward secure, provided that g is pseudorandom. As this process is deterministic, two entities who share an initial common state can use this method to produce a forward-secure sequence of shared keys without any communication overheads.

In the constrained environment of a WSN, however, the use of a provably secure generator is likely to prove too computationally expensive. Also, the need to store the generator's internal state as well as the current key represents an additional overhead. In order to realise a significant gain in efficiency, it may therefore be deemed acceptable in a sensor network context to consider a weaker form of forward security, namely: given a version of a key, it should be computationally infeasible to decrypt any ciphertexts produced with prior versions of the key. This can be achieved by the use of a one-way function. This is a standard technique that can be described as follows.

Standard Refreshing. Suppose that nodes Alice and Bob share a symmetric key k taken from a key space $\mathcal{K}$. Let $f : \mathcal{K} \to \mathcal{K}$ be a public one-way function (so f can be efficiently computed, but it is difficult to find an inverse image under f). In practice, we may build a one-way function f from a secure hash function.

Define the ith *version* k_i of the key k by $k_0 = k$ and $k_i = f(k_{i-1})$ for $i \geq 1$. Initially, both Alice and Bob store version 0 of the key. Whenever they exchange an encrypted message, they use the current version of the key. After exchanging the message, they replace their key k_i by $k_{i+1} = f(k_i)$, and destroy the original key k_i. This process is known as *refreshing* the key. Note that if Alice or Bob are compromised, the adversary only comes into possession of the most up-to-date version k_i of the key. The adversary is unable to compute any previous version k_j of the key, where $j < i$, because f is one-way, and so cannot decrypt any ciphertexts intercepted before the node compromise. This method therefore satisfies the restricted notion of forward security (although it does not achieve Bellare and Yee's indistinguishability property, as the function f can be used to distinguish a sequence of keys from a random sequence). Both standard and provably secure refreshing require no communication overhead. The former technique is a little more efficient, but the latter technique has the advantage of a more precisely defined security model. In our schemes, which we describe in Sect. 4 and 5, either technique can be used.

2.2 Forward Security in Sensor Networks

The literature contains examples of schemes for refreshing pairwise keys that have been proposed specifically for WSNs. In [9], Mauw, van Vessem and Bos consider a network in which each node communicates directly with a base station. Each node n shares a unique initial key x_n^0 with the base station, and the standard refreshing technique described in Subsect. 2.1 is used, with key x_n^i being generated as $\mathcal{H}(x_n^{i-1})$, where $\mathcal{H}$ is a one-way hash function (the authors suggest the use of SHA-1).

Klonowski, Kutyłowski, Ren and Rybarczyk consider the scenario in which every node "shares a separate pairwise key with each neighbour" [6]. Their scheme also employs a one-way function F but, based on a key distribution mechanism in [11], incorporates an element of randomness. In their scheme, if nodes A and B share key k_{AB} and A wants to send a message to B, then A encrypts the message using a key $k' = F(k_{AB}, i)$, where i is chosen uniformly at random from the set $\{0, 1, \ldots, l\}$ for some small l. Node B then has to perform several trial decryptions in order to determine the precise value of i and hence k' that was used. This is more computationally expensive than the standard pairwise refreshing technique, and has the complication that B must succeed in receiving and decrypting the message in order for key refreshing to occur successfully. The presence of the randomness does, however, provide the additional property that an adversary that possesses an old version of a key will eventually be unable to determine newer versions of the key unless it has continued to monitor all the messages sent using intermediate versions of that key. Note that real randomness, rather than pseudorandomness, must be used for this additional property to hold (as we may assume that node compromise reveals the state of any pseudorandom generator used by the node). This limits the applicability of the scheme. Note also that the computational burden of trial decryptions may be eliminated from this scheme at the expense of a little more communication complexity by appending the random bits used in key refresh to the message from A to B.

Since randomness is not needed for forward security, and a security model where the randomness has benefits must involve a weakening of the standard model considered for sensor networks (in which an adversary is capable of intercepting all communication), we do not consider randomness in the schemes we present later in the paper.

The schemes we have considered so far all involve refreshing keys that are shared by exactly two entities. As discussed in the introduction, however, many sensor network applications involve keys that are shared by more than two participants. Refreshing keys in this situation becomes more complicated; in the following subsection we discuss some of the issues that arise.

2.3   Problems That Arise When Widely Shared Keys Are Refreshed

When seeking to maintain forward security when a key k is shared by more than two nodes, a pairwise key refreshing scheme cannot be used without some modifications. If user X is currently storing version i of the key k, we write $\mathrm{vn}_k(X) = i$. In the standard two node schemes discussed in Subsect. 2.1, it is clear that $\mathrm{vn}_k(\text{Alice}) = \mathrm{vn}_k(\text{Bob})$ at all times, whereas this will not usually be the case if more than two nodes use the same key. If communicating nodes simply refresh their keys after each message, other nodes using the same key will not necessarily be aware that a message has been transmitted and so will not refresh their key appropriately. This causes two problems:

- (*Undecipherable messages*) If users X and Y are such that $\mathrm{vn}_k(X) < \mathrm{vn}_k(Y)$, we have a problem if X sends a message to Y using version $\mathrm{vn}_k(X)$ of k (since Y cannot decrypt). So we need to have a mechanism to ensure that the version numbers of X and Y are synchronised.
- (*Degradation of forward security*) Suppose some node Z has refreshed its key less than communicating nodes X and Y, so $\mathrm{vn}_k(Z) < \mathrm{vn}_k(X) = \mathrm{vn}_k(Y)$. Then the compromise of Z allows an adversary to decipher any messages exchanged by X and Y using versions of the key lying between $\mathrm{vn}_k(Z)$ and $\mathrm{vn}_k(X)$. So we need to have a mechanism to ensure that no node stores a "very old" version of a key.

The first problem could be solved by requiring nodes to use a different version number of the key for each pairwise communication link they maintain. A node would have to store a set of version numbers (one for each link) together with the version of the key corresponding to the lowest of these version numbers. But this causes a proliferation of version numbers and so this solution is often unrealistic because of storage constraints in the WSN model. Moreover, the second problem becomes worse.

In this paper we propose two alternative classes of solutions. In Sect. 4 we address the problems of undecipherable messages and degradation of forward security by describing mechanisms to ensure that all nodes update their copy of

k at essentially the same time (*synchronised key refreshing*). However, in some applications this approach is unrealistic, and so in Sect. 5 we describe a method whereby a pair of communicating nodes determines which version number of the key to use (*asynchronous key refreshing*, addressing the first problem) and then describe several mechanisms to ensure that no node stores a low version number of a key (*key resynchronisation*, addressing the second problem). First, however, we discuss several applications for sensor networks. These give rise to five categories of network environment, in which our different schemes are appropriate.

3   Sensor Network Environments and Applications

The vast array of applications that have been proposed for WSNs leads to networks with widely varying properties. In order to provide a context for the key refreshing schemes we propose in this paper, we consider five distinct sensor network application environments. The differing characteristics of these situations mean that the most appropriate method of key refreshing varies between examples. Here we describe these environments, and give examples of possible applications for which they are appropriate.

1. (**Synchronised clocks**). In many applications, the nodes in the network have synchronised clocks. As discussed in Römer et al. [12], clock synchronisation comes at a cost. However, in networks where it is provided for the purposes of the application, we can exploit clock synchronisation for performing key refreshing. Examples of applications for which clock synchronisation is necessary include an intruder detection system in which records of events are timestamped by individual sensors, or a system for monitoring volcanic activity in which the network is used to provide a global picture of a volcano's behaviour at a given time.

2. (**Frequent flooding**). Many environments do not require nodes to have synchronised clocks, but frequent flooding of messages through the network should take place. This might be the case, for example, in a disaster recovery scenario in which sensors attached to medical personnel flood real-time updates on their status to others in the area.

3. (**Infrequent network-wide events**). Some applications call for networks in which synchronised clocks and regular flooding are not present, but in which there is an occasional event that can be detected by the entire network. For example, the data sink could consist of a helicopter that flies over the network occasionally and broadcasts a request to retrieve data to the entire network. In some applications an infrequent flooding of the network might take place (for example, an intruder detection system in a warehouse might be armed or disarmed by a flooded message that is triggered by the locking or unlocking of a door).

4. (**Infrequent local events**). Our fourth category consists of networks in which no global events occur with sufficient frequency or regularity and no

regular flooding takes place, but whose communication capacity can support an occasional flooded message. This is the case in networks measuring events that occur locally, and in which there is a low amount of (mostly local) communication between nodes.

5. **(Regular disconnection).** The final network environment that we address consists of networks that have a high likelihood of becoming disconnected, but in which the separate components continue functioning independently until the network is later reconnected. This might occur in sparse networks in which nodes are sited at the very edge of their communication capacities, or networks in which clusters of nodes are associated with moving objects, such as vehicles.

4   Schemes to Synchronise Key Refreshing

This section contains two schemes that can be used to synchronise key refreshing throughout a network; they can be applied in the first two application environments respectively. The schemes can either be used to refresh a fixed key from the keypool, or a subset of keys.

4.1   Synchronous Event-Driven Key Refreshing

The simplest means of maintaining synchronicity of key version numbers is:

Scheme 1 (Event-driven refreshing). *Nodes refresh their keys in response to some event that can be observed by the whole network.*

In our first application scenario, in which nodes have synchronised clocks, the network can simply refresh their keys every five minutes, say, thus providing forward security for messages more than five minutes old. Alternatively, if nodes are capable of detecting some network-wide event that happens with sufficient frequency, then they can refresh their keys every time such an event is detected, thus removing the requirement that their internal clocks be strictly synchronised. Finally, in networks possessing a base station capable of broadcasting directly to each node, the base station can simply send regular messages prompting the nodes to refresh their keys.

This scheme is very desirable in that there are no communication overheads. The existence of a suitable network-wide event is a strong (but widely satisfied) requirement: the more complex schemes discussed in subsequent sections are intended to be used when this requirement is not met.

4.2   Flooded Refreshing

Another solution to the problem of version number synchronisation is for a node to flood a key refresh signal throughout the network each time a key needs to be refreshed. The resulting communication overhead makes this infeasible in many instances; however, in our second scenario where much of the traffic involves messages being flooded throughout the entire network, the refresh signal can be 'piggy-backed' onto a flooded message. Each such flood then acts as a signal for all keys to be updated (hence the same version number is maintained for each key). The following scheme illustrates how this can be carried out, taking into account the fact that the flooding of separate messages may be simultaneously initiated at differing points of the network. The only communication overhead associated with refreshing in this manner is the need to append the version number to the encrypted message. (Even this overhead could be eliminated at the cost of nodes potentially having to perform several trial decryptions to determine the correct version number.)

Scheme 2 (Flooded refreshing)

1. *Before initiating the flooding of a message, a node first updates all its keys. It then encrypts the message under the new version of its keys before broadcasting it.*
2. *A node X receiving a flooded message encrypted with a version $i > \mathrm{vn}_k(X)$ of key k must update k in order to decrypt the message; it similarly updates the rest of its keys, then encrypts the message under these new versions before forwarding it. (Note that a node only forwards each message once; if it receives additional copies of the same message it simply ignores them.)*
3. *A node keeps a particular version of its keys until after it has broadcast a message using a higher version number. If a node receives several messages encrypted with different version numbers before it is able to forward them, it encrypts all the messages using the highest of these version numbers before rebroadcasting them. Once the messages have been sent it deletes all older versions of its keys.*

This scheme ensures that nodes only have to store multiple versions of the same key for the brief time between receiving a message and rebroadcasting it. If we assume that the media access control employed by the WSN prevents two neighbouring nodes from broadcasting simultaneously, then this manner of key updating prevents problems arising from nodes needing to use old versions of keys that they have already deleted. (Note that because of the small distances involved, we suppose that a message sent directly to a node by its neighbour is received instantaneously.)

Theorem 1. *If synchronous key refreshing is performed using Scheme 2 then no node receives a message encrypted with a version of a key that it has already deleted.*

Proof. Suppose a node A receives a message m rebroadcast by a neighbouring node B encrypted with version $\mathrm{vn}_k(B)$ of a key k possessed by A. Then A has version $\mathrm{vn}_k(A)$, and $\mathrm{vn}_k(A) \leq \mathrm{vn}_k(B)$, unless A has already rebroadcast some message using a version number higher than $\mathrm{vn}_k(B)$. However, in that case, A's neighbour B would have received that message prior to sending m, and thus $\mathrm{vn}_k(B) \geq \mathrm{vn}_k(A)$, which is a contradiction.   □

In environments where a significant proportion of communication is local, Scheme 2 would incur an undesirable communication overhead. So we need to find schemes that flood the network less frequently.

5   The Asynchronous Case

The synchronous schemes discussed in Sect. 4 all have the advantage of ensuring that nodes sharing a given key maintain the same numbered version of that key. In our last three network environments, however, there are no sufficiently frequent network-wide events that would enable these schemes to be employed. In Subsect. 5.1, we discuss an asynchronous scheme that can be used in these environments. The nature of the scheme means that we need to resynchronise the version numbers across the network occasionally, to prevent undue degradation of forward security. Subsect. 5.2, 5.3 and 5.4 discuss methods for resynchronisation appropriate in environments 3, 4 and 5 respectively.

5.1   Asynchronous Key Refreshing

A simple method of *asynchronous key refreshing*, in which different nodes refresh their keys at different rates, is described as follows:

Scheme 3 (Message-driven refreshing)

1. *When two neighbouring nodes X and Y want to communicate using key k, X sends $\mathrm{vn}_k(X)$ to Y and Y sends $\mathrm{vn}_k(Y)$ to X.*
2. *X and Y each compute*

$$\mathrm{newvn} = 1 + \max\{\mathrm{vn}_k(X), \mathrm{vn}_k(Y)\}.$$

3. *X and Y each update their copy of k by applying f an appropriate number of times, so that*

$$\mathrm{vn}_k(X) = \mathrm{vn}_k(Y) = \mathrm{newvn}.$$

Then they use the updated key k to encrypt any information they wish to send to each other.

This scheme works well if all the nodes are more-or-less equally active, and hence update k at similar rate[1]. Even so, it is still possible that relatively inactive nodes do not update k very often. Thus, to avoid the degradation of forward security, a resynchronisation scheme must be deployed. Again, the method employed will depend on the network environment: we now discuss some possible methods.

---

[1] Due to the broadcast nature of wireless communication, it is also possible for any neighbours of the nodes involved in this exchange to learn the version number reached and refresh their own keys if necessary.

5.2   Periodic Resynchronisation

The third category of networks discussed in Sect. 3 consists of those that experience regular events (such as a helicopter fly-past) that would be suitable for event-based key refreshing except that they do not happen with sufficient frequency. In such a context, the asynchronous refreshing Scheme 3 can be applied, but with the version numbers held by nodes being resynchronised each time the infrequent event is observed. A simple resynchronisation scheme requires all nodes to update their keys to a pre-specified version number upon detection of the event. For example, the jth occurrence of the regular event could trigger each node to update their version number to the value $100j$ (assuming that no node will transmit more than 100 times between events). Thus less active nodes will "catch up" with highly active nodes once a day, maintaining some level of sychronicity on a regular basis. This technique is suitable as long as the amount of traffic likely to occur between consecutive occurrences of the event in question does not vary greatly and can be reasonably estimated. It has the advantage of incurring no communication overheads.

5.3   Resynchronisation by a Flood

In applications where there are no network-wide events and the network can only support occasional flooding (see our fourth environment), a flooding technique could be used for resynchronisation rather than key refresh. So whenever a node has refreshed its key 100 times (say), it uses the flooded key refresh scheme from Sect. 4 to flood the network with a message requiring all nodes to update their keys to its version number. Flooding places an extra communication burden on the network, but this can be made manageable since the frequency of the floods is much lower than the frequency of key refresh operations. This scheme trades a degradation of forward security for an improvement in communication complexity.

5.4   Resynchronisation Via a Leader Election

A third approach towards resynchronising keys in the absence of an appropriate network-wide event would be to periodically execute a protocol to resynchronise the network, by determining which node has the highest version number of a key k. (This is similar to the *leader election problem* that is studied in distributed systems.) Then every node would update their keys to this version[2]. This technique is useful in the fifth application environment of Sect. 3, in which the network may be temporarily disconnected. If the amount of traffic in each

---

[2] In general, it is not necessary for the refreshing of two distinct keys to be synchronised. For the sort of applications we are considering, however, it simplifies matters if all keys are refreshed at the same time. In particular this avoids any problems arising when the set of nodes that share a given key is disconnected.

component varies then the key versions possessed by nodes in different components will differ. In order to resynchronise these versions once the components are reconnected, it will be necessary to excute a protocol of this nature.

There is a large literature describing algorithms for leader election in different settings. For our purposes, a variation of the algorithms described in Peleg [10] is appropriate, and we describe this algorithm below (Algorithm 1). This approach to resynchronisation is appropriate in situations when the network needs to run a protocol to establish some of its global properties (such as the shortest path to a sink node) in cases when the network is dynamic.

The algorithm has time complexity $O(D)$ and message complexity $O(DE)$, where D is the diameter of the network and E is the number of edges in the network. We describe an algorithm for leader election that can be initiated by any node x. The algorithm does not require that message transmissions be synchronised. The number of rounds (or *pulses*) is determined by the maximum distance of a node from the initiating node x, which we denote by dmax. The value of dmax does not have to be known ahead of time; indeed, the algorithm will compute it. We do not require that nodes have any knowledge of the structure of the network, except for the requirement that every node is assumed to know who all of its neighbours are. Note that if two nodes initiate the protocol simultaneously, it is easy to avoid any resulting conflicts by enforcing a standard rule for deciding which algorithm to drop.

Every node i has a value v_i; at the end of the algorithm, every node should know the value

$$\mathsf{vmax} = \max\{v_i\}.$$

In this algorithm, nodes broadcast tuples of the form (s, y, d, v), whose components are defined as follows:

- s is the node who is broadcasting the tuple, ($s = 0$ denotes a termination condition for the algorithm)
- y is the node at maximum distance (which is denoted by d) from the initiating node x, according to the current knowledge of s,
- v is the value of vmax, according to the current knowledge of s.

Algorithm 1

1. *The first time node s receives a broadcast from any of its neighbours, it increments d by one and specifies itself as the node of maximum distance from x. It sets the value of v to be the maximum of v_s and the received value of v, then it broadcasts the tuple (s, s, d, v). This represents the first pulse for node s.*

2. *In subsequent pulses, the node s waits until it receives broadcasts from all of its neighbours (subsequent to its last broadcast). Then it updates d and v (and y, if necessary) based on the most recent set of tuples received, and broadcasts an updated tuple.*

3. *The initialising node x terminates the algorithm once there are two consecutive pulses in which the maximum received d-value does not change. This*

allows x to conclude that it has received information from every other node. It broadcasts the terminating condition (s = 0) in the form of the tuple (0, y, d, v) in which d = dmax, v = vmax, and y has distance dmax from x.

4. Whenever a node receives a broadcasted tuple with s = 0, it rebroadcasts this tuple and terminates.

Algorithm 1 can be used in conjunction with our asynchronous key refreshing scheme (Scheme 3). As it requires a substantial amount of communication between nodes it is perhaps most useful when performed occasionally, in response to a change in network conditions. For example, in the context of our fifth application environment, if the network becomes disconnected then Algorithm 1 can be applied in order to resynchronise key version numbers once connectivity is restored. We now give an example that demonstrates its behaviour.

Example 1. We present an example illustrating Algorithm 1. We use the graph in vertex set $\{1, \ldots, 6\}$ with edges 12, 15, 23, 24, 25, 34, 46 (Fig. 1). The values stored in the nodes are $v_1 = 8$, $v_2 = 6$, $v_3 = 17$, $v_4 = 11$, $v_5 = 12$, $v_6 = 17$, and the initialising node is $x = 1$.

Fig. 1. A network in which the nodes possess different versions of a key

The tuples that will be broadcast during the execution of the algorithm are shown in Table 1. During the first pulse node 1 broadcasts the tuple $(1, 1, 0, 8)$ to initiate the algorithm. This is received by its neighbours, nodes 2 and 5. Node 2 has a lower version number than node 1, so it broadcasts the tuple $(2, 2, 1, 8)$. The first 2 denotes that the tuple is being sent by node 2, the second 2 and the 1 indicate that node 2 is at distance 1 from the initiating node, and that as yet it does not know of any nodes located further away. The 8 is the highest version number that node 2 has encountered so far. Similarly, during this second pulse node 5 broadcasts $(5, 5, 1, 12)$ to indicate that it is at distance 1 from node 1, including its own value for v as it is higher than that of node 1. This process continues until node 1 has received tuples with $d = 3$ in two consecutive pulses. Node 1 now knows that node 6 is the farthest node, and that the highest version number in the network is 17. It thus broadcasts the termination message $(0, 6, 3, 17)$, which is then rebroadcast by the other nodes in the network, until all nodes have received and rebroadcast this message.

6   Discussion

We have seen that the behaviour of a key refreshing scheme depends on the network environment in which it is to be applied. In Table 2 we summarise

Table 1. Example of the Leader Election Algorithm

	1	2	3	4	5	6
send	$(1,1,0,8)$					
receive		$(1,1,0,8)$			$(1,1,0,8)$	
send		$(2,2,1,8)$			$(5,5,1,12)$	
receive	$(2,2,1,8)$ $(5,5,1,12)$	$(5,5,1,12)$	$(2,2,1,8)$	$(2,2,1,8)$	$(2,2,1,8)$	
send	$(1,2,1,12)$		$(3,3,2,17)$	$(4,4,2,11)$		
receive		$(1,2,1,12)$ $(3,3,2,17)$ $(4,4,2,11)$	$(4,4,2,11)$	$(3,3,2,17)$	$(1,2,1,12)$	$(4,4,2,11)$
send		$(2,3,2,17)$			$(5,2,1,12)$	$(6,6,3,11)$
receive	$(2,3,2,17)$ $(5,2,1,12)$	$(5,2,1,12)$	$(2,3,2,17)$	$(2,3,2,17)$ $(6,6,3,11)$	$(2,3,2,17)$	
send	$(1,3,2,17)$		$(3,3,2,17)$	$(4,6,3,17)$		
receive		$(1,3,2,17)$ $(3,3,2,17)$ $(4,6,3,17)$	$(4,6,3,17)$	$(3,3,2,17)$	$(1,3,2,17)$	$(4,6,3,17)$
send		$(2,6,3,17)$			$(5,3,2,17)$	$(6,6,3,17)$
receive	$(2,6,3,17)$ $(5,3,2,17)$	$(5,3,2,17)$	$(2,6,3,17)$	$(2,6,3,17)$ $(6,6,3,17)$	$(2,6,3,17)$	
send	$(1,6,3,17)$		$(3,6,3,17)$	$(4,6,3,17)$		
receive		$(1,6,3,17)$ $(3,6,3,17)$ $(4,6,3,17)$	$(4,6,3,17)$	$(3,6,3,17)$	$(1,6,3,17)$	$(4,6,3,17)$
send		$(2,6,3,17)$			$(5,6,3,17)$	$(6,6,3,17)$
receive	$(2,6,3,17)$ $(5,6,3,17)$	$(5,6,3,17)$	$(2,6,3,17)$	$(2,6,3,17)$ $(6,6,3,17)$	$(2,6,3,17)$	
send	$(0,6,3,17)$		$(3,6,3,17)$	$(4,6,3,17)$		
receive		$(0,6,3,17)$	$(4,6,3,17)$	$(3,6,3,17)$	$(0,6,3,17)$	$(4,6,3,17)$
send		$(0,6,3,17)$			$(0,6,3,17)$	
receive			$(0,6,3,17)$	$(0,6,3,17)$		$(0,6,3,17)$
send			$(0,6,3,17)$	$(0,6,3,17)$		
receive						$(0,6,3,17)$

the properties of the schemes we have proposed for key refreshing and resynchronisation, as well as prior schemes appearing in the literature. The first four schemes have the advantage of incurring no communication overheads, although the scheme of [6] does involve a slight computational overhead, due to the need for trial decryptions. In the case of a network where there is pairwise communication with a base station, our event-driven scheme essentially reduces to the scheme of [9]; however, it is applicable in a wider range of environments, particularly any network where the nodes have synchronised clocks.

The remaining schemes do require extra communication, but are applicable in environments in which the first four schemes cannot be used. In the case of the flooded scheme this overhead is slight, as it is only necessary to append a key version number to each message that is flooded through the network. The final refreshing scheme (message-driven refreshing) is more costly, as two version numbers have to be transmitted before each message is sent. However, it can be used in any network environment, and hence can be employed in networks that do not have the necessary properties for the other schemes to be applied. Similar observations can be made regarding the resynchronisation schemes.

Table 2. A comparison of key refreshing and resynchronisation schemes. $+vn=key$ version number appended to each message; $x \times vn=x$ additional transmissions of vn per message; n=number of nodes; D=diameter of network; E=number of edges in network graph; for description of applications, see Sect. 3.

Scheme	Required Network Properties	Suitable Application Environments
Key Refreshing		
pairwise keys [9]	nodes communicate directly with the base station	
base station [6]	keys are shared by pairs of nodes	
1. Event-driven	frequent occurrence of a network-wide event	synchronised clocks
2. Flooded	frequent flooding of messages	frequent flooding
3. Message-driven	-	any
Resynchronisation		
Periodic	occasional network-wide event	infrequent network-wide events
Flooded	capable of supporting occasional flooded messages	infrequent local events
Leader Election	-	regular disconnection

There are several issues concerning key refreshing in a WSN context that merit further research. In some WSNs it is customary to deploy an excess of nodes that then spend part of their time in a 'sleep' state. Such nodes have the potential to degrade forward security if they are asleep through several key refresh events. One solution might be to mandate that nodes refresh their keys numerous times before entering the sleep state, however overall network-wide management of this process requires further investigation. Also, nodes in a WSN have relatively high failure probabilities, whether due to battery exhaustion, destruction, or simple malfunction. It would be interesting to investigate ways of limiting the degradation of forward security due to the results of node failure. Finally, many WSNs have specific topologies (such as hierarchal networks) for which it may be possible to devise dedicated key refreshing schemes that perform more efficiently than the general ones proposed in this paper.

References

1. Bellare, M., Yee, B.: Forward-Security in Private-Key Cryptography. In: Joye, M. (ed.) CT-RSA 2003. LNCS, vol. 2612, pp. 1–18. Springer, Heidelberg (2003)
2. Blum, L., Blum, M., Shub, M.: A Simple Unpredictable Pseudo-random Number Generator. SIAM J. Comput. 15(2), 364–383 (1986)
3. Çamtepe, S.A., Yener, B.: Key Distribution Mechanisms for Wireless Sensor Networks: a Survey. Technical report, Rensselaer Polytechnic Inst. TR-05-07 (2005)
4. Eschenauer, L., Gligor, V.D.: A Key-Management Scheme for Distributed Sensor Networks. In: Atluri, V. (ed.) CCS 2002, pp. 41–47. ACM, New York (2002)
5. Günter, C.G.: An Identity-Based Key-Exchange Protocol. In: Quisquater, J.-J., Vandewalle, J. (eds.) EUROCRYPT 1989. LNCS, vol. 434, pp. 29–37. Springer, Heidelberg (1990)
6. Klonowski, M., Kutyłowski, M., Ren, M., Rybarczyk, K.: Forward-Secure Key Evolution in Wireless Sensor Networks. In: Bao, F., Ling, S., Okamoto, T., Wang, H., Xing, C. (eds.) CANS 2007. LNCS, vol. 4856, pp. 102–120. Springer, Heidelberg (2007)
7. Lee, J., Stinson, D.R.: On the Construction of Practical Key Predistribution Schemes for Distributed Sensor Networks Using Combinatorial Designs. ACM Trans. Inf. Syst. Secur. 11(2), 1–35 (2008)
8. Martin, K.M., Paterson, M.B.: An Application-Oriented Framework for Wireless Sensor Network Key Establishment. In: WCAN, ENTCS (to appear, 2007)
9. Mauw, S., van Vessen, I., Bos, B.: Forward Secure Communication in Wireless Sensor Networks. In: Clark, J.A., Paige, R.F., Polack, F.A.C., Brooke, P.J. (eds.) SPC 2006. LNCS, vol. 3934, pp. 32–43. Springer, Heidelberg (2006)
10. Peleg, D.: Time-Optimal Leader Election in General Networks. J. Parallel Distr. Com. 8, 96–99 (1990)
11. Ren, M., Das, T.K., Zhou, J.: Diverging Keys in Wireless Sensor Networks. In: Katsikas, S.K., López, J., Backes, M., Gritzalis, S., Preneel, B. (eds.) ISC 2006. LNCS, vol. 4176, pp. 257–269. Springer, Heidelberg (2006)
12. Römer, K., Blum, P., Meier, L.: Time Synchronization and Calibration in Wireless Sensor Networks. In: Stojmenovic, I. (ed.) Handbook of Sensor Networks: Algorithms and Architectures, pp. 199–237. Wiley and Sons, Chichester (2005)
13. Römer, K., Mattern, F.: The Design Space of Wireless Sensor Networks. Wirel. Commun. 11(6), 54–61 (2004)
14. Xiao, Y., Rayi, V.K., Sun, B., Du, X., Hu, F., Galloway, M.: A Survey of Key Management Schemes in Wireless Sensor Networks. Comput. Commun. 30, 2314–2341 (2007)

Efficient Traitor Tracing from Collusion Secure Codes

Olivier Billet[1] and Duong Hieu Phan[2]

[1] Orange Labs, Issy-les-Moulineaux, France
[2] Université Paris 8, Saint-Denis, France
olivier.billet@orange-ftgroup.com, hieu.phan@univ-paris8.fr

Abstract. In this paper, we describe a new traitor tracing scheme which relies on Tardos' collusion secure codes to achieve *constant size* ciphertexts. Our scheme is also equipped with a black-box tracing procedure against pirates that are allowed to decrypt with some (possibly high) error rate while keeping the decoders of the lowest possible size when using collusion secure codes, namely of size proportional to the length of Tardos' code.

1 Introduction

One common issue in digital content distribution is the problem of broadcasting data to several legitimate users in a secure way. Therefore, the broadcaster usually encrypts its data for the legitimate users. This is for example the case in pay-TV systems which allow to restrict access to the content to subscribers only, or when distributing digital media such as DVDs encrypted such that they can be used with compliant readers only [1]. In these scenarios and many others, the legitimate users rely on a decryption box containing the secrets that are necessary to obtain the digital content from the broadcasted information; this decryption box can be a tamper resistant device such as a smart card, a firmware for an electronic appliance, or a software on a personal computer. Tamper resistant devices are hard and expensive since they are designed to withstand a large range of attacks from side-channels attacks to invasive attacks. This raises the following issue: What if legitimate users are able to extract the secrets from their decryption box and redistribute them?

Traitor tracing is a well known cryptographic means to discourage such indelicate users (hereafter called traitors) from redistributing their secrets: It provides a way of embedding different secrets into each user's decryption box so that even if several traitors collude to produce a pirate decoder from their shared secrets, an authority is able to trace at least one of them. The efficiency of a traitor tracing scheme can be evaluated through several parameters: the maximum size c of tolerated coalitions, the size of the broadcasted ciphertext, and the size of the decoders. While it is obvious to design a traitor tracing scheme with a ciphertext size linear in the total number N of users, efficiently resisting collusions when traitors have full access to their decoders is not straightforward. Since its introduction by Chor, Fiat, and Naor [7], several techniques have been proposed.

R. Safavi-Naini (Ed.): ICITS 2008, LNCS 5155, pp. 171–182, 2008.
© Springer-Verlag Berlin Heidelberg 2008

A first class of schemes that we might call combinatorial is based on carefully choosing some subset of a set of master keys to be put in each decryption box. By analyzing the keys found in a pirate decoder, it is possible to trace one of the traitors. The schemes [7, 8, 12, 18, 19] belong to this family. Another class of schemes is the public key traitor tracing schemes first introduced in [16] by Kurosawa and Desmedt. To this family belong for instance [2, 4, 6, 9, 17, 20]. A third class of schemes relying on the use of collusion secure codes (and thus combining ideas from the two previous classes) has been introduced by Kiayias and Yung in [15]. The schemes [3, 10, 22, 29] belong to this class. Several of these works also provided additional features apart from the basic traitor tracing properties. It has been shown how to cope with decoders that decrypt correctly only with some (non-negligible) probability [19]. Tracing the traitors using black-box access only to the pirate decoders has been first proposed in [8]. The notion of public traceability has been proposed in [6, 21].

Our work, as for instance [10, 15, 29], is based on the use of collusion secure codes. These schemes enjoy many nice and desirable properties: they support black-box tracing and the ratio between the ciphertexts and the plaintexts is constant. However, since these schemes use collusion secure codes for both the ciphertext and the key used in the decoders, the size of the ciphertexts and decoders is quite large, namely $O(c^4 \log(N/\epsilon))$ for resisting coalitions of at most c traitors with probability $1 - \epsilon$. Another drawback of [15] comes from the use of an all-or-nothing transform (AONT [24]) to prevent deletion of keys from the pirate decoders as a way to escape the tracing procedure based on the underlying collusion secure code. This AONT renders the scheme quite rigid and prevents the reduction of the ciphertext's size since it requires to use *every* key from the decoder in order to decrypt a ciphertext, and thus slows down the decryption process. Safavi-Naini and Wang propose in [26] to use collusion secure codes that support random deletion in any position. In [29], Sirvent constructs new collusion secure codes which support deletion of a number of positions chosen by the adversary in addition to the usual properties: this results in a black-box tracing procedure which accommodates even more powerful pirates than [15, 26] and allows to remove the need for AONT. However, codewords from collusion secure codes supporting adversarial erasure have length $\Omega(c^4 \log(N/\epsilon))$ and the size of the ciphertexts and decoders remains large. In this paper, we propose a scheme based on Tardos' collusion secure code with *constant size ciphertexts* and thus resolve a first issue with code based traitor tracing schemes. The independent work [3] also proposes a scheme with constant size ciphertexts, but to be able to trace pirate decoders with non-negligible error rate δ, the size of the decoders is $\Omega(c^4/(1 - \delta)^2 \log(N/\epsilon))$ and tracing is accordingly expensive. This large complexity comes from the fact that the authors in [3] built a collusion secure code with the strong property of resisting erasure. While this might lead to useful applications in settings other than traitor tracing, we show that such a strong collusion secure code is not required here: Our scheme takes advantage of the specific setting of traitor tracing where it is possible to distinguish between erased and unreadable positions. As a result our scheme can rely on Tardos' code and, in addition to bring constant size ciphertexts, also allows decoders of size $O(c^2 \log(N/\epsilon))$ even when considering pirate decoders with high error rates δ.

2   Tardos' Collusion Secure Codes

Fingerprinting with collusion secure codes allows to uniquely identify a digital document among several copies of it by embedding a fingerprint (a codeword). Such an identification scheme must be resilient to collusions of traitors trying to remove their fingerprints so as to escape identification. Therefore, collusion secure codes share some properties with traitor tracing; However, the main assumption here (called the marking assumption) is that the traitors from a coalition are only able to identify the positions where the digits from their respective codewords differ; Such positions are called *detectable positions*. This assumption especially makes sense when fingerprinting data: apart from the codewords, the documents are identical, and it is easy to uncover places where two copies of a document differ.

Among the first collusion secure codes are the identifiable parent property (IPP) codes introduced in [7]; However, these codes are defined over large alphabets and are resilient in a restricted attack model. The marking assumption and a way to construct randomized collusion secure codes has first been proposed by Boneh and Shaw in [5]; The length of the codewords is $O(N^3 \log(N/\epsilon))$ for fully-collusion resistant codes and $O(c^4 \log(N/\epsilon))$ for codes resisting coalitions of at most c traitors. Tardos later introduced a new construction in [31] and proved that the size of its codewords is optimal: a length of $O(c^2 \log(N/\epsilon))$ is enough to resist coalitions of at most c traitors. This obviously gives fully-collusion secure codes of length $O(N^2 \log(N/\epsilon))$.

2.1   Tardos' Construction

We now briefly describe the generation of a Tardos collusion secure code as proposed in [31]. We additionally describe the associated tracing procedure.

Code generation. In order to generate a code for N users that resists to c-collusions, set the length $\ell = 100c^2 \log(\frac{N}{\epsilon})$ where ϵ is the false-positive error probability (that is, the probability that an innocent user is accused) of the tracing algorithm and randomly draw a sequence of probabilities p_i as follows:

$$p_i = \sin^2(r_i), \qquad i \in [\![1, \ell]\!] \tag{1}$$

where r_i is randomly drawn from $[t, \pi/2 - t]$ and $0 < t < \pi/4$ is chosen so that $300\, c \sin^2 t = 1$.

Each binary codeword w of the code is then constructed by choosing its i-th digit to be either '1' or '0' according to the probability p_i, that is: $\Pr[w_i = 1] = p_i$.

Tracing procedure. The authority traces a subset of the traitors from a coalition (of at most c traitors) that has produced some binary word v by computing an accusation sum Z_w for each possible codeword w via:

$$Z_w = \sum_{i=1}^{\ell} v_i \cdot \left(\bar{w}_i \sqrt{\frac{1 - p_i}{p_i}} + (\bar{w}_i - 1) \sqrt{\frac{p_i}{1 - p_i}} \right) \; ,$$

where $\bar{w}_i$ is the bit w_i viewed as an integer. Then, users corresponding to codewords w such that $Z_w > 20 \, c \log(\frac{N}{\epsilon})$ are declared as traitors. Tardos proves that the probability of false-negative alarms (that is, the probability that no traitor is found) is then $\epsilon^{c/4}$.

2.2   Note about the Marking Assumption

Here we make some basic remark that will be used later on in this paper. Think about Tardos' code as a matrix containing the codewords in its rows. We note that the columns in Tardos' code are all treated identically: they are generated the same way and contribute to the accusation sum following the same rule. Moreover, these columns have been generated *independently*. This very simple fact allows one to use codewords of bigger length, say, twice or four times the length of Tardos' original codewords (i.e. $L = 2\ell$ or $L = 4\ell$) and still allows to trace the traitors by using *any* subset of positions of size ℓ. We stress here that the traitors can make an educated choice of the subset of positions instead of choosing them randomly. However, even in this case, the resulting set of codeword remains a perfectly valid instance of Tardos' code.

This remark is motivated by the usual marking assumption for collusion secure codes. Indeed, the most commonly used marking assumption is that traitors are able to identify positions in their code words only where the digits differ: this fits a wide range of settings, such as watermarking of digital content. However, in the following, we additionally consider that some of the positions—regardless of the fact that they can be identified or not—might be deleted by the traitors, so that this position does not hold the original digit anymore. This issue motivated the introduction of AONT in [15] and the introduction of collusion secure codes resisting erasure in [3, 29]. However, our above remark shows that expanding a Tardos' code of length ℓ to a length $L = \frac{1}{\beta}\ell$ allows to cope with collusions of at most c traitors that are able to delete up to $(1 - \beta)L$ digits from their pirate word, and then fall back to the *classical* marking assumption on the untouched subset of $\beta L = \ell$ positions.

3   Traitor Tracing Schemes from Collusion Secure Codes

3.1   Construction

Building the Decoders. The main idea to build the decoder is to use two different set of keys, viewed as a pair of tables denoted $T^{(0)}$ and $T^{(1)}$, each consisting of L randomly drawn n-bit elements and to use them to recover u random values $k_1, \ldots, k_u$ broadcasted (in an encrypted form) to the users in order to derive the corresponding session key SK from the HEADER for the data encapsulation mechanism: Obviously, the idea of using such a pair of tables is to allow

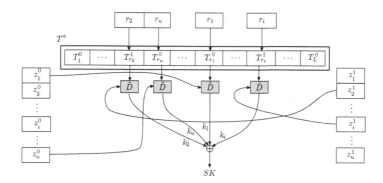

Fig. 1. The HEADER is made of the values r_i, $z_i^{(0)}$ and $z_i^{(1)}$ and the decoder of user a has access to table T^a. Using its bit string I^a, user a selects the correct values z_i to be decrypted: here, user a selects $z_1^{(0)}$, $z_2^{(1)}$, ..., $z_i^{(1)}$, ..., $z_u^{(0)}$. User a then decrypts these values with the corresponding keys $T^a[k_1]$, ..., $T^a[k_u]$ from table T^a. The decrypted keys k_1, ..., k_u are further combined together to form the session key $SK = k_1 \oplus \cdots \oplus k_u$.

the embedding of the identity of the user a in her personal decoder: if I^a is an L-bit string carrying the identity of user a, then we create a table T^a specific to user a by choosing as the i-th element $T^a[i]$ the key $T^{(I_i^a)}[i]$. (Here, I_i^a denotes the i-th bit of the bit string I^a.)

Coming back to the derivation of the session key SK from HEADER, since each decoder either embeds a key from $T^{(0)}$ or a key from $T^{(1)}$, the above-mentioned values k_i must be encrypted under both of these keys. The derivation of the session key is then performed from an HEADER $= (r_1, \ldots, r_u, z_1^{(0)}, z_1^{(1)}, \ldots, z_u^{(0)}, z_u^{(1)})$ where the r_i are u randomly chosen indices from $[\![1, L]\!]$ and the z_i are values obtained by encrypting u randomly chosen n-bit values k_1, ..., k_u using an encryption scheme $\tilde{E}$ as follows:

$$\forall i \in [\![1, u]\!], \qquad z_i^{(0)} = \tilde{E}_{T^{(0)}[r_i]}(k_i) \quad \text{and} \quad z_i^{(1)} = \tilde{E}_{T^{(1)}[r_i]}(k_i) \ .$$

Note that the number u of elements of the table T entering in the derivation of the session key SK also depends on other system parameters in a way that is going to be discussed later on. A brief description of how these elements fit together into our proposal for an implementation of the function F_K to be used in our key encapsulation mechanism within each decoder is given in Figure 1.

Then, the data encapsulation mechanism is implemented as:

Encryption of M by broadcaster:

1. Draw $(r_1, r_2, \ldots, r_u)$ from $[\![1, L]\!]^u$ randomly;
2. Draw u elements k_1, k_2, ..., k_u from $\{0, 1\}^n$ randomly;
3. Encrypt the random values k_i as $z_i^{(0)} = \tilde{E}_{T^{(0)}[r_i]}(k_i)$ and $z_i^{(1)} = \tilde{E}_{T^{(1)}[r_i]}(k_i)$, for $i \in [\![1, u]\!]$;
4. Set HEADER $= (r_1, \ldots, r_u; z_1^{(0)}, z_1^{(1)}, z_2^{(0)}, z_2^{(1)}, \ldots, z_u^{(1)})$;

5. Derive the session key as $SK = k_1 \oplus k_2 \oplus \cdots \oplus k_u$;
6. Encrypt M with the underlying encryption algorithm E and the secret key SK: $C = E_{SK}(M)$;
7. Output the ciphertext $E'(M) = (\text{HEADER}, C)$.

Decryption of (HEADER, C) *in decoders:*

1. Extract $r_1, \ldots, r_u$ from HEADER;
2. Depending on the value I_i^a of the i-th bit of the user's identifying string I^a, compute
$$k_i = \tilde{D}_{T^a[r_i]}\left(z_i^{(I_i^a)}\right) \quad \forall i \in [\![1, u]\!] \ .$$
3. Derive the temporary secret key $SK = k_1 \oplus k_2 \oplus \cdots \oplus k_u$;
4. Use the underlying decryption algorithm to decrypt C with SK: $M = D_{SK}(C)$;
5. Output the plaintext $D'(C) = M$.

Pirate Decoders. A pirate decoder is only required to decrypt valid ciphertexts with some probability τ. This is meant to take into account the case of coalitions of pirates dropping some of the secrets required to decrypt so as to help concealing their identity, which is highly critical in the setting of decoders based on collusion secure codes.

The Tracing Procedure. There are two main types of decoders: stateless decoders and stateful decoders. Stateless decoders do not record information between two decryption attempts whereas stateful decoders might memorize some information in order to help escaping the tracing procedure. We first describe a procedure against stateless decoders.

Our tracing procedure is derived from the general black-box tracing strategy for stateless decoders described in [8]: In order to decide if the decoder embeds the key $T^{(0)}[r]$ or the key $T^{(1)}[r]$ for some position r, the tracer provides the information to derive SK only for one of the key, that is, broadcasts $\tilde{E}_{T^{(0)}[r]}(k_1)$ and $\tilde{E}_{T^{(1)}[r]}(0)$; Therefore, if the decoder decrypts correctly this (invalid) ciphertext, the tracer deduces that the decoder knows $T^{(0)}[r]$.

Our tracing procedure also heavily relies on the property that the pirate decoders always embed at least ℓ digits that have been produced through the *classical* marking assumption (traitors can only put unreadable digits on detectable positions, the other positions are untouched) where ℓ is the required length for Tardos' code to be secure. We give sufficient conditions on the parameters u and β for this property to hold in Theorem 2 of the next paragraph.

We first describe the tracing procedure for $u = 1$. In this case, HEADER only consists of three values (r, z^0, z^1) where $\tilde{D}_{T^0[r]} = \tilde{D}_{T^1[r]}$. We call a 0-invalid header a header $(r, z^0, *)$ produced from a valid header (r, z^0, z^1) by replacing z^1 by a randomly chosen value '*' and similarly call $(r, *, z^1)$ a 1-invalid header. One can easily detect if the cell r of a decoder is coming from $T^{(0)}[r]$, $T^{(1)}[r]$ is unreadable or is wrong/erased; as noted previously, the ability to decide between unreadable cells (i.e. where the decoder knows the two possible keys) and the wrong/erased cells (i.e. where the decoder knows none of the keys) is fundamental to the tracing procedure. In order to distinguish these two types of positions, just follow the procedure:

- Input a number L/τ of valid headers with randomly chosen positions r (where τ is the decryption threshold of the decoder); every possible position therefore occurs τ^{-1} times on the average. Every position for which the decoder decrypted at least once, is declared an *inhabited* position. (Thus, inhabited position are the positions r for which the tracer knows for sure that the decoder embeds at least one of the values $T^{(0)}[r], T^{(1)}[r]$.)
- For every inhabited position r, input a number τ^{-1} of 0/1-invalid headers. As soon as the decoder correctly decrypts a b-invalid header, deduce that cell r is coming from table $T^{(b)}$. If the decoder never decrypts b-invalid headers, deduce that the position r corresponds to a detectable position in the collusion secure code, that is, assume that the decoder knows both $T^{(0)}[r]$ and $T^{(1)}[r]$ and call this position an *unveiled* position.

(Note that the above procedure declares a position r to be '0', '1', or unveiled even though the pirate decoder refused to use the corresponding key $T^{(i)}[r]$ all of the time but once, i.e. used a probabilistic strategy to hide its choices.) Since the pirate decoder embeds at least ℓ digits (either from detectable positions or untouched from the traitors' original codewords) we are able to trace the traitors by applying Tardos' tracing procedure to these ℓ positions as explained in Section 2.

This procedure naturally extends to the case of $u > 1$. Remember that the pirate decoder must decrypt correctly with probability greater than the threshold τ the well formed headers. Therefore, for $\tau^{-1}L$ choices of the u-tuples, the tracer knows about every inhabited position (each time the decoder refuses to decrypt during this first phase no assumption is made, but when the decoder decrypts, u inhabited positions are learnt). Then, for every inhabited position r, the tracer considers 0/1-invalid headers corresponding to position r and chooses the remaining $u - 1$ positions among the set of inhabited positions (discovered in the previous phase) randomly; the type ('0', '1', or unveiled) of position r is then determined as in the case $u = 1$ and the tracing procedure ends as before.

It is also possible to trace stateful decoders. Indeed, Kiayias and Yung proposed in [14] a generic strategy to convert a tracing procedure against stateless decoders into a tracing procedure against stateful decoders by using two versions of the plaintext watermarked differently. This strategy can be applied with a slight modification of our scheme: instead of encrypting k_1 under $T^{(0)}[r_1]$ and $T^{(1)}[r_1]$, the broadcaster encrypts k_1 under $T^{(0)}[r_1]$ and $\tilde{k}_1$ under $T^{(1)}[r_1]$; Then instead of $E_{SK}(M)$, the broadcaster encrypts the plaintext watermarked in two different ways M_1 and M_2 under $SK = k_1 \oplus k_2 \oplus \cdots \oplus k_u$ and under $\widetilde{SK} = \tilde{k}_1 \oplus k_2 \oplus \cdots \oplus k_u$ respectively, that is, provides $E_{SK}(M_1)$ and $E_{\widetilde{SK}}(M_2)$.

3.2   Security

In this paragraph we provide two results. The first one, given by Theorem 1, is that the encryption scheme we propose is secure. The second one is that our proposed implementation of the decoders is indeed resistant to coalitions of at most c-traitors and is given in Theorem 2.

Semantic Security of a Symmetric Encryption Scheme. The semantic security of a symmetric encryption SKE = (KeyGen, Enc, Dec) is defined as follows:

Definition 1. *Let A be an adversary against SKE and λ be some security parameter. The adversary A chooses two messages, m_0 and m_1, of equal length, and gives them to an encryption oracle. The key generation $KeyGen(\lambda)$ generates a random key K, draws a random value $\sigma \in \{0,1\}$, and encrypts the corresponding message m_σ using the key K. The resulting ciphertext $c^\star = Enc_K(m_\sigma)$ is then provided to the adversary A. Finally, the adversary outputs $\hat{\sigma} \in \{0,1\}$. We define the advantage of A against SKE to be*

$$\mathsf{Adv}_A^{SKE}(\lambda) = \left| \Pr\left[\sigma = \hat{\sigma}\right] - \frac{1}{2} \right|$$

in the above attack game. We also define $\mathsf{Adv}^{SKE}(\lambda)$ as the maximum of all advantages $\mathsf{Adv}_A^{SKE}(\lambda)$ for all probabilistic, polynomial-time machines A. We say that SKE is semantically secure if $\mathsf{Adv}^{SKE}(\lambda)$ is negligibly for a security level λ.

Theorem 1. *Assume that the encryption schemes $(\tilde{E}, \tilde{D})$ and (E, D) are semantically secure. Let us assume that adversaries know for a fraction of at most 2α positions the corresponding entry from at least one of the two tables $T^{(0)}$ and $T^{(1)}$, and let $u(\lambda)$ be chosen so that $\pi_u(\lambda) = \binom{\alpha L}{u} / \binom{L}{u}$ is negligible for the security level λ. Then*

$$\mathsf{Adv}^{E'}(\lambda) \leq \pi_u(\lambda) + 2\mathsf{Adv}^{\tilde{E}}(\lambda) + \mathsf{Adv}^E(\lambda)$$

and thus (E', D') is semantically secure against the above adversaries.

Proof. First, note that for each choice of the tuple of indices $r_1, r_2, \ldots, r_u$, either the adversary knows at least one value in every of the u pairs $(T^{(0)}[r_1], T^{(1)}[r_1])$, ..., $(T^{(0)}[r_u], T^{(1)}[r_u])$, or she does not know $T^{(0)}[r_i]$ and $T^{(1)}[r_i]$ for at least one index r_i among $r_1, \ldots, r_u$. The first case happens at most $\pi_u = \binom{\alpha L}{u} / \binom{L}{u}$ of the times over the random choices of $r_1, \ldots, r_u$. In the other case, we can assume without loss of generality that the adversary A knows the $u-1$ remaining indices and (by renaming the indices) that the unknown values correspond to r_1, that is she does not know $T^{(0)}[r_1]$ nor $T^{(0)}[r_1]$. Let us note $s_0 = T^{(0)}[r_1]$ and $s_1 = T^{(1)}[r_1]$. As the keys to encrypt $k_2, \ldots, k_u$ are known to the adversary, the encryption of a message m of E' can be expressed, under the adversary's view, as $\big(\tilde{E}_{s_0}(k_1), \tilde{E}_{s_1}(k_1), k_2, \ldots k_u, E_{SK}(m)\big)$, where $SK = k_1 \oplus k_2 \oplus \cdots \oplus k_u$. Let $\kappa = k_2 \oplus \cdots \oplus k_u$ so that $SK = k_1 \oplus \kappa$.

We now wish to bound the advantage of the adversary in breaking (E', D'). To this end, let Game_0 be the original attack game played by the adversary A against (E', D'). We denote by $\psi = (e_0^\star, e_1^\star, k_2^\star, \ldots, k_u^\star, c^\star)$ the target ciphertext, we denote by σ the hidden bit generated by the encryption oracle, and we let $\hat{\sigma}$ be the bit outputted by A. Let T_0 be the event where $\sigma = \hat{\sigma}$. Also, let $k_1^\star$ denote the underlying message corresponding to the ciphertexts $e_0^\star$, $e_1^\star$ and $SK^\star$ denote the symmetric key used to encrypt m_σ, that is: $e_0^\star = \tilde{E}_{s_0}(k_1^\star)$, $e_1^\star = \tilde{E}_{s_1}(k_1^\star)$, and $c^\star = E_{SK}(m_\sigma)$.

We also define a modified game Game_1 which behaves just like game G_1, except that a completely random symmetric key SK^+ is used in place of the key $SK^\star$. Let T_1 be the event that $\sigma = \hat{\sigma}$ in this game Game_1.

It is straightforward to see that there is an oracle query machine A_1, whose running time is essentially the same as that of A, such that:

$$\left| \Pr[T_1] - \Pr[T_0] \right| \leq 2\mathsf{Adv}_{A_1}^{\tilde{E}}(\lambda) \ . \tag{2}$$

Indeed, the adversary A_1 just uses adversary A to play two independent games against $\tilde{E}$: one under the key s_0 and another under the key s_1. In the attack games that A_1 are playing against $\tilde{E}$, the challenged message k_1 is equal to $SK^\star \oplus k_2^\star \oplus \cdots \oplus k_u^\star$ in game Game_0, and is equal to $SK^+ \oplus k_2^\star \oplus \cdots \oplus k_u^\star$ in game Game_1.

Finally, we observe that in this modified game Game_1, the key SK^+ is used to encrypt message m_σ and does not play any other role. Thus, in game Game_1, the adversary A is essentially carrying out an attack against E:

$$\left| \Pr[T_1] - \frac{1}{2} \right| \leq \mathsf{Adv}^E(\lambda) \ . \tag{3}$$

By combining Eq. (2) and Eq. (3) in the case where the adversary lacks at least one pair, we get:

$$\mathsf{Adv}^{E'}(\lambda) \leq \pi_u(\lambda) + (1 - \pi_u)\left(2\mathsf{Adv}^{\tilde{E}}(\lambda) + \mathsf{Adv}^E(\lambda)\right)$$

which proves the theorem. $\qquad\square$

An immediate corollary of the previous theorem is that the encryption scheme prevents an attacker from dropping too many cells of its pirate decoder without dramatically dropping its probability of correctly decrypting. The following theorem in turn shows that this can be exploited to rely on the collusion secure code to trace at least one of the traitors.

Theorem 2. *Consider our construction for a traitor tracing scheme given in Sec. 3.1 with master tables $T^{(0)}$, $T^{(1)}$ of n-bit cells and length L, a number u of keys k_i, and where the identifying strings are taken from the c-collusion secure code for N users derived from Tardos' fingerprinting scheme such as explained in Sec. 2, that is of size $L = \frac{100}{\beta}c^2 \log\left(\frac{N}{\epsilon}\right)$. We claim that no coalition of less than c traitors can produce a pirate decoder with a decryption probability greater* *than 2^{-t} that can not be traced to at least one of the traitors as soon as β and u are chosen so that:*

$$\binom{\beta L}{u} \leq 2^{-t}\binom{L}{u}. \tag{4}$$

Proof. The idea of the proof is as follows: for the underlying fingerprint code to work, we need to ensure that at least (say) one fourth of the cells of the tables has to be kept. Forcing the pirate decoder to embed this number of cells to be able to decrypt correctly can be achieved by increasing the number u of required cells to derive the session key SK.

First of all, note that for a cell from the table T^P of the pirate decoder to be useful to the pirate, more than $n - t$ bits must be exact. (The remaining t bits can be guessed on the fly for a price of at most 2^{-t}, but more than t unknown bits would be too costly.) Therefore, either the pirate decoder stores $n - t$ bits or more of some cell (and thus the corresponding bit from the fingerprinting code can be deduced) or the decoder stores less than $n - t$ bits of the cell (and thus it is useless for the derivation of the session key).

From the above we deduce that we can assume that only a certain fraction $0 < \alpha \leq 1$ of the cells of the table are kept in the pirate decoder. Now the probability that the decoder is able to decrypt correctly is: $\pi_u = \binom{\alpha L}{u}/\binom{L}{u}$, so that the pirate decoder can not decrypt with probability higher than 2^{-t} by the hypothesis made at Eq. 4 if $\alpha < \beta$. Therefore the pirate decoder embeds more than βL digits and since the underlying Tardos' fingerprint code of length L has been expanded to $\frac{100}{\beta}c^2\log(\frac{N}{\epsilon})$, there remains $100c^2\log(\frac{N}{\epsilon})$ digits in the pirate word which allows Tardos' tracing algorithm to output a list of traitors as usual. $\qquad\square$

3.3 Efficiency and Sample Parameters

We now propose a set of parameters for a sample implementation with the AES as the underlying encryption schemes (E, D) and $(\tilde{E}, \tilde{D})$. The key size is therefore chosen to be $n = 128$. For a number of users $N = 2^{30}$, setting $\beta = \frac{1}{2}$, and considering coalitions of at most $c = 100$ traitors, the expanded code has length $L \simeq 2^{24}$, and Theorem 2 gives the following data:

	$2^{-t} = \frac{10}{100}$	$2^{-t} = \frac{1}{100}$	$2^{-t} = \frac{1}{1000}$
u	4	7	10

4 Conclusion

The long series of work about traitor tracing schemes based on collusion secure codes shows that they can provide many interesting properties such as constant size ciphertexts, black-box tracing procedures against stateful (and possibly high error rate) pirate decoders. In contrast, the intriguing question of whether achieving trace and revoke capabilities is possible or not remains open.

References

1. AACS, http://www.aacsla.com
2. Boneh, D., Franklin, M.K.: An efficient public key traitor tracing scheme. In: Wiener, M.J. (ed.) CRYPTO 1999. LNCS, vol. 1666, pp. 338–353. Springer, Heidelberg (1999)
3. Boneh, D., Naor, M.: Traitor tracing with constant size ciphertexts (February 2008), http://crypto.stanford.edu/~dabo/papers/
4. Boneh, D., Sahai, A., Waters, B.: Fully collusion resistant traitor tracing with short ciphertexts and private keys. In: Vaudenay, S. (ed.) EUROCRYPT 2006. LNCS, vol. 4004, pp. 573–592. Springer, Heidelberg (2006)
5. Boneh, D., Shaw, J.: Collusion-secure fingerprinting for digital data. In: Coppersmith, D. (ed.) CRYPTO 1995. LNCS, vol. 963, pp. 452–465. Springer, Heidelberg (1995)
6. Chabanne, H., Phan, D.H., Pointcheval, D.: Public traceability in traitor tracing schemes. In: Cramer, R.J.F. (ed.) EUROCRYPT 2005. LNCS, vol. 3494, pp. 542–558. Springer, Heidelberg (2005)
7. Chor, B., Fiat, A., Naor, M.: Tracing traitors. In: Desmedt, Y.G. (ed.) CRYPTO 1994. LNCS, vol. 839, pp. 257–270. Springer, Heidelberg (1994)
8. Chor, B., Fiat, A., Naor, M., Pinkas, B.: Tracing traitors. IEEE Transactions on Information Theory 46(3), 893–910 (2000)
9. Dodis, Y., Fazio, N.: Public key trace and revoke scheme secure against adaptive chosen ciphertext attack. In: Desmedt, Y.G. (ed.) PKC 2003. LNCS, vol. 2567, pp. 100–115. Springer, Heidelberg (2002)
10. Fazio, N., Nicolosi, A., Phan, D.H.: Traitor tracing with optimal transmission rate. In: Juan, A., Garay, A.K. (eds.) ISC 2007. LNCS, vol. 4779, pp. 71–88. Springer, Heidelberg (2007)
11. Fiat, A., Naor, M.: Broadcast encryption. In: Stinson, D.R. (ed.) CRYPTO 1993. LNCS, vol. 773, pp. 480–491. Springer, Heidelberg (1994)
12. Fiat, A., Tassa, T.: Dynamic traitor training. In: Wiener, M.J. (ed.) CRYPTO 1999. LNCS, vol. 1666, pp. 354–371. Springer, Heidelberg (1999)
13. Kiayias, A., Yung, M.: Self protecting pirates and black-box traitor tracing. In: Kilian, J. (ed.) CRYPTO 2001. LNCS, vol. 2139, pp. 63–79. Springer, Heidelberg (2001)
14. Kiayias, A., Yung, M.: Digital Rights Management ACM CCS Workshop – DRM 2001. In: Sander, T. (ed.) DRM 2001. LNCS, vol. 2320, pp. 22–39. Springer, Heidelberg (2002)
15. Kiayias, A., Yung, M.: Traitor tracing with constant transmission rate. In: Knudsen, L.R. (ed.) EUROCRYPT 2002. LNCS, vol. 2332, pp. 450–465. Springer, Heidelberg (2002)
16. Kurosawa, K., Desmedt, Y.: Optimum traitor tracing and asymmetric schemes. In: Nyberg, K. (ed.) EUROCRYPT 1998. LNCS, vol. 1403, pp. 145–157. Springer, Heidelberg (1998)
17. Matsushita, T., Imai, H.: A public-key black-box traitor tracing scheme with sublinear ciphertext size against self-defensive pirates. In: Lee, P.J. (ed.) ASIACRYPT 2004. LNCS, vol. 3329, pp. 260–275. Springer, Heidelberg (2004)
18. Naor, D., Naor, M., Lotspiech, J.: Revocation and tracing schemes for stateless receivers. In: Kilian, J. (ed.) CRYPTO 2001. LNCS, vol. 2139, pp. 41–62. Springer, Heidelberg (2001)

19. Naor, M., Pinkas, B.: Threshold traitor tracing. In: Krawczyk, H. (ed.) CRYPTO 1998. LNCS, vol. 1462, pp. 502–517. Springer, Heidelberg (1998)
20. Naor, M., Pinkas, B.: Efficient trace and revoke schemes. In: Frankel, Y. (ed.) FC 2000. LNCS, vol. 1962, pp. 1–20. Springer, Heidelberg (2001)
21. Pfitzmann, B.: Trials of traced traitors. In: Anderson, R. (ed.) IH 1996. LNCS, vol. 1174, pp. 49–64. Springer, Heidelberg (1996)
22. Phan, D.H.: Traitor tracing for stateful pirate decoders with constant ciphertext rate. In: Nguyên, P.Q. (ed.) VIETCRYPT 2006. LNCS, vol. 4341, pp. 354–365. Springer, Heidelberg (2006)
23. Phan, D.H., Safavi-Naini, R., Tonien, D.: Generic construction of hybrid public key traitor tracing with full-public-traceability. In: Bugliesi, M., Preneel, B., Sassone, V., Wegener, I. (eds.) ICALP 2006. LNCS, vol. 4052, pp. 264–275. Springer, Heidelberg (2006)
24. Rivest, R.L.: All-or-nothing encryption and the package transform. In: Biham, E. (ed.) FSE 1997. LNCS, vol. 1267, pp. 210–218. Springer, Heidelberg (1997)
25. Safavi-Naini, R., Wang, Y.: Collusion secure q-ary fingerprinting for perceptual content. In: Sander, T. (ed.) DRM 2001. LNCS, vol. 2320, pp. 57–75. Springer, Heidelberg (2002)
26. Safavi-Naini, R., Wang, Y.: Traitor tracing for shortened and corrupted fingerprints. In: Feigenbaum, J. (ed.) DRM 2002. LNCS, vol. 2696, pp. 81–100. Springer, Heidelberg (2003)
27. Silverberg, A., Staddon, J., Walker, J.L.: Efficient traitor tracing algorithms using list decoding. In: Boyd, C. (ed.) ASIACRYPT 2001. LNCS, vol. 2248, pp. 175–192. Springer, Heidelberg (2001)
28. Silverberg, A., Staddon, J., Walker, J.L.: Applications of list decoding to tracing traitors. IEEE Transactions on Information Theory 49(5), 1312–1318 (2003)
29. Sirvent, T.: Traitor tracing scheme with constant ciphertext rate against powerful pirates. In: Augot, D., Sendrier, N., Tillich, J.-P. (eds.) Workshop on Coding and Cryptography – WCC 2007, April 2007, pp. 379–388 (2007)
30. Stinson, D.R., Wei, R.: Key preassigned traceability schemes for broadcast encryption. In: Tavares, S., Meijer, H. (eds.) SAC 1998. LNCS, vol. 1556, pp. 144–156. Springer, Heidelberg (1999)
31. Tardos, G.: Optimal probabilistic fingerprint codes. In: ACM Symposium on Theory of Computing – STOC 2003, pp. 116–125. ACM Press, New York (2003)

Revisiting the Karnin, Greene and Hellman Bounds

Yvo Desmedt[1], Brian King[2], and Berry Schoenmakers[3]

[1] Department of Computer Science
University College London
[2] Dept. of Elec. & Comp. Eng.
Indiana University - Purdue University Indianapolis
briking@iupui.edu
[3] Dept. of Mathematics and Computer Science
Technical University of Eindhoven
berry@win.tue.nl

Abstract. The algebraic setting for threshold secret sharing scheme can vary, dependent on the application. This algebraic setting can limit the number of participants of an *ideal secret sharing scheme*. Thus it is important to know for which thresholds one could utilize an *ideal threshold sharing scheme* and for which thresholds one would have to use non-ideal schemes. The implication is that more than one share may have to be dealt to some or all parties. Karnin, Greene and Hellman constructed several bounds concerning the maximal number of participants in threshold sharing scheme. There has been a number of researchers who have noted the relationship between k-arcs in projective spaces and ideal linear threshold secret schemes, as well as between MDS codes and ideal linear threshold secret sharing schemes. Further, researchers have constructed optimal bounds concerning the size of k-arcs in projective spaces, MDS codes, etc. for various finite fields. Unfortunately, the application of these results on the Karnin, Greene and Hellamn bounds has not been widely disseminated. Our contribution in this paper is revisiting and updating the Karnin, Greene, and Hellman bounds, providing optimal bounds on the number of participants in ideal linear threshold secret sharing schemes for various finite fields, and constructing these bounds using the same tools that Karnin, Greene, and Hellman introduced in their seminal paper. We provide optimal bounds for the maximal number of players for a t out of n ideal linear threshold scheme when $t = 3$, for all possible finite fields. We also provide bounds for infinitely many t and infinitely many fields and a unifying relationship between this problem and the MDS (maximum distance separable) codes that shows that any improvement on bounds for ideal linear threshold secret sharing scheme will impact bounds on MDS codes, for which there is a number of conjectured (but open) problems.

1 Introduction

Threshold secret sharing is an important cryptographic tool that is used in many applications in cryptography. It provides group access control of secret

R. Safavi-Naini (Ed.): ICITS 2008, LNCS 5155, pp. 183–198, 2008.
© Springer-Verlag Berlin Heidelberg 2008

keys, and it can be used to provide group signatures and group authentication, it is used in e-voting, e-government, as well as many other applications. The problem that we will consider is to determine the maximal number of players (participants) that can participate in a t out of n linear threshold sharing scheme over a finite field. This number depends on both t and the field $\mathbb{F}$. Bounds for this problem were introduced almost 25 years ago in [14], but since then few improvements have been made. Meanwhile, there has been considerable work on the bounds of the size of shares for sharing schemes over general access structures, for example [7, 8, 12]. Moreover, there has been significant amount of work concerning bounds on information rate [3, 22, 18]. However, our focus is on *ideal threshold schemes*. An ideal threshold scheme is a threshold sharing scheme for which the size of the shares is the same as the size of the secret.

The problem of determining the maximal number of participants in a t out of n ideal linear threshold scheme is related to a coding theory problem, but the goals are different. In a t out of n threshold scheme we require completeness (any t or more participants can compute the secret) and privacy (any $t - 1$ or less participants learn nothing about the secret). Whereas in coding theory the goal is primarily a "completeness problem". In [16], McEliece and Sarwate first discussed the relationship between coding theory and secret sharing, however they did not provide any bounds concerning the limitations on the number of participants. In Section 7 we discuss the relationship to the problem we pose and the problem concerning the maximal size of a MDS code for a finite field $\mathbb{F}$. A considerable amount of research has been conducted on the problem concerning the maximal size of a MDS code for a finite field $\mathbb{F}$, in particular for many finite fields the maximal size has been known [17, 20, 11], as we discuss in Section 7. Further there is a direct relationship between MDS codes and ideal linear threshold secret sharing schemes. Unfortunately, as far as we know, the Karnin, Greene and Hellman bounds. were not updated. Several other problems, such as k-arcs in a projective space [13], and orthogonal arrays [6] have been shown to be equivalent to MDS codes and/or ideal linear threshold secret sharing schemes, and thus under the equivalence, results concerning maximal size in a finite field would impact the problem of determining the maximal number of participants in a t out of n ideal linear threshold scheme.

Summary of Our Results. The problem posed in this paper is to determine the maximal n for t out of n linear, ideal threshold sharing scheme over a finite field $\mathbb{F}$, which we denote by $n_{max,t}$ or in short n_{max}. Our results provide improved bounds on the maximal number of participants in a perfect ideal linear secret sharing scheme. Moreover, we are able to construct these bounds using many of the "tools" that Karnin, Greene and Hellman introduced in their ground breaking paper on secret sharing [14]. In this paper we provide optimal solutions for $n_{max,t}$ for $t = 3$ for both fields of characteristic 2 and odd characteristic. We provide upper bounds for $n_{max,t}$ for infinitely many cases of t and $\mathbb{F}$. We provide a unification of this problem to a coding theory problem and pose open problems that have an implication in threshold secret sharing and coding theory.

2   Background

Shamir [21] and Blakley [1] independently introduced the concept of threshold secret sharing over a finite field.

Definition 1. *[22] A t out of n threshold sharing scheme is a scheme for sharing a secret key k to n participants in such a way that any t participants can reconstruct the key but no group of t − 1 or less can reconstruct the key. A t out of n threshold sharing scheme will consist of two phases: the distribution phase where some entity called the dealer, using a distribution algorithm D, constructs shares $s_1, \ldots, s_n$ and for $i = 1, \ldots, n$. For each i, the dealer privately sends share s_i to participant P_i. The second phase called the reconstruction phase, occurs when t participants $P_{i_1}, \ldots, P_{i_t}$ want to reconstruct the secret key. Using reconstruction algorithm R and shares $s_{i_1}, \ldots, s_{i_t}$ they reconstruct the secret key k.*

Definition 2. *[22] A t out of n threshold sharing scheme is called a perfect sharing scheme provided that given a secret k, any set of at least t participants can compute k, and any subset of t − 1 or less participants gain no information about k. That is, if $s_1, \ldots, s_n$ represent the shares distributed to the n participants, then the security conditions are:*

(i) (completeness) $Prob(\mathbf{k} = k | \mathbf{s}_{i_1} = s_{i_1}, \ldots, \mathbf{s}_{i_t} = s_{i_t}) = 1$
(ii) (privacy) $Prob(\mathbf{k} = k | \mathbf{s}_{i_1} = s_{i_1}, \ldots, \mathbf{s}_{i_{t-1}} = s_{i_{t-1}}) = Prob(\mathbf{k} = k)$

The set Γ which consists of all sets of t or more participants is called the access structure for a threshold scheme.

A *linear secret sharing scheme* is such that the reconstruction of the secret key by the t participants is performed by taking linear combination of the t shares [22]. In a t out of n linear threshold sharing scheme over finite field $\mathbb{F}$ the shares $\{s_1, \ldots, s_n\}$ can be constructed using the *distribution matrix D* as follows.

$$\begin{bmatrix} s_1 \\ s_2 \\ \vdots \\ s_n \end{bmatrix} = \begin{bmatrix} x_{11} & x_{12} & x_{13} & \cdots & x_{1m} \\ x_{21} & x_{22} & x_{23} & \cdots & x_{2m} \\ \vdots & \vdots & \vdots & \ddots & \vdots \\ x_{n1} & x_{n2} & x_{n3} & \cdots & x_{nm} \end{bmatrix} \cdot \begin{bmatrix} k \\ a_1 \\ \vdots \\ a_{m-1} \end{bmatrix} \quad (1)$$

Here k is the secret. Equation (1) can be abbreviated as $\overline{S} = D \cdot \overline{y}$ (we use $\overline{y}$ to denote the column matrix). Note that if a perfect linear scheme is defined over a finite field then the number of columns of D will be t.

An *ideal threshold sharing scheme* is a threshold sharing scheme such that the size of the shares is the same as the size of the secret.

Note. In the context of this paper, all threshold sharing schemes that are discussed will be perfect, ideal and linear t out on n threshold sharing schemes. We will use the acronym t **out of** n **PIL threshold sharing scheme** to denote a perfect, ideal and linear t out on n threshold sharing scheme.

Since a t out of n PIL threshold secret sharing scheme must satisfy Definition 1, we can restate the requirements in terms of characteristics of the distribution matrix D.

1. *Completeness.* Any set of participants containing at least t participants can compute the secret k. Thus any t rows of the distributor's matrix D given in (1) must have a row span that includes the row $[1,0,0,..,0]$.

2. *Privacy.* No subset of less than t participants can determine any information about the secret k. Thus any $t-1$ or less rows of D cannot have a row span that includes $[1,0,0,..,0]$.

An important tool used in many threshold schemes is the Vandermonde matrix. The Vandermonde matrix is a matrix of the form

$$\begin{bmatrix} 1 & x_1 & x_1^2 & \cdots & x_1^{l-1} \\ 1 & x_2 & x_2^2 & \cdots & x_2^{l-1} \\ \vdots & \vdots & \vdots & \ddots & \vdots \\ 1 & x_l & x_l^2 & \cdots & x_l^{l-1} \end{bmatrix}.$$

The determinant of the Vandermonde matrix denoted by $\Delta(x_1, x_2, \ldots, x_l)$, over a finite field $\mathbb{F}$ is non-zero provided $x_i \neq x_j$, for $i \neq j$. Thus the Vandermonde matrix is invertible over any field.

Shamir Secret Sharing scheme is an effective tool to share out the secret key whenever the key space is isomorphic to some finite field $\mathbb{F}$. The essential tool used in Shamir Secret Sharing is the Lagrange interpolation polynomial. Shamir's scheme constructs a t our of n threshold sharing scheme as follows. For secret k belonging to finite field $\mathbb{F}$, a dealer selects $t-1$ random elements from $\mathbb{F}$, denoted by $a_1, \ldots, a_{t-1}$, and computes the polynomial $f(x) = k + a_1 x + \cdots + a_{t-1} x^{t-1}$. The dealer selects n distinct non-zero elements from $\mathbb{F}$, $x_1, x_2, \ldots x_n$ and computes $f(x_i)$, for $i = 1, \ldots, n$. The dealer then privately sends each participant P_i the share $f(x_i)$. Later when t participants $P_{i_1}, P_{i_2}, \ldots, P_{i_t}$ wish to reconstruct the secret key k, they send their shares to a combiner who computes the secret using Lagrange Interpolation: $k = \sum_{j=1}^{t} f(x_i) \cdot \prod_{\substack{l=1 \\ l \neq j}}^{t} \frac{-x_{i_l}}{x_{i_j} - x_{i_l}}$. Observe that the distribution matrix of Shamir's scheme is the Vandermonde matrix. A limitation imposed by the Shamir secret sharing scheme concerns the limit on the number of participants of a threshold sharing scheme over finite field $\mathbb{F}$, that is there is an implicit bound that $n \leq |\mathbb{F}| - 1$.

In [14], Karnin, Greene and Hellman described the following threshold sharing scheme which we will call the *Karnin-Greene-Hellman secret sharing scheme*. The scheme is as follows. Consider the finite field $GF(q^m)$. Let α be a primitive element of $GF(q^m)$, and let α_i denote α^i, for $i = 1, \ldots, q^m - 1$. The dealer selects $a_1, a_2, \ldots, a_{t-1}$ at random from $GF(q^m)$. The dealer then constructs the n shares s_i as follows

$$\begin{bmatrix} s_1 \\ s_2 \\ \vdots \\ s_r \\ s_{r+1} \end{bmatrix} = \begin{bmatrix} 1 & \alpha_1 & \alpha_1^2 & \ldots & \alpha_1^{t-1} \\ 1 & \alpha_2 & \alpha_2^2 & \ldots & \alpha_2^{t-1} \\ \vdots & \vdots & \vdots & \ddots & \vdots \\ 1 & \alpha_r & \alpha_r^2 & \ldots & \alpha_r^{t-1} \\ 0 & 0 & 0 & \ldots & 1 \end{bmatrix} \begin{bmatrix} k \\ a_1 \\ a_2 \\ \vdots \\ a_{t-1} \end{bmatrix} \qquad (2)$$

Here $n = r + 1$ and $r \le q^m - 1$. The dealer then sends s_i privately to participant P_i. Observe that given any t rows of D, denoted by $D_{i_1, i_2, \ldots, i_t}$, the resulting matrix is a $t \times t$ invertible matrix. Hence $\bar{y} = D^{-1}_{i_1, i_2, \ldots, i_t} \cdot \bar{S}_{i_1, i_2, \ldots, i_t}$, here $\bar{S}_{i_1, i_2, \ldots, i_t}$ denotes the column vector consisting of the shares $s_{i_1}, s_{i_2}, \ldots, s_{i_t}$. Thus the secret k can be computed. Further, given any $t - 1$ rows of D, the row $[\gamma, 0, 0, \ldots, 0]$ for all $\gamma \in GF(q^m) \setminus \{0\}$, will not be in the row span of $D_{i_1, i_2, \ldots, i_{t-1}}$. Thus no information concerning the secret k will be revealed by $t - 1$ or less shares. Consequently, one can construct a t out of $r + 1$ threshold sharing, where $r + 1 = |\mathbb{F}|$. Thus the number of participants n can be as large as the field and so from the perspective of determining the maximal n that can be used in a t out of n threshold secret sharing scheme, we see that the Karnin-Green-Hellman secret sharing scheme is more efficient than the Shamir secret sharing scheme.

We define $n_{max,t}$ to be the largest n for which one can construct a t out of n PIL threshold sharing scheme over finite field $\mathbb{F}$.

In [14], Karnin, Greene and Hellman established the following.

Theorem 1 (KGH). [14] Suppose the secret space $\mathcal{S} = \mathbb{F} = GF(q^m)$, then $n_{max,t}$ satisfies

$$|\mathbb{F}| \le n_{max,t} \le |\mathbb{F}| + t - 2, \quad q^m > t, \tag{3}$$

$$n_{max,t} = t, \quad q^m \le t, \tag{4}$$

The proof of this result is provided in [14]. The lower bound given in (3) is established by using the sharing scheme constructed by Karnin, Greene and Hellman. The upper bound can be understood by applying the following representation described by Karnin, Green and Hellman in [14], which we define as the *KGH normal form.*

Definition 3. *Let D be the distribution matrix of a t out of n PIL threshold sharing scheme over finite field $\mathbb{F}$. Then D is in KGH normal form provided that the distribution matrix D satisfies the following equation.*

$$D = \begin{bmatrix} 1 & x_{12} & x_{13} & \cdots & x_{1t} \\ 1 & x_{22} & x_{23} & \cdots & x_{2t} \\ \vdots & \vdots & \vdots & \ddots & \vdots \\ 1 & x_{r2} & x_{r3} & \cdots & x_{rt} \\ 1 & 1 & 1 & \cdots & 1 \\ 0 & 1 & 0 & \cdots & 0 \\ 0 & 0 & 1 & \cdots & 0 \\ \vdots & \vdots & \vdots & \ddots & \vdots \\ 0 & 0 & 0 & \cdots & 1 \end{bmatrix}. \tag{5}$$

Recall that the shares are computed via the matrix equation $\bar{s} = D \cdot \bar{y}$, where $\bar{y}^T = [k, a_1, \ldots, a_l]$. Observe that the first column of the matrix D given in (5) represents the use of the secret key k.

Lemma 1 (KGH). *[14] For every t out of n PIL threshold sharing scheme over a finite field, one can always express the distribution matrix D in KGH normal form (as illustrated in equation (5)).*

Lemma 1 and its proof are provided in [14, proof of Theorem 4, p. 39].

There exists a great similarity between linear codes and threshold secret sharing schemes.

Definition 4. *[17, 20] A linear code of length n and rank k is a linear subspace with dimension k of the vector space $\mathbb{F}_q^n$ where $\mathbb{F}_q$ is the finite field with q elements The linear code of length n and rank k is often denoted as a [n, k, d] linear code, where d is the minimum distance between codes.*

As noted above, there is a similarity between linear codes and the completeness property of a t out of n linear threshold sharing schemes. The threshold t in a t out of n threshold sharing scheme corresponds to the k of a $[n, k, d]$ linear code, and the distribution matrix D corresponds to the transpose of the generator matrix of the linear code. The difference between threshold sharing scheme and a linear code is that the privacy condition is also a necessary requirement for a t out of n PIL threshold sharing schemes.

Example 1. Consider a $[3, 2, 2]$ linear code with generator matrix G, given by:

$$G = \begin{bmatrix} 1 & 0 & 1 \\ 0 & 1 & 1 \end{bmatrix}$$

Consider the matrix G^T, and interpret it as a distribution matrix of a 2 out of 3 threshold secret sharing scheme. Clearly it would satisfy the completeness property, Since any two rows would contain the row span [1,0]. However it violates the privacy condition since one row would generate [1,0].

3   Some Preliminary Results

Consider the distribution matrix D written in KGH normal form, as described in (5). Then D can be represented as

$$D = \left[\begin{array}{c} A \\ \hline 0_{1\times(t-1)} \quad I_{(t-1)\times(t-1)} \end{array} \right] = \begin{bmatrix} 1 & x_{12} & x_{13} & \cdots & x_{1t} \\ 1 & x_{22} & x_{23} & \cdots & x_{2t} \\ \vdots & \vdots & \vdots & \ddots & \vdots \\ 1 & x_{r2} & x_{r3} & \cdots & x_{rt} \\ 1 & 1 & 1 & \cdots & 1 \\ 0 & 1 & 0 & \cdots & 0 \\ 0 & 0 & 1 & \cdots & 0 \\ \vdots & \vdots & \vdots & \ddots & \vdots \\ 0 & 0 & 0 & \cdots & 1 \end{bmatrix} \tag{6}$$

where A is a $(r+1) \times t$ matrix (here $r = n - t$), $0_{1 \times (t-1)}$ is the column matrix consisting of zeros, and $I_{(t-1) \times (t-1)}$ is the $(t-1) \times (t-1)$ identity matrix.

A necessary and sufficient condition for a t out of n PIL threshold sharing scheme is the following.

Lemma 2 (KGH). *[14] Let D be a matrix in KGH normal form (6), then D is the distribution matrix of a t out of n PIL threshold scheme if and only if every $j \times j$ minor of A (for $j = 1, \ldots, \min(t, n - t + 1)$) is nonzero.*

The proof is provided in [14, proof of Theorem 4, p. 39].

The *dual* of a t out of n threshold scheme is a $n - t + 1$ out of n threshold scheme. The dual has been studied extensively in literature, for more information on the dual see [10]. It is straightforward to go from a t out of n threshold scheme and construct its dual, with the same number of players. In [10], Cramer and Fehr provided the algebraic conditions for constructing the dual of a t out of n threshold scheme which is defined over a ring (such conditions would of course have to be satisfied for a dual over a field). The distribution matrix of the dual is related to the *reconstruction matrix*. That is, a series of matrix operations including a transpose of the reconstruction matrix will provide the distribution matrix of the dual.

Thus if $v = n_{max,t} - t + 1$ then there exists a v out of $n_{max,t}$ PIL threshold scheme. Therefore $n_{max,v} \geq n_{max,t}$.

We now discuss a result concerning the properties of a distribution matrix written in KGH form.

Lemma 3. *Let D be a matrix in KGH normal form. If D is a distribution matrix of a t out of n threshold scheme the following must be true.*

(1) for all i,j, with $1 \leq i \leq r$ and $2 \leq j \leq t$, the i,j entry of A satisfies $x_{i,j} \neq 0$ and $x_{ij} \neq 1$.

(2) for $i, v \in \{1, \ldots, r\}$, $i \neq v$, and for each $j = 2, \ldots, t$, we have $x_{ij} \neq x_{vj}$.

(3) for $j, l \in \{2, \ldots, t\}$, $j \neq l$. and for each $i = 1, \ldots, r$, we have $x_{ij} \neq x_{il}$, and

(4) for $i, v \in \{1, \ldots, r\}$, $i \neq v$, and for $j, l \in \{1, \ldots, t\}$, $j \neq l$, the field elements $\dfrac{x_{vj}}{x_{vl}} \neq \dfrac{x_{ij}}{x_{il}}$.

Proof. In [14] Karnin, Greene and Hellman established that every $j \times j$ minor of A is nonzero. The proof of Lemma 3 is established by considering various 1×1 and 2×2 minors of A.

For example to establish that every $x_{i,j}$ is nonzero, consider a 1×1 minor of A. To establish that $x_{i,j}$ does not equal 1, consider a 2×2 minor consisting of the ith row, the $r + 1^{st}$ row, the 1st column and the jth column of D. The resulting minor $\begin{vmatrix} 1 & x_{i,j} \\ 1 & 1 \end{vmatrix} \neq 0$, which implies $x_{i,j} \neq 1$. The remaining cases (2), (3), and (4) of Lemma 3 can be established in a similar manner.

Theorem 2. *Let $\mathbb{F}$ be a finite field and let $t \geq 2$, then*

(1) $n_{max,t} \leq 1 + n_{max,t-1}$, and

(2) for positive integer θ and $t \geq \theta + 1$, $n_{max,t} \leq \theta + n_{max,t-\theta}$.

Proof. To prove (1) let D represent a distribution matrix written in KGH form for a t out of $n_{max,t}$ PIL threshold secret sharing scheme over field $\mathbb{F}$. Let $\widetilde{D}$ represents the matrix formed by removing the tth column of D and the last row of D. The last row of D is of the form $[0, 0, \ldots, 0, 1]$. Thus $\widetilde{D}$ is a $(n_{max,t} - 1) \times (t-1)$ matrix. Therefore, it is trivial that any $t - 1$ rows of $\widetilde{D}$ contain the row $[1, 0, \ldots, 0]$ in its row span. Further it is trivial that any $t - 2$ or less rows of $\widetilde{D}$ do not contain $[\gamma, 0, 0, \ldots, 0]$ with $\gamma \neq 0$, in its row span. Thus $\widetilde{D}$ is a $t - 1$ out of $n_{max,t} - 1$ threshold scheme. Hence $n_{max,t-1} \geq n_{max,t} - 1$.

The proof of (2) follows from (1), by applying it θ many times.

Note: the Karnin-Green-Hellman [14] bounds (see Theorem 1) are tight for $t = 2$, so we focus on $t > 2$.

4   An $n_{max,t}$ Optimal Scheme for $GF(2^m)$ When $t = 3$

We now construct a 3 out of n PIL threshold sharing scheme over the field $GF(2^m)$ for which $n = n_{max,3}$. Important tools in our construction will be the KGH normal form and the Vandermonde matrix.

Theorem 3. *Let $\mathbb{F} = GF(2^m)$ be a finite field and let $n = |\mathbb{F}| + 1$, then there exists a secure 3 out of n PIL threshold sharing scheme over $\mathbb{F}$.*

Proof. Since the characteristic of $\mathbb{F} = GF(2^m)$ is 2, all nonzero nontrivial elements (elements not equal to 0 or 1) of $\mathbb{F}$ have (multiplicative) order[1] greater than 2. Let $x_1, x_2, \ldots x_{|\mathbb{F}|-2}$ denote the distinct elements of $\mathbb{F}$ not equal to 0 or 1. Consider the following matrix

$$D = \begin{bmatrix} 1 & x_1 & x_1^2 \\ \vdots & \vdots & \vdots \\ 1 & x_{|\mathbb{F}|-2} & x_{|\mathbb{F}|-2}^2 \\ 1 & 1 & 1 \\ 0 & 1 & 0 \\ 0 & 0 & 1 \end{bmatrix} \tag{7}$$

Thus D is a $(|\mathbb{F}| + 1) \times 3$ matrix. We now establish that D is a distribution matrix of a 3 out of n PIL threshold sharing scheme.

We first consider *completeness*. We will show that any three participants can construct the secret. Label the rows of the distribution matrix (7) from 1 to n in a top-to-down manner.

case (i) Given any 3 rows from $\{1, \ldots, n - 2\}$, the secret can be constructed due to the invertibility of the Vandermonde matrix.

case (ii) Suppose we are given the row $[0,1,0]$ and the row $[0,0,1]$ and one additional row selected from $\{1, \ldots, n - 2\}$ then it is trivial that one can construct the secret.

---

[1] The order of an element $a \in \mathbb{F}^*$ is the smallest positive integer e such that $a^e = 1$.

case (iii) Suppose one of the rows belongs to $\{[0,1,0],[0,0,1]\}$ and the two other rows selected from rows $\{1,\ldots,n-2\}$. Then reduce the system by using row operations utilizing the row from the set $\{[0,1,0],[0,0,1]\}$. The resulting system is a 2 by 2 Vandermonde system and hence invertible.

So the completeness property is established. The proof for *privacy* follows in a very similar manner.

Thus for all fields $\mathbb{F}$ of characteristic 2, we have $n_{max,3} = |\mathbb{F}|+1 = |\mathbb{F}|+3-2 = |\mathbb{F}|+t-2$. Consequently for fields of characteristic 2, we find that the Karnin, Greene, and Hellman upper bound given in equation (3) for $n_{max,3}$ is tight.

Recall the *dual* of a t out of n threshold scheme is a $n-t+1$ out of n threshold scheme. Suppose D is the distribution matrix of a t out of $n_{max,t}$ scheme. Then $Dual(D)$ is a distribution matrix for a $n_{max,t}-t+1$ out of $n_{max,t}$ scheme. Thus if we let $v = n_{max,t}-t+1$, then $Dual(D)$ is the distribution matrix of a v out of $n_{max,t}$ scheme. Hence $n_{max,v} \geq n_{max,t}$. Consequently we have $n_{max,|\mathbb{F}|-2} \geq |\mathbb{F}|+1$ (since $|\mathbb{F}|-2 = n_{max,3}-3+1$. It is trivial to show that $n_{max,|\mathbb{F}|-2} \leq |\mathbb{F}|+1$ Therefore we have:

Corollary 1. *Let $\mathbb{F}$ be a field of characteristic 2, and consider a $|\mathbb{F}|-2$ out of n PIL threshold sharing scheme, then $n_{max,|\mathbb{F}|-2} \geq |\mathbb{F}|+1$.*

5   Bounds of $n_{max,t}$ for Fields of Odd Characteristic When $t = 3$

The construction of a 3 out of $|\mathbb{F}|+1$ PIL threshold sharing scheme (where characteristic of $\mathbb{F}$ is even) is such that the upper $|\mathbb{F}|-2$ rows of the distribution matrix D (what we denoted earlier as matrix A) is a Vandermonde matrix. This construction does not violate Lemma 3 because no element of $\mathbb{F}$ has order 2. In a finite field with odd characteristic, we are guaranteed to have the element -1 (the additive inverse of 1) and $-1 \neq 1$ (a condition that is false in fields of characteristic 2). Thus attempting to utilize this construction for 3 out of $|\mathbb{F}|+1$ scheme, would violate Lemma 3. This observation does not imply anything about $n_{max,3}$ for a field of odd characteristic. However the following result establishes the precise value for $n_{max,3}$.

Theorem 4. *Consider a field $\mathbb{F} = GF(p^m)$, where p is prime with $p > 2$, and consider all 3 out of n PIL threshold sharing schemes, then $n \leq |\mathbb{F}|$. Thus we have that $n_{max,3} = |\mathbb{F}|$.*

Proof. Without loss of generality assume that $\mathbb{F} = \mathbb{Z}_p$ for p prime > 2. The proof for the case where $\mathbb{F} = GF(p^m)$ with $m > 1$ follows in a similar manner.

By Theorem 1, $n_{max,3}$ satisfies that $|\mathbb{F}| \leq n_{max,3} \leq |\mathbb{F}|+3-2 = |\mathbb{F}|+1$. So we are left to show that $n_{max,3} < |\mathbb{F}|+1$. Suppose $n_{max,3} = |\mathbb{F}|+1$. If $n_{max,3} = |\mathbb{F}|+1$ where $t = 3$, then r as described in the equation (5) satisfies $r = |\mathbb{F}|+1-3 = |\mathbb{F}|-2$. Note that $|\mathbb{F}|-2$ is the number of elements of $\mathbb{F}$ that are not equal to 0 or 1. By Lemma 3 the $(i, 1)$ entry x_{i1} of A is unique and is not equal to 0 or 1, for $i = 1, \ldots, r$. Then the set of x_{i1}, for $i = 1, \ldots, r$, represents the $|\mathbb{F}| - 2$ elements not equal to 0 or 1. Similarly the set of x_{i2}, for $i = 1, \ldots, r$, represents the $|\mathbb{F}| - 2$ elements not equal to 0 or 1 and the set of $\frac{x_{i2}}{x_{i1}}$, for $i = 1, \ldots, r$, represents the $|\mathbb{F}| - 2$ elements not equal to 0 or 1. By Wilson's Theorem [4], the product all the nonzero elements of $\mathbb{Z}_p$ reduced modulo p will equal -1. Therefore the product of all the elements x_{i1} satisfies $\prod_{i=1}^{r} x_{i1} = -1 \mod p$. Similarly both $\prod_{i=1}^{r} x_{i2} = -1 \mod p$ and $\prod_{i=1}^{r} \frac{x_{i2}}{x_{i1}} = -1 \mod p$. Then

$$\prod_{i=1}^{r} \frac{x_{i2}}{x_{i1}} = -1 = (\prod_{i=1}^{r} x_{i1}) / (\prod_{i=1}^{r} x_{i2}) = (-1)/(-1) = 1$$

Therefore we have a contradiction and so $n_{max,3} \neq |\mathbb{F}| + 1$. Hence $n_{max,3} = |\mathbb{F}|$ when $\mathbb{F} = \mathbb{Z}_p$. The proof will be valid for all fields $\mathbb{F} = GF(p^m)$ where p prime and $p > 2$.

Thus $n_{max,3} = |\mathbb{F}|$ for fields of odd characteristic. Consequently, for 3 out of n PIL threshold sharing schemes, the characteristic of the field does affect the maximal number of participants that can participate in the threshold scheme.

Corollary 2. *The optimal scheme with $n = n_{max,t}$ for fields of odd characteristic when $t = 3$ is given by the Karnin, Greene and Hellman secret sharing scheme.*

Because we have reduced the bound for $n_{max,3}$ to $|\mathbb{F}|$ and since $1 + n_{max,t-1} \geq n_{max,t}$, we see that $n_{max,4} \leq |\mathbb{F}| + 1 = |\mathbb{F}| + 4 - 3 < |\mathbb{F}| + 4 - 2$ (the latter is the KGH upper bound). We can continue this process. For example $n_{max,5} \leq 1 + n_{max,4} \leq 2 + n_{max,3}$. We then have the following bound.

Corollary 3. *Suppose $\mathbb{F}$ is a finite field of odd characteristic, then $n_{max,t} \leq |\mathbb{F}| + t - 3$.*

The bound is an improvement of the upper bound given Theorem 1 (as derived in [14]). Thus we have demonstrated an improved upper bound for $n_{max,t}$ for fields of odd characteristic when $t \geq 3$.

6   Implications of $n_{max,t}$ for $t \geq 4$

Recall that the nonzero elements of $\mathbb{F}$ form a multiplicative cyclic group. Let α be a primitive element then for all $x \in \mathbb{F} \setminus \{0\}$ there exists an i such that $x = \alpha^i$.

We can then apply the fact that the multiplicative group of $\mathbb{F}$ is cyclic, since the matrix A (submatrix of D) consists of nonzero elements they can each be expressed as α to a power. Further all elements in each row of A are distinct and all elements in each column j of A $(j = 2, \ldots, t)$ are distinct. We can interpret each power (the discrete log with respect to α) as a function of the row number i and that the column number j determines a permutation of the possible powers $\{1, \ldots, |\mathbb{F}| - 2\}$, i.e. we can view it as $\pi_i(j)$. That is, the condition $x_{ij} \neq x_{il}$ (where neither is 0 or 1) can be interpreted as $\alpha^{\pi_j(i)} \neq \alpha^{\pi_l(i)}$ and that $\pi_j(i) \neq \pi_l(i)$.

As a motivating example, consider the distribution matrix D of a 4 out of n PIL threshold sharing scheme. Then

$$D = \begin{bmatrix} 1 & x_{12} & x_{13} & x_{14} \\ \vdots & \vdots & \vdots & \vdots \\ 1 & x_{r2} & x_{r3} & x_{r4} \\ 1 & 1 & 1 & 1 \\ 0 & 1 & 0 & 0 \\ 0 & 0 & 1 & 0 \\ 0 & 0 & 0 & 1 \end{bmatrix} = \begin{bmatrix} 1 & \alpha^{\pi_2(1)} & \alpha^{\pi_3(1)} & \alpha^{\pi_4(1)} \\ \vdots & \vdots & \vdots & \vdots \\ 1 & \alpha^{\pi_2(r)} & \alpha^{\pi_3(r)} & \alpha^{\pi_4(r)} \\ 1 & 1 & 1 & 1 \\ 0 & 1 & 0 & 0 \\ 0 & 0 & 1 & 0 \\ 0 & 0 & 0 & 1 \end{bmatrix} \qquad (8)$$

Here π_w is a permutation of the set $\{1, 2, \ldots, |\mathbb{F}| - 2\}$ and $\pi_w(i)$ is the ith term of this function. Note we are only interested in the first $n - t$ terms of the function π_w (we view a function on $|\mathbb{F}| - 2$ terms as an $(|\mathbb{F}| - 2)$-tuple).

We can then generalize equation (8) to any t out of n threshold scheme and then generalize Lemma 3 as follows.

Theorem 5. *Let D be a matrix in KGH normal form. If D is a distribution matrix of a t out of n threshold scheme for each of the columns $w = 2, \ldots, t$ there exists a permutation π_w of the set $\{1, 2, ., |\mathbb{F}| - 2\}$ such that for $i = 1, \ldots n - t$ the (i, w) entry of D is $\alpha^{\pi_w(i)}$. Then each of the following must be true.*

(1) for all $i \in \{1, \ldots, n - t\}$ and $w \in \{2, .., t\}$, the discrete log of the i, w entry of A satisfies $\pi_w(i) \neq 0$,

(2) for $j, l \in \{2, \ldots t\}$, with $j \neq l$ and for each row $i \in \{1 \ldots, n - t\}$, we have $\pi_j(i) \neq \pi_l(i)$,

(3) for $i, v \in \{1, \ldots n - t\}$, with $i \neq v$, and for $j, l \in \{2, \ldots t\}$, with $j \neq l$, we have $\pi_j(i) - \pi_l(i) \neq \pi_j(v) - \pi_l(v)$, and

(4) $\pi_w^{-1} \circ \pi_j$ is a derangement on the first $n - t$ elements of the function $\pi_w^{-1} \circ \pi_j$.

Here a *derangement* π is a permutation on the set $\{1, \ldots, T\}$ such that $\pi(i) \neq i$ for all i, we require derangement condition (4) to be satisfied on only the first $n - t$ elements of π.

The proof of Theorem 5 follows immediately from Lemma 2.

7 Unifying Threshold Sharing Schemes with MDS Codes

We now describe the relationship between the maximum $n_{max,t}$ for t out of n PIL threshold sharing schemes and $n_{MDS,max,t}$ MDS codes. Bounds on the maximal number of participants in a perfect ideal linear t out of n threshold sharing scheme and bounds on maximal size of MDS codes are very similar, where the former appears to be one less than the latter. In Theorem 6 we prove that this is true. First we introduce some terminology.

Recall the definition of a $[n, k, d]$ linear code. The Singleton Bound gives

$$d \leq n - k + 1. \qquad (9)$$

A $[n, k, d]$ linear code is called a *maximum distance separable (MDS) code* if $d = n - k + 1$ [17, 20].

We now introduce some combinatorial constructions of MDS codes.

Some Combinatorial Constructions of MDS Codes

An n-arc is a set of points in the projective geometry $PG(k-1, q)$ such that no k points lie in a hyperplane $PG(k-2, q)$, where $3 \leq k \leq n$. An $[n, k]$ MDS code over field $\mathbb{F}_q$ exists iff there exists an n-arc in $PG(k-1, q)$.

Also, an $[n, k]$ MDS code over field $\mathbb{F}_q$ exists iff the rows of a (q^k, n, q, k) linear orthogonal array of index unity and symbols from $\mathbb{F}_q$ exists.

We now define $n_{MDS,max,k}$ as the maximum value of n for a $[n, k, d]$ MDS code for finite field $\mathbb{F}$.

Theorem 6. *For finite field* $\mathbb{F}$, $n_{max,t} = n_{MDS,max,t} - 1$.

We establish Theorem 6 via the following lemmas, Lemma 4 and Lemma 5. These lemmas have been established previously in [11] (other sources for similar arguments include [17, 19, 13]). We state the lemmas in a manner to fit the context of this paper and we provide the proof using our tools (KGH tools) and terminology.

Lemma 4. *Consider a* $[n, k, d]$ *linear MDS code* C *for which* n *is maximum and* $d \geq 2$, *then there exists a generator matrix* G *of the code* C *and a row* R *of* G^T *such that if* D *is the matrix formed by using all but the* R^{th} *row of* G^T. *Then* D *is a distribution matrix of a* k *out of* $n_{max,k}$ *PIL threshold sharing scheme.*

Proof. Consider

$$G^T = \begin{bmatrix} B_1 \\ B_2 \end{bmatrix}$$

where B_2 is a $k \times k$ matrix, and due to completeness invertible. Thus

$$G^T B_2^{-1} = \begin{bmatrix} B_1 \\ B_2 \end{bmatrix} B_2^{-1} = \begin{bmatrix} B_1 B_2^{-1} \\ I \end{bmatrix}$$

where I is the $k \times k$ identity matrix. Therefore we may assume without loss of generality that G^T is expressed in systematic form (i.e. the last k rows form the identity matrix). Label the columns of G^T from 1 to k and label the rows of G^T from 1 to n in a top to down fashion. Let R denote the row consisting of $[1, 0, 0, \ldots, 0]$ and remove R from G^T and denote this matrix by D. Then clearly any k rows of D are invertible. Further, each $j \times j$ minor of D is nonzero. This follows from the fact that every k rows of D are invertible and that the last $k-1$ rows of D possess the form $[0, 0, \ldots, 0, 1, 0, \ldots, 0]$ where the 1 occurs in the ℓ columns for $\ell = 2, \ldots k$.

Thus every bound on a $[n, k, d]$ linear MDS code infers a bound on $n_{max,k}$ of a k out of n PIL threshold sharing scheme.

Lemma 5. *Let D be a distribution matrix of a k out of $n_{max,k}$ PIL threshold sharing scheme written in KGH normal form. Then by adding a row R to D, the resulting matrix is the transpose of a generator matrix for a $[n, k, d]$ MDS code.*

Proof. Since D is written in KGH normal form, it satisfies (3). We now add the row $[1, 0, \ldots, 0]$ to D, denote this matrix by D'. Then

$$D' = \begin{bmatrix} 1 & x_{12} & x_{13} & \cdots & x_{1k} \\ 1 & x_{22} & x_{23} & \cdots & x_{2k} \\ \vdots & \vdots & \vdots & \ddots & \vdots \\ 1 & x_{r2} & x_{r3} & \cdots & x_{rk} \\ 1 & 1 & 1 & \cdots & 1 \\ 1 & 0 & 0 & \cdots & 0 \\ 0 & 1 & 0 & \cdots & 0 \\ 0 & 0 & 1 & \cdots & 0 \\ \vdots & \vdots & \vdots & \ddots & \vdots \\ 0 & 0 & 0 & \cdots & 1 \end{bmatrix}.$$

Now, $(D')^T$ forms a generator matrix of a $[n, k, d]$ MDS code where $n = n_{max,k} + 1$, as we now explain. We need to show that $(D')^T$ forms a $[n, k, d]$ linear code where $d = n - k + 1$. A codeword is a member of the row span of $(D')^T$. Recall that d is the minimum distance between codewords. Observe that column 1 of D' consists of $1 + n_{max,k} - (k - 1) = 1 + n_{max,k} - k + 1 = n - k + 1$ many nonzero elements. Thus $d \leq n - k + 1$. Since $[0, 0, \ldots, 0]$ is a code word, and the code a linear code, we are left to show that any nontrivial linear combination of rows of $(D')^T$ consists of at least $d = n - k + 1$ nonzero elements. Now observe that $(D')^T = [A^T | I_{k \times k}]$ where A^T is a $k \times n - k$ matrix and $I_{k \times k}$ is the $k \times k$ identity matrix. Since there are only k rows of $(D')^T$, we need to show that any nontrivial linear combination of ρ many rows of $(D')^T$, contains at least $d = n - k + 1$ nonzero elements, where $\rho \leq k$. We partition the argument into two parts: if one takes a linear combination of ρ many rows from $I_{k \times k}$, then one is going to have exactly ρ many nonzero entries. Thus we are left to show that if one takes a linear combination of ρ many rows from A^T then one has at least $d - \rho$ many nonzero entries. Here $d = n - k + 1$ and there are $n - k$ many columns of A^T. We claim that any row which is a linear combination of ρ many rows of A^T contains at most $\rho - 1$ zero elements. This implies that there are at least $n - k - (\rho - 1) = n - k + 1 - \rho = d - \rho$ many nonzero elements. To prove this claim, suppose there is a linear combination ρ many rows of A^T for which there are at least ρ many zeros. Thus there is a $\rho \times \rho$ matrix formed by ρ many rows and ρ many columns of A^T for which a nontrivial linear combination of rows is $[0, 0, \ldots, 0]$. This implies that there is a $\rho \times \rho$ minor of A^T which is zero. However, this contradicts a result noted in the proof of Lemma 3, that every $j \times j$ minor of A is nonzero. Hence there are at most $\rho - 1$ many zero elements of the linear combination of ρ many rows of A^T and so there are at least $d - \rho$

many nonzero elements. Consequently $(D')^T$ is a generator matrix of a MDS $[n, k, d]$ code.

Therefore bounds on $n_{max,k}$ of a k out of n PIL threshold sharing scheme infers bounds on $[n, k, d]$ linear MDS code.

The proof of Theorem 6 follows from the above Lemmas.

Thus we see that bounds concerning $n_{max,t}$ for t out of n PIL threshold sharing schemes directly impact bounds on linear MDS codes and vice versa. There are several open problems concerning bounds on MDS codes. It is possible that the problem concerning constructing bounds for $n_{max,t}$ may be easier than problems concerning constructing bounds on MDS codes (since there are more constraints to this problem, i.e. both "completeness" and "privacy" must be satisfied for threshold sharing schemes). Thus any improvements in bounds concerning $n_{max,t}$ will directly impact bounds concerning linear MDS codes.

Some Known Results Concerning MDS Codes. The following is some results that are known concerning the maximal size of MDS codes for finite fields. Our work, which was derived using KGH tools, agree with the known results. If we let $n_{MDS,max,k}$ denote the maximum value of n for a $[n, k, d]$ MDS code for finite field $\mathbb{F}_q$, then by [11, 20]

$$n_{MDS,max,k} = \begin{cases} q+1 \text{ when } k = 2 \\ q+1 \text{ when } k = 3 \text{ or } k = q-1 \text{ and } q \text{ odd} \\ q+2 \text{ when } k = 3 \text{ and } q \text{ is even} \\ k+1 \text{ when } k \geq q \end{cases}$$

For $k \geq q$ it is known that $n_{MDS,max,k} = k + 1$. The *well-known MDS conjecture* states that for $2 \leq k < q$,

$$n_{MDS,max,k} = \begin{cases} q+2, q \text{ even and } k = 3 \text{ or } k = q-1, \\ q+1, \text{ otherwise.} \end{cases}$$

This conjecture has been proved for small values of k (for example for $k \leq 5$), it has also been established for small values of q (for $q \leq 27$) and has been established for some other cases, see [11].

The following upper bounds for $n_{MDS,max,k}$ have been proved by Bush [5]. For $2 \leq k < q$,

$$n_{MDS,max,k} \leq \begin{cases} q+k-2, k \geq 3 \text{ and } q \text{ odd}, \\ q+k-1, \text{ otherwise,} \end{cases}$$

These general upper bounds have been improved slightly according to [23] where it states that $q + k - 3$ is an upper bound in the case $k >= 4$ and q even. They refer to [15].

As noted there exists a relationship between MDS codes and k-arcs in projective geometry. Thus there exists a relationship exists between linear threshold schemes and k-arcs in projective geometry. There is also a relationship between linear threshold schemes and orthogonal arrays. In [6], Dawson et. al. established several results concerning orthogonal arrays and threshold schemes, in particular that all linear threshold schemes are equivalent to orthogonal arrays.

8   Conclusion

We have discussed several bounds on the maximal number of players, $n_{max,t}$, in t out of n threshold schemes over a finite field. We have derived these bounds using the same tools that Karnin, Greene and Hellamn described in their original paper. We have formalized the notation for this problem and derived several results. We have also unified this problem to a problem in coding theory, namely linear MDS codes and have noted that improvements in constructing bounds on $n_{max,t}$ directly impact bounds concerning MDS codes.

References

1. Blakley, G.R.: Safeguarding cryptographic keys. In: Proceedings of the National Computer Conference, 1979, American Federation of Information Processing Societies Proceedings, vol. 48, pp. 313–317 (1979)
2. Brickell, E.F., Davenport, D.M.: On the classification of ideal secret sharing schemes. J. Cryptology 4, 123–134 (1991)
3. Brickell, E.F., Stinson, D.R.: Some improved bounds on the information rate of perfect secret sharing schemes. Journal of Cryptology 5, 153–166 (1992)
4. Bach, E., Shallit, J.: Algorthmic Number Theory, vol. 1. MIT Press, Cambridge (1996)
5. Bush, K.A.: Orthogonal Arrays of Index Unity. The Annals of Mathematical Statistics 23(3), 426–434 (1952)
6. Dawson, E., Mahmoodian, E.S., Rahilly, A.: Orthogonal arrays and ordered threshold schemes. Australasian Journal of Combinatorics 8, 27–44 (1993)
7. Capocelli, R.M., De Santis, A., Gargana, L., Vaccaro, U.: On the Size of shares for secret sharing schemes. Journal of Cryptology 6, 157–167 (1993)
8. Charnes, C., Pieprzyk, J.: Generalized cumulative arrays and their applications to secret sharing schemes. Proceeding of the 18th Australasian Computer Science Conference, Australasian Computer Science Communications 17(1), 61–65 (1995)
9. Cramer, R., Fehr, S., Stam, M.: Primitive Sets over Number Fields and Black-Box Secret Sharing. In: Shoup, V. (ed.) CRYPTO 2005. LNCS, vol. 3621, pp. 344–360. Springer, Heidelberg (2005)
10. Cramer, R., Fehr, S.: Optimal Black-Box Secret Sharing over Arbitrary Abelian Groups. In: Yung, M. (ed.) CRYPTO 2002. LNCS, vol. 2442, pp. 272–287. Springer, Heidelberg (2002)
11. Hirschfeld, J.W.P., Storme, L.: The packing problem in statistics, coding theory and finite projective spaces: update 2001. In: Blokhuis, A., Hirschfeld, J.W.P., Jungnickel, D., Thas, J.A. (eds.) Finite Geometries: Proceedings of the Fourth Isle of Thorns Conference (Chelwood Gate, 2000), July 16–21, 2001. Developments in Mathematics, vol. 3, pp. 201–246. Kluwer Academic Publishers, Dordrecht (2001)
12. Ito, M., Saito, A., Nishizeki, T.: Secret sharing schemes realizing general access structures. In: Proc. IEEE Global Telecommunications Conf., Globecom 1987, pp. 99–102. IEEE Communications Soc. Press, Los Alamitos (1987)
13. Jackson, W., Martin, K., O'Keefe, C.: Geometrical contributions to secret sharing theory. Journal of Geometry 79, 102–133 (2004)
14. Karnin, E.D., Greene, J.W., Hellman, M.E.: On secret sharing systems. IEEE Transactions on Information Theory 29, 35–41 (1983)

15. Kounias, S., Petros, C.I.: Orthogonal arrays of strength three and four with index unity. Sankhya: The Indian Journal of Statistics 37, 228–240 (1975)
16. McEliece, R.J., Sarwate, D.V.: On Sharing Secrets and Reed-Solomon Codes. Comm. ACM 24(9), 583–584 (1981)
17. MacWilliams, F.J., Sloane, N.J.A.: The Theory of Error-Correcting Codes. North-Holland, Amsterdam (1977)
18. Pieprzyk, J., Hardjono, T., Seberry, J.: Fundamantals of Computer Security. Springer, Heidelberg (2003)
19. Pieprzyk, J., Zhang, X.: Characterisations of Ideal Threshold Schemes. Journal of Descrete Mathematics and Theoretical Computer Science (DMTCS) 6(2), 471–482 (2004)
20. Roth, R.: Introduction to Coding Theory. Cambridge Press, NY (2006)
21. Shamir, A.: How to share a secret. Communications of the ACM 22, 612–613 (1979)
22. Stinson, D.R.: Cryptography: Theory and Practice. CRC, Boca Raton (1995)
23. Bound for OAs with Index Unity, http://mint.sbg.ac.at/desc_CBoundTO.html

Simple Direct Reduction of String $(1,2)$-OT to Rabin's OT without Privacy Amplification

Kaoru Kurosawa[1] and Takeshi Koshiba[2]

[1] Department of Computer and Information Sciences, Ibaraki University,
4-12-1 Nakanarusawa, Hitachi, Ibaraki, 316-8511, Japan
kurosawa@mx.ibaraki.ac.jp
[2] Division of Mathematics, Electronics and Informatics,
Graduate School of Science and Engineering, Saitama University,
255 Shimo-Okubo, Sakura, Saitama 338-8570, Japan
koshiba@mail.saitama-u.ac.jp

Abstract. It is known that string $(1,2)$-OT and Rabin's OT are equivalent. Actually, there have been many reductions between them. Many of them use the privacy amplification technique as a basic tool. The privacy amplification technique essentially involves some post-processing of sending random objects (e.g., random indices of pairwise independent hash functions) per each invocation of Rabin's OT is necessary. In this paper, we show a simple direct reduction of string $(1,2)$-OT to Rabin's OT by using a deterministic randomness extractor for bit-fixing sources. Our reduction can be realized without privacy amplification and thus our protocol is simpler and more efficient with respect to the communication complexity than the previous reductions.

Keywords: oblivious transfer, reduction, privacy amplification, deterministic randomness extractor.

1 Introduction

Suppose that Alice (database company) has two secret strings, s_0 and s_1. Bob (user) wants to buy one s_c among them. But he wants to keep his choice private. That is, it must be that Alice does not know which one Bob bought. On the other hand, Alice wants to keep her privacy. That is, it must be that Bob does not know s_{1-c}. A two-party protocol which realizes the above goal is called a 1-out-of-2 string *oblivious transfer*, denoted string $(1,2)$-OT [19]. If s_0 and s_1 are single bits, the protocol is called a *bit* $(1,2)$-OT. On the other hand, suppose that Alice wants to send a mail to Bob. However, the mail system is so bad that Bob receives the mail with probability $1/2$. Notice that Alice does not know if Bob received or not. A two-party protocol which realizes the above situation is called Rabin's OT [27].

It is known that a string $(1,2)$-OT, a bit $(1,2)$-OT and Rabin's OT are all equivalent. That is, there is a reduction between any two of them. Reductions

R. Safavi-Naini (Ed.): ICITS 2008, LNCS 5155, pp. 199–209, 2008.
© Springer-Verlag Berlin Heidelberg 2008

especially of string $(1,2)$-OT to simpler bit $(1,2)$-OT have been extensively studied in the literature. A reduction of 1-bit $(1,2)$-OT to Rabin's OT was shown by Crépeau [12]. After that, the notion of *universal* OT was introduced by Brassard and Crépeau [5] and the reductions to universal OT have been intensively studied [5,8,15,29]. (Those reductions immediately imply corresponding reductions to Rabin's OT as the universal OT gives the dishonest receiver only more power.) Recently, Imai, Morozov and Nascimento [22] gave a direct efficient reduction of string $(1,2)$-OT to Rabin's OT.

One of the techniques for reductions of string $(1,2)$-OT to bit $(1,2)$-OT is known as a notion of *zigzag functions*, based on particular types of error-correcting codes called *self-intersecting codes*. This technique was used in earlier literature [7,6]. In the reductions, a predetermined zigzag function f is supposed. The underlying idea is as follows: if x_0 (resp., x_1) is a random preimage of s_0 (resp., s_1), and if Bob is given to choose the i-th bit of either x_0 or x_1 by using bit $(1,2)$-OT, then no information on either x_0 or x_1 can be obtained. Another technique for reductions of string $(1,2)$-OT to bit $(1,2)$-OT is known as *privacy amplification*, originally used in the context of key agreement [3,2]. It is rather standard and used in recent literature, e.g., [8]. In the reduction, Alice uses a transformation of a string x into a shorter string s so as not to recover x from s even if Bob know the transformation. To implement string $(1,2)$-OT with two secrets s_0 and s_1, Alice executes a sequence of bit $(1,2)$-OT with the i-th bit of x_0 and the i-th bit of x_1. Subsequently, Alice informs Bob how to transform x_0 (resp., x_1) to s_0 (resp., s_1) via privacy amplification. The important difference between zigzag functions and privacy amplification is when Alice reveals "the trick" to Bob. While zigzag functions is known *before* the execution of bit $(1,2)$-OT, in the construction based on privacy amplification the function is revealed *after* the execution of bit $(1,2)$-OT. Because of this difference, constructions based on privacy amplification in general are simpler and more efficient. On the other hand, constructions based on privacy amplification must generate a new function (e.g., a hash key of pairwise independent hash functions) and send it at each execution of the protocol. Since string $(1,2)$-OT is an important building block in cryptography, the communication cost of the post-processing may not be negligible.

Since Rabin's OT is as simple as bit $(1,2)$-OT, it is also important to consider reductions of string $(1,2)$-OT to Rabin's OT. Also note that since Rabin's OT can be seen as an erasure channel, the direct reduction can be a construction of string $(1,2)$-OT based on the erasure channel. As we mentioned, almost all previous reductions use privacy amplification technique. A reduction by Imai et al [22] is one of such reductions and invokes about the number $4L$ of Rabin's OT to implement L-bit $(1,2)$-OT.

Our Contribution

In this paper, we show a simple direct reduction of string $(1,2)$-OT to Rabin's OT by using a *deterministic randomness extractor*, i.e., without privacy amplification[1]. Our reduction is as efficient as the direct reduction by Imai et al.[22] from the view point of the number of invocations of smaller primitives. That is, our construction of L-bit $(1,2)$-OT also uses about the number $4L$ of invocations of Rabin's OT. The advantage of our reduction is the use of deterministic randomness extractor. It enables us to enjoy the advantages of both zigzag functions and privacy amplification. Since the deterministic randomness extractor to be used in the reduction can be predetermined, any post-processing is not necessary. This property, which implies the reduction of the communication cost, is quite important because string $(1,2)$-OT is a basic cryptographic building block and such a building block can be used many times. In addition, our construction is rather simple than the previous results based on privacy amplification.

Note that Bennett, Brassard and Robert [3] have already studied the privacy amplification in the "deterministic" scenario. But, just a replacement of (randomized) privacy amplification technique with some deterministic privacy amplification does not work in general. The deterministic extractor we use is tailored for specific sources, say, bit-fixing sources. The use of deterministic extractors for bit-fixing sources plays an essential role in our protocol.

Remarks on Deterministic Extractors for Bit-Fixing Sources

An (n,k)-*bit-fixing* source introduced by Chor et al. [11] was a distribution over $\{0,1\}^n$ where some k bits out of n bits are uniformly distributed and the other $n - k$ bits are constant. One of the motivations for studying deterministic extractors for bit-fixing sources is a connection to cryptography. Consider the following cryptographic scenario: even if the adversary obtains some bits of an n-bit secret key, he learns almost nothing about the secret key. Such *exposure resilient* property in cryptology was studied in [24,28,4,16,10,18]. Relations of exposure resilient cryptography to deterministic extractors for bit-fixing sources were discussed in [24,16].

Kurosawa, Johansson and Stinson showed the first deterministic extractor under the name of almost $(n - k)$-resilient functions [24]. Canetti, Dodis, Halevi, Kushilevitz and Sahai showed a probabilistic construction of deterministic extractors [10]. Kamp and Zuckerman [23] showed an explicit construction of deterministic extractors for bit-fixing sources by adapting random walks on regular graphs. After that Gabizon, Raz and Shaltiel [20] improved Kamp-Zuckerman's extractor by coupling with *samplers* and *seeded* extractors. The deterministic extractor of [20] extracts $(1 - o(1))k$ bits from (n,k)-bit-fixing sources whenever $k > (\log n)^c$ for some universal constant $c > 0$. For $k \gg \sqrt{n}$, the extracted bits have statistical distance $2^{-n^{\Omega(1)}}$ from uniform, and for $k \leq \sqrt{n}$, the extracted bits have statistical distance $k^{-\Omega(1)}$ from uniform.

---

[1] Since extractors are one of privacy amplification techniques, deterministic extractors can be seen as a kind of privacy amplification. However, since the deterministic extractor is a deterministic machinery, we would like to claim that the term "amplification" is not appropriate in our setting.

Our protocol uses deterministic extractors for bit-fixing sources differently from the standard usage. Thus, our protocol is not only an improvement of the previous reduction but also another cryptographic application of deterministic extractor for bit-fixing sources.

2   Preliminaries

2.1   (1, 2)-Oblivious Transfer

In L-bit $(1,2)$-OT, Alice has two secret strings $s_0, s_1 \in \{0,1\}^L$ and Bob has a secret bit c. Then the following three conditions must be satisfied.

- At the end of the protocol, Bob receives s_c. This condition is called *correctness*.
- But Bob learns no information other than s_c. This condition is called *sender's privacy*.
- On the other hand, Alice has no information on c. This condition is called *receiver's privacy*.

We give more formal definitions for the above conditions in the following. Though there is a definition based on the universal composability [14], we adopt an information theoretic one due to Brassard, Crépeau and Wolf [8] since it is suitable to our discussion. (Actually, defining OT is a subtle problem. See [15,14] for the topic. We have considered the problem in our definitions).

Let A be Alice's (probabilistic) algorithm for the protocol and B Bob's. Let $[A; B](a; b)$ be the random variable that describes the outputs obtained by Alice and Bob when they execute together the programs A and B on respective inputs a and b. Similarly, let $[A; B]^*(a; b)$ be the random variable that describes the total information (including messages exchanged between Alice and Bob and the results of any local random sampling) they may have performed acquired during the protocol $[A; B]$ on respective inputs a and b. Let $[A; B]_P(a; b)$ and $[A; B]_P^*(a; b)$ be the marginal random variables obtained by restricting the above to only one party P, i.e., either Alice or Bob. The latter random variable is also known as *view* of P.

Definition 1. A protocol $[A; B]$ for L-bit $(1,2)$-OT is $(1 - \varepsilon)$-*correct* if we have

$$\Pr\{[A; B](s_0, s_1; c) \neq (\bot, s_c)\} \leq \varepsilon$$

for every $s_0, s_1 \in \{0,1\}^L$ and $c \in \{0,1\}$, where $\bot$ denotes the empty output.

Let (S_0, S_1) and C be random variables taking values over $\{0,1\}^{2L}$ and $\{0,1\}$ that describe Alice's and Bob's respective inputs. Also we denote, by $\mathcal{V}(\{0,1\}^{2L})$ and $\mathcal{V}(\{0,1\})$, all the random variables over $\{0,1\}^{2L}$ and $\{0,1\}$, respectively. We assume that both Alice and Bob are aware of the arbitrary joint probability distribution of these random variables $P_{S_0, S_1, C}$. A sample (s_0, s_1, c) is generated from the distribution and (s_0, s_1) is given to Alice as her secret input while c is given to Bob as his secret input.

Let $H(X)$ be the Shannon entropy of a random variable X. The mutual information of two random variables X and Y is denoted by $I(X; Y) = H(X) - H(X \mid Y)$ and conditioned by a third random variable Z as $I(X; Y \mid Z) = H(X \mid Z) - H(X \mid Y, Z)$.

Definition 2. A protocol $[A; B]$ for L-bit $(1, 2)$-OT satisfies *receiver's* $(1 - \varepsilon)$-*privacy* if for all $(S_0, S_1) \in \mathcal{V}(\{0, 1\}^{2L})$, $C \in \mathcal{V}(\{0, 1\})$, for all $s_0, s_1 \in \{0, 1\}^L$, for all dishonest A',

$$I(C; [A'; B]^*_{A'}(S_0, S_1; C) \mid (S_0, S_1) = (s_0, s_1)) \leq \varepsilon.$$

The random variable C in the above definition may depend on the random variables S_0 and S_1.

Definition 3. A protocol $[A; B]$ for L-bit $(1, 2)$-OT satisfies *sender's* $(1 - \varepsilon)$-*privacy* if for all $(S_0, S_1) \in \mathcal{V}(\{0, 1\}^{2L})$, $C \in \mathcal{V}(\{0, 1\})$, for all $c \in \{0, 1\}$, for all dishonest B', there exists $C' \in \mathcal{V}(\{0, 1\})$ such that

$$I(S_{1-C'}; [A, B']^*_{B'}(S_0, S_1; C) \mid C', S_{C'}, C = c)/L \leq \varepsilon$$

where the random variable C' is independent of (S_0, S_1) conditioned on C.

2.2 Rabin's Oblivious Transfer

In Rabin's OT, Alice has a secret bit b. At the end of the protocol, Bob receives b with probability $1/2$. On the other hand, Alice does not know if Bob received b or not. (Rabin's OT can be viewed as an erasure channel.)

2.3 Previous Reductions

Crépeau showed a reduction of 1-bit $(1, 2)$-OT to Rabin's OT [12]. In his reduction, Rabin's OT must be invoked at least $64s/3 > 21s$ times, where s is a security parameter such that

- $(1 - 2^{-s})$-correctness, and
- Sender's $(1 - 2^{-s})$-privacy is satisfied.

Also there is a direct direction of *string* $(1, 2)$-OT to Rabin's OT due to Imai et al [22]. They gave only a simple sketch of the analysis. Since their protocol is similar to ours, our analysis shown later may be applicable to the analysis of their protocol.

3 Deterministic Extractor

An (n, k)-bit-fixing source is a distribution X on $\{0, 1\}^n$ on which $n - k$ bits are fixed and the remaining k bits are uniform and independent each other. A deterministic bit-fixing source extractor is a function $E : \{0, 1\}^n \to \{0, 1\}^L$ which on input an arbitrary (n, k)-bit-fixing source, outputs L bits that are statistically-close to uniform.

Definition 4. (bit-fixing source on S). A distribution $X = (X_{i_1}, X_{i_2}, \cdots, X_{i_n})$ over $\{0,1\}^n$ is a bit-fixing source on $S = \{i_1, \cdots, i_k\} \subseteq \{1, \cdots, n\}$ if the joint distribution of $X_{i_1}, X_{i_2}, \cdots, X_{i_k}$ is uniformly distributed over $\{0,1\}^k$ and for every $i \notin S$, X_i is a fixed constant.

Definition 5. $((n, k)$-bit-fixing source). A distribution X over $\{0,1\}^n$ is an (n, k)-bit-fixing source if there exists a subset $S = \{i_1, \cdots, i_k\} \subseteq \{1, \cdots, n\}$ such that X is a bit-fixing source on S.

Definition 6. (deterministic extractor). A function $E : \{0,1\}^n \to \{0,1\}^L$ is a deterministic (k, ε)-bit-fixing source extractor if for every (n, k)-bit-fixing source X, the distribution $E(X)$ (obtained by sampling x from X and computing $E(x)$) is ε-close to the uniform distribution on L bit strings.

Gabizon, Raz and Shaltiel [20] gave a deterministic extractor for bit-fixing sources as follows.

Proposition 1. *For every constant $0 < \gamma < 1/2$, there exists an integer n' (depending on γ) such that: for any $n > n'$ and any k, there is an explicit deterministic (k, ε)-bit-fixing source extractor $E : \{0,1\}^n \to \{0,1\}^L$, where $L = k - n^{1/2+\gamma}$ and $\varepsilon = 2^{-\Omega(n^{\gamma})}$.*

Consider $k = n^{1/2+\alpha}$ for some constant $0 < \alpha < 1/2$. We can choose any $\gamma < \alpha$ and extract $L = n^{1/2+\alpha} - n^{1/2+\gamma}$ bits.

4   Direct Reduction of *String* $(1, 2)$-OT to Rabin's OT

Only known direct reduction of *string* $(1, 2)$-OT to Rabin's OT uses the technique of *privacy amplification*. In this section, we show a direct and simple reduction of *string* $(1, 2)$-OT to Rabin's OT *without* privacy amplification. In general, constructions (of string $(1, 2)$-OT from bit $(1, 2)$-OT) based on privacy amplification is simpler. While we use a different technique (i.e., deterministic extractor) than privacy amplification, our construction is rather simpler.

4.1   Proposed Reduction

We show how to realize *string* $(1, 2)$-OT from p-OT directly and efficiently, where p-OT is a generalization of Rabin's OT. In p-OT, Alice has a secret bit b. At the end of the execution of the protocol, Bob receives b with probability p. On the other hand, Alice does not know if Bob received b or not. Rabin's OT is a special case such that $p = 1/2$.

Alice and Bob agree on a positive integer n and $0 < \delta < \sqrt{2}p/3$. Let $N = n(p - \delta/\sqrt{2})$ and $k = n(p - 3\delta/\sqrt{2})/2$. Suppose that there exists a deterministic (k, ε)-bit-fixing source extractor $E : \{0,1\}^N \to \{0,1\}^L$.

Then our L-bit $(1, 2)$-OT is described as follows.

1. Alice chooses $x_1, \cdots, x_n \in \{0,1\}$ randomly.
2. For $i = 1, \cdots, n$, Alice and Bob execute p-OT on x_i.
3. Bob chooses $U_0, U_1 \subseteq \{1, \cdots, n\}$ such that $|U_0| = |U_1| = N$, $U_0 \cap U_1 = \varnothing$ and he knows x_i for each $i \in U_c$. He then sends (U_0, U_1) to Alice.
4. Suppose that

$$U_0 = \{i_1, \cdots, i_N\}, \quad U_1 = \{j_1, \cdots, j_N\}.$$

Define

$$R_0 = (x_{i_1}, \cdots, x_{i_N}), \quad R_1 = (x_{j_1}, \cdots, x_{j_N}).$$

Alice sends $y_0 = E(R_0) \oplus s_0$ and $y_1 = E(R_1) \oplus s_1$ to Bob.
5. Bob computes $s_c = E(R_c) \oplus y_c$.

4.2   Security

Now we will prove the security of the above protocol implementing L-bit $(1,2)$-OT. More formally, we have the following.

Theorem 1. *The protocol above implements L-bit $(1,2)$-OT with the following properties.*

- $(1 - 2e^{-n\delta^2})$-correctness,
- sender's $(1 - (\varepsilon + 2e^{-n\delta^2}))$-privacy, and
- receiver's 1-privacy,

where ε is the statistical difference between extractor outputs and the uniform distribution.

Proposition 2. (Hoeffding Bound [21]) *Let $x_1, x_2, \cdots, x_n$ be independent Bernoulli random variables. If $\Pr(x_i = 1) = p$ for $1 \leq i \leq n$, then for all $0 \leq \gamma \leq 1$, we have*

$$\Pr\left(\left|\frac{\sum_{i=1}^{n} x_i}{n} - p\right| \geq \gamma\right) \leq 2e^{-2n\gamma^2}.$$

Let

$$X = \{x_i \mid \text{Bob received } x_i \text{ at step 2}\}.$$

Note that $\mathbf{E}[|X|] = np$. Then by applying the Hoeffding Bound,

$$n\left(p - \frac{\delta}{\sqrt{2}}\right) \leq |X| \leq n\left(p + \frac{\delta}{\sqrt{2}}\right) \tag{1}$$

with probability more than $1 - 2e^{-n\delta^2}$. Therefore,

1. There exists $U_c \subseteq \{1, \cdots, n\}$ such that $N \stackrel{\text{def}}{=} n(p - \delta/\sqrt{2}) = |U_c|$ and he knows x_i for each $i \in U_c$, since, at step 2, he receives elements enough to constitute U_c. Hence honest Bob can receive s_c with probability more than $1 - 2e^{-n\delta^2}$. Thus the protocol satisfies $(1 - 2e^{-n\delta^2})$-correctness.

2. Again from eq.(1), Bob knows at most $M \stackrel{\text{def}}{=} n(p + \delta/\sqrt{2})$ bits among $x_1, \cdots, x_n$ with probability more than $1 - 2e^{-n\delta^2}$. On the other hand, $|U_0| + |U_1| = 2n(p - \delta/\sqrt{2})$. Hence Bob has no information on the rest of

$$|U_0| + |U_1| - M = 2n\left(p - \frac{\delta}{\sqrt{2}}\right) - n\left(p + \frac{\delta}{\sqrt{2}}\right) = n\left(p - \frac{3\delta}{\sqrt{2}}\right) = 2k$$

bits, because he does not receive any of them at step 2. Let us consider more precisely. Now, we assume that at step 3 Bob sends U_d and U_{1-d} such that $|U_d \cap X| \geq |U_{1-d} \cap X|$ (and $|U_d| = |U_{1-d}| = N$ and $U_d \cap U_{1-d} = \varnothing$). Then k indices out of U_{1-d} are unknown to Bob. That is R_{1-d} is an (N, k)-bit-fixing source for Bob. Here, we can define the random variable C' (appeared in Definition 3) as Bob's choice d, which is independent of (S_0, S_1) conditioned on C. Then he has (almost) no information on s_{1-d} (regardless of the knowledge on d, s_d and c) because E is a deterministic (k, ε)-bit-fixing source extractor and $y_i = E(R_i) \oplus s_i$ for $i = 0, 1$. It means that sender's $(1 - \varepsilon)$-privacy is satisfied on conditioning that Bob receives s_c as expected. After all, sender's $(1 - (\varepsilon + 2e^{-n\delta^2}))$-privacy is satisfied.

3. Receiver's 1-privacy immediately follows from the construction.

4.3   Comparison

Rabin's OT is a special case such that $p = 1/2$. Suppose that $p = 1/2$ in our protocol. Then we obtain L-bit $(1, 2)$-OT which satisfies sender's $(1 - (\varepsilon + 2e^{-n\delta^2}))$-privacy for any $0 < \delta < \sqrt{2}/6$ if there exists a deterministic (k, ε)-bit-fixing source extractor $E : \{0, 1\}^N \rightarrow \{0, 1\}^L$ with $N = n(0.5 - \delta/\sqrt{2})$ and $k = n(0.5 - 3\delta/\sqrt{2})$.

If we use a deterministic extractor for bit-fixing sources due to Gabizon, Raz and Shaltiel [20][2], then we have

$$L = (1 - o(1))k = (1 - o(1))n\left(\frac{1}{2} - \frac{3}{\sqrt{2}}\delta\right)/2.$$

We consider the case where L-bit $(1, 2)$-OT satisfies both $(1 - 2^{-s})$-correctness and sender's $(1 - 2^{-s})$-privacy. Let $s = n\delta^2 \ln 2$. (For simplicity, we assume that $\varepsilon = 0$.) Then,

---

[2] Their extractor consists of the Kamp-Zuckerman extractor[23] based on almost random walk on cycle graphs, a sampler (that can be realized by almost k-wise independent random variables[1]) and a standard seeded extractor. The computational cost of the seeded extractor is relatively expensive. So, we may use another deterministic extractor for bit-fixing sources if exists. For example, a generalization by Lee, Lu and Tsai [26] is a more efficient deterministic extractor for bit-fixing sources. What we care in the paper is on the communication cost, so we do not consider the running cost of extractors.

$$L \approx n/4 - O(\sqrt{sn}).$$

It means that we invoke Rabin's OT approximately $n \approx 4L + O(\sqrt{sL})$ times to construct L-bit $(1, 2)$-OT.

On the other hand, the previous reduction of L-bit $(1, 2)$-OT to Rabin's OT requires 2-step reduction. In the first step, we can construct a 1-bit $(1, 2)$-OT from Rabin's OT by using the reduction of Crépeau [12]. In the second step, we can construct an L-bit $(1, 2)$-OT from the 1-bit $(1, 2)$-OT. The first step requires at least $21s$ invocations of Rabin's OT as shown in Sec.2.3, where s is the security parameter. Brassard, Crépeau and Wolf showed the second step which runs $n = 2L + s'$ instances of 1-bit $(1, 2)$-OT, where s' is a security parameter [8]. Hence the previous reduction requires at least $21sL$ invocations of Rabin's OT.

See the following table for comparison. From this table, we see that our reduction is more efficient with respect to the communication complexity than the previous reduction, since our protocol does not use post-processing (i.e., sending random matrices and so on) for privacy amplification.

	the number of invocations of Rabin's OT to construct L-bit $(1, 2)$-OT
Previous 2-step reduction	at least $21sL$
Imai et al [22]	$4L + O(\sqrt{sL})$ (with post-processing each)
This paper	$4L + O(\sqrt{sL})$ (without post-processing)

5 Discussion

5.1 Technical Difference from Previous Reductions

Technical differences between our reduction and Crépeau's reduction [12] are as follows. The main difference is that we use a deterministic extractor for bit-fixing sources $E : \{0, 1\}^N \to \{0, 1\}^L$ while Crépeau used a deterministic function $E : \{0, 1\}^N \to \{0, 1\}$ such that

$$E(x_1, \cdots, x_N) = x_1 \oplus \cdots \oplus x_N.$$

In a sense, the usage of deterministic extractor for bit-fixing sources might be seen as a generalization. The reduction by Imai et al is also similar to Crépeau's reduction. They introduced privacy amplification as usual because their reduction is from string OT but from bit OT. Using predetermined deterministic extractors allows us to construct a direct and efficient reduction of L-bit $(1, 2)$-OT to Rabin's OT because ours does not need post-processing for each invocation as well as Crépeau's reduction from 1-bit $(1, 2)$-OT to Rabin's OT.

Another (but slight) difference from Crépeau's is that he used Bernshtein's Law of large numbers while we use Hoeffding bound which is tighter. While Imai et al. did not give the analysis, similar analysis may be applicable since our protocol is similar to theirs.

6 Concluding Remark

It is very hard to derive a lower bound on the number t of invocations of Rabin's OT to construct L-bit $(1,2)$-OT. Imai et al. [22] showed that a lower bound on the number t of invocations of Rabin's OT to construct L-bit $(1,2)$-OT *in the semi-honest model* is $2L$. Thus, a trivial lower bound *in the malicious model* is also $2L$. As we have shown, the upper bound is almost $4L$. So, there is still a gap between upper and lower bounds. It remains open to look for the matching bound. In case of the OT reduction from string $(1,2)$-OT to bit $(1,2)$-OT, the lower bounds have been extensively studied [17,30,25]. The techniques therein may be helpful to improve the lower bound in [22].

Acknowledgements

We would like to thank Serge Fehr and other PC members for ICITS 2008 for guiding us to a right definition of OT and suggestions to improve presentations. We also thank anonymous reviewers for valuable comments.

References

1. Alon, N., Goldreich, O., Håstad, J., Peralta, R.: Simple constructions of almost k-wise independent random variables. Random Structures and Algorithms 3(3), 289–304 (1992)
2. Bennett, C.H., Brassard, G., Crépeau, C., Maurer, U.M.: Generalized privacy amplification. IEEE Transactions on Information Theory 41(6), 1915–1923 (1995)
3. Bennett, C.H., Brassard, G., Robert, J.-M.: Privacy amplification by public discussion. SIAM Journal on Computing 17(2), 210–229 (1988)
4. Boyko, V.: On the security properties of OAEP as an all-or-nothing transform. In: Wiener, M.J. (ed.) CRYPTO 1999. LNCS, vol. 1666, pp. 503–518. Springer, Heidelberg (1999)
5. Brassard, G., Crépeau, C.: Oblivious transfers and privacy amplification. In: Fumy, W. (ed.) EUROCRYPT 1997. LNCS, vol. 1233, pp. 334–347. Springer, Heidelberg (1997)
6. Brassard, G., Crépeau, C., Robert, J.-M.: Information theoretic reductions among disclosure problems. In: Proc. 27th IEEE Symposium on Foundations of Computer Science, pp. 168–173 (1986)
7. Brassard, G., Crépeau, C., Santha, M.: Oblivious transfers and intersecting codes. IEEE Transactions on Information Theory 42(6), 1769–1780 (1996)
8. Brassard, G., Crépeau, C., Wolf, S.: Oblivious transfers and privacy amplification. Journal of Cryptology 16(4), 219–237 (2003)
9. Cachin, C.: On the foundations of oblivious transfer. In: Nyberg, K. (ed.) EUROCRYPT 1998. LNCS, vol. 1403, pp. 361–374. Springer, Heidelberg (1998)
10. Canetti, R., Dodis, Y., Halevi, S., Kushilevitz, E., Sahai, A.: Exposure-resilient functions and all-or-nothing transforms. In: Preneel, B. (ed.) EUROCRYPT 2000. LNCS, vol. 1807, pp. 453–469. Springer, Heidelberg (2000)
11. Chor, B., Goldreich, O., Håstad, J., Friedman, J., Rudich, R., Smolensky, R.: The bit extraction problem or t-resilient functions. In: Proc. 26th IEEE Symposium on Foundations of Computer Science, pp. 396–407 (1985)

12. Crépeau, C.: Equivalence between two flavours of oblivious transfers. In: Pomerance, C. (ed.) CRYPTO 1987. LNCS, vol. 293, pp. 350–354. Springer, Heidelberg (1988)
13. Crépeau, C.: Efficient cryptographic protocols based on noisy channels. In: Fumy, W. (ed.) EUROCRYPT 1997. LNCS, vol. 1233, pp. 306–317. Springer, Heidelberg (1997)
14. Crépeau, C., Savvides, G., Schaffner, C., Wullschleger, J.: Information-theoretic conditions for two-party secure function evaluation. In: Vaudenay, S. (ed.) EUROCRYPT 2006. LNCS, vol. 4004, pp. 538–554. Springer, Heidelberg (2006)
15. Damgård, I.B., Fehr, S., Salvail, L., Schaffner, C.: Oblivious transfer and linear functions. In: Dwork, C. (ed.) CRYPTO 2006. LNCS, vol. 4117, pp. 427–444. Springer, Heidelberg (2006)
16. Dodis, Y.: Exposure-Resilient Cryptography. PhD thesis, Dept. Electrical Engineering and Computer Science, MIT (2000)
17. Dodis, Y., Micali, S.: Lower bounds for oblivious transfer reductions. In: Stern, J. (ed.) EUROCRYPT 1999. LNCS, vol. 1592, pp. 42–55. Springer, Heidelberg (1999)
18. Dodis, Y., Sahai, A., Smith, A.: On perfect and adaptive security in exposure-resilient cryptography. In: Pfitzmann, B. (ed.) EUROCRYPT 2001. LNCS, vol. 2045, pp. 299–322. Springer, Heidelberg (2001)
19. Even, S., Goldreich, O., Lempel, A.: A randomized protocol for signing contracts. Communications of ACM 28(6), 637–647 (1985)
20. Gabizon, A., Raz, R., Shaltiel, R.: Deterministic extractors for bit-fixing sources by obtaining an independent seed. SIAM Journal on Computing 36(4), 1072–1094 (2006)
21. Hoeffding, W.: Probability inequalities for sum of bounded random variables. Journal of the American Statistical Association 58, 13–30 (1963)
22. Imai, H., Morozov, K., Nascimento, A.: On the oblivious transfer capacity of the erasure channel. In: Proc. 2006 IEEE International Symposium on Information Theory, pp.1428–1431 (2006)
23. Kamp, J., Zuckerman, D.: Deterministic extractors for bit-fixing sources and exposure-resilient cryptography. SIAM Journal on Computing 36(5), 1231–1247 (2007)
24. Kurosawa, K., Johansson, T., Stinson, D.: Almost k-wise independent sample spaces and their cryptologic applications. Journal of Cryptology 14(4), 231–253 (2001)
25. Kurosawa, K., Kishimoto, W., Koshiba, T.: A combinatorial approach to deriving lower bounds for perfectly secure oblivious transfer reductions. IEEE Transactions on Information Theory 54(6), 2566–2571 (2008)
26. Lee, C.-J., Lu, C.-J., Tsai, S.-C.: Deterministic extractors for independent-symbol sources. In: Bugliesi, M., Preneel, B., Sassone, V., Wegener, I. (eds.) ICALP 2006. LNCS, vol. 4051, pp. 84–95. Springer, Heidelberg (2006)
27. Rabin, M.O.: How to exchange secrets by oblivious transfer. Technical Memo TR-81, Aiken Computation Laboratory, Harvard University (1981)
28. Rivest, R.: All-or-nothing encryption and the package transform. In: Biham, E. (ed.) FSE 1997. LNCS, vol. 1267, pp. 210–218. Springer, Heidelberg (1997)
29. Wolf, S.: Reducing oblivious string transfer to universal oblivious transfer. In: Proc. 2000 IEEE International Symposium on Information Theory, p.465 (2000)
30. Wolf, S., Wullschleger, J.: New monotones and lower bounds in unconditional two-party computation. In: Shoup, V. (ed.) CRYPTO 2005. LNCS, vol. 3621, pp. 467–477. Springer, Heidelberg (2005)

The Complexity of Distinguishing Distributions (Invited Talk)

Thomas Baignères[*] and Serge Vaudenay

EPFL
CH-1015 Lausanne, Switzerland
http://lasecwww.epfl.ch

Abstract. Cryptography often meets the problem of distinguishing distributions. In this paper we review techniques from hypothesis testing to express the advantage of the best distinguisher limited to a given number of samples. We link it with the Chernoff information and provide a useful approximation based on the squared Euclidean distance. We use it to extend linear cryptanalysis to groups with order larger than 2.[1]

1 Preliminaries

1.1 Best Distinguisher

The hypothesis testing problem can be considered as a simple game in which a first player uses a *source* to generate independent random samples in some given finite set $\mathcal{Z}$ with a distribution P which follows either a *null hypothesis* H_0 or an alternate hypothesis H_1. The second player, often called *distinguisher*, must determine which hypothesis was used by using the samples. In the simplest testing problem, the source follows a distribution $\mathsf{P} \in \{\mathsf{P}_0, \mathsf{P}_1\}$ chosen among two distributions, both being known to the distinguisher. He faces two hypotheses, namely $\mathsf{H}_0 : \mathsf{P} = \mathsf{P}_0$ and $\mathsf{H}_1 : \mathsf{P} = \mathsf{P}_1$. This situation is commonly referred to as the *simple hypothesis testing problem* since both alternatives fully determine the distribution. A more complex situation arises when one of the two hypotheses is *composite*, i.e., when the distinguisher has to guess whether the distribution followed by the source is one particular distribution ($\mathsf{H}_0 : \mathsf{P} = \mathsf{P}_0$) or if it belongs to a set of several distributions ($\mathsf{H}_1 : \mathsf{P} \in \{\mathsf{P}_1, \ldots, \mathsf{P}_d\}$). Finally, the difficulty of the game can be increased from the point of view of the distinguisher if the exact description of the alternate hypothesis is not available. In that case, it shall guess whether the source follows a specific (known) distribution ($\mathsf{H}_0 : \mathsf{P} = \mathsf{P}_0$) or not ($\mathsf{H}_1 : \mathsf{P} \neq \mathsf{P}_0$).

In all cases, the adversary is assumed to be computationally unbounded[2] and to be only limited by the number q of samples available, so that we will referred to it as a q-limited distinguisher and denote it A_q. If $\boldsymbol{Z}^q = Z_1, \ldots, Z_q$ are the q samples available to A_q, we define the type I error α and the type II error β by:

$$\alpha = \mathrm{Pr}_{\mathsf{H}_0}[\mathsf{A}_q(\boldsymbol{Z}^q) = 1] \qquad \beta = 1 - \mathrm{Pr}_{\mathsf{H}_1}[\mathsf{A}_q(\boldsymbol{Z}^q) = 1]$$

---

[*] Supported by the Swiss National Science Foundation, 200021-107982/1.
[1] These results will be part of [1].
[2] So that we can assume w.l.o.g. that the adversary is fully deterministic.

R. Safavi-Naini (Ed.): ICITS 2008, LNCS 5155, pp. 210–222, 2008.
© Springer-Verlag Berlin Heidelberg 2008

For composite hypotheses, these probabilities make sense when distributions are assigned weights (following the Bayesian approach). We measure the ability to distinguish between hypothesis H_0 and H_1 by the *advantage* defined as

$$\mathrm{Adv}_{A_q}(H_0, H_1) = |\mathrm{Pr}_{H_0}[A_q(\boldsymbol{Z}^q) = 1] - \mathrm{Pr}_{H_1}[A_q(\boldsymbol{Z}^q) = 1]| = |1 - \alpha - \beta|.$$

In the simple hypothesis case we denote the advantage by $\mathrm{Adv}_{A_q}(P_0, P_1)$. We let

$$P_{\boldsymbol{Z}^q}[z] = \frac{n_z}{q},$$

be the relative proportion of occurrences of each symbol of $\mathcal{Z}$ ($P_{\boldsymbol{Z}^q}$ is also called *type* of $\boldsymbol{Z}^q$ [4]), where n_z is the number of occurrences of the symbol z in the sequence $\boldsymbol{Z}^q = Z_1, \dots, Z_q$. Since the samples are assumed to be mutually independent, their particular order must be irrelevant. Consequently, the final distinguishing decision can be solely based on the type $P_{\boldsymbol{Z}^q}$ of the sequence. Denoting $\mathcal{P}$ the set of all probability distributions over $\mathcal{Z}$, we can completely describe any distinguisher by an *acceptance region* $\Pi \subset \mathcal{P}$ such that

$$A_q(\boldsymbol{Z}^q) = 1 \quad \Leftrightarrow \quad P_{\boldsymbol{Z}^q} \in \Pi.$$

For $q = 1$ we can easily show (see [2]) that $\mathrm{Adv}_{A_q}(P_0, P_1)$ reaches a maximum equal to

$$\mathrm{BestAdv}_1(P_0, P_1) = \frac{1}{2}\|P_0 - P_1\|_1$$

where the norm $\|\cdot\|_1$ of a function f is defined by $\|f\|_1 = \sum_x |f(x)|$. We can apply this result to the probability distribution of $\boldsymbol{Z}^q$. By using the equality

$$2(aa' - bb') = (a - b)(a' + b') + (a' - b')(a + b)$$

we deduce that

$$\mathrm{BestAdv}_q(P_0, P_1) \leq \frac{q}{2}\|P_0 - P_1\|_1$$

The first concern of the present paper is to obtain a more precise expression for $\mathrm{BestAdv}_q(P_0, P_1)$.

Notations. The natural logarithm is denoted $\ln$ while $\log$ refers to basis 2 logarithm. The *support* of a distribution P is the set $\mathrm{Supp}(P)$ of all z for which $P[z] > 0$. In this paper, P_0 and P_1 will be two distinct distributions on a finite set $\mathcal{Z}$ such that $\mathrm{Supp}(P_0) \cup \mathrm{Supp}(P_1) = \mathcal{Z}$. We will denote $\mathcal{Z}' = \mathrm{Supp}(P_0) \cap \mathrm{Supp}(P_1)$. In the case where both P_0 and P_1 are of full support we have $\mathcal{Z} = \mathcal{Z}'$, otherwise $\mathcal{Z}' \subsetneq \mathcal{Z}$. The *Chernoff information*[3] between P_0 and P_1 is

$$C(P_0, P_1) = -\inf_{0 < \lambda < 1} \log \sum_{z \in \mathcal{Z}'} P_0[z]^{1-\lambda} P_1[z]^{\lambda}.$$

---

[3] Note that our definition differs from that sometimes given (e.g., in [4, p.314]), namely $C(P_0, P_1) = -\min_{0 \leq \lambda \leq 1} \log \sum_{z \in \mathcal{Z}} P_0[z]^{1-\lambda} P_1[z]^{\lambda}$, since the latter is not well defined when $\mathrm{Supp}(P_0) \neq \mathrm{Supp}(P_1)$.

The Kullback-Leibler divergence between P_0 and P_1 is

$$D(P_0\|P_1) = \sum_{z \in \mathsf{Supp}(P_0)} P_0[z] \log \frac{P_0[z]}{P_1[z]}$$

with the convention that $D(P_0\|P_1) = +\infty$ when $\mathsf{Supp}(P_0) \not\subseteq \mathsf{Supp}(P_1)$. The notation $f(q) \doteq g(q)$ for $q \to +\infty$ means that $f(q) = g(q)e^{o(q)}$ or equivalently that

$$\lim_{q \to +\infty} \frac{1}{q} \log \frac{f(q)}{g(q)} = 0.$$

We denote $f(q) \sim g(q)$ for $f(q) = g(q)(1 + o(1))$.

1.2 Neyman-Pearson

Given 3 distributions P_0, P_1, P, let us define

$$L(P) = \sum_{z \in \mathsf{Supp}(P)} P[z] \log \frac{P_0[z]}{P_1[z]}$$

with the natural convention that $\log 0 = -\infty$ and $\frac{1}{0} = +\infty$. (Note that if P has a support either included in the one of P_0 or in the one of P_1 then we never encounter an illegal operation such as $\frac{0}{0}$ or $\infty - \infty$.) The best distinguisher between P_0 and P_1 can be expressed as follows. Given a sample vector Z^q we compute $L(P_{Z^q})$ (which is nothing but the logarithmic likelihood ratio). The distinguisher is defined by a threshold τ and outputs 1 iff $L(P_{Z^q}) \le \log \tau$. The Neyman-Pearson Lemma [6] says that for any distinguisher achieving error probabilities α and β, there exists τ such that the above distinguisher has error probabilities not larger than α and β respectively. This means that for any distinguisher there exists one based on the likelihood ratio which is at least as good in terms of error probabilities.

If one is concerned with maximizing the advantage (or equivalently in minimizing $\alpha + \beta$) then the best distinguisher is defined by $\tau = 1$. It can be defined by the acceptance region

$$\Pi = \{P \in \mathcal{P} \ : \ L(P) \le 0\}.$$

A classical result (see [4, Section 12.9]) gives a precise asymptotic expression for α and β when P_0 and P_1 have the *same support*.

Theorem 1. *Let P_0 and P_1 be two distributions of finite support $\mathcal{Z}$. Let $\mathsf{BestAdv}_q(P_0, P_1)$ denote the best advantage for distinguishing P_0 from P_1 with q samples and α and β the type I and type II errors of the distinguisher, respectively. We have*

$$1 - \mathsf{BestAdv}_q(P_0, P_1) \doteq \alpha \doteq \beta \doteq 2^{-q\mathsf{C}(P_0, P_1)}.$$

Unfortunately, this expression of α and β is not correct if the supports do not match as the following example shows.

Example 2. We can consider $\mathcal{Z} = \{1, 2, 3\}$ and

$$\mathsf{P}_0 = \left(\tfrac{1}{3} \ \tfrac{1}{3} \ \tfrac{1}{3} \right) \qquad \mathsf{P}_1 = \left(a \ b \ 0 \right)$$

with $a + b = 1$, $\tfrac{1}{3} > a > \tfrac{1}{7}$. We have

$$\mathsf{L}(\mathsf{P}) = \begin{cases} \mathsf{P}[1] \log \tfrac{1}{3a} + \mathsf{P}[2] \log \tfrac{1}{3b} & \text{if } \mathsf{P}[3] = 0 \\ +\infty & \text{if } \mathsf{P}[3] \neq 0 \end{cases}$$

The Chernoff information is computed from the minimum over $]0, 1[$ of

$$F(\lambda) = \frac{1}{3}(3a)^\lambda + \frac{1}{3}(3b)^\lambda.$$

This is a convex function such that $F(0) = \tfrac{2}{3}$ and $F(1) = 1$. Assuming that $a \in]\tfrac{1}{3}, \tfrac{1}{7}[$, since $a + b = 1$ we have $9ab > 1$ thus $F'(0) > 0$. We deduce that F is increasing over $]0, 1[$ so the minimum is $F(0) = \tfrac{2}{3}$: we have $\mathsf{C}(\mathsf{P}_0, \mathsf{P}_1) = -\log \tfrac{2}{3}$. Since $F(\lambda) \to +\infty$ when $\lambda \to -\infty$ the minimum of F is reached for some $\lambda < 0$ which we call λ_0. We have $2^{-q\mathsf{C}(\mathsf{P}_0,\mathsf{P}_1)} = \left(\tfrac{2}{3}\right)^q$. The type I error α is the probability that $\mathsf{L}(\mathsf{P}_{\mathbf{Z}^q}) \leq 0$ under distribution P_0 which mandates that 3 never occurs. This holds with probability $\left(\tfrac{2}{3}\right)^q$. When this happens, the number of occurrences of 1 and 2 are roughly similar so $\mathsf{L}(\mathsf{P}_{\mathbf{Z}^q}) \leq 0$. We can indeed show that $\alpha \doteq \left(\tfrac{2}{3}\right)^q$, which matches the result of Theorem 1. However, the type II error β is the probability that $\mathsf{L}(\mathsf{P}_{\mathbf{Z}^q}) > 0$ under distribution P_1 which is the probability that $n_1 \log 3a + n_2 \log 3b < 0$. This means that 2 must occur much less than 1 although its probability b is higher than a. As a consequence of Theorem 3 below we can show that $\beta \doteq F(\lambda_0)^q$ which does not match Theorem 1. The expression is thus correct for α but incorrect for β. In what follows we show that the expression is always correct for $\max(\alpha, \beta)$ so it is still correct for the advantage.

2   Best Advantage for Simple Hypothesis Testing

2.1   Result

Theorem 3. *Let P_0 and P_1 be two distributions of finite supports with union $\mathcal{Z}$ and intersection $\mathcal{Z}'$. Given a distribution P over $\mathcal{Z}$ we define*

$$\mathsf{L}(\mathsf{P}) = \sum_{z \in \mathsf{Supp}(\mathsf{P})} \mathsf{P}[z] \log \frac{\mathsf{P}_0[z]}{\mathsf{P}_1[z]} \quad \text{and} \quad F(\lambda) = \sum_{z \in \mathcal{Z}'} \mathsf{P}_0[z]^{1-\lambda} \mathsf{P}_1[z]^\lambda.$$

Let $\Pi = \{\mathsf{P} \in \mathcal{P} : \mathsf{L}(\mathsf{P}) \leq 0\}$ be the acceptance region of the best distinguisher. Its type I error α satisfies

$$\alpha \doteq \left(\inf_{\lambda > 0} F(\lambda) \right)^q.$$

If there exists $z \in \mathcal{Z}'$ such that $0 < \mathsf{P}_1[z] < \mathsf{P}_0[z]$ then

$$\beta \doteq \left(\inf_{\lambda < 1} F(\lambda) \right)^q .$$

Otherwise, $\beta = 0$.

If for all $z \in \mathcal{Z}'$ we have $\mathsf{P}_1[z] \geq \mathsf{P}_0[z]$ then β is clearly zero and $\inf_{\lambda > 0} F(\lambda) = F(0)$ so $\max(\alpha, \beta) = \alpha \doteq 2^{-q C(\mathsf{P}_0, \mathsf{P}_1)}$. Otherwise, we note that

$$\max \left(\inf_{]0, +\infty[} F, \inf_{]-\infty, 1[} F \right) = \inf_{]0, 1[} F$$

because F is a convex function. Hence, we still have

$$\max(\alpha, \beta) \doteq 2^{-q C(\mathsf{P}_0, \mathsf{P}_1)} .$$

We deduce the following result.

Corollary 4. *Let P_0 and P_1 be two distributions of finite support with intersection $\mathcal{Z}'$. We have*

$$1 - \mathrm{BestAdv}_q(\mathsf{P}_0, \mathsf{P}_1) \doteq 2^{-q C(\mathsf{P}_0, \mathsf{P}_1)} = \left(\inf_{0 < \lambda < 1} \sum_{z \in \mathcal{Z}'} \mathsf{P}_0[z]^{1-\lambda} \mathsf{P}_1[z]^{\lambda} \right)^q .$$

2.2 Proof of Theorem 3

We first recall Sanov's theorem. To do this, we recall some notions of topology. The set of all functions from the finite set $\mathcal{Z}$ to $\mathbf{R}$ is a vector space of finite dimension thus all norms $\| \cdot \|$ define the same topology. An *open set* is a union of open balls, i.e. a set of functions f satisfying $\| f - f_0 \| < r$ for a given function f_0 and a given radius $r \in \mathbf{R}$. The *interior* of a set Π is the union $\overset{\circ}{\Pi}$ of all open sets included in Π. A *closed set* is an intersection of closed balls. The *closure* of a set Π is the intersection $\overline{\Pi}$ of all closed sets containing Π.

Theorem 5 (Sanov [7]). *Let P_0 be a distribution over a finite set $\mathcal{Z}$ and $\mathbf{Z}^q = Z_1, \ldots, Z_q$ be q mutually independent random variables following distribution P_0. Let Π be a set of distributions over $\mathcal{Z}$ such that $\overset{\circ}{\Pi} = \overline{\Pi}$. We have*

$$\Pr[\mathsf{P}_{\mathbf{Z}^q} \in \Pi] \doteq 2^{-q D(\Pi \| \mathsf{P}_0)}$$

where $D(\Pi \| \mathsf{P}_0) = \inf_{\mathsf{P} \in \Pi} D(\mathsf{P} \| \mathsf{P}_0)$.

Intuitively, the $\overset{\circ}{\Pi} = \overline{\Pi}$ assumption means that Π has no isolated point which could substantially influence $D(\mathsf{P} \| \mathsf{P}_0)$ but would exceptionally (if ever) be reached by $\mathsf{P}_{\mathbf{Z}^q}$.

Lemma 6. *Let P_0 be a distribution of finite support $\mathcal{Z}$. Let g be a function such that $g(z) > 0$ for all $z \in \mathcal{Z}$. Given a distribution P over $\mathcal{Z}$ we define*

$$\mathsf{L}(\mathsf{P}) = \sum_{z \in \mathsf{Supp}(\mathsf{P})} \mathsf{P}[z] \log \frac{\mathsf{P}_0[z]}{g(z)} \quad and \quad F(\lambda) = \sum_{z \in \mathcal{Z}} \mathsf{P}_0[z]^{1-\lambda} g(z)^\lambda.$$

Let Π be the set of distributions over $\mathcal{Z}$ such that $\mathsf{L}(\mathsf{P}) \leq 0$ and consider the distinguisher A_q who accepts $\mathbf{Z}^q$ (i.e., returns 1) iff $\mathsf{P}_{\mathbf{Z}^q} \in \Pi$. We have

$$\Pr[\mathsf{A}_q(\mathbf{Z}^q) = 1] = \Pr[\mathsf{P}_{\mathbf{Z}^q} \in \Pi] \doteq \left(\inf_{\lambda > 0} F(\lambda) \right)^q.$$

If Π is now the set of all distributions such that $\mathsf{L}(\mathsf{P}) < 0$ and there exists z such that $0 < \mathsf{P}_0[z] < g(z)$ the result still holds. Otherwise, the probability is zero.

Proof. We first assume that $\mathsf{P}_0[z] \geq g(z)$ for all z. If Π is defined by $\mathsf{L}(\mathsf{P}) \leq 0$, the probability is $\mathsf{P}_0(\mathcal{Z}'')^q$ where $\mathcal{Z}''$ is the set of all z's such that $\mathsf{P}_0[z] = g(z)$, and the result easily comes. If Π is defined by $\mathsf{L}(\mathsf{P}) < 0$, the probability is clearly zero.

We now assume that we have $0 < \mathsf{P}_0[z] < g(z)$ for some z. Clearly, the distribution P such that $\mathsf{P}(z) = 1$ verifies $\mathsf{L}(\mathsf{P}) < 0$ so Π is nonempty. Considering the topology of distributions over $\mathcal{Z}$, we notice that L is continuous. Since $\mathsf{L}(\mathsf{P}) < 0$ for some $\mathsf{P} \in \Pi$, for $\varepsilon > 0$ small enough all distributions within a distance to P smaller than ε are in Π as well. This means that the interior of Π is nonempty. We note that Π is a convex set. Consequently, we have $\overset{\circ}{\Pi} = \overline{\Pi}$ so that Sanov's theorem applies and we have

$$\Pr[\mathsf{P}_{\mathbf{Z}^q} \in \Pi] \doteq 2^{-q\mathsf{D}(\Pi\|\mathsf{P}_0)}.$$

What remains to be shown is that $\mathsf{D}(\Pi\|\mathsf{P}_0)$ is equal to $-\inf_{\lambda > 0} \log F(\lambda)$ for both possible definitions of Π.

The set $\overline{\Pi}$ is bounded and topologically closed in a real vector space of finite dimension and therefore compact. We notice that $\mathsf{P} \mapsto \mathsf{D}(\mathsf{P}\|\mathsf{P}_0)$ is continuous on $\overline{\Pi}$. We deduce that $\mathsf{D}(\Pi\|\mathsf{P}_0) = \mathsf{D}(\mathsf{P}\|\mathsf{P}_0)$ for some P in $\overline{\Pi}$: we do have global minima for this function in $\overline{\Pi}$. Furthermore, the function $\mathsf{P} \mapsto \mathsf{D}(\mathsf{P}\|\mathsf{P}_0)$ is convex since

$$\mathsf{D}((1-t)\mathsf{P} + t\mathsf{P}'\|\mathsf{P}_0) \leq (1-t)\mathsf{D}(\mathsf{P}\|\mathsf{P}_0) + t\mathsf{D}(\mathsf{P}'\|\mathsf{P}_0)$$

so we deduce that there is no local minimum which is not global as well. Since the set of P's such that $\mathsf{D}(\mathsf{P}\|\mathsf{P}_0) \leq r$ is a convex set for any radius r, the set of global minima is indeed a convex set as well. Finally, if P reaches a minimum, then the segment between P_0 and P except P contains distributions "closer" (in the sense of D) to P_0 which must then be outside of Π. Thus their L value are positive. So, either the segment is reduced to P_0 (meaning that $\mathsf{L}(\mathsf{P}_0) \leq 0$) or we must have $\mathsf{L}(\mathsf{P}) = 0$ due to the continuity of L. Hence, the closest P in Π is either P_0 (if $\mathsf{P}_0 \in \overline{\Pi}$) or some P such that $\mathsf{L}(\mathsf{P}) = 0$.

We consider the differentiable function $P \mapsto D(P\|P_0)$ over the open space $\{P : \mathcal{Z} \longrightarrow \mathbf{R}_+^*\}$ with constraints $N(P) = 1$ and $L(P) = \text{cste}$ where $N(P) = \sum_z P(z)$. By looking at the differentials, we have

$$\frac{\partial D(P\|P_0)}{\partial P(a)} = \log \frac{P(a)}{P_0[a]} + \frac{1}{\ln 2}$$

so $\frac{\partial^2 D(P\|P_0)}{\partial P(a)\partial P(b)} = 0$ for $a \neq b$ and is strictly positive otherwise. Hence the second differential of $D(P\|P_0)$ is a strictly positive quadratic form. Thus, P is a local minimum for $D(\cdot\|P_0)$ over the distributions whose L value is constant iff the first differential is a linear combination of dN and dL. This is the case iff P is of form P_λ for some λ where

$$P_\lambda[z] = \frac{P_0[z]^{1-\lambda}g(z)^\lambda}{\sum_a P_0[a]^{1-\lambda}g(a)^\lambda}.$$

We deduce that for all $\lambda \in \mathbf{R}$, P_λ is *the* closest (in the sense of D) distribution to P_0 with this $L(P_\lambda)$ value. We look for the one for which this is zero.

We observe that F is a convex function such that $F(0) = 1$ and $F'(0) = -L(P_0)\ln 2$. More precisely, we have $F'(\lambda) = -L(P_\lambda)F(\lambda)\ln 2$. Since there exists z such that $P_0[z] < g(z)$ the limit of F at $+\infty$ is $+\infty$. We note that

$$D(P_\lambda\|P_0) = -\lambda L(P_\lambda) - \log F(\lambda).$$

If the closest P is not P_0 we have $L(P_0) \geq 0$ hence $F'(0) \leq 0$, so there must be a $\lambda \geq 0$ such that $F'(\lambda) = 0$ and for which $F(\lambda)$ is minimal. Clearly, this minimum is $\inf_{\lambda>0} F(\lambda)$. We deduce $L(P_\lambda) = 0$ thus P_λ is the closest distribution to P_0 in Π. The above expression of the distance yields the announced result in this case.

When P_0 is in $\overline{\Pi}$ we have $L(P_0) \leq 0$ thus $F'(0) \geq 0$. Since F is convex, F is increasing on $[0, +\infty[$ so $\inf_{\lambda>0} F(\lambda) = F(0) = 1$. Since $0 = D(\Pi\|P_0)$ the result holds in this case as well.   □

Proof (of Theorem 3). Let $\tilde{P}_0[z] = P_0[z]/P_0(\mathcal{Z}')$ for $z \in \mathcal{Z}'$ and $\tilde{P}_0[z] = 0$ otherwise. Let $g(z) = P_1[z]/P_0(\mathcal{Z}')$ for $z \in \mathcal{Z}'$ and $g(z) = 0$ otherwise. Applying Lemma 6 to $\tilde{P}_0$ and g over $\mathcal{Z}'$ defines two functions $\tilde{L}$ and $\tilde{F}$ and a set $\tilde{\Pi}$ of distributions over $\mathcal{Z}'$ satisfying $\tilde{L}(P) \leq 0$. Clearly, we have $\tilde{L}(P) = L(P)$ for any distribution over $\mathcal{Z}'$. Indeed, Π consists of $\tilde{\Pi}$ plus all the distributions of support included in the one of P_1 but not in $\mathcal{Z}'$. The probability to reach one of these latter distributions when sampling z's following P_0 is clearly zero. Hence, the probability of accepting $\mathbf{Z}^q$ is the probability that $P_{\mathbf{Z}^q} \in \tilde{\Pi}$, under H_0. It is $P_0(\mathcal{Z}')^q$ times the probability that $P_{\mathbf{Z}^q} \in \tilde{\Pi}$ when sampling the Z_i's according to $\tilde{P}_0$. By applying Theorem 1 we immediately obtain the result.   □

3   Approximations for "Close" Distributions

We assume in this section that P_1 is *close* to P_0 of full support $\mathcal{Z}$. More precisely, we assume that P_0 is fixed of support $\mathcal{Z}$ and that P_1 tends towards P_0.

Eventually, both distributions have the same support $\mathcal{Z}$, and for all $z \in \mathcal{Z}$ we have $x_z = o(1)$ as $\mathsf{P}_1 \to \mathsf{P}_0$ where

$$x_z = \frac{\mathsf{P}_1[z] - \mathsf{P}_0[z]}{\mathsf{P}_0[z]}.$$

3.1   Computing the Chernoff Information

Theorem 7. *Let P_0 be a distribution of support $\mathcal{Z}$. If the distribution P_1 over $\mathcal{Z}$ tends towards P_0, then*

$$\mathsf{C}(\mathsf{P}_0, \mathsf{P}_1) \sim \frac{1}{8 \ln 2} \sum_{z \in \mathcal{Z}} \frac{(\mathsf{P}_1[z] - \mathsf{P}_0[z])^2}{\mathsf{P}_0[z]}.$$

Proof. We let $x = (x_z)_{z \in \mathcal{Z}}$ and consider

$$F(\lambda, x) = \sum_{z \in \mathcal{Z}} \mathsf{P}_0[z](1 + x_z)^\lambda$$

$$g(\lambda, x) = \sum_{z \in \mathcal{Z}} \mathsf{P}_0[z](1 + x_z)^\lambda \ln(1 + x_z).$$

We define $\lambda^* \in [0, 1]$ as the value verifying $g(\lambda^*, x) = 0$. In terms of λ, $F(\lambda, x)$ is strictly convex of derivative $g(\lambda, x)$. Clearly, $\mathsf{C}(\mathsf{P}_0, \mathsf{P}_1) = -\log F(\lambda^*, x)$. We will approximate $F(\lambda^*, x)$ when x is small and subject to $\sum_z \mathsf{P}_0[z]x_z = 0$. We first have

$$g(\lambda, x) = \sum_z \mathsf{P}_0[z](1 + \lambda x_z + o(x_z)) \left(x_z - \frac{x_z^2}{2} + o(x_z^2) \right)$$

$$= \sum_z \mathsf{P}_0[z] \left(\lambda - \frac{1}{2} \right) x_z^2 + o\left(\|x\|_2^2 \right)$$

since $\sum_z \mathsf{P}_0[z]x_z$ is zero. As $g(\lambda^*, x) = 0$ we deduce that λ^* tends towards $\frac{1}{2}$ as x tends towards 0. We now let

$$F(\lambda^*, x) = F\left(\frac{1}{2}, x \right) + \left(\lambda^* - \frac{1}{2} \right) F'_\lambda \left(\frac{1}{2}, x \right) + \frac{1}{2} \left(\lambda^* - \frac{1}{2} \right)^2 R$$

with $|R| \leq \max_\lambda F''_\lambda(\lambda, x)$ for $\lambda \in [0, 1]$. As $F'_\lambda(\lambda, x) = g(\lambda, x)$, previous computations immediately lead to $F'_\lambda(\frac{1}{2}, x) = g(\frac{1}{2}, x) = o(\|x\|_2^2)$. Similarly we have

$$F''_\lambda(\lambda, x) = \sum_{z \in \mathcal{Z}} \mathsf{P}_0[z](1 + x_z)^\lambda \left(\ln(1 + x_z) \right)^2$$

$$= \sum_{z \in \mathcal{Z}} \mathsf{P}_0[z](1 + o(1)) \left(x_z + o(x_z) \right)^2$$

$$= \sum_{z \in \mathcal{Z}} \mathsf{P}_0[z]x_z^2 + o(\|x\|^2)$$

which is a $O(\|x\|^2)$, hence

$$F(\lambda^*, x) = F\left(\frac{1}{2}, x\right) + o(\|x\|^2).$$

Now, we have

$$F\left(\frac{1}{2}, x\right) = \sum_{z \in \mathcal{Z}} \mathsf{P}_0[z]\sqrt{1 + x_z}$$

$$= \sum_{z \in \mathcal{Z}} \mathsf{P}_0[z]\left(1 + \frac{1}{2}x_z - \frac{1}{8}x_z^2 + o(x_z^2)\right)$$

$$= 1 - \frac{1}{8}\sum_{z \in \mathcal{Z}} \mathsf{P}_0[z]x_z^2 + o(\|x\|_2^2)$$

and therefore

$$F(\lambda^*, x) = 1 - \frac{1}{8}\sum_{z \in \mathcal{Z}} \mathsf{P}_0[z]x_z^2 + o(\|x\|_2^2),$$

which can be written

$$F(\lambda^*, x) = 1 - \frac{1}{8}\sum_{z \in \mathcal{Z}} \frac{(\mathsf{P}_1[z] - \mathsf{P}_0[z])^2}{\mathsf{P}_0[z]} + o\left(\sum_{z \in \mathcal{Z}}\left(\frac{\mathsf{P}_1[z] - \mathsf{P}_0[z]}{\mathsf{P}_0[z]}\right)^2\right).$$

$\square$

Our computations were based on the assumption that $x_z = o(1)$ for all z. In practice however, both distribution are fixed. Yet we can use Theorem 7 to approximate $C(\mathsf{P}_0, \mathsf{P}_1)$ when $|\mathsf{P}_1[z] - \mathsf{P}_0[z]| \ll \mathsf{P}_0[z]$ for all z.

3.2 Close-to-Uniform Distributions

In the particular case where P_0 is the uniform distribution over $\mathcal{Z}$ of cardinality n, Theorem 7 yields

$$C(\mathsf{P}_0, \mathsf{P}_1) \sim \frac{n}{8\ln 2}\|\mathsf{P}_1 - \mathsf{P}_0\|_2^2$$

for the Euclidean norm $\|\cdot\|_2$, which can be used as the approximation

$$C(\mathsf{P}_0, \mathsf{P}_1) \approx \frac{n}{8\ln 2}\|\mathsf{P}_1 - \mathsf{P}_0\|_2^2$$

when $|\mathsf{P}_1[z] - \frac{1}{n}| \ll \frac{1}{n}$ for all z. When $\mathcal{Z}$ has a group structure, this can be expressed as

$$C(\mathsf{P}_0, \mathsf{P}_1) \approx \frac{1}{8\ln 2}\|\hat{\mathsf{P}}_1 - \hat{\mathsf{P}}_0\|_2^2 \quad \text{or even} \quad C(\mathsf{P}_0, \mathsf{P}_1) \approx \frac{1}{8\ln 2}\sum_{\chi \in \hat{\mathcal{Z}}} \mathsf{LP}(\chi)$$

where $\hat{\mathcal{Z}}$ is the dual group of $\mathcal{Z}$ (i.e., the set of all group homomorphisms χ between $\mathcal{Z}$ and the non-zero complex numbers) and where $\hat{\mathsf{P}}$ is the Fourier transform of P, i.e.

$$\hat{\mathsf{P}}(\chi) = \sum_{z \in \mathcal{Z}} \mathsf{P}[z]\bar{\chi}(z) \quad \text{and} \quad \mathsf{LP}(\chi) = |\hat{\mathsf{P}}_1(\chi)|^2 = |\mathsf{E}(\chi(Z))|^2$$

where Z follows the distribution P_1. This formally proves a heuristic result from Baignères, Stern, and Vaudenay [3] by showing that the best advantage is approximately

$$1 - e^{-\frac{q}{8}\|\hat{\mathsf{P}}_1 - \hat{\mathsf{P}}_0\|_2^2}$$

for q large and $\|\hat{\mathsf{P}}_1 - \hat{\mathsf{P}}_0\|_2$ small.

4 A Case of Composite Hypothesis Testing

So far, we considered the problem of testing the null hypothesis $\mathsf{H}_0 : \mathsf{P} = \mathsf{P}_0$ against the simple alternate hypothesis $\mathsf{H}_1 : \mathsf{P} = \mathsf{P}_1$ where P_0 and P_1 were fully specified. We now consider the problem of distinguishing the case where P is equal to a specified distribution P_0 (the null hypothesis H_0) from the case where P belongs to a set $\mathcal{D} = \{\mathsf{P}_1, \ldots, \mathsf{P}_d\}$ of d fully specified distributions (the hypothesis H_1). Under H_1 we assume that the selection of P_i is taken with an *a priori* weight of π_i to define the advantage for distinguishing H_0 from H_1. For simplicity we assume that all distributions have the same support $\mathcal{Z}$.

4.1 Complex Hypothesis Testing

Theorem 8. *Let P_0 be a distribution of support $\mathcal{Z}$ and $\mathcal{D} = \{\mathsf{P}_1, \ldots, \mathsf{P}_d\}$ be a finite set of distributions of support $\mathcal{Z}$. In order to test the null hypothesis $\mathsf{H}_0 : \mathsf{P} = \mathsf{P}_0$ against $\mathsf{H}_1 : \mathsf{P} \in \mathcal{D}$, the advantage of the best q-limited distinguisher is such that*

$$1 - \mathrm{BestAdv}_q(\mathsf{P}_0, \mathcal{D}) \doteq \max_{1 \leq i \leq d} 2^{-q\mathrm{C}(\mathsf{P}_0, \mathsf{P}_i)}.$$

It is reached by the distinguisher accepting Z^q iff

$$\min_{1 \leq i \leq d} \sum_{z \in \mathcal{Z}} \mathsf{P}_{Z^q}[z] \log \frac{\mathsf{P}_0[z]}{\mathsf{P}_i[z]} \leq 0.$$

Proof. Consider a q-limited distinguisher A_q defined by an acceptance region Π and denote by Adv_q its advantage. We have

$$1 - \mathrm{Adv}_q = \mathrm{Pr}_{\mathsf{H}_0}[\mathsf{A}_q(Z^q) = 1] + \sum_{i=1}^{d} \pi_i \mathrm{Pr}[\mathsf{A}_q(Z^q) = 0 | \mathsf{P} = \mathsf{P}_i]$$

thus $1 - \mathrm{Adv}_q$ is at least the average of all $1 - \mathrm{BestAdv}_q(\mathsf{P}_0, \mathsf{P}_i)$ with weight π_i, which are (asymptotically) $2^{-q\mathrm{C}(\mathsf{P}_0, \mathsf{P}_i)}$. We deduce that

$$1 - \mathrm{Adv}_q \stackrel{.}{>} \sum_{i=1}^{d} \pi_i 2^{-q\mathrm{C}(\mathsf{P}_0, \mathsf{P}_i)} \quad \text{thus} \quad 1 - \mathrm{Adv}_q \stackrel{.}{>} \max_{1 \leq i \leq d} 2^{-q\mathrm{C}(\mathsf{P}_0, \mathsf{P}_i)}.$$

We define

$$\mathsf{L}_i(\mathsf{P}) = \sum_{z \in Z} \mathsf{P}[z] \log \frac{\mathsf{P}_0[z]}{\mathsf{P}_i[z]}$$

and consider the distinguisher based on the likelihood ratio between P_0 and P_i which is the closest to P_{Z^q}. We have

$$D(P\|P_i) = \sum_{z \in \mathcal{Z}} P[z] \log \frac{P[z]}{P_i[z]}$$

so that $D(P\|P_i) \leq D(P\|P_j)$ is equivalent to $L_i(P) \leq L_j(P)$. Finally, this distinguisher is based on $L(P) = \min_i L_i(P)$ and accepts H_1 iff $L(P) \leq 0$. Let Π_i be the set of all P's such that $L_i(P) \leq 0$ and Π be the union of all Π_i's. The best distinguishers simply checks whether $P_{Z^q} \in \Pi$.

Looking at the proof of Theorem 1, we can first see that the probability that $P_{Z^q} \in \Pi$ under the null hypothesis is equivalent to $2^{-qD(\Pi\|P_0)}$ which is the maximum of $2^{-qD(\Pi_i\|P_0)}$, itself equal to $2^{-qC(P_i,P_0)}$. We deduce that

$$\Pr_{H_0}[A_q(\mathbf{Z}^q) = 1] \doteq \max_{1 \leq i \leq d} 2^{-qC(P_0,P_i)}.$$

When the Z_i's are sampled according to P_i under hypothesis H_1, the probability of rejection is the probability that $P_{Z^q} \notin \Pi$. This is less than the probability that $P_{Z^q} \notin \Pi_i$ and we know that it is equivalent to $2^{-qC(P_0,P_i)}$. Since this is less than the maximum of $2^{-qC(P_0,P_j)}$, the advantage Adv_q is such that

$$1 - \text{Adv}_q \doteq \max_{1 \leq i \leq d} 2^{-qC(P_0,P_i)}$$

Therefore, this distinguisher has the best advantage, asymptotically.   □

4.2   Example: Generalized Linear Cryptanalysis

Let X be a random variable over G, an Abelian group. Let χ be a character over G such that the group $\mathcal{Z} = \chi(G)$ is of order d. Let $Z = \chi(X)$. Let P_0 be the uniform distribution over $\mathcal{Z}$. For each $u \in \mathcal{Z}$ we consider the distribution P_u defined by $P_u[u] = \frac{1-\varepsilon}{d} + \varepsilon$ and $P_u[z] = \frac{1-\varepsilon}{d}$ for all $z \in \mathcal{Z}$ such that $z \neq u$. Note that $\text{LP}(\chi) = \varepsilon^2$ when Z follows distribution P_u for any u. These distributions have the property that $\hat{P}_u$ is flat in the sense that for all $\varphi \neq 1$, $|\hat{P}_u(\varphi)| = \varepsilon$. In linear cryptanalysis [5,3], χ is the product of several characters with "independent" biased distributions. It thus inherits of a distribution P such that $\hat{P}$ is the product of "independent" Fourier transforms (this is the Piling-up Lemma) and is flattened as such. We have the following result.

Theorem 9. *If $Z = \chi(X)$ where χ is a character of order d, the best distinguisher between the null hypothesis that Z is uniformly distributed in the range of χ and the alternate hypothesis that Z follows some distribution P_u with u unknown is defined by*

$$A_q(\mathbf{Z}^q) = 1 \Leftrightarrow \max_u P_{Z^q}[u] \geq \frac{\log(1-\varepsilon)}{\log(1-\varepsilon) - \log(1 + (d-1)\varepsilon)}$$

where the right-hand side is approximated by $\frac{1}{d}(1 + (d-1)\frac{\varepsilon}{2})$. This distinguisher has an advantage such that $1 - \text{Adv}_q \doteq 2^{-qC(P_0,P_1)}$ which is approximated by

$$1 - \text{Adv}_q \approx e^{-q\frac{d-1}{8}\varepsilon^2}.$$

Proof. We use the distinguisher which outputs 1 iff $\min_u L_u(\mathsf{P}_{\mathbf{Z}^q}) \leq 0$ (as suggested by Theorem 8). Clearly, $\min_u L_u$ is reached for the value of u which maximizes $\mathsf{P}_{\mathbf{Z}^q}[u]$. We obtain that $\mathbf{Z}^q$ is accepted iff

$$\max_u \mathsf{P}_{\mathbf{Z}^q}[u] \geq \frac{\log(1-\varepsilon)}{\log(1-\varepsilon) - \log(1+(d-1)\varepsilon)}$$

which is approximately $\frac{1}{d}(1+(d-1)\frac{\varepsilon}{2})$. As it is surprising enough, we stress that the best distinguisher is based on $\|\hat{\mathsf{P}}_{\mathbf{Z}^q}\|_\infty$ and not on the statistical average of $\chi(X)$ as one would expect. We can now focus on its advantage. By Theorem 8 we have

$$1 - \mathrm{Adv}_q \doteq \max_{u \in \mathcal{Z}} 2^{-qC(\mathsf{P}_0, \mathsf{P}_u)}.$$

Since all $C(\mathsf{P}_0, \mathsf{P}_u)$ are equal, we can focus on $C(\mathsf{P}_0, \mathsf{P}_1)$. Assuming that $\varepsilon \ll \frac{1}{d}$, we obtain

$$C(\mathsf{P}_0, \mathsf{P}_1) = -\inf_\lambda \log \frac{1}{d}\left((1+(d-1)\varepsilon)^\lambda + (d-1)(1-\varepsilon)^\lambda\right) \approx \frac{d-1}{8\ln 2}\varepsilon^2.$$

The advantage is thus roughly $1 - e^{-\frac{d-1}{8}q\varepsilon^2}$. $\qquad\square$

Another problem consists in distinguishing the null hypothesis that Z is uniformly distributed in the range of χ from the alternate hypothesis that Z follows some arbitrary distribution of known *flatness* ζ. We define the flatness of a distribution P_1 by $\|\hat{\mathsf{P}}_1 - \hat{\mathsf{P}}_0\|_2$. (Previously, we had $\zeta = \varepsilon\sqrt{d-1}$.) For such distributions, the Chernoff information is approximated by $C(\mathsf{P}_0, \mathsf{P}_1) \approx \frac{\zeta^2}{8\ln 2}$. By Theorem 8, the best distinguisher satisfies $1 - \mathrm{Adv}_q \approx e^{-\frac{q}{8}\zeta^2}$. It is defined by accepting $\mathbf{Z}^q$ iff we have $L(\mathsf{P}_{\mathbf{Z}^q}) \leq 0$ for

$$L(\mathsf{P}_{\mathbf{Z}^q}) = \min_{\substack{\mathsf{P}_1 \\ \|\hat{\mathsf{P}}_1 - \hat{\mathsf{P}}_0\|_2 = \zeta}} \sum_{z \in \mathcal{Z}} \mathsf{P}_{\mathbf{Z}^q}[z] \log \frac{\mathsf{P}_0[z]}{\mathsf{P}_1[z]}.$$

Since $\|f\|_2^2 = \frac{1}{d}\|\hat{f}\|_2^2$ for any function $f : \mathcal{Z} \to \mathbf{R}$, by writing $\mathsf{P}_0[z] = \frac{1}{d}$ and assuming that $\mathsf{P}_{\mathbf{Z}^q}[z] - \mathsf{P}_0[z]$ and $\mathsf{P}_1[z] - \mathsf{P}_0[z]$ are negligible to the first order, the above sum approximates to

$$L(\mathsf{P}_{\mathbf{Z}^q}) \approx \frac{d}{\ln 2}\left(\frac{1}{2}\|\mathsf{P}_1 - \mathsf{P}_0\|_2^2 - \max_{\mathsf{P}_1}\sum_{z \in \mathcal{Z}}\left(\mathsf{P}_{\mathbf{Z}^q}[z] - \frac{1}{d}\right)\left(\mathsf{P}_1[z] - \frac{1}{d}\right)\right)$$

which is clearly reached when $\mathsf{P}_1[z] - \frac{1}{d}$ is proportional to $\mathsf{P}_{\mathbf{Z}^q}[z] - \frac{1}{d}$. It is negative iff $\|\mathsf{P}_{\mathbf{Z}^q} - \mathsf{P}_0\|_2 \geq \frac{1}{2}\|\mathsf{P}_1 - \mathsf{P}_0\|_2$. So the best distinguisher accepts $\mathbf{Z}^q$ iff $\|\mathsf{P}_{\mathbf{Z}^q} - \mathsf{P}_0\|_2 \geq \frac{\zeta}{2\sqrt{d}}$. We conclude by the following heuristic result.

Theorem 10. *If $Z = \chi(X)$ where χ is a character of order d, the best distinguisher between the null hypothesis that Z is uniformly distributed in the range*

*of χ and the alternate hypothesis that Z follows some unknown distribution P_1
of known flatness $\zeta = \|\hat{\mathsf{P}}_1 - \hat{\mathsf{P}}_0\|_2$ is defined by*

$$A_q(\mathbf{Z}^q) = 1 \Leftrightarrow \sum_z \frac{\left(\mathsf{P}_{\mathbf{Z}^q}[z] - \frac{1}{d}\right)^2}{\frac{1}{d}} \geq \frac{\zeta^2}{4}.$$

It has an advantage approximated by

$$1 - \mathrm{Adv}_q \approx e^{-\frac{q}{8}\zeta^2}.$$

All in all, this is nothing but a χ^2 test on the frequencies with threshold $\frac{\zeta^2}{4}$.

5   Conclusion

We provided a precise asymptotic expression for the best distinguisher between
two given distributions. We gave a simple approximation of this in terms of
the Euclidean distance between the two distributions. We derived a link to the
spectral analysis of distributions. We studied the problem of distinguishing one
distribution from a set of distributions. This lead us to generalize linear cryptanalysis to arbitrary Abelian groups with order not necessarily equal to 2.

References

1. Baignères, T.: Quantitative Security of Block Ciphers: Design and Cryptanalysis
   Tools. PhD Thesis, EPFL (expected, 2008)
2. Baignères, T., Junod, P., Vaudenay, S.: How Far Can We Go Beyond Linear Cryptanalysis? In: Lee, P.J. (ed.) ASIACRYPT 2004. LNCS, vol. 3329, pp. 432–450.
   Springer, Heidelberg (2004)
3. Baignères, T., Stern, J., Vaudenay, S.: Linear cryptanalysis of non binary ciphers.
   In: Adams, C.M., Wiener, M.J. (eds.) Selected Areas in Cryptography - SAC 2007.
   LNCS, vol. 4876, pp. 184–211. Springer, Heidelberg (2007)
4. Cover, T.M., Thomas, J.A.: Elements of Information Theory. Wiley Series in
   Telecommunications. John Wiley & Sons, Chichester (1991)
5. Matsui, M.: Linear cryptanalysis method for DES cipher. In: Helleseth, T. (ed.)
   EUROCRYPT 1993. LNCS, vol. 765, pp. 386–397. Springer, Heidelberg (1994)
6. Neyman, J., Pearson, E.S.: On the problem of the most efficient tests of statistical
   hypotheses. Philosophical Transactions of the Royal Society of London. Series A,
   Containing Papers of a Mathematical or Physical Character 231, 289–337 (1933)
7. Sanov, I.N.: On the probability of large deviations of random variables. Mat.
   Sbornik 42, 11–44 (1957)

Some Information Theoretic Arguments for Encryption: Non-malleability and Chosen-Ciphertext Security (Invited Talk)

Goichiro Hanaoka

Research Center for Information Security,
National Institute of Advanced Industrial Science and Technology (AIST), Japan

Abstract. In this paper, we briefly review two independent studies: (1) an information-theoretic definition and constructions of non-malleable encryption, and (2) applications of information-theoretically secure tools for enhancing security of computationally secure cryptographic primitives.

1 Introduction

In this paper, we review two security notions, i.e. *non-malleability* and *chosen-ciphertext security*, from the viewpoint of information theory. Specifically, in Sec. 2 we first discuss how we can define non-malleability in an information-theoretic manner, and construct perfectly non-malleable encryption schemes. Next, in Sec. 3 we discuss how we can upgrade semantically secure encryption [10] to have (bounded) chosen-ciphertext security by using information-theoretically secure tools. It should be noticed that these two security notions have been mainly discussed in the context of computational security. We hope that these observations will be helpful for finding out novel applications of information-theoretically secure cryptographic tools.

2 Perfect Non-malleability

Frankly, non-malleability means an adversary's inability: given a challenge ciphertext c, to generate a different ciphertext $\hat{c}$ such that the plaintexts $m, \hat{m}$ underlying these two ciphertexts are meaningfully related. The notion was originally proposed by Dolev, Dwork, and Naor [6], and the discussion that followed after their original proposal was mainly given from a computationally secure perspective, e.g. [1,17,18]. The first formalization of information-theoretic non-malleability was given by Hanaoka et al. [13], and this was then extended by McAven, Safavi-Naini, and Yung [16]. In this section, we dicuss how we can define non-malleability in an information-theoretic manner by mainly explaining the definition by Hanaoka et al. [13].

2.1 Malleability of the "Classical" One-Time Pad

It is well known that the classical one-time pad does not provide non-malleability (in any possible definition). For understanding (information-theoretic)

R. Safavi-Naini (Ed.): ICITS 2008, LNCS 5155, pp. 223–231, 2008.
© Springer-Verlag Berlin Heidelberg 2008

non-malleability, here we briefly review this observation. Let $c = m \oplus k$, where c, m, and k are a ciphertext, a plaintext, and a secret key, respectively. For this simple encryption, Shannon proved that it is perfectly impossible to extract any information about the plaintext from any ciphertext, assuming that $m \in \{0,1\}^{\ell}$ and k is picked from $\{0,1\}^{\ell}$ uniformly at random. However, it is malleable since for any given ciphertext $c(= m \oplus k)$, we can generate another ciphetext $\hat{c}$ whose plaintext is $m \oplus r$ by modifying it as $\hat{c} = c \oplus r$, where r is any ℓ-bit binary string.

2.2 Towards Information-Theoretic Non-malleability

Intuitively, if an encryption scheme is malleable, then it is always vulnerable against chosen-ciphertext attacks (this is a reason why the one-time pad cannot be used as the DEM part for CCA-secure hybrid encryption under the standard KEM/DEM composition theorem [21]). More precisely, for a given malleable (deterministic, symmetric) encryption scheme S, a plaintext-ciphertext pair (m, c), and another ciphertext $c'(\neq c)$ of S under the same secret key, an adversary can always extract some information on the plaintext of c' as follows: Since S is malleable, there exists a meaningful relation $\mathcal{R}$ such that the adversary can generate another ciphertext $\hat{c}$ whose plaintext $\hat{m}$ satisfies $\mathcal{R}(m, \hat{m}) = 1$. Then, the plaintext of c' is considered $\hat{m}$ if $c' = \hat{c}$, or it is not otherwise. Hence, we observe that information on the plaintext of c' is leaked.

From the above observation, we notice that if it is impossible to extract any information on the plaintext of c', then it is also information-theoretically impossible to generate $\hat{c}$ for any meaningful relation $\mathcal{R}$. Therefore, we can define that an encryption scheme S' is *non-malleable* if for any given plaintext-ciphertext pair (m, c) and another ciphetext c' of S' (under the same secret key), any information on the plaintext of c' is not leaked.

2.3 Perfect Non-malleability

Now, we formally define *perfect* non-malleability [13] for unconditionally secure encryption with two parties, i.e. a sender S and a receiver R. In our model, S and R (or one of them) generate an encryption key e for S, and a decryption key d for R. (The decryption key d may be the same as e.) To send a plaintext m to R with data confidentiality, S encrypts m by using e and transmits the ciphertext c to R. R decrypts c by using d and recovers m. Throughout this paper, we let a random variable be $\mathcal{X}$ and $H(\mathcal{X})$ denote the entropy of $\mathcal{X}$. For $\mathcal{X}$, let $X := \{x | \Pr[\mathcal{X} = x] > 0\}$. $|X|$ is the cardinality of X.

Definition 1. Let $\mathcal{E}$, $\mathcal{D}$, $\mathcal{M}$ and $\mathcal{C}$ denote the random variables induced by e, d, m and c, respectively. We say that $S = (\mathcal{E}, \mathcal{D}, \mathcal{M}, \mathcal{C})$ has *perfect secrecy* (PS) if

1. R correctly decrypts m from c, that is, $H(\mathcal{M}|\mathcal{C}, \mathcal{D}) = 0$.
2. Any outsider cannot obtain any information on m from c, that is, $H(\mathcal{M}|\mathcal{C}) = H(\mathcal{M})$.

It will also satisfy *perfect non-malleability* (NM) if

3. Any outsider cannot generate a ciphertext whose plaintext is meaningfully related to m, that is,

$$H(\hat{\mathcal{M}}|\mathcal{C},\hat{\mathcal{C}},\mathcal{M}) = H(\hat{\mathcal{M}}|\mathcal{C},\mathcal{M}),$$

where $\hat{c}(\neq c)$ be another ciphertext which can be generated by S instead of c, $\hat{m}(\neq m)$ be a plaintext corresponding $\hat{c}$, and $\hat{\mathcal{C}}$ and $\hat{\mathcal{M}}$ denote random variables induced by $\hat{c}$ and $\hat{m}$, respectively.

Then, we say that $S = (\mathcal{E},\mathcal{D},\mathcal{M},\mathcal{C})$ has PS&NM if it satisfies both PS and NM.

Remark. There are also other different definitions of information-theoretic non-malleability.[1] Here, we mainly focus on the above definition due to its simplicity. In [16], a stronger definition is given without using the entropy measure. However, we note that for the most of interesting cases, the above definition is sufficient. On the other hand, the above definition of perfect non-malleability seems stronger than the minimum requirement since it overkills some existing schemes which are considered likely to be non-malleable, e.g. the one-time pad plus authentication codes. Finding out the most appropriate definition of information-theoretic non-malleability is considered as an interesting research topic.

2.4 A Generic Construction Via Chaffing-and-Winnowing

In [11], Hanaoka et al. presented a generic construction of encryption schemes with perfect non-malleability from authentication codes (A-codes) [9,22] by using the *chaffing-and-winnowing* framework [19]. In this subsection, we review Hanaoka et al.'s construction.

A-Codes. In the model of A-codes, there are three participants, a sender S, a receiver R and a trusted initializer TI. TI generates secret information u and v for S and R, respectively. In order to send a plaintext m to R, S generates an authenticated message (m,α) from m by using u and transmits (m,α) to R. R verifies validity of α using m and v. We note that S and/or R may generate u and v themselves to remove TI.

Definition 2. Let $\mathcal{U},\mathcal{V},\mathcal{M}$ and $\mathcal{A}$ denote the random variables induced by u,v,m and α, respectively. We say that $A = (\mathcal{U},\mathcal{V},\mathcal{M},\mathcal{A})$ is *p-impersonation secure (p-Imp)* if

1. Any set of outsiders (which do not include S, R or TI) can perform impersonation with probability at most p. Namely,

$$\max_{(m,\alpha)} \Pr[R \text{ accepts } (m,\alpha)] \leq p,$$

it is also *p-substitution secure (p-Sub)* if

---

[1] For computational non-malleability, there exist some different definitions. See, for example, [18] for such definitions.

2. Any set of outsiders can perform substitution with probability at most p. Namely, letting (m', α') be an authenticated message generated by S,

$$\max_{(m',\alpha')} \max_{(m,\alpha)(\neq(m',\alpha'))} \Pr[R \text{ accepts } (m,\alpha)|(m',\alpha')] \leq p.$$

We say that $\mathsf{A} = (\mathcal{U}, \mathcal{V}, \mathcal{M}, \mathcal{A})$ is *p-impersonation&substitution secure (p-Imp&Sub)* if it is both p-Imp and p-Sub secure.

Construction methods for A-codes are given in, for example, [9,22,12,20]. In the rest of the paper, for simplicity, we let $f : \mathcal{M} \times \mathcal{U} \to \mathcal{A}$ denote a mapping such that $f(m, u) = \alpha$.

Chaffing-and-Winnowing. In [19], Rivest proposed a novel and interesting cryptographic technique called *"chaffing-and-winnowing"*. Remarkable property of this cryptographic technique is that it can provide data confidentiality by using only authentication when sending data over an insecure channel. In brief, chaffing-and-winnowing can be constructed as follows. In the setup phase, a sender S and a receiver R prepare their keys for message authentication. When S sends a plaintext m to R, S adds "dummy" plaintext m' (with an invalid authentication tag) so that "dummy" m' obscure the intended message m, so that only the authorized receiver R can distinguish the "real" from the "dummy". On receiving the message, R removes the dummy m' by checking its tag. As long as an adversary does not distinguish the valid tag from the invalid tag, it cannot tell which one of m and m' is real and not real. In [11], via the chaffing-and-winnowing framework, Hanaoka et al. presented a generic construction of encryption schemes with perfect secrecy from weakly secure A-codes, and another one with perfect non-malleability from fully secure A-codes. Stinson [23] improved Hanaoka et al.'s scheme (with perfect secrecy) with shorter ciphertext length.

The Construction. We next show Hanaoka et al.'s encryption scheme with PS&NM from p-Imp&Sub A-codes. For simplicity, we consider only *optimal p-Imp&Sub* A-codes such that $p = 1/|A| = 1/|U|^{1/2}$. It should be noticed that if an A-code is p-Imp&Sub, then $|A| \geq 1/p$ and $|U| \geq 1/p^2$ [15]. Many of such optimal A-codes have been known. Then, Hanaoka et al.'s construction [11] is as follows:

KEY GENERATION. For a given A-code $\mathsf{A} = (\mathcal{U}, \mathcal{V}, \mathcal{M}, \mathcal{A})$, S and R generate $u \in U$ and $v \in V$ as an encryption key for S and a decryption key for R, respectively. Let the plaintext space be M. S picks $|M|$ distinct keys $u_1, ..., u_{|M|}$ from $U \backslash \{u\}$ such that

$$\forall u_i, u_j (\neq u_i), \ \forall m \in M, \ f(m, u_i) \neq f(m, u_j).$$

ENCRYPTION. Let a plaintext be $m^* \in M$. S sets $\alpha := f(m^*, u)$ and finds u_i such that $f(m^*, u_i) = \alpha$. Then, S sends $c := (m||\alpha_m)_{m \in M}$ to R, where $\alpha_m := f(m, u_i)$.

DECRYPTION. On receiving c', R parses c' as $c' := (m||\alpha_m)_{m \in M}$ and selects m' such that m' is accepted as valid (by using v). Finally, R outputs m'.

For any given A-code, the above scheme properly works with perfect secrecy and perfect non-malleability due to the following lemmas [11].

Lemma 1. *If* A *is a* $1/|M|$-Imp&Sub *A-code, then, for all* $u \in U$ *there exist* $u_1, ..., u_{|M|} \in U \setminus \{u\}$ *such that for all* $u_i, u_j (\neq u_i) \in \{u_1, ..., u_{|M|}\}$ *and* $m \in M$, $f(m, u_i) \neq f(m, u_j)$.

Lemma 2. *For any* $u \in U$, *any* $u_1, ..., u_{|M|}$ *chosen as in above, and any* $m \in M$, $|\{u_i | f(m, u_i) = f(m, u), \ u_i \in \{u_1, ..., u_{|M|}\}\}| = 1$.

Lemma 3. *The above scheme has* PS, *i.e.* $H(\mathcal{M}^*) = H(\mathcal{M}^* | \mathcal{C})$, *where* $\mathcal{M}^*$ *is a random variable induced by* m^*.

Lemma 4. *The above scheme has* NM, *i.e.* $H(\hat{\mathcal{M}} | \mathcal{C}, \hat{\mathcal{C}}, \mathcal{M}^*) = H(\hat{\mathcal{M}} | \mathcal{C}, \mathcal{M}^*)$, *where* $\hat{c} (\neq c)$ *is another ciphertext which can be generated by* S *instead of* c, $\hat{m} (\neq m^*)$ *be a plaintext underlying* $\hat{c}$, *and* $\hat{\mathcal{C}}$ *and* $\hat{\mathcal{M}}$ *denote random variables induced by* $\hat{c}$ *and* $\hat{m}$, *respectively.*

2.5   A Practical Instantiation

Here, we introduce a practical instantiation [13,14] of a perfectly non-malleable encryption from the above methodology with specific (but well-known) A-codes. As seen in the construction, a ciphertext essentially consists of $(f(m, u_i))_{m \in M}$, and consequently, this can be compressed as a single $f(m^*, u)$ if $f(m, u_i)$ always takes the same value for all $m \in M$. More formally, it is sufficient to send one authentication tag instead of $|M|$ tags if the underlying A-code has the following property: For all $\alpha \in A$, there exists at least one $u \in U$ such that for all messages $m \in M$, $f(m, u) = \alpha$, that is,

$$\forall \alpha \in A, \exists u \in U \ s.t. \ \forall m \in M, f(m, u) = \alpha.$$

Let $\hat{U}$ denote a subset of U such that $\hat{U} = \cup_{\alpha \in A} \{u | \forall m \in M, f(m, u) = \alpha\}$.

Now, we present a method for compressing ciphertexts by using such $\hat{U}$. If in the encryption scheme in the previous subsection, for all u there exist $u_1, \ldots, u_{|M|}$ such that for all $m_0, m_1 \in M, f(m_0, u_i) = f(m_1, u_i)$, then a ciphertext becomes $(m_j || \alpha)_{m_j \in M}$ where $\alpha = f(m^*, u)$, and therefore, a full ciphertext can be reconstructed from only α. Hence, it is sufficient to send only one authentication tag α as a ciphertext. For implementing this idea, we pick u from $U \setminus \hat{U}$, and always use $\hat{U}$ as $\{u_1, \cdots, u_{|M|}\}$.

The concrete construction is as follows:

KEY GENERATION. For a given A-code $A = (\mathcal{U}, \mathcal{V}, \mathcal{M}, \mathcal{A})$, S and R generates $u \in U \setminus \hat{U}$ and $v \in V$ as an encryption key for S and a decryption key for R, respectively. Let the plaintext space be M.

ENCRYPTION. Let a plaintext be $m^* \in M$. S sets $c := f(m^*, u)$, and sends c to R.

DECRYPTION. On receiving c', R selects m' such that c' is accepted as valid (by using m', v). Finally, R outputs m'.

Since the above construction is a special case of that in the previous subsection, it also provides PS&NM. An example of A-codes with the above property is as follows: Let $M = A = GF(p)$ and $U = V = GF(p)^2$. Let an authentication tag for message m be $\alpha = k_1 m + k_2$, where $(k_1, k_2) \in GF(p)^2$ is a shared secret between S and R. For simplicity, we assume that p is a prime. Then, we can set $\hat{U} = \{(0,0), \ldots, (0, p-1)\}$.

Based on the above A-code, we can construct a very simple non-malleable one-time pad [13,14] as follows:

KEY GENERATION. Let the plaintext space be $GF(p)$. S and R generate $(k_1, k_2) \in (GF(p) \backslash \{0\}) \times GF(p)$ as their common key.

ENCRYPTION. Let a plaintext be $m^* \in GF(p)$. S sets $c = k_1 m^* + k_2$, and sends c to R.

DECRYPTION. On receiving $c'(= \alpha)$, R computes $m' = (c' - k_2) \cdot k_1^{-1}$, and outputs m'.

In the above construction, we notice that the ciphertext length is the same as the plaintext length.

3 Chosen-Ciphertext Security

In this section, (as an independent interest to the previous section) we briefly point out that information-theoretically secure tools can be also used as powerful building blocks for computationally secure encryption schemes, and present, for example, how security of public key encryption (PKE) schemes can be enhanced via information-theoretic discussions. Specifically, we introduce Cramer et al.'s method [4] which generically converts any chosen-plaintext (CPA) secure PKE scheme [10] into another one which provides security against chosen-ciphertext (CCA) adversaries with some restrictions, i.e. *bounded CCA* (BCCA) security (see below).

3.1 General Observation

In the security proof of CCA-security of a PKE scheme P, for any given algorithm $\mathcal{A}$ which breaks CCA-security of P, we construct another algorithm $\mathcal{B}$ which solves the underlying hard problem, e.g. the decisional Diffie-Hellman problem, by using $\mathcal{A}$ as a subroutine. The main technical hurdle for the proof is (usually) that $\mathcal{B}$ has to respond to any decryption query from $\mathcal{A}$ without knowing the witness of the given hard problem. It should be noticed that $\mathcal{A}$ may be *computationally unlimited*, and therefore, $\mathcal{B}$ has to deceive such a powerful adversary. Hence, even in the arguments for computational CCA-security, information-theoretic arguments are still important.

3.2   Bounded CCA-Security

Here, we give a brief review of BCCA-security [4]. We say that a PKE scheme P is q-BCCA-secure if it is CCA-secure in the standard sense [6,1] except that the number of decryption queries is known to be at most q a priori. If q is infinite or zero, then this is equivalent to the standard CCA-security or CPA-security, respectively. For simplicity, we consider only *non-adaptive* BCCA-security in the following subsections rather than adaptive BCCA-security.

3.3   BCCA-Security from Cover Free Families (and CPA-Security)

In this subsection, we show how we can upgrade a CPA-secure PKE scheme to have BCCA-security via *an information-theoretic argument* [4]. For the construction, we utilize *cover free families* (CFF) as such an information-theoretic tool which is defined as follows:

Cover Free Family. Let $\mathcal{L}$ be a set with $|\mathcal{L}| = u$ and $\mathcal{F} = \{\mathcal{F}_1, ..., \mathcal{F}_v\}$ be a family of subsets of $\mathcal{L}$.

Definition 3. We say $(\mathcal{L}, \mathcal{F})$ is a (u, v, w)-*cover free family* (CFF) if $\mathcal{F}_i \not\subseteq \cup_{j \in \mathcal{S}_i} \mathcal{F}_j$ for all $i \in \{1, ..., v\}$ and for all $\mathcal{S}_i \subseteq \{1, ..., v\} \setminus \{i\}$ such that $|\mathcal{S}_i| \leq w$.

There exist nontrivial constructions of CFF with $u = O(w^2 \log^2 v)$ and $|\mathcal{F}_i| = O(w \log v)$ for all $i \in \{1, ..., v\}$. This implies that there exists a (u, v, w)-CFF such that $u = O(\mathsf{poly}(k))$ and $v = \Omega(\exp(k))$ if $w = O(\mathsf{poly}(k))$ for a security parameter k. It should be noticed that for given $\mathcal{L}$ and index i, one can efficiently generate $\mathcal{F}_i$. An example of concrete methods for generating CFF [7,8] is as follows. Consider a code $\mathcal{C}$ of length N on an alphabet $\mathcal{Q}$ with $|\mathcal{Q}| = t$. Let a codeword $c \in \mathcal{C}$ be $(c_1, ..., c_N) \in \mathcal{Q}^N$, and $\mathcal{F}_c$ be $\{(i, c_i)\}_{1 \leq i \leq N}$. Let $\mathcal{F}$ denote $\{\mathcal{F}_c\}_{c \in \mathcal{C}}$, and $\mathcal{L}$ be $\{1, ..., N\} \times \mathcal{Q}$. When applying Reed-Solomon code as $\mathcal{C}$, $(\mathcal{L}, \mathcal{F})$ becomes a CFF.

Proposition 1. *For given N, t and w where t is a prime power and $N \leq t+1$, there exists a $(tN, t^{\lceil (N+w-1)/w \rceil}, w)$-CFF.*

The Construction. Let P $=$ (Gen, Enc, Dec) be a PKE scheme where Gen, Enc, and Dec are a key generation algorithm, an encryption algorithm, and a decryption algorithm, respectively. These algorithms are defined as usual. Let $(\mathcal{L}, \mathcal{F})$ be a (u, v, q)-CFF such that $u = O(\mathsf{poly}(k))$, $v = \Omega(\exp(k))$, and $q = O(\mathsf{poly}(k))$ for a security parameter k. Then, a non-adaptive q-CCA-secure PKE scheme P$'$ is constructed as follows:

KEY GENERATION. For a given security parameter k, a receiver generates a (u, v, q)-CFF $(\mathcal{L}, \mathcal{F})$ such that $\mathcal{L} = \{1, ..., u\}$ and $(dk_i, ek_i) \leftarrow$ Gen(1^k) for $1 \leq i \leq u$, and outputs a private decryption key $dk = ((dk_i)_{1 \leq i \leq u}, (\mathcal{L}, \mathcal{F}))$ and a public encryption key $ek = ((ek_i)_{1 \leq i \leq u}, (\mathcal{L}, \mathcal{F}))$.

ENCRYPTION. For given ek and a plaintext $M \in \mathcal{M}$, a sender picks r from $\{1, ..., v\}$ uniformly at random, divides M into $(M_i)_{i \in \mathcal{F}_r}$ such that $\bigoplus_{i \in \mathcal{F}_r} M_i = M$, computes $C_i \leftarrow$ Enc(ek_i, M_i) for all $i \in \mathcal{F}_r$, and outputs $C = (r, (C_i)_{i \in \mathcal{F}_r})$.

DECRYPTION. For given dk and a ciphertext $C' = (r', (C'_i)_{i \in \mathcal{F}_{r'}})$, the receiver calculates $M'_i \leftarrow \mathsf{Dec}(dk_i, C_i)$ for all $i \in \mathcal{F}_{r'}$ and $M' \leftarrow \bigoplus_{i \in \mathcal{F}_{r'}} M_i$, and outputs M'.

Theorem 1 ([4]). *The above scheme* P' *is non-adaptively* q-*BCCA-secure if* P *is CPA-secure.*

An intuitive explanation of the role of CFF for deceiving a BCCA adversary is as follows: Let $\mathcal{B}$ is an algorithm whose goal is to break CPA-security of P by using another algorithm $\mathcal{A}$ which breaks q-BCCA-security of P'. For a given public key ek', $\mathcal{B}$ picks random j from $\{1, ..., u\}$, sets $ek_j = ek'$, and generates (dk_i, ek_i) for all $i \in \{1, ..., u\} \backslash \{j\}$. Then, $\mathcal{B}$ inputs $ek = ((ek_i)_{1 \le i \le u}, (\mathcal{L}, \mathcal{F}))$ to $\mathcal{A}$. When $\mathcal{A}$ submits a query $C = (r, (C_i)_{i \in \mathcal{F}_r})$, $\mathcal{B}$ can respond to it by straightforward decryption if $j \notin \mathcal{F}_r$. Finally, $\mathcal{B}$ inputs $C^* = (r^*, (C_i)_{i \in \mathcal{F}_{r^*}})$ as a challenge ciphertext where r^* is picked from $\{1, ..., v\}$ uniformly at random. Due to CFF, it is *information-theoretically* guaranteed that $[\mathcal{A}$ never submits a query such that $j \notin \mathcal{F}_r] \wedge [j \in \mathcal{F}_{r^*}]$ with probability at least $1/u$, which is non-negligible.

Remark. The above construction is a simplified version of adaptive q-BCCA-secure construction in [4], and it is constructed based on Dodis, Katz, Xu, and Yung's key-insulated encryption scheme [5] along with Canetti, Halevi, and Katz's IBE-to-PKE transform [2]. It is possible to enhance security of the above scheme with fully adaptive BCCA-security by using one-time signatures [4] (similarly to [2]). Following the work by Cramer et al., Choi, Dachman-Soled, Malkin, and Wee [3] presented another black-box construction of q-BCCA-secure PKE schemes with non-malleability by using *error-correcting codes*.

References

1. Bellare, M., Desai, A., Pointcheval, D., Rogaway, P.: Relations among notions of security for public-key encryption schemes. In: Krawczyk, H. (ed.) CRYPTO 1998. LNCS, vol. 1462, pp. 26–45. Springer, Heidelberg (1998)
2. Canetti, R., Halevi, S., Katz, J.: Chosen-ciphertext security from identity-based encryption. In: Cachin, C., Camenisch, J.L. (eds.) EUROCRYPT 2004. LNCS, vol. 3027, pp. 207–222. Springer, Heidelberg (2004)
3. Choi, S.-G., Dachman-Soled, D., Malkin, T., Wee, H.: Black-box construction of a non-malleable encryption scheme from any semantically secure one. In: Canetti, R. (ed.) TCC 2008. LNCS, vol. 4948, pp. 427–444. Springer, Heidelberg (2008)
4. Cramer, R., Hanaoka, G., Hofheinz, D., Imai, H., Kiltz, E., Pass, R., Shelat, A., Vaikuntanathan, V.: Bounded CCA2-Secure Encryption. In: Kurosawa, K. (ed.) ASIACRYPT 2007. LNCS, vol. 4833, pp. 502–518. Springer, Heidelberg (2007)
5. Dodis, Y., Katz, J., Xu, S., Yung, M.: Key-insulated public key cryptosystems. In: Knudsen, L.R. (ed.) EUROCRYPT 2002. LNCS, vol. 2332, pp. 65–82. Springer, Heidelberg (2002)
6. Dolev, D., Dwork, C., Naor, M.: Non-malleable cryptography. In: Proc. of STOC 1991, pp. 542–552 (1991)
7. Erdös, P., Frankl, P., Furedi, Z.: Families of finite sets in which no sets is covered by the union of two others. Journal of Combin. Theory Ser. A 33, 158–166 (1982)

8. Erdös, P., Frankl, P., Furedi, Z.: Families of finite sets in which no sets is covered by the union of r others. Israel Journal of Math. 51, 79–89 (1985)
9. Gilbert, E.N., MacWilliams, F.J., Sloane, N.J.A.: Codes which detect deception. Bell System Technical Journal 53, 405–425 (1974)
10. Goldwasser, S., Micali, S.: Probabilistic encryption. Journal of Computer and System Science 28, 270–299 (1984)
11. Hanaoka, G., Hanaoka, Y., Hagiwara, M., Watanabe, H., Imai, H.: Unconditionally secure Chaffing-and-Winnowing: A Relationship Between Encryption and Authentication. In: Fossorier, M.P.C., Imai, H., Lin, S., Poli, A. (eds.) AAECC 2006. LNCS, vol. 3857, pp. 154–162. Springer, Heidelberg (2006)
12. Hanaoka, G., Shikata, J., Zheng, Y., Imai, H.: Unconditionally secure digital signature schemes admitting transferability. In: Okamoto, T. (ed.) ASIACRYPT 2000. LNCS, vol. 1976, pp. 130–142. Springer, Heidelberg (2000)
13. Hanaoka, G., Shikata, J., Hanaoka, Y., Imai, H.: Unconditionally secure anonymous encryption and group authentication. In: Zheng, Y. (ed.) ASIACRYPT 2002. LNCS, vol. 2501, pp. 81–99. Springer, Heidelberg (2002)
14. Kitada, W., Hanaoka, G., Matsuura, K., Imai, H.: Unconditionally secure chaffing-and-winnowing for multiple use. In: Proc. of ICITS 2007 (to appear)
15. Maurer, U.M.: A unified and generalized treatment of authentication theory. In: Puech, C., Reischuk, R. (eds.) STACS 1996. LNCS, vol. 1046, pp. 387–398. Springer, Heidelberg (1996)
16. McAven, L., Safavi-Naini, R., Yung, M.: Unconditionally secure encryption under strong attacks. In: Wang, H., Pieprzyk, J., Varadharajan, V. (eds.) ACISP 2004. LNCS, vol. 3108, pp. 427–439. Springer, Heidelberg (2004)
17. Pass, R., Shelat, A., Vaikuntanathan, V.: Construction of a non-malleable encryption scheme from any semantically secure one. In: Dwork, C. (ed.) CRYPTO 2006. LNCS, vol. 4117, pp. 271–289. Springer, Heidelberg (2006)
18. Pass, R., Shelat, A., Vaikuntanathan, V.: Relations among notions of non-malleability for encryption. In: Kurosawa, K. (ed.) ASIACRYPT 2007. LNCS, vol. 4833, pp. 519–535. Springer, Heidelberg (2007)
19. Rivest, R.: Chaffing and winnowing: confidentiality without encryption, http://theory.lcs.mit.edu/rivest/publication.html
20. Shikata, J., Hanaoka, G., Zheng, Y., Imai, H.: Security notions for unconditionally secure signature schemes. In: Knudsen, L.R. (ed.) EUROCRYPT 2002. LNCS, vol. 2332, pp. 434–449. Springer, Heidelberg (2002)
21. Shoup, V.: Using hash functions as a hedge against chosen ciphertext attack. In: Preneel, B. (ed.) EUROCRYPT 2000. LNCS, vol. 1807, pp. 275–288. Springer, Heidelberg (2000)
22. Simmons, G.J.: Authentication theory/coding theory. In: Blakely, G.R., Chaum, D. (eds.) CRYPTO 1984. LNCS, vol. 196, pp. 411–431. Springer, Heidelberg (1985)
23. Stinson, D.R.: Unconditionally secure chaffing and winnowing with short authentication tags. Advances in Mathematics of Communication 1, 269–280 (2007)

A Proof of Security in $O(2^n)$ for the Xor of Two Random Permutations

Jacques Patarin

Université de Versailles
45 avenue des Etats-Unis, 78035 Versailles Cedex, France
jacques.patarin@prism.uvsq.fr

Abstract. Xoring two permutations is a very simple way to construct pseudorandom functions from pseudorandom permutations. The aim of this paper is to get precise security results for this construction. Since such construction has many applications in cryptography (see [2,3,4,6] for example), this problem is interesting both from a theoretical and from a practical point of view. In [6], it was proved that Xoring two random permutations gives a secure pseudorandom function if $m \ll 2^{\frac{2n}{3}}$. By "secure" we mean here that the scheme will resist all adaptive chosen plaintext attacks limited to m queries (even with unlimited computing power). More generally in [6] it is also proved that with k Xor, instead of 2, we have security when $m \ll 2^{\frac{kn}{k+1}}$. In this paper we will prove that for $k = 2$, we have in fact already security when $m \ll O(2^n)$. Therefore we will obtain a proof of a similar result claimed in [2] (security when $m \ll O(2^n/n^{2/3})$). Moreover our proof is very different from the proof strategy suggested in [2] (we do not use Azuma inequality and Chernoff bounds for example), and we will get precise and explicit O functions. Another interesting point of our proof is that we will show that this (cryptographic) problem of security is directly related to a very simple to describe and purely combinatorial problem. An extended version of this paper can be obtained on eprint [8].

Keywords: Pseudorandom functions, pseudorandom permutations, security beyond the birthday bound, Luby-Rackoff backwards.

1 Introduction

The problem of converting pseudorandom permutations (PRP) into pseudorandom functions (PRF) named "Luby-Rackoff backwards" was first considered in [3]. This problem is obvious if we are interested in an asymptotical polynomial versus non polynomial security model (since a PRP is then a PRF), but not if we are interested in achieving more optimal and concrete security bounds. More precisely, the loss of security when regarding a PRP as a PRF comes from the "birthday attack" which can distinguish a random permutation from a random function of n bits to n bits, in $2^{\frac{n}{2}}$ operations and $2^{\frac{n}{2}}$ queries. Therefore different ways to build PRF from PRP with a security above $2^{\frac{n}{2}}$ and by performing very few computations have been suggested (see [2,3,4,6]). One of the simplest way

R. Safavi-Naini (Ed.): ICITS 2008, LNCS 5155, pp. 232–248, 2008.
© Springer-Verlag Berlin Heidelberg 2008

(and the way that gives so far our best security result) is simply to Xor k independent pseudorandom permutations, for example with $k = 2$. In [6] (Theorem 2 p.474), it has been proved, with a simple proof, that the Xor of k independent PRP gives a PRF with security at least in $O(2^{\frac{k}{k+1}n})$. (For $k = 2$ this gives $O(2^{\frac{2}{3}n})$). In [2], a much more complex strategy (based on Azuma inequality and Chernoff bounds) is presented. It is claimed that with this strategy we may prove that the Xor of two PRP gives a PRF with security at least in $O(2^n/n^{\frac{2}{3}})$ and at most in $O(2^n)$, which is much better than the birthday bound in $O(2^{\frac{n}{2}})$. However the authors of [2] present a very general framework of proof and they do not give every details for this result. For example, page 9 they wrote "we give only a very brief summary of how this works", and page 10 they introduce O functions that are not easy to express explicitly. In this paper we will use a completely different proof strategy, based on the "coefficient H technique" (see Section 3 below), simple counting arguments and induction. We will need a few pages, but we will get like this a self contained proof of security in $O(2^n)$ for the Xor of two permutations with a very precise O function. Since building PRF from PRP has many applications (see [2,3,4]), we think that these results are really interesting both from theoretical and from practical point of view. It may be also interesting to notice that there are many similarities between this problem and the security of Feistel schemes built with random round functions (also called Luby-Rackoff constructions). In [7], it was proved that for L-R constructions with k rounds functions we have security that tends to $O(2^n)$ when the number k of rounds tends to infinity. Then in [11], it was proved that security in $O(2^n)$ was obtained not only for $k \rightarrow +\infty$, but already for $k = 7$. Similarly, we have seen that in [6] it was proved that for the Xor of k PRP we have security that tends $O(2^n)$ when $k \rightarrow +\infty$. In this paper, we show that security in $O(2^n)$ is not only for $k \rightarrow +\infty$, but already for $k = 2$.

Remark: in this paper, we concentrate on proofs of security while in paper [9] we present the best known attacks for the Xor of k random permutations.

2 Notation and Aim of This Paper

In all this paper we will denote $I_n = \{0, 1\}^n$. F_n will be the set of all applications from I_n to I_n, and B_n will be the set of all permutations from I_n to I_n. Therefore $|I_n| = 2^n$, $|F_n| = 2^{n \cdot 2^n}$ and $|B_n| = (2^n)!$. $x \in_R A$ means that x is randomly chosen in A with a uniform distribution.

The aim of this paper is to prove the theorem below, with an explicit O function (to be determined).

Theorem 1. *For all CPA-2 (Adaptive chosen plaintext attack) ϕ on a function G of F_n with m chosen plaintext, we have: $\mathrm{Adv}_\phi^{\mathrm{PRF}} \leq O(\frac{m}{2^n})$ where $\mathrm{Adv}_\phi^{\mathrm{PRF}}$ denotes the advantage to distinguish $f \oplus g$, with $f, g \in_R B_n$ from $h \in_R F_n$.*

By "advantage" we mean here, as usual, for a distinguisher, the absolute value of the difference of the two probabilities to output 1. This theorem says that there is no way (with an adaptive chosen plaintext attack) to distinguish with a good probability $f \oplus g$ when $f, g \in_R B_n$ from $h \in_R F_n$ when $m \ll 2^n$. Therefore, it implies that the number λ of computations to distinguish $f \oplus g$ with $f, g \in_R B_n$ from $h \in_R F_n$ satisfies: $\lambda \geq O(2^n)$. We say also that there is no generic CPA-2 attack with less than $O(2^n)$ computations for this problem, or that the security obtained is greater than or equal to $O(2^n)$. Since we know (for example from [2]) that there is an attack in $O(2^n)$, Theorem 1 also says that $O(2^n)$ is the exact security bound for this problem.

3   The General Proof Strategy

We will use this general Theorem:

Theorem 2. *Let α and β be real numbers, $\alpha > 0$ and $\beta > 0$. Let E be a subset of I_n^m such that $|E| \geq (1 - \beta) \cdot 2^{nm}$. If:*

1. *For all sequences a_i, $1 \leq i \leq m$, of pairwise distinct elements of I_n and for all sequences b_i, $1 \leq i \leq m$, of E we have:*

$$H \geq \frac{|B_n|^2}{2^{nm}}(1 - \alpha)$$

   where H denotes the number of $(f, g) \in B_n^2$ such that

$$\forall i, 1 \leq i \leq m, \ (f \oplus g)(a_i) = b_i$$

   Then
2. *For every CPA-2 with m chosen plaintexts we have: $p \leq \alpha + \beta$ where $p = \mathrm{Adv}_\phi^{\mathrm{PRF}}$ denotes the advantage to distinguish $f \oplus g$ when $(f, g) \in_R B_n^2$ from a function $h \in_R F_n$.*

By "advantage" we mean here, as usual, for a distinguisher, the absolute value of the difference of the two probabilities to output 1.

Proof of Theorem 2
It is not very difficult to prove Theorem 2 with classical counting arguments. This proof technique is sometimes called the "Coefficient H technique". A complete proof of Theorem 2 can also be found in [10] page 27 and a similar Theorem was used in [11] p.517. In order to have access to all the proofs, Theorem 2 is also included in the eprint extended version of this paper [8].

How to get Theorem 1 from Theorem 2

In order to get Theorem 1 from Theorem 2, a sufficient condition is to prove that for " most" (most since we need β small) sequences of values b_i, $1 \leq i \leq m$, $b_i \in I_n$, we have: the number H of $(f, g) \in B_n^2$ such that $\forall i, 1 \leq i \leq m$, $f(a_i) \oplus g(a_i) = b_i$ satisfies: $H \geq \frac{|B_n|^2}{2^{nm}}(1 - \alpha)$ for a small value α (more precisely with $\alpha \ll O(\frac{m}{2^n})$). For this, we will evaluate $E(H)$ the mean value of H when the b_i values are randomly chosen in I_n^m, and $\sigma(H)$ the standard deviation of H when the b_i values are randomly chosen in I_n^m. (Therefore we can call our general proof strategy the "Hσ technique", since we use the coefficient H technique plus the evaluation of $\sigma(H)$). We will prove that $E(H) = \frac{|B_n|^2}{2^{nm}}$ and that $\sigma(H) = \frac{|B_n|^2}{2^{nm}} O(\frac{m}{2^n})^{\frac{3}{2}}$, with an explicit O function, i.e. that $\sigma(H) \ll E(H)$ when $m \ll 2^n$. From Bienayme-Tchebichev Theorem, we have

$$Pr\big(|H - E(H)| \le \alpha E(H)\big) \ge 1 - \frac{\sigma^2(H)}{\alpha^2 E^2(H)}$$

So

$$Pr\big[H \ge E(H)(1 - \alpha)\big] \ge 1 - \frac{\sigma^2(H)}{\alpha^2 E^2(H)}$$

Therefore from Theorem 2 we will have for all $\alpha > 0$: $\mathrm{Adv}_\phi^{\mathrm{PRF}} \le \alpha + \frac{\sigma^2(H)}{\alpha^2 E^2(H)}$.

With $\alpha = \big(\frac{\sigma(H)}{E(H)}\big)^{2/3}$, this gives $\mathrm{Adv}_\phi^{\mathrm{PRF}} \le 2\big(\frac{\sigma(H)}{E(H)}\big)^{2/3} = 2\big(\frac{V(H)}{E^2(H)}\big)^{1/3}$. So if $\frac{\sigma(H)}{E(H)} = O(\frac{m}{2^n})^{3/2}$, and $E(H) = \frac{|B_n|^2}{2^{nm}}$, Theorem 1 comes from Theorem 2.

Introducing N instead of H

H is (by definition) the number of $(f, g) \in B_n^2$ such that $\forall i$, $1 \le i \le m$, $f(a_i) \oplus g(a_i) = b_i$. $\forall i$, $1 \le i \le m$, let $x_i = f(a_i)$. Let N be the number of sequences x_i, $1 \le i \le m$, $x_i \in I_n$, such that:

1. The x_i are pairwise distinct, $1 \le i \le m$.
2. The $x_i \oplus b_i$ are pairwise distinct, $1 \le i \le m$. We see that $H = N \cdot \frac{|B_n|^2}{\big(2^n(2^n-1)\dots(2^n-m+1)\big)}$. (Since when x_i is fixed, f and g are fixed on exactly m pairwise distinct points by $\forall i$, $1 \le i \le m$, $f(a_i) = x_i$ and $g(a_i) = b_i \oplus x_i$).

Thus we have $\mathrm{Adv}_\phi^{\mathrm{PRF}} \le 2\big(\frac{\sigma(H)}{E(H)}\big)^{2/3} = 2\big(\frac{\sigma(N)}{E(N)}\big)^{2/3}$ (3.1). Therefore, instead of evaluating $E(H)$ and $\sigma(H)$, we can evaluate $E(N)$ and $\sigma(N)$, and our aim is to prove that

$$E(N) = \frac{(2^n(2^n - 1)\dots(2^n - m + 1))^2}{2^{nm}} \text{ and that } \sigma(N) \ll E(N) \text{ when } m \ll 2^n$$

As we will see, the most difficult part will be the evaluation of $\sigma(N)$. (We will see in Section 5 that this evaluation of $\sigma(N)$ leads us to a purely combinatorial problem: the evaluation of values that we will call λ_α).

Remark: We will not do it, nor need it, in this paper, but it is possible to improve slightly the bounds by using a more precise evaluation than the Bienayme-Tchebichev Theorem: instead of

$$Pr(|N - E(N)| \ge t\sigma(N)) \le \frac{1}{t^2},$$

it is possible to prove that for our variables N, and for $t \gg 1$, we have something like this:

$$Pr(|N - E(N)| \geq t\sigma(N)) \leq \frac{1}{e^t}$$

(For this we would have to analyze more precisely the law of distribution of N: it follows almost a Gaussian and this gives a better evaluation than just the general $\frac{1}{t^2}$).

4   Computation of $E(N)$

Let $b = (b_1, \ldots, b_m)$, and $x = (x_1, \ldots, x_m)$. For $x \in I_n^m$, let

$$\delta_x = 1 \Leftrightarrow \begin{cases} \text{The } x_i \text{ are pairwise distinct,} & 1 \leq i \leq m \\ \text{The } x_i \oplus b_i \text{ are pairwise distinct,} & 1 \leq i \leq m \end{cases}$$

and $\delta_x = 0 \Leftrightarrow \delta_x \neq 1$. Let J_n^m be the set of all sequences x_i such that all the x_i are pairwise distinct, $1 \leq i \leq m$. Then $|J_n^m| = 2^n(2^n - 1)\ldots(2^n - m + 1)$ and $N = \sum_{x \in J_n^m} \delta_x$. So we have $E(N) = \sum_{x \in J_n^m} E(\delta_x)$. For $x \in J_n^m$,

$$E(\delta_x) = Pr_{b \in_R I_n^m}(\text{All the } x_i \oplus b_i \text{ are pairwise distinct})$$

$$= \frac{2^n(2^n - 1)\ldots(2^n - m + 1)}{2^{nm}}$$

Therefore

$$E(N) = |J_n^m| \cdot \frac{2^n(2^n - 1)\ldots(2^n - m + 1)}{2^{nm}} = \frac{(2^n(2^n - 1)\ldots(2^n - m + 1))^2}{2^{nm}}$$

as expected.

5   First Results on $V(N)$

We denote by $V(N)$ the variance of N when $b \in_R I_n^m$. We have seen that our aim (cf(3.1)) is to prove that $V(N) \ll E^2(N)$ when $m \ll 2^n$ (with $E^2(N) = \frac{(2^n(2^n - 1)\ldots(2^n - m + 1))^4}{2^{2nm}}$). With the same notations as in Section 4 above, $N = \sum_{x \in J_n^m} \delta_x$. Since the variance of a sum is the sum of the variances plus the sum of all covariances we have:

$$V(N) = \sum_{x \in J_n^m} V(\delta_x) + \sum_{\substack{x, x' \in J_n^m \\ x \neq x'}} \left[E(\delta_x \delta_{x'}) - E(\delta_x) E(\delta_{x'}) \right] \tag{5.1}$$

We will now study the 3 terms in (5.1), i.e. the terms in $V(\delta_x)$, the terms in $E(\delta_x \delta_{x'})$ and the terms in $E(\delta_x) E(\delta_{x'})$.

Terms in $V(\delta_x)$

$$V(\delta_x) = E(\delta_x^2) - (E(\delta_x))^2 = E(\delta_x) - (E(\delta_x))^2$$

$$V(\delta_x) = \frac{2^n(2^n - 1)\ldots(2^n - m + 1)}{2^{nm}} - \frac{(2^n(2^n - 1)\ldots(2^n - m + 1))^2}{2^{2nm}}$$

So $\sum_{x \in J_n^m} V(\delta_x) = \frac{(2^n(2^n - 1)\ldots(2^n - m + 1))^2}{2^{nm}} - \frac{(2^n(2^n - 1)\ldots(2^n - m + 1))^3}{2^{2nm}}$

This term is less than $E(N)$ and therefore is much less than $E^2(N)$.   (5.2)

Terms in $E(\delta_x)\,E(\delta_{x'})$

$$E(\delta_x)\,E(\delta_{x'}) = \frac{(2^n(2^n - 1)\ldots(2^n - m + 1))^2}{2^{2nm}}$$

$$\sum_{\substack{x,x' \in J_n^m \\ x \neq x'}} E(\delta_x)E(\delta_{x'}) = \frac{[2^n(2^n - 1)\ldots(2^n - m+1) - 1][2^n(2^n - 1)\ldots(2^n - m + 1)]^3}{2^{2nm}}$$

$$\simeq \frac{(2^n(2^n - 1)\ldots(2^n - m + 1))^4}{2^{2nm}} = E^2(N)   \qquad (5.3)$$

Terms in $E(\delta_x\,\delta_{x'})$

Therefore the last term A_m that we have to evaluate in (5.1) is

$$A_m =_{def} \sum_{\substack{x,x' \in J_n^m \ x \neq x'}} E(\delta_x\,\delta_{x'}) =$$

$$\sum_{\substack{x,x' \in J_n^m \\ x \neq x'}} Pr_{b \in I_n^m}\left(\left\{ \begin{array}{ll} \text{The } x_i \text{ are pairwise distinct,} & 1 \leq i \leq m \\ \text{The } x_i \oplus b_i \text{ are pairwise distinct,} & 1 \leq i \leq m \end{array} \right. \right)$$

Let $\lambda_m =_{def}$ the number of sequences (x_i, x_i', b_i), $1 \leq i \leq m$ such that

1. The x_i are pairwise distinct, $1 \leq i \leq m$.
2. The x_i' are pairwise distinct, $1 \leq i \leq m$.
3. The $x_i \oplus b_i$ are pairwise distinct, $1 \leq i \leq m$.
4. The $x_i' \oplus b_i$ are pairwise distinct, $1 \leq i \leq m$.

We have $A_m = \frac{\lambda_m}{2^{nm}}$ (5.4). Therefore from (5.1), (5.2), (5.3), (5.4), we have obtained:

$$V(N) \leq E(N) + E^2(N) - \frac{\lambda_m}{2^{nm}}   \qquad (5.5)$$

We want to prove that $V(N) \ll E^2(N)$. Therefore, our aim is to prove that

$$\lambda_m \simeq 2^{nm} \cdot E^2(N) = \frac{(2^n(2^n - 1)\ldots(2^n - m + 1))^4}{2^{nm}}   \qquad (5.6)$$

Change of variables

Let $f_i = x_i$ and $g_i = x_i'$, $h_i = x_i \oplus b_i$. We see that λ_m is also the number of sequences (f_i, g_i, h_i), $1 \leq i \leq m$, $f_i \in I_n$, $g_i \in I_n$, $h_i \in I_n$, such that

1. The f_i are pairwise distinct, $1 \leq i \leq m$.
2. The g_i are pairwise distinct, $1 \leq i \leq m$.
3. The h_i are pairwise distinct, $1 \leq i \leq m$.
4. The $f_i \oplus g_i \oplus h_i$ are pairwise distinct, $1 \leq i \leq m$.

We will call these conditions 1.2.3.4. the "conditions λ_α". (Examples of λ_m values are given in Appendix A). In order to get (5.6), we see that a sufficient condition is finally to prove that

$$\lambda_m = \frac{(2^n(2^n - 1)\ldots(2^n - m + 1))^4}{2^{nm}}(1 + O(\frac{m}{2^n})) \tag{5.7}$$

with an explicit O function. So we have transformed our security proof against all CPA-2 for $f \oplus g$, $f, g \in_R B_n$, to this purely combinatorial problem (5.7) on the λ_m values. (We can notice that in $E(N)$ and $\sigma(N)$ we evaluate the values when the b_i values are randomly chosen, while here, on the λ_m values, we do not have such b_i values anymore). The proof of this combinatorial property is given below and in the eprint version. (Unfortunately the proof of this combinatorial property (5.7) is not obvious: we will need a few pages. However, fortunately, the mathematics that we will use are simple).

6   First Results in λ_α

The values λ_α have been introduced in Section 5. Our aim is to prove (5.7), (or something similar, for example with $O(\frac{m^{k+1}}{2^{nk}})$ for any integer k) with explicit O functions. For this, we will proceed like this: in this Section 6 we will give a first evaluation of the values λ_α. Then, in Section 7, we will prove an induction formula (7.2) on λ_α. Finally, in the Appendices, we will use this induction formula (7.2) to get our property on λ_α.

Let $U_\alpha = \frac{[2^n(2^n - 1)\ldots(2^n - \alpha + 1)]^4}{2^{n\alpha}}$. We have $U_{\alpha+1} = \frac{(2^n - \alpha)^4}{2^n}U_\alpha$.

$$U_{\alpha+1} = 2^{3n}(1 - \frac{4\alpha}{2^n} + \frac{6\alpha^2}{2^{2n}} - \frac{4\alpha^3}{2^{3n}} + \frac{\alpha^4}{2^{4n}})U_\alpha \tag{6.1}$$

Similarly, we want to obtain an induction formula on λ_α, i.e. we want to evaluate $\frac{\lambda_{\alpha+1}}{\lambda_\alpha}$. More precisely our aim is to prove something like this: $\frac{\lambda_{\alpha+1}}{\lambda_\alpha} = \frac{U_{\alpha+1}}{U_\alpha}(1 + O(\frac{1}{2^n}) + O(\frac{\alpha}{2^{2n}}))$ (6.2)

Notice that here we have $O(\frac{\alpha}{2^{2n}})$ and not $O(\frac{\alpha}{2^n})$. Therefore we want something like this:

$$\frac{\lambda_{\alpha+1}}{2^{3n} \cdot \lambda_\alpha} = (1 - \frac{4\alpha}{2^n} + \frac{6\alpha^2}{2^{2n}} - \frac{4\alpha^3}{2^{3n}} + \frac{\alpha^4}{2^{4n}})(1 + O(\frac{1}{2^n}) + O(\frac{\alpha}{2^{2n}})) \tag{6.3}$$

(with some specific O functions)

Then, from (6.2) used for all $1 \leq i \leq \alpha$ and since $\lambda_1 = U_1 = 2^{3n}$, we will get

$$\lambda_\alpha = (\frac{\lambda_\alpha}{\lambda_{\alpha-1}})(\frac{\lambda_{\alpha-1}}{\lambda_{\alpha-2}})\ldots(\frac{\lambda_2}{\lambda_1})\lambda_1 = U_\alpha(1 + O(\frac{1}{2^n}) + O(\frac{\alpha}{2^{2n}}))^\alpha$$

and therefore we will get property (5.4): $\lambda_\alpha = U_\alpha\left(1 + O\left(\frac{\alpha}{2^n}\right)\right)$ as wanted. Notice that to get here $0\left(\frac{\alpha}{2^n}\right)$ we have used $0\left(\frac{\alpha}{2^{2n}}\right)$ in (6.2). By definition $\lambda_{\alpha+1}$ is the number of sequences (f_i, g_i, h_i), $1 \le i \le \alpha + 1$ such that we have:

1. The conditions λ_α
2. $f_{\alpha+1} \notin \{f_1, \ldots, f_\alpha\}$
3. $g_{\alpha+1} \notin \{g_1, \ldots, g_\alpha\}$
4. $h_{\alpha+1} \notin \{h_1, \ldots, h_\alpha\}$
5. $f_{\alpha+1} \oplus g_{\alpha+1} \oplus h_{\alpha+1} \notin \{f_1 \oplus g_1 \oplus h_1, \ldots, f_\alpha \oplus g_\alpha \oplus h_\alpha\}$

We will denote by $\beta_1, \ldots, \beta_{4\alpha}$ the 4α equalities that should not be satisfied here: $\beta_1 : f_{\alpha+1} = f_1$, $\beta_2 : f_{\alpha+1} = f_2, \ldots$, $\beta_{4\alpha} : f_{\alpha+1} \oplus g_{\alpha+1} \oplus h_{\alpha+1} = f_\alpha \oplus g_\alpha \oplus h_\alpha$.

First evaluation
When f_i, g_i, h_i values are fixed, $1 \le i \le \alpha$, such that they satisfy conditions λ_α, for $f_{\alpha+1}$ that satisfy 2), we have $2^n - \alpha$ solutions and for $g_{\alpha+1}$ that satisfy 3) we have $2^n - \alpha$ solutions. Now when f_i, g_i, h_i, $1 \le i \le \alpha$, and $f_{\alpha+1}$, $g_{\alpha+1}$ are fixed such that they satisfy 1), 2), 3), for $h_{\alpha+1}$ that satisfy 4) and 5) we have between $2^n - \alpha$ and $2^n - 2\alpha$ possibilities. Therefore (first evaluation for $\frac{\lambda_{\alpha+1}}{\lambda_\alpha}$) we have:

$$\lambda_\alpha(2^n - \alpha)^2(2^n - 2\alpha) \le \lambda_{\alpha+1} \le \lambda_\alpha(2^n - \alpha)^2(2^n - \alpha)$$

Therefore, $1 - \dfrac{4\alpha}{2^n} \le \dfrac{\lambda_{\alpha+1}}{2^{3n} \cdot \lambda_\alpha} \le 1$ (6.4). This an approximation in $O\left(\frac{\alpha}{2^n}\right)$ and from it we get $\lambda_\alpha = U_\alpha\left(1 + O\left(\frac{\alpha}{2^n}\right)\right)^\alpha$, i.e. $\lambda_\alpha = U_\alpha\left(1 + O\left(\frac{\alpha^2}{2^n}\right)\right)$, i.e. we get security until $\alpha^2 \ll 2^n$, i.e. until $\alpha \ll \sqrt{2^n}$. However, we want security until $\alpha \ll 2^n$ and not only $\alpha \ll \sqrt{2^n}$, so we want a better evaluation for $\frac{\lambda_{\alpha+1}}{2^{3n} \cdot \lambda_\alpha}$ (i.e. we want something like (6.3) instead of (6.4)).

7 An Induction Formula on λ_α

A more precise evaluation
For each i, $1 \le i \le 4\alpha$, we will denote by B_i the set of $(f_1, \ldots, f_{\alpha+1}, g_1, \ldots, g_{\alpha+1}, h_1, \ldots, h_{\alpha+1})$, that satisfy the conditions λ_α and the conditions β_i. Therefore we have: $\lambda_{\alpha+1} = 2^{3n}\lambda_\alpha - |\cup_{i=1}^{4\alpha} B_i|$.

We know that for any set A_i and any integer μ, we have:

$$\left| \cup_{i=1}^{\mu} A_i \right| = \sum_{i=1}^{\mu} |A_i| - \sum_{i_1 < i_2} |A_{i_1} \cap A_{i_2}|$$

$$+ \sum_{i_1 < i_2 < i_3} |A_{i_1} \cap A_{i_2} \cap A_{i_3}| + \ldots + (-1)^{\mu+1}|A_1 \cap A_2 \cap \ldots \cap A_\mu|$$

Moreover, each set of 5 (or more) equations β_i is in contradiction with the conditions λ_α because we will have at least two equations in f, or two in g, or two in h, or two in $f \oplus g \oplus h$ (and $f_{\alpha+1} = f_i$ and $f_{\alpha+1} = f_j$ gives $f_i = f_j$ with $i \neq j$ and $1 \leq \alpha$, $j \leq \alpha$, in contradiction with λ_α).

Therefore, we have:

$$\lambda_{\alpha+1} = 2^{3n}\lambda_\alpha - \sum_{i=1}^{4\alpha}|B_i| + \sum_{i<j}|B_i \cap B_j| - \sum_{i<j<k}|B_i \cap B_j \cap B_k| + \sum_{i<j<k<l}|B_i \cap B_j \cap B_k \cap B_l|$$

- **1 equation**

In B_i, we have the conditions λ_α plus the equation β_i, and β_i will fix $f_{\alpha+1}$, or $g_{\alpha+1}$, or $h_{\alpha+1}$ from the other values. Therefore, $|B_i| = 2^{2n}\lambda_\alpha$ and $-\sum_{i=1}^{4\alpha}|B_i| = -4\alpha \cdot 2^{2n}\lambda_\alpha$.

- **2 equations**

First Case: β_i and β_j are two equations in f (or two in g, or two in h, or two in $f \oplus g \oplus h$. (For example: $f_{\alpha+1} = f_1$ and $f_{\alpha+2} = f_2$). Then these equations are not compatible with the conditions λ_α, therefore $|B_i \cap B_j| = 0$.

Second Case: we are not in the first case. Then two variables (for example f_α and g_α) are fixed from the others. Therefore: $|B_i \cap B_j| = 2^n\lambda_\alpha$ and $\sum_{i<j}|B_i \cap B_j| = 6\alpha^2 \cdot 2^n\lambda_\alpha$.

- **3 equations**

If we have two equations in f, or in g, or in h, or in $f \oplus g \oplus h$, we have $|B_i \cap B_j \cap B_k| = 0$. If we are not in these cases, then $f_{\alpha+1}$, $g_{\alpha+1}$ and $h_{\alpha+1}$ are fixed by the three equations from the other variables, and then $|B_i \cap B_j \cap B_k| = \lambda_\alpha$. Therefore: $-\sum_{i<j<k}|B_i \cap B_j \cap B_k| = -4\alpha^3\lambda_\alpha$.

- **4 equations**

This value is different from 0 only if we have one equation $f_{\alpha+1} = f_i$, one equation $g_{\alpha+1} = g_j$, one equation $h_{\alpha+1} = h_k$ and one equation $f_{\alpha+1} \oplus g_{\alpha+1} \oplus h_{\alpha+1} = f_l \oplus g_l \oplus h_l$. Then $|B_i \cap B_j \cap B_k \cap B_l| = $ number of f_a, g_b, h_c, with $a, b, c \in \{1, \ldots, \alpha\}$, that satisfy the conditions λ_α plus the equation X: $f_i \oplus g_j \oplus h_k = f_l \oplus g_l \oplus h_l$.

Case 1. i, j, k, l are pairwise distinct. Here we have $\alpha(\alpha-1)(\alpha-2)(\alpha-3) = \alpha^4 - 6\alpha^3 + 11\alpha^2 - 6\alpha$ possibilities for i, j, k, l and from the symmetries of all indexes in the conditions λ_α, all the $\lambda'_\alpha(X)$ of this case 1 are equal. We denote by $\lambda'^{(4)}_\alpha$ this value of $\lambda'_\alpha(X)$. (The (4) here is to remember that we have exactly 4 indexes i, j, k, l).

Case 2. In $\{i, j, k, l\}$, we have exactly 3 indexes. Here we have $6\alpha(\alpha-1)(\alpha-2) = 6\alpha^3 - 18\alpha^2 + 12\alpha$ possibilities for i, j, k, l (since there are 6 possibilities to choose an equality). From the symmetries in the conditions λ_α, all the $\lambda'_\alpha(X)$ of this case 2 are equal. We denote by $\lambda'^{(3)}_\alpha$ this value of $\lambda'_\alpha(X)$.

Case 3. In $\{i, j, k, l\}$, 3 indexes have the same value (example $i = j = k$) and the other one has a different value. Then X is not compatible with the conditions λ_α.

Case 4. In i, j, k, l, we have 2 indexes and we are not in the Case 3 (for example $i = j$ and $k = l$). Here we have $3\alpha(\alpha-1) = 3\alpha^2 - 3\alpha$ possibilities for i, j, k, l. From the symmetries in the conditions λ_α all the $\lambda'_\alpha(X)$ of this case 4 are equal. We denote by $\lambda'^{(2)}_\alpha$ this value of $\lambda'_\alpha(X)$.

Case 5. We have $i = j = k = l$. Here we have α possibilities for i, j, k, l. Here X is always true, and $\lambda'_\alpha(X) = \lambda_\alpha$.

From these 5 cases we get:

$$\sum_{i<j<k<l} |B_i \cap B_j \cap B_k \cap B_l| = \alpha(\alpha-1)(\alpha-2)(\alpha-3)\lambda'^{(4)}_\alpha$$

$$+6\alpha(\alpha-1)(\alpha-2)\lambda'^{(3)}_\alpha + 3\alpha(\alpha-1)\lambda'^{(2)}_\alpha + \alpha\lambda_\alpha$$

Therefore

$$\lambda_{\alpha+1} = (2^{3n} - 4\alpha \cdot 2^{2n} + 6\alpha^2 \cdot 2^n - 4\alpha^3 + \alpha)\lambda_\alpha + (\alpha^4 - 6\alpha^3 + 11\alpha^2 - 6\alpha)\lambda'^{(4)}_\alpha$$

$$+(6\alpha^3 - 18\alpha^2 + 12\alpha)\lambda'^{(3)}_\alpha + (3\alpha^2 - 3\alpha)\lambda'^{(2)}_\alpha \qquad (7.1)$$

We will denote by $[\lambda'_\alpha]$ any value of $\lambda'_\alpha(X)$ such that X is compatible with the conditions λ_α and such that X is not always true (X is not $0 = 0$). Then, from (7.1) we write

$$\lambda_{\alpha+1} = (2^{3n} - 4\alpha \cdot 2^{2n} + 6\alpha^2 \cdot 2^n - 4\alpha^3 + \alpha)\lambda_\alpha + (\alpha^4 - 4\alpha^2 + 3\alpha)[\lambda'_\alpha] \quad (7.2)$$

where $A \cdot [\lambda'_\alpha]$ is just a notation to mean that we have A terms λ'_α but each of these λ'_α may have different values. Our aim is to get (6.3) from (7.2). For this we see that we have to prove that

$$[\lambda'_\alpha] = \frac{\lambda_\alpha}{2^n}(1 + O(\frac{1}{2^n}) + O(\frac{\alpha}{2^{2n}})) \qquad (7.3)$$

for "most" values $[\lambda'_\alpha]$ or for the values $\lambda'^{(4)}_\alpha$. This is what we started in Appendix B and the complete result is in the Appendices of the eprint version of this paper [8].

8   From $[\epsilon_\alpha]$ to $\mathrm{Adv}_\phi^{\mathrm{PRF}}$

Let $[\epsilon_\alpha] = \frac{2^n[\lambda'_\alpha]}{\lambda_\alpha} - 1$. Therefore, $[\lambda'_\alpha] = \frac{\lambda_\alpha}{2^n}(1 + [\epsilon_\alpha])$. From the analysis of the previous sections, we know that if we can prove that $\|[\epsilon_\alpha]\|$ is small, then $\mathrm{Adv}_\phi^{\mathrm{PRF}}$ will be small. Let evaluate more precisely the links between $\|[\epsilon_\alpha]\|$ and $\mathrm{Adv}_\phi^{\mathrm{PRF}}$ that we have. From formula (7.2), we have:

$$\lambda_{\alpha+1} = 2^{3n}\left[1 - \frac{4\alpha}{2^n} + \frac{6\alpha^2}{2^{2n}} - \frac{4\alpha^3}{2^{3n}} + \frac{\alpha}{2^{3n}} + \frac{(\alpha^4 - 4\alpha^2 + 3\alpha)}{2^{4n}} + A\right]\lambda_\alpha$$

with

$$A \le \frac{\alpha^4[\epsilon_\alpha]}{2^n \cdot 2^{3n}} \qquad (8.1)$$

Therefore, by using U_α of section 6 we have:

$$\frac{\lambda_{\alpha+1}}{\lambda_\alpha} = \frac{U_{\alpha+1}}{U_\alpha} \cdot \frac{(1 - \frac{4\alpha}{2^n} + \frac{6\alpha^2}{2^{2n}} - \frac{4\alpha^3}{2^{3n}} + \frac{\alpha}{2^{3n}} + \frac{(\alpha^4 - 4\alpha^2 + 3\alpha)}{2^{4n}} + A)}{(1 - \frac{4\alpha}{2^n} + \frac{6\alpha^2}{2^{2n}} - \frac{4\alpha^3}{2^{3n}} + \frac{\alpha^4}{2^{4n}})}$$

$$\frac{\lambda_{\alpha+1}}{\lambda_\alpha} = \frac{U_{\alpha+1}}{U_\alpha} \cdot \left(1 + \frac{\frac{\alpha}{2^{3n}} - \frac{4\alpha^2}{2^{4n}} + \frac{3\alpha}{2^{4n}} + A}{1 - \frac{4\alpha}{2^n} + \frac{6\alpha^2}{2^{2n}} - \frac{4\alpha^3}{2^{3n}} + \frac{\alpha^4}{2^{4n}}}\right) \tag{8.2}$$

Therefore, with (8.1) we have

$$\frac{\lambda_{\alpha+1}}{\lambda_\alpha} = \frac{U_{\alpha+1}}{U_\alpha} \cdot \left(1 + O_1(\frac{\alpha}{2^{3n}}) + O_2(A)\right)$$

with

$$|O_1(\frac{\alpha}{2^{3n}})| \le \frac{\alpha}{2^{3n}(1 - \frac{4\alpha}{2^n})} \tag{8.3}$$

and

$$|O_2(A)| \le \frac{A}{(1 - \frac{4\alpha}{2^n})} \tag{8.4}$$

Since $\lambda_1 = U_1 = 2^{3n}$, we have

$$\lambda_\alpha = \left(\frac{\lambda_\alpha}{\lambda_{\alpha-1}}\right)\left(\frac{\lambda_{\alpha-1}}{\lambda_{\alpha-2}}\right)\ldots\left(\frac{\lambda_2}{\lambda_1}\right)\lambda_1 = U_\alpha\left[1 + O(\frac{\alpha}{2^{3n}}) + O(A)\right]^\alpha$$

$$\lambda_\alpha = \frac{[2^n(2^n - 1)\ldots(2^n - \alpha + 1)]^4}{2^{n\alpha}}\left(1 + O(\frac{\alpha^2}{2^{3n}}) + \alpha O(A)\right) \tag{8.5}$$

Now from (8.5) and (5.5) we get:

$$V(N) \le E(N) + (E(N))^2\left(O(\frac{\alpha^2}{2^{3n}}) + \alpha O(A)\right)$$

Therefore, from (3.1) we get that the best CPA-2 attacks ϕ satisfy:

$$\text{Adv}_\phi^{PRF} \le 2\left(\frac{V(N)}{E^2(N)}\right)^{1/3} \le 2\left(\frac{1}{E(N)} + O(\frac{\alpha^2}{2^{3n}}) + \alpha O(A)\right)^{1/3}$$

More precisely, by using (8.3) and (8.4) we get:

$$\text{Adv}_\phi^{PRF} \le 2\left(\frac{1}{E(N)} + \frac{m^2}{2^{3n}(1 - \frac{4m}{2^n})} + \frac{\alpha^5 \cdot [\epsilon_\alpha]}{2^{4n} \cdot (1 - \frac{4\alpha}{2^n})}\right)^{1/3} \tag{8.6}$$

Here we have $\frac{1}{E(N)} = \frac{2^{nm}}{(2^n(2^n-1)\ldots(2^n-m+1))^2}$ and this is much smaller than $\frac{m^3}{2^{3n}}$ for example, thanks to Stirling Formula. From formula (8.6) we see clearly that a bound on $\|[\epsilon_\alpha]\|$ gives immediately a precise bound on Adv_ϕ^{PRF}. Now, in the Appendices of the extended version ([8]), we present good bounds for $\|[\epsilon_\alpha]\|$. More precisely, we proceed progressively: first, in Appendix B, we get a bound for $\|[\epsilon_\alpha]\|$ in $O(\frac{\alpha}{2^n})$ and therefore a security (from (8.6)) in $O(2^{\frac{5n}{6}})$. Then, in Appendix D we get a bound for $\|[\epsilon_\alpha]\|$ in $O(\frac{\alpha^5}{2^{5n}})$ and therefore a security (from (8.6)) in $O(2^{\frac{9n}{10}})$. Finally, in Appendix E, we iterate the process in order to obtain security in $m \ll O(2^n)$ as wanted.

9   A Simple Variant of the Schemes with Only One Permutation

Instead of $G = f_1 \oplus f_2, f_1, f_2 \in_R B_n$, we can study $G'(x) = f(x\|0) \oplus f(x\|1)$, with $f \in_R B_n$ and $x \in I_{n-1}$. This variant was already introduced in [2] and it is for this that in [2] p.9 the security in $\frac{m}{2^n} + O(n)\left(\frac{m}{2^n}\right)^{3/2}$ is presented. In fact, from a theoretical point of view, this variant G' is very similar to G, and it is possible to prove that our analysis can be modified to obtain a similar proof of security for G'.

10   A Simple Property about the Xor of Two Permutations and a New Conjecture

I have conjectured this property:

$$\forall f \in F_n, \text{ if } \bigoplus_{x \in I_n} f(x) = 0, \text{ then } \exists (g, h) \in B_n^2, \text{ such that } f = g \oplus h.$$

Just one day after this paper was put on eprint, J.F. Dillon pointed to us that in fact this was proved in 1952 in [5]. We thank him a lot for this information. (This property was proved again independently in 1979 in [12]).

A new conjecture. However I conjecture a stronger property. Conjecture:

$$\forall f \in F_n, \text{ if } \bigoplus_{x \in I_n} f(x) = 0, \text{ then the number } H \text{ of } (g, h) \in B_n^2,$$

$$\text{such that } f = g \oplus h \text{ satisfies } H \geq \frac{|B_n|^2}{2^{n2^n}}.$$

Variant: I also conjecture that this property is true in any group, not only with Xor.

Remark: in this paper, I have proved weaker results involving m equations with $m \ll O(2^n)$ instead of all the 2^n equations. These weaker results were sufficient for the cryptographic security wanted.

11   Conclusion

The results in this paper improve our understanding of the PRF-security of the Xor of two random permutations. More precisely in this paper we have proved that the Adaptive Chosen Plaintext security for this problem is in $O(2^n)$, and we have obtained an explicit O function. These results belong to the field of finding security proofs for cryptographic designs above the "birthday bound". (In [1,7,11], some results "above the birthday bound" on completely different cryptographic designs are also given). Our proofs need a few pages, so are a bit hard to read, but the results obtained are very easy to use and the mathematics used are elementary (essentially combinatorial and induction arguments). Moreover, we have proved (in Section 5) that this cryptographic problem of security is directly related to a very simple to describe and purely combinatorial problem. We have obtained this transformation by combining the "coefficient H technique" of [10,11] and a specific computation of the standard deviation of H. (In a way, from a cryptographic point of view, this is maybe the most important result, and all the analysis after Section 5 can be seen as combinatorial mathematics and not cryptography anymore). Since building PRF from PRP has many practical applications,we believe that these results are of real interest both from a theoretical point of view and a practical point of view.

References

1. Aiello, W., Venkatesan, R.: Foiling Birthday Attacks in Length-Doubling Transformations - Benes: A Non-Reversible Alternative to Feistel. In: Ueli, M. (ed.) EUROCRYPT 1996. LNCS, vol. 1070, pp. 307–320. Springer, Heidelberg (1996)
2. Bellare, M., Impagliazzo, R.: A Tool for Obtaining Tighter Security Analyses of Pseudorandom Function Based Constructions, with Applications to PRP to PRF Conversion; ePrint Archive 1999/024: Listing for 1999
3. Bellare, M., Krovetz, T., Rogaway, P.: Luby-Rackoff Backwards: Increasing Security by Making Block Ciphers Non-invertible.. In: Nyberg, K. (ed.) EUROCRYPT 1998. LNCS, vol. 1403, pp. 266–280. Springer, Heidelberg (1998)
4. Hall, C., Wagner, D., Kelsey, J., Schneier, B.: Building PRFs from PRPs.. In: Krawczyk, H. (ed.) CRYPTO 1998. LNCS, vol. 1462, pp. 370–389. Springer, Heidelberg (1998)
5. Hall Jr., M.: A Combinatorial Problem on Abelian Groups. Proceedings of the Americal Mathematical Society 3(4), 584–587 (1952)
6. Lucks, S.: The Sum of PRPs Is a Secure PRF. In: Preneel, B. (ed.) EUROCRYPT 2000. LNCS, vol. 1807, pp. 470–487. Springer, Heidelberg (2000)
7. Maurer, U., Pietrzak, K.: The Security of Many-Round Luby-Rackoff Pseudo-Random Permutations. In: Biham, E. (ed.) EUROCRYPT 2003. LNCS, vol. 2656, pp. 544–561. Springer, Heidelberg (2003)
8. Patarin, J.: A Proof of Security in $O(2^n)$ for the Xor of Two Random Permutations - Extended Version; Cryptology ePrint archive: 2008/010: Listing for 2008
9. Patarin, J.: Generic Attacks for the Xor of k Random Permutations; Cryptology ePrint archive: 2008/009: Listing for 2008
10. Patarin, J.: Etude de Générateurs de Permutations Basés sur les Schémas du DES. In: Ph. Thesis. Inria, Domaine de Voluceau, France (1991)
11. Patarin, J.: Luby-Rackoff: 7 Rounds are Enough for $2^{n(1-\epsilon)}$ Security. In: Boneh, D. (ed.) CRYPTO 2003. LNCS, vol. 2729, pp. 513–529. Springer, Heidelberg (2003)
12. Salzborn, F., Szekeres, G.: A Problem in Combinatorial Group Theory. Ars Combinatoria 7, 3–5 (1979)

Appendices

A   Examples: $\lambda_1, \lambda_2, \lambda_3$

As examples, we present here the exact values for $\lambda_1, \lambda_2, \lambda_3$.

Computation of λ_1

$$\lambda_1 =_{def} \text{ Number of } (f_1, g_1, h_1) \text{ with } f_1, g_1, h_1 \in I_n$$

Therefore $\lambda_1 = 2^{3n}$.

Computation of λ_2 from (7.2)

$$\lambda_2 =_{def} \text{ Number of } (f_1, g_1, h_1), (f_2, g_2, h_2) \text{ such that}$$

$$f_2 \neq f_1, \ g_2 \neq g_1, \ h_2 \neq h_1, \ f_2 \oplus g_2 \oplus h_2 \neq f_1 \oplus g_1 \oplus h_1$$

From the general formula (7.1) or (7.2) of Section 7, we have (with $\alpha = 1$):

$$\lambda_2 = [2^{3n} - 4 \cdot 2^{2n} + 6 \cdot 2^n - 3]\lambda_1 + 0$$

(here $[\lambda_1'] = 0$ since we have only one indice and in X we must have at least two indices).

$$\lambda_2 = [2^{3n} - 4 \cdot 2^{2n} + 6 \cdot 2^n - 3] \cdot 2^{3n}$$

Computations of λ_2 from the β_i equations

$$\lambda_2 = 2^{3n}\lambda_1 - \sum_{i=1}^{4} |B_i| + \sum_{i<j} |B_i \cap B_j| - \sum_{i<j<k} |B_i \cap B_j \cap B_k| + \sum_{i<j<k<l} |B_i \cap B_j \cap B_k \cap B_l|$$

1 equation: $\sum_{i=1}^{4} |B_i| = 4 \cdot 2^{2n}\lambda_1$.
2 equations: $\sum_{i<j} |B_i \cap B_j| = 6 \cdot 2^n \lambda_1$.
3 equations: $\sum_{i<j<k} |B_i \cap B_j \cap B_k| = 4\lambda_1$.
4 equations: $\sum_{i<j<k<l} |B_i \cap B_j \cap B_k \cap B_l| = \lambda_1$.
Therefore $\lambda_2 = (2^{3n} - 4 \cdot 2^{2n} + 6 \cdot 2^n - 3)\lambda_1$ (as expected we obtain the same result as above).

Computation of λ_3 from (7.2)

From the general formulas (7.1) and (7.2), we have (with $\alpha = 2$):

$$\lambda_3 = (2^{3n} - 8 \cdot 2^{2n} + 24 \cdot 2^n - 30)\lambda_2 + 6\lambda_2'^{(2)}$$

where $\lambda_2'^{(2)}$ is the number of (f_1, g_1, h_1), (f_2, g_2, h_2) such that $f_2 \neq f_1$, $g_2 \neq g_1$, $h_2 \neq h_1$, $f_2 \oplus g_2 \oplus h_2 \neq f_1 \oplus g_1 \oplus h_1$ and $f_1 \oplus g_1 = f_2 \oplus g_2$ (all the other equations X of the type $\lambda_2'^{(2)}$ give the same value $\lambda_2'^{(2)}$). When f_1, g_1, h_1 are fixed (we have 2^{3n} possibilities) then we will choose $f_2 \neq f_1$, $h_2 \neq h_1$, and $g_2 = f_1 \oplus f_2 \oplus g_1$ (so we have $g_2 \neq g_1$ and $f_2 \oplus g_2 \oplus h_2 \neq f_1 \oplus g_1 \oplus h_1$). Therefore $\lambda_2'^{(2)} = 2^{3n} \cdot (2^n - 1)^2$ and the exact value of λ_3 is:

$$\lambda_3 = (2^{3n} - 8 \cdot 2^{2n} + 24 \cdot 2^n - 30)\lambda_2 + 6 \cdot 2^{3n} \cdot (2^n - 1)^2$$

(with $\lambda_2 = (2^{3n} - 4 \cdot 2^{2n} + 6 \cdot 2^n - 3) \cdot 2^{3n}$ as seen above).

Computation of $\lambda_\alpha'^{(2)}$ from the β_i equations

$$\lambda_2' = 2^{2n}\lambda_1 - \sum_{i=1}^{4}|B_i'| + \sum_{i<j}|B'i \cap B_j'| - \sum_{i<j<k}|B_i' \cap B_j' \cap B_k'| + \sum_{i<j<k<l}|B_i' \cap B_j' \cap B_k' \cap B_l'|$$

Here X is: $f_1 \oplus f_2 = g_1 \oplus g_2$

- $X + 1$ **equations**

$$\sum_{i=1}^{4}|B_i'| = 4 \cdot 2^n \lambda_1$$

- $X + 2$ **equations.** If the 2 equations β_i are ($f_1 = f_2$ and $g_1 = g_2$), or ($h_1 = h_2$ and $f_1 \oplus g_1 \oplus h_1 = f_2 \oplus g_2 \oplus h_2$), then X is the Xor of these equations. Therefore

$$\sum_{i<j}|B'i \cap B_j'| = 4 \cdot \lambda_1 + 2 \cdot 2^n \lambda_1$$

- $X+3$ **equations.** X is always a consequence of the 3 equations, $\sum_{i<j<k}|B_i' \cap B_j' \cap B_k'| = 4\lambda_1$.
- $X + 4$ **equations.** $\sum_{i<j<k<l}|B_i' \cap B_j' \cap B_k' \cap B_l'| = \lambda_1$.
Therefore

$$\lambda_\alpha'^{(2)} = (2^{2n} - 4 \cdot 2^n + 4 - 2 \cdot 2^n - 4 + 1)\lambda_1$$

$$\lambda_\alpha'^{(2)} = (2^{2n} - 2 \cdot 2^n + 1)\lambda_1$$

(as expected we obtain the same result as above).

Remark. Here

$$\frac{2^n \lambda_2'^{(2)}}{\lambda_2} = \frac{1 - \frac{2}{2^n} + \frac{1}{2^{2n}}}{1 - \frac{4}{2^n} + \frac{6}{2^{2n}} - \frac{3}{2^{3n}}} = 1 + \frac{2}{2^n} + \frac{3}{2^{2n}} + O(\frac{1}{2^{3n}})$$

Therefore we see that in $\dfrac{2^n[\lambda_\alpha']}{\lambda_\alpha}$, we have sometimes a term in $O(\frac{1}{2^n})$. However this is exceptional: here $f_1 \oplus g_1 = f_2 \oplus g_2$ is the Xor of the conditions $f_1 \neq f_2$ and $g_1 \neq g_2$, or of the conditions $h_1 \neq h_2$ and $f_2 \oplus g_2 \oplus h_2 \neq f_1 \oplus g_1 \oplus h_1$. Moreover here we have only 2 indices.

B   Evaluations of $[\lambda_\alpha']/\lambda_\alpha$ in $O(\frac{\alpha}{2^n})$, Security in $m \ll 2^{\frac{5n}{6}}$

By definition $[\lambda_\alpha']$ denotes (as we have seen in Section 7) the number of

$$(f_1, \ldots, f_\alpha, g_1, \ldots, g_\alpha, h_1, \ldots, h_\alpha) \text{ of } I_n^{3\alpha}$$

that satisfy the conditions λ_α plus an equation X of the type:

$$f_j \oplus g_j \oplus h_j = f_k \oplus g_l \oplus h_i$$

with $i, j, k, l \in \{1, \dots, \alpha\}$ such that X is compatible with the conditions λ_α and such that X is not $0 = 0$ (i.e. we do not have $i = j = k = l$). We have seen in Section 7 that $[\lambda'_\alpha]$ is not a fixed value: it can be $\lambda_\alpha^{'(4)}$ (by symmetries of the hypothesis for this case we can assume X to be: $f_\alpha \oplus g_\alpha \oplus h_\alpha = h_{\alpha-1} \oplus g_{\alpha-2} \oplus f_{\alpha-3}$) or $\lambda_\alpha^{'(3)}$ (for this case we can assume X to be: $f_\alpha \oplus g_\alpha = f_{\alpha-1} \oplus g_{\alpha-2}$) or $\lambda_\alpha^{'(2)}$ (for this case we can assume X to be: $f_\alpha \oplus g_\alpha = f_{\alpha-1} \oplus g_{\alpha-1}$). However, as we will see all these three values $[\lambda'_\alpha]$ are very near, and they are very near $\frac{\lambda_\alpha}{2^n}$. (Remark: we are mainly interested in $\lambda_\alpha^{'(4)}$ very near $\frac{\lambda_\alpha}{2^n}$ since in formula (7.1) of Section 7 we have a term in $\alpha^4 \lambda_\alpha^{'(4)}$).

Theorem 3. *For all values* $[\lambda'_\alpha]$ *we have:*

$$1 - \frac{8\alpha}{2^n} \le \frac{2^n [\lambda'_\alpha]}{\lambda_\alpha} \le 1 + \frac{8\alpha}{(1 - \frac{8\alpha}{2^n})2^n}$$

Proof of Theorem 3
We will present here the proof with $X : f_\alpha \oplus g_\alpha \oplus h_\alpha = h_{\alpha-1} \oplus g_{\alpha-2} \oplus f_{\alpha-3}$. The proof is exactly similar for all the other cases. From (6.4), we have:

$$1 - \frac{4(\alpha - 1)}{2^n} \le \frac{\lambda_\alpha}{2^{3n} \lambda_{\alpha-1}} \le 1$$

and

$$1 - \frac{4(\alpha - 2)}{2^n} \le \frac{\lambda_{\alpha-1}}{2^{3n} \lambda_{\alpha-2}} \le 1$$

Therefore

$$2^{6n} \lambda_{\alpha-2} \left(1 - \frac{4(\alpha - 1)}{2^n}\right)^2 \le \lambda_\alpha \le 2^{6n} \lambda_{\alpha-2} \tag{B1}$$

We will now evaluate $[\lambda'_\alpha]$ from $\lambda_{\alpha-2}$.
In $[\lambda'_\alpha]$ we have the condition $\lambda_{\alpha-2}$ plus

1. $f_{\alpha-1} \notin \{f_1, \dots, f_{\alpha-2}\}$
2. $g_{\alpha-1} \notin \{g_1, \dots, g_{\alpha-2}\}$
3. $h_{\alpha-1} \notin \{h_1, \dots, h_{\alpha-2}\}$
4. $f_{\alpha-1} \oplus g_{\alpha-1} \oplus h_{\alpha-1} \notin \{f_1 \oplus g_1 \oplus h_1, \dots, f_{\alpha-2} \oplus g_{\alpha-2} \oplus h_{\alpha-2}\}$
5. $f_\alpha \notin \{f_1, \dots, f_{\alpha-1}\}$
6. $g_\alpha \notin \{g_1, \dots, g_{\alpha-1}\}$
7. $h_\alpha \notin \{h_1, \dots, h_{\alpha-1}\}$
8. $f_\alpha \oplus g_\alpha \oplus h_\alpha \notin \{f_1 \oplus g_1 \oplus h_1, \dots, f_{\alpha-1} \oplus g_{\alpha-1} \oplus h_{\alpha-1}\}$
9. (Equation X): $f_\alpha \oplus g_\alpha \oplus h_\alpha = f_{\alpha-3} \oplus g_{\alpha-2} \oplus h_{\alpha-1}$

We can decide that X will fix h_α from the other values: $h_\alpha = f_\alpha \oplus g_\alpha \oplus f_{\alpha-3} \oplus g_{\alpha-2} \oplus h_{\alpha-1}$, and we can decide that conditions 2, 3, 4 and 8 will be written in $h_{\alpha-1}$ and $g_{\alpha-1}$:

$$h_{\alpha-1} \notin \{h_1, \ldots, h_{\alpha-2},$$
$$f_1 \oplus g_1 \oplus h_1 \oplus f_{\alpha-1} \oplus g_{\alpha-1}, \ldots, f_{\alpha-2} \oplus g_{\alpha-2} \oplus h_{\alpha-2} \oplus f_{\alpha-1} \oplus g_{\alpha-1},$$
$$f_1 \oplus g_1 \oplus h_1 \oplus f_{\alpha-3} \oplus g_{\alpha-2}, \ldots, f_{\alpha-2} \oplus h_{\alpha-2} \oplus f_{\alpha-3}\}$$

In this set we have between $\alpha - 2$ and $3(\alpha - 2)$ elements when $h_1, \ldots, h_{\alpha-2}$ are pairwise distinct.

$$g_{\alpha-1} \notin \{g_1, \ldots, g_{\alpha-2}, \ f_{\alpha-1} \oplus f_{\alpha-3} \oplus g_{\alpha-2}\}$$

In this set we have between $\alpha - 2$ and $\alpha - 1$ elements when $g_1, \ldots, g_{\alpha-2}$ are pairwise distinct ($g_{\alpha-1} \neq f_{\alpha-1} \oplus f_{\alpha-3} \oplus g_{\alpha-2}$ comes from the last condition 8).

Similarly, we can write conditions 6 and 7 in g_α:

$$g_\alpha \notin \{g_1, \ldots, g_{\alpha-1}, h_1 \oplus f_\alpha \oplus f_{\alpha-3} \oplus g_{\alpha-2} \oplus h_{\alpha-1}, \ldots, h_{\alpha-1} \oplus f_\alpha \oplus f_{\alpha-3} \oplus g_{\alpha-2} \oplus h_{\alpha-1}\}$$

In this set we have between $\alpha - 1$ and $2(\alpha - 1)$ elements when $g_1, \ldots, g_{\alpha-1}$ are pairwise distinct. Therefore we get:

$$[\lambda'_\alpha] \geq \lambda_{\alpha-2} \underbrace{(2^n - (\alpha-2))}_{f_{\alpha-1}} \underbrace{(2^n - (\alpha-1))}_{g_{\alpha-1}} \underbrace{(2^n - 3(\alpha-2))}_{h_{\alpha-1}} \underbrace{(2^n - (\alpha-1))}_{f_\alpha} \underbrace{(2^n - 2(\alpha-1))}_{g_\alpha}$$

and

$$[\lambda'_\alpha] \leq \lambda_{\alpha-2} \underbrace{(2^n - (\alpha-2))}_{f_{\alpha-1}} \underbrace{(2^n - (\alpha-2))}_{g_{\alpha-1}} \underbrace{(2^n - (\alpha-2))}_{h_{\alpha-1}} \underbrace{(2^n - (\alpha-1))}_{f_\alpha} \underbrace{(2^n - (\alpha-1))}_{g_\alpha}$$

So

$$\left(1 - \frac{(\alpha-2)}{2^n}\right)\left(1 - \frac{(\alpha-1)}{2^n}\right)^2 \left(1 - \frac{3(\alpha-2)}{2^n}\right)\left(1 - \frac{2(\alpha-1)}{2^n}\right) \leq \frac{[\lambda'_\alpha]}{2^{5n}\lambda_{\alpha-2}}$$
$$\leq \left(1 - \frac{(\alpha-2)}{2^n}\right)^3\left(1 - \frac{(\alpha-1)}{2^n}\right)^2$$

So we have: $1 - \frac{8\alpha}{2^n} \leq \frac{[\lambda'_\alpha]}{2^{5n}\lambda_{\alpha-2}} \leq 1$ and with $(B1)$ this gives:

$$\frac{2^{5n}\lambda_\alpha}{2^{6n}}\left(1 - \frac{8\alpha}{2^n}\right) \leq [\lambda'_\alpha] \leq \frac{2^{5n}\lambda_\alpha}{2^{6n}(1 - \frac{4(\alpha-1)}{2^n})^2} \leq \frac{\lambda_\alpha}{2^n(1 - \frac{8\alpha}{2^n})}$$

So $1 - \frac{8\alpha}{2^n} \leq \frac{2^n[\lambda'_\alpha]}{\lambda_\alpha} \leq 1 + \frac{8\alpha}{2^n(1 - \frac{8\alpha}{2^n})}$ as claimed.

Theorem 4. *We have* $\mathrm{Adv}_\phi^{\mathrm{PRF}} \leq 2\left(\frac{1}{E(N)} + \frac{m^2}{2^{3n}(1 - \frac{4m}{2^n})} + \frac{8m^6}{2^{5n}(1 - \frac{12m}{2^n})}\right)^{1/3}$ $(B.2)$

Proof of Theorem 4

This proof follows immediately from Theorem 3 and formula (8.6) of Section 8.

Remark: If $m >> \sqrt{2^n}$ (these are the only difficult cases), then in this expression, the main term is $\left(\frac{8m^6}{2^{5n}(1 - \frac{12m}{2^n})}\right)^{1/3}$ in $O(\frac{m^2}{2^{5n/3}})$.

In order to get security in $m << 2^n$, instead of $m << 2^{5n/6}$, we need to have a better evaluation of $[\lambda'_\alpha]$ (i.e. we need $||[\epsilon_\alpha]|| = O(\frac{\alpha}{2^{2n}})$ instead of $O(\frac{\alpha}{2^n})$).

Author Index

Lecture Notes in Computer Science

Sublibrary 4: Security and Cryptology

For information about Vols. 1– 3958
please contact your bookseller or Springer

Vol. 4631: B. Christianson, B. Crispo, J.A. Malcolm, M. Roe (Eds.), Security Protocols. IX, 347 pages. 2007.

Vol. 4622: A. Menezes (Ed.), Advances in Cryptology - CRYPTO 2007. XIV, 631 pages. 2007.

Vol. 4593: A. Biryukov (Ed.), Fast Software Encryption. XI, 467 pages. 2007.

Vol. 4586: J. Pieprzyk, H. Ghodosi, E. Dawson (Eds.), Information Security and Privacy. XIV, 476 pages. 2007.

Vol. 4582: J. López, P. Samarati, J.L. Ferrer (Eds.), Public Key Infrastructure. XI, 375 pages. 2007.

Vol. 4579: B.M. Hämmerli, R. Sommer (Eds.), Detection of Intrusions and Malware, and Vulnerability Assessment. X, 251 pages. 2007.

Vol. 4575: T. Takagi, T. Okamoto, E. Okamoto, T. Okamoto (Eds.), Pairing-Based Cryptography – Pairing 2007. XI, 408 pages. 2007.

Vol. 4567: T. Furon, F. Cayre, G. Doërr, P. Bas (Eds.), Information Hiding. XI, 393 pages. 2008.

Vol. 4521: J. Katz, M. Yung (Eds.), Applied Cryptography and Network Security. XIII, 498 pages. 2007.

Vol. 4515: M. Naor (Ed.), Advances in Cryptology - EUROCRYPT 2007. XIII, 591 pages. 2007.

Vol. 4499: Y.Q. Shi (Ed.), Transactions on Data Hiding and Multimedia Security II. IX, 117 pages. 2007.

Vol. 4464: E. Dawson, D.S. Wong (Eds.), Information Security Practice and Experience. XIII, 361 pages. 2007.

Vol. 4462: D. Sauveron, K. Markantonakis, A. Bilas, J.-J. Quisquater (Eds.), Information Security Theory and Practices. XII, 255 pages. 2007.

Vol. 4450: T. Okamoto, X. Wang (Eds.), Public Key Cryptography – PKC 2007. XIII, 491 pages. 2007.

Vol. 4437: J.L. Camenisch, C.S. Collberg, N.F. Johnson, P. Sallee (Eds.), Information Hiding. VIII, 389 pages. 2007.

Vol. 4392: S.P. Vadhan (Ed.), Theory of Cryptography. XI, 595 pages. 2007.

Vol. 4377: M. Abe (Ed.), Topics in Cryptology – CT-RSA 2007. XI, 403 pages. 2006.

Vol. 4356: E. Biham, A.M. Youssef (Eds.), Selected Areas in Cryptography. XI, 395 pages. 2007.

Vol. 4341: P.Q. Nguyên (Ed.), Progress in Cryptology - VIETCRYPT 2006. XI, 385 pages. 2006.

Vol. 4332: A. Bagchi, V. Atluri (Eds.), Information Systems Security. XV, 382 pages. 2006.

Vol. 4329: R. Barua, T. Lange (Eds.), Progress in Cryptology - INDOCRYPT 2006. X, 454 pages. 2006.

Vol. 4318: H. Lipmaa, M. Yung, D. Lin (Eds.), Information Security and Cryptology. XI, 305 pages. 2006.

Vol. 4307: P. Ning, S. Qing, N. Li (Eds.), Information and Communications Security. XIV, 558 pages. 2006.

Vol. 4301: D. Pointcheval, Y. Mu, K. Chen (Eds.), Cryptology and Network Security. XIII, 381 pages. 2006.

Vol. 4300: Y.Q. Shi (Ed.), Transactions on Data Hiding and Multimedia Security I. IX, 139 pages. 2006.

Vol. 4298: J.K. Lee, O. Yi, M. Yung (Eds.), Information Security Applications. XIV, 406 pages. 2007.

Vol. 4296: M.S. Rhee, B. Lee (Eds.), Information Security and Cryptology – ICISC 2006. XIII, 358 pages. 2006.

Vol. 4284: X. Lai, K. Chen (Eds.), Advances in Cryptology – ASIACRYPT 2006. XIV, 468 pages. 2006.

Vol. 4283: Y.Q. Shi, B. Jeon (Eds.), Digital Watermarking. XII, 474 pages. 2006.

Vol. 4266: H. Yoshiura, K. Sakurai, K. Rannenberg, Y. Murayama, S.-i. Kawamura (Eds.), Advances in Information and Computer Security. XIII, 438 pages. 2006.

Vol. 4258: G. Danezis, P. Golle (Eds.), Privacy Enhancing Technologies. VIII, 431 pages. 2006.

Vol. 4249: L. Goubin, M. Matsui (Eds.), Cryptographic Hardware and Embedded Systems - CHES 2006. XII, 462 pages. 2006.

Vol. 4237: H. Leitold, E.P. Markatos (Eds.), Communications and Multimedia Security. XII, 253 pages. 2006.

Vol. 4236: L. Breveglieri, I. Koren, D. Naccache, J.-P. Seifert (Eds.), Fault Diagnosis and Tolerance in Cryptography. XIII, 253 pages. 2006.

Vol. 4219: D. Zamboni, C. Krügel (Eds.), Recent Advances in Intrusion Detection. XII, 331 pages. 2006.

Vol. 4189: D. Gollmann, J. Meier, A. Sabelfeld (Eds.), Computer Security – ESORICS 2006. XI, 548 pages. 2006.

Vol. 4176: S.K. Katsikas, J. López, M. Backes, S. Gritzalis, B. Preneel (Eds.), Information Security. XIV, 548 pages. 2006.

Vol. 4117: C. Dwork (Ed.), Advances in Cryptology - CRYPTO 2006. XIII, 621 pages. 2006.

Vol. 4116: R. De Prisco, M. Yung (Eds.), Security and Cryptography for Networks. XI, 366 pages. 2006.

Vol. 4107: G. Di Crescenzo, A. Rubin (Eds.), Financial Cryptography and Data Security. XI, 327 pages. 2006.

Vol. 4083: S. Fischer-Hübner, S. Furnell, C. Lambrinoudakis (Eds.), Trust and Privacy in Digital Business. XIII, 243 pages. 2006.

Vol. 4064: R. Büschkes, P. Laskov (Eds.), Detection of Intrusions and Malware & Vulnerability Assessment. X, 195 pages. 2006.

Vol. 4058: L.M. Batten, R. Safavi-Naini (Eds.), Information Security and Privacy. XII, 446 pages. 2006.

Vol. 4047: M. Robshaw (Ed.), Fast Software Encryption. XI, 434 pages. 2006.

Vol. 4043: A.S. Atzeni, A. Lioy (Eds.), Public Key Infrastructure. XI, 261 pages. 2006.

Vol. 4004: S. Vaudenay (Ed.), Advances in Cryptology - EUROCRYPT 2006. XIV, 613 pages. 2006.

Vol. 3995: G. Müller (Ed.), Emerging Trends in Information and Communication Security. XX, 524 pages. 2006.

Vol. 3989: J. Zhou, M. Yung, F. Bao (Eds.), Applied Cryptography and Network Security. XIV, 488 pages. 2006.

Vol. 3969: Ø. Ytrehus (Ed.), Coding and Cryptography. XI, 443 pages. 2006.